YOUR DESTINY AND SCIENTIFIC HAND ANALYSIS

Your Destiny and Scientific Hand Analysis

YASCHPAULE

MOTILAL BANARSIDASS PUBLISHERS
PRIVATE LIMITED • DELHI

2nd Revised Edition : Delhi, 2009
Reprint : Delhi, 2000
First Indian Edition : Delhi, 1996

ISBN : 978-81-208-1347-2

MOTILAL BANARSIDASS
41 U.A. Bungalow Road, Jawahar Nagar, Delhi 110 007
8 Mahalaxmi Chamber, 22 Bhulabhai Desai Road, Mumbai 400 026
203 Royapettah High Road, Mylapore, Chennai 600 004
236, 9th Main III Block, Jayanagar, Bangalore 560 011
Sanas Plaza, 1302 Baji Rao Road, Pune 411 002
8 Camac Street, Kolkata 700 017
Ashok Rajpath, Patna 800 004
Chowk, Varanasi 221 001

PRINTED IN INDIA

BY JAINENDRA PRAKASH JAIN AT SHRI JAINENDRA PRESS,
A-45, NARAINA, PHASE-I, NEW DELHI 110 028
AND PUBLISHED BY NARENDRA PRAKASH JAIN FOR
MOTILAL BANARSIDASS PUBLISHERS PRIVATE LIMITED,
BUNGALOW ROAD, DELHI 110 007

Dedication

To my son Jaipal Singh, the sages of India, the thousands of Malaysian and foreign clients who have consulted me and been a source of encouragement to me, and my teacher, Mr. T.S. Vasan of Bangalore.

Contents

Preface
Revised Edition

This book has met with gratifying success. This was clearly shown in my palms and horoscope. The first edition has seen eight reprints. The book is also published in India by a leading international Indian publisher, called Motilal Banarsidass Publishers Private Limited, based in Delhi. The Indian edition is sold in Delhi, Mumbai, Chennai, Pune, Calcutta, Patna and Varanasi [Benares].

Certain parts of Chapter 19, titled 'Remedial Measures in Scientific Hand Analysis' have been updated. I have learned the Science of Gemmology from a leading Malaysian gemmologist. Thus I have learned the finer points of recommending astrological gemstones to clients. This certainly has made the chapter on the selection of gemstones very professional in the presentation of this topic.

I have attended many astrological conferences in India. I have attended two such conferences in Bangladesh. The book has been praised by some leading astrologers and hand analysts in India and Bangladesh. Indian hand analysis is world famous and Indian hand analysts have written some of the best books in the world on Scientific Hand Analysis. India is the cradle of Astrology and Scientific Hand Analysis.

It is thus a source of justified pride that the book has been favourably reviewed in 'Express Star Teller', a highly prestigious astrological magazine, sold in India and Malaysia. This very professional magazine is published at 'Express Star Teller, Express Estates, Mount Road, Chennai 600 002, India.'

The book was reviewed by S. Sridaran in the February 1997 issue of 'Express Star Teller', on Page 50. Among other favourable remarks, this is what was published:

'The book under review is undoubtedly one of the better ones on Palmistry available today. His work encompasses the Indian, Western, and Egyptian schools of thought with greater emphasis on the first mentioned. The treatise is not an outcome of bookish knowledge, but one of actual verification of thousands of hands from various walks of life from beggars to businessmen and murderers to academicians. The chapters are interspersed with case studies and examples to make the subject easy to understand and assimilate. The author, a believer in remedial measures, has included a chapter on gem remedies, which he says can lessen the evil influence of planets and also alter the course of some lives in the hand too. The presentation is tidy, the diagrams are neatly done, and the print is easy on the eye.'

The book has been an eye-opener to many a sceptic. After reading the book, the sharp differences between 'fortune telling' and Scientific Hand Analysis will be clear to even a hard-core sceptic. Chapter 2 proves decisively that the hand lines clearly come from the Mind. They are not formed by physical hand movements.

The Laws of Destiny are mysterious but it is possible to lift the veil of the Unknown to a significant degree through the genius of hand analysis.

May all readers grow in Wisdom by studying this book and having their hands analyzed by experienced, learned Scientific Hand Analysts.

Foreword

By

DR. BANGALORE VENKATA RAMAN
Editor: *The Astrological Magazine*

Mr. Yaschpaule gives a fascinating exposition of the art and science of palmistry or *Hastasamudrika*.

Palmistry is an interesting subject not only in itself but because it can be a reliable guide to life. Milestones in life can be foreseen with accuracy years in advance. However, the precise details are a little difficult to glean but not always elusive.

A scientific analysis of the hand can not only help in marital and emotional problems but also play a decisive role in determining academic and vocational aptitude.

Mr. Yaschpaule's systematic treatment of palmistry is backed by years of experience. The art of palm interpretation is difficult and, in the wrong hands, even dangerous. However, a diligent study of this volume can give a good knowledge of the subject and enable one to become a skilled interpreter.

As the author rightly points out, a correct analysis is possible if, in addition to the technical knowledge of the science, one is also intuitive. The intuitive powers can be developed through simple living, a tranquil and equanimous disposition, honesty in all mundane transactions and above all *mantra siddhi* or spiritual attainment.

The chapter on the history of the science is particularly striking for touching on points usually overlooked by other authors on the subject.

The author Mr. Yaschpaule is a noted palmist. He has been doing commendable work in the propagation of palmistry and astrology through his lectures, books and articles in newspapers and periodicals in Malaysia. As a columnist in one of Malaysia's leading newspapers, he has regularly analysed countless palm-prints of people from all walks of life. He has systematically tried to enlighten the educated public of the scientific foundations of palmistry. Both professionals and amateurs will, I am sure, gain immensely from a diligent study of this book.

The subject receives comprehensive treatment at the hands of the author who spares no pains to simplify the presentation with illustrative diagrams.

I wish the author all success.

Bangalore
15.4.1985

B. V. RAMAN

Preface

This book is designed to convince the healthy and scientific-minded sceptic that hand analysis is a science worthy of serious consideration. The laws of scientific hand analysis are presented in a very simple manner, and are amply illustrated by diagrams. This book is also intended for those who do not have the faintest concept of what hand analysis or astrology is all about, so that no previous knowledge is required for its understanding. At the same time the subject of hand analysis is comprehensively covered and its close connections with astrology have been emphasized. As such this book will be of interest to professional astrologers. In many Eastern countries leading astrologers have a good knowledge of hand analysis. Where the horoscope does not give clear guidance on a particular aspect, they consult the palms in order to obtain clarification.

The benefits of studying this sublime science are clearly set out. The scientific basis of hand analysis is explained in great detail at the beginning of this book and incorporates some of my own research over the past nine years. I may add that practically every law of scientific hand analysis has been tested many times, and that in my experience they have always been found to be reliable and accurate.

The ideas put forward in this book are based on the Indian, Western and Egyptian schools of hand analysis, although the Indian system has been used the most. For instance, the views of Indian hand analysts on 'fate' and 'free will' are set out in the early chapters of this book. The scientific rationale behind the wearing of particular gems in order to ward off evil planetary influences is also succinctly described. It is not sufficient merely to give the correct diagnosis: the practitioner of hand analysis must also be able to suggest constructive remedial measures.

Above all, this is meant to be an eminently straightforward and practical work. The sceptic has only to study his* own palms to be pleasantly surprised at how accurately hand analysis reveals his own particular case.

I am passionately opposed to the abuse of this sublime science as a means of providing a diverting pastime at garden parties. Would one dare to reduce another science such as medicine to such frivolous ends?

I take this opportunity to express my deep gratitude to my clients, who have come from various corners of the earth to consult me. I have learned as much from them as they have learned from me. I would also like to convey my special thanks here to Miss Frances Liew Lee Sooi and Miss Szuniewycz for typing the manuscript.

Kuala Lumpur, 1981. Yaschpaule

*I have used the words 'he' and 'his' very frequently in this book. This has been done merely out of convenience, and is not due to any 'male chauvinism' on my part.

Chapter One

How the Science of Hand Analysis Can Change Your Life for the Better. A Word to Parents

> Dr. Albert Einstein, the world famous scientist, said that chirology (scientific hand analysis) may be one of the vital sciences of the future.

Two paediatricians, Pamela A. Davies and Victoria Smallpiece, writing in an American medical journal[1], speak of 'the single transverse palmar crease in infants and children'. Actually the line referred to is the Simian Line, which is a fusion of the Heart and Head Lines. Normally, the Heart and Head Lines are separated, but in the case of the Single Transverse Palmar Crease or Simian Line, the Heart and Head Lines are joined together. The two doctors found that this peculiar combination could be associated with mongolism. To quote the two doctors:[2]

> The association of such a crease with mongolism has been known for some time (Langdon Down, 1909), but it is not so widely appreciated that it may be found with other abnormalities, as well as in normal people.[3]

Scientific hand analysis does not call such a formation a crease, but rather a line of the hand.

---

[1] *Developmental Medicine and Child Neurology,* 1963, V, pp.491–6.

[2] *ibid.*, p.491

[3] for supporting statistics, see *ibid.*, p.492

The article concludes thus:

> Although our numbers are small, we believe that the clinical associations of this single crease are of sufficient interest to merit the inclusion of a brief assessment of the palms in the routine examination of the infant and child. This can be done in a few seconds, and does not require any special apparatus.

So these two well-known paediatricians feel that scientific hand analysis could be a useful tool for the medical diagnosis of mongolism.

According to Dr. Louis Cohen at the University of Chicago every part of the body will in certain circumstances give a clue to something happening in another part of the body. The hands especially are a most valuable source of information and some doctors have accepted medical hand analysis as a science.[4] Dr. Cohen affirms that there is basic truth in hand analysis.

All your prospects concerning business, career, finance, travel, and emotional matters are accurately revealed by scientific hand analysis. Marriage compatibility can be assessed with the most remarkable accuracy through this science. There would be fewer marital tragedies if couples consulted hand analysts before rushing into marriage and repenting at leisure. The hands also show hidden talents, and what profession or hobby the subject is best suited for. It is truly a comprehensive science.

Let us now analyse the benefits every individual in the world can enjoy as a result of this science of the hand. The palms reveal the mental, moral and physical tendencies of the subject accurately. There is a close link

---

In an article entitled: What Your Hands Say about Your Health', condensed from *Today's Health* by Don A. Schanche, in *Reader's Digest,* December, 1975.

between the hands and the mind. This is why the lines alter due to the direction of the mind. Medical science will benefit by the extensive use of Medical Hand Analysis. Parents will know exactly how to guide their children correctly as regards vocations. Couples wishing to get married will be able to assess future marital harmony with extraordinary insight through Scientific Hand Analysis. School teachers will understand their pupils much better by means of this science.

In every school, there should be an expert hand analyst teacher to periodically analyse the hands of pupils. A regular, systematic record of the character, temperament, family background, health indications and latent talents, if any, of each pupil could prove a boon to both educational authorities and parents alike. The teacher, in particular, will be able to gain a deep insight into the true nature and possibilities of his pupils. Psychological and intelligence tests could be carried out as well, in order to confirm the results yielded by scientific hand analysis.

These analyses should also be done at university level, so as to draw out the best from university students. Doubtless in the long run such procedures will prove to be a tremendous gain for the country, and perhaps even for the world at large. This proposal might appear to be revolutionary, but the proof of the pudding is in the eating of it. Let all those who are sceptical of the claims of this ancient science subject it to the acid test.

Let us consider the question of marriage. Parents all over the world are concerned about the future happiness of their sons and daughters. In India it is the custom to compare the horoscopes of the intending couple, and for a reliable hand analyst to examine the hands of the boy and girl. In innumerable cases, in many countries, marriage is neither a union of hearts nor of mentally compatible individuals. It is therefore most advisable for a woman to analyse her beloved's hands very thoroughly indeed before she commits herself to a life-long union. Such a process may take the glamour and excitement out of courtship, but then every woman desires a happy marriage, and since scientific hand analysis can show the way to such a union, the so-called glamour and excitement can be safely left out, since all too often these do not make for a wise choice in matrimony.

Marriage is a milestone in the life of an individual. Marriage not only affects both parties, but it also affects society. It has to be considered in relation to diverse factors, such as health, mentality, heredity, sexual compatibility and social and economic status. After analysing all these factors, the ancients decide whether the couple can stand the stress and strain of marriage. The sciences of astrology and hand analysis take all these factors into consideration, and it is at once clear that the custom of consulting a good astrologer or hand analyst is truly scientific. There is nothing superstitious about it. The judicious use of hand analysis would result in fewer marriage break-ups and social tragedies. For instance, in many cases, marriages end in disaster because of the impotence or sterility of one partner. There are specific and reliable indications of sterility in hand analysis, and the intending couple, after consulting a good hand analyst, will know whether or not they can have children. This saves a lot of disappointment and mutual recrimination later on, as it is no use complaining after the holy bonds of matrimony have been tied.

Astrology is now becoming popular in various Western countries, especially in the USA and Australia. In order to be reliable, astrology has to be based on the correct date and time of birth. If this is lacking, the horoscopic analysis is likely to be misleading.

This is where hand analysis has the upper hand over astrology. It is not necessary to know the exact time of birth. A close examination of the hands will reveal all the necessary information pertaining to a happy marriage.

Let us now turn to vocational analysis. The science of hand analysis, since it is a science that can reveal latent talents, reveals to each individual his most suitable career or line of work. Beyond any shadow of doubt, the hand reveals the mental calibre, innate temperament, and natural flair and talent, latent or otherwise, for a specific vocation. This knowledge is priceless, and could be used by each individual to choose a career yielding the most fruitful results both for himself and for society. Hand analysis is most accurate in showing an individual the correct vocation to pursue. There are specific signs and marks in the hand associated with particular vocations. By a thorough, scientific analysis of these signs as well as the shape of the hand, it is possible to state with authority the profession which any given individual is most suited for. Half of life's tragedies would disappear if individuals knew what they were best suited for in life. Hand analysis can reveal a lot more than only aptitude for a particular vocation, but this one aspect alone is so vitally important as to merit a deep study of this science. The marks in the palms show the path an individual should pursue, but the important point is that one should know how to interpret these symbols.

The need is pressing and of great moment. The coming generation has a keen desire to know what vocations to pursue. There has been a criminal waste of educational talent in the past, and this must be prevented in the future. Parents should be in a position to know what their children are best suited for. The answer lies in hand analysis.

The hand is the mirror of the MIND. It reflects the

intelligence of the brain. Hand analysts are clearly justified in relying on the hand for knowledge of vocational analysis. The misplacement of human beings is a tragedy with incalculable consequences. Let us therefore seek solace and light from hand analysis, a great science, lest we misplace ourselves.

Let us now consider medical hand analysis in some depth. Medical hand analysis is a wide and deep subject. It is entirely true to assert that the hand betrays the cause and progress of disease. Medical hand analysis can be used in conjunction with accepted medical techniques, and the diagnosis will be even more accurate. The hand can reveal intestinal disorders, rheumatic conditions, heart conditions, chest and lung complications, brain disorders, and diseases of the spine. Eye troubles, deafness and dumbness are also revealed by this science. In the field of pyschological hand analysis, a hypersensitive disposition as well as hysterical temperaments can also be discovered. By any standards, this is an impressive list. The hand analyst is in a position to know when, unless precautions are taken beforehand to overcome undesirable indications, a certain disease will develop strongly. So, through this science, it is possible to nip a developing disease in the bud.

There is a reliable specific system of calculating ages to within six months or one year either way. Thus, by such calculations, it is possible to pin-point the ages and years when such and such a disease will afflict the individual. It is also within the power of the hand analyst to say how long the illness will last, and with what effects on the subject's career. A master of hand analysis will also know whether the patient will survive the illness or not. A doctor, who is also competent in medical hand analysis, will gain a deeper insight into a patient's state of health.

The time will come when doctors have a thorough

knowledge of medical hand analysis, as well as medical astrology. In America, doctors have done research in Medical Hand Analysis. Their thorough research has led them to the conclusion that an experienced physician's careful study of the hands will reveal important clues which a stethoscope or even an electrocardiograph do not disclose.

Plato, Anaxagoras and Galen state that the hand is an important organ in the study of human beings. Hippocrates, Aristotle, Paracelsus, and Dr. Charles Bell, father of modern neurology, all used the human hand as an aid to diagnosis.

Today scientific hand analysis is coming of age. It is increasingly being recognised as a great aid in medical diagnosis. Leading institutions, outstanding medical men, and highly respected medical journals are becoming aware of the role of the hand in medical diagnosis.

Can the hand really reveal the future? Can the veil of the unknown really be lifted by hand analysis? Let us study a few examples, and then make up our own minds as to whether there is truth in the assertion of hand analysts that the future is revealed by the lines of the hand.

Harvey Day, a noted British writer on yoga and the occult, has written a very interesting book called *Seeing into the Future.*[5] Any open-minded person who wants to know whether the future can be seen by hand analysis, astrology, and dreams, should read this fascinating book.

Harvey Day describes[6] how a sceptic was convinced by a renowned Indian hand analyst and astrologer. There was an Indian prince, before India attained indepen-

---

[5] H. Day, *Seeing into the Future,* Thorsons Publishers, Wellingborough, 1966, pp.138-140.

[6] *ibid.,* p.138

dence, by the name of Ranji. The British Government would not entertain his claim to the throne of the State of Nawanagar in India. Ranji underwent a bad planetary period and a rival claimant to the throne (*gadi*) appeared on the scene. So Ranji, who was in England at the time, returned to India. In Bombay, his friends sang the praises of a wonderful *joshi* (seer). Ranji at first said that he did not believe in such unadulterated rubbish as seeing the future. Eventually, he was persuaded to visit the famous astro-hand analyst, Pandit Hareshwar. But Ranji wanted to test this great seer, so he did not reveal his name. An appointment was made through a third party, so that Pandit Hareshwar would be kept in the dark as to the identity of his client, and the astro-palmist was asked to come to a humble house outside Bombay.

When Pandit Hareshwar arrived, he met four persons, with a servant wielding a fan behind them. After some small talk, one of the four asked whether there was any possibility of one of them becoming one day a ruler of men? Hareshwar analysed their palms and asked for their birth dates. After deep analysis, he pronounced that none of them would sit on the throne. Then he requested that the servant show his hands. On seeing the servant's palms, Pandit Hareshwar said that the servant would twice be a king, and, that he would also be a ruler in another field, probably in sports. The servant was Ranji in disguise, and the great hand analyst had not been led up the garden path by this trap laid for him by the sceptics. It was also a fact that Ranji, while in England, had made a big name for himself in cricket.

Ranji was delighted at the skill of Hareshwar and believed in his predictions. His legal advisers presented his case to the British government. However, his claim was not considered, and Jassaji, his rival, became powerful. In 1903, Jassaji was proclaimed *Jam Saheb*, which was the title of the ruler of Nawanagar. It now looked as if the predictions of the great seer were hollow.

Very perturbed, Ranji visited Hareshwar again. Hareshwar did a thorough check, and said, 'If you do not sit on the *gadi* (throne) of Nawanagar by 11 March 1907, I shall not only award two thousand rupees to charity, but also relinquish my work, for it will be proof that I am a charlatan.'

Ranji was still doubtful of this firm prediction. In 1906 a typhoid epidemic swept Nawanagar. Jassaji contracted the disease and passed away. The British government was then forced to raise Ranji to the *gadi*, and he was installed as *Jam Saheb* on 10 March 1907. By any standards, this was truly a brilliant prediction by Hareshwar, who, during his time, was one of the best hand analysts and astrologers in the world.

Let us consider further examples of accurate forecasts in the world of scientific hand analysis. Let us now consider a famous Western hand analyst, now deceased, called Madam Mamlok. She called herself a chirologist. (This word is obtained from the Greek word Kheir = hand.) Harvey Day also writes about her skill in his book.[7] Madam Mamlok was married to Professor Hans J. Mamlok of the University of Berlin. Through her skill in medical hand analysis, she was respected in medical circles in Germany. The head of a cancer hospital in Amsterdam used to write to Madam Mamlok asking her to diagnose the illnesses of some of his patients from their handprints alone. This she did with superlative accuracy. Harvey Day describes one instance where this hand analyst changed the entire course of life of the subject for the better.

In 1937 Madam Mamlok and her husband left Germany for America, where she set up a busy practice in New York.

---

[7] *ibid.*, pp.98-101

One day, in New York, a young lady came to consult Madam Mamlok. This lady had a tyrannical mother, who had crushed her independence. She was almost a nervous wreck from the mental tortures inflicted on her by her mother, and could not even develop a warm relationship with the man she loved. The love relationship could not possibly flower under such adverse planetary aspects.

The hand analyst saw, through her science, that the over-bearing mother's pernicious influence was the root cause of all the trouble. The young lady was advised to break away from her mother, and start leading an independent life of her own. The girl was trying to succeed as a writer of fiction. She was advised to give this up and to concentrate on newspaper work.

The young lady followed the suggestions of the expert hand analyst. She took courage in both hands, and with resolution, broke away from the mother, left home and secured a job on a newspaper. A different, more conducive environment resulted in a vast improvement, both physically and mentally. The young lady carved a niche for herself as a highly respected and successful newspaper woman in America. This accurate forecast shows the great service scientific hand analysis performs in the field of vocational guidance.

Madam Mamlok certainly was very prominent in her field of work. Distinguished personalities consulted her. Among these were Dr. Albert Einstein, Alfred Steiglitz, Sir John Barbirolli, Raymond Gram Swing and Dorothy Parker.

Let us consider another example of an accurate prediction narrated by Harvey Day in the same book. Gypsies have traditionally been associated with hand analysis, astrology and face reading. Many of these gypsies have been charlatans, and have given these sciences an evil reputation especially in Europe. But quacks can be found in any field, even in fields where there is strict government control and legislation. There have been a few gypsies who have been serious students of hand analysis and who have made remarkably accurate predictions.

Harvey Day describes how Bette Davis was stunned at the remarkable accuracy of the forecast of a gypsy. Bette Davis tells of her encounter in her autobiography, *The Lonely Life*. When in her teens, she did not know what vocation to pursue. She went to a gypsy lady who analysed palms in the nearby town of York, Maine. The gypsy promised Bette Davis that one day she would become world famous. The gypsy shook her own head when she made this prediction. This is because Bette Davis was poor at the time of consultation, and the gypsy found it difficult to reconcile this fact with the brilliant promise shown in the hands of the eighteen-year-old girl.

Bette Davis and her mother were incredulous, and did not know what to make of this forecast. It is a well-known fact that expert hand analysts and astrologers cannot see the precise details which will make their predictions come true in the distant future. At that time, motion pictures, one way by which one could achieve world fame, never crossed the minds of mother and daughter. Most readers in the Western world will know that Bette Davis achieved enormous success in motion pictures, and her name became famous in five continents of the world. This most unlikely prediction of the gypsy was fulfilled with uncanny accuracy.

A thousand and one examples of really brilliant predictions by hand analysts could be given, but this would serve no useful purpose. The prejudiced will keep on mumbling, 'It's all sheer coincidence.' Even when expert statisticians point out that the chances of coincidence are exceptionally remote or downright impossible, the prejudiced will not be convinced in the least. This holds good in practically every field of scientific research. My aim in this elementary work on scientific hand analysis is to present the facts to readers with open minds. As for the prejudiced, even if angels came down to earth, they would still not be convinced, not even when faced with the cold, hard facts.

Let us conclude this chapter by studying a few quotations on hand analysis:

> In the case of men or women, everything that happens to them — life and death, gain and loss, joy and sorrow — mostly happens through the lines of the palm.
>
> *Samudrika Shastra (an Indian treatise)*

> Among the limbs, the hand is considered more important than even the head.
>
> *Anga Vidya (a Sanskrit treatise)*

> Contrary to common conception, the study of the hand has occupied some of the greatest minds in all ages. Its beginnings are lost in the night of antiquity that has no dawn.
>
> *Cheiro*

> Success in all worldly affairs depends upon the laws of destiny controlled by the actions of mortals in their previous lives and the conduct of the individual; the decrees of destiny are a mystery. We must, therefore, have recourse to means which depend upon man.
>
> *Maharishi Manu, a famous Indian sage*

> The hand is the organ of organs, the active agent of the passive powers of the entire system.
>
> *Aristotle*

> The superiority of Man is owing to his hands.
>
> *Anaxagoras*

There is no doubt that this science (of hand analysis) is of eminently practical value in the choice of a vocation.

Joseph Ranald

One may be deceived in a face — but in a hand, never.

Napoleon

We ought to define the hand as belonging exclusively to Man, corresponding in its sensibility and emotion, to the endowment of the mind.

It is a remarkable fact that we cannot feel the pulse with the tongue, but we can with the fingers.

Sir Charles Bell

Chapter Two

The Scientific Basis of Hand Analysis

Most people who do not believe in hand analysis are under the misconception that the lines on the palms are caused by the physical movements of folding the hands. At first glance this seems plausible enough. But let us probe deeper. An issue of *Lancet,* the august British medical journal, included an article by the late Professor Lionel Penrose, seeking to stimulate interest in the use of hand analysis in diagnosis. The lines of the palm are not strictly creases in the hand, according to the professor. They are formed at about the twelfth week of embryonic life when the hands of the foetus are not flexed, although they also appear in areas which will later be folded.

Most readers of this book, on closer examination of their palms, will be able to see signs and marks which look like squares, triangles, crosses, stars and half-moons. These intricate designs could not have been formed by folding movements of the hands. Could any sceptic show the precise movements of the palm capable of producing a star on the first phalange of the third (Sun) finger? Figure 2-1 will be helpful in this context.

Let us, for one moment, concede that the lines on the palm could possibly be formed by hand movements. Assuming this is correct, it stands to reason that people who do a lot of manual labour should have more lines on their hands than people who do not. Let us observe if this is really so.

We will take the observable cases of a baby three minutes after birth, and of a labourer of fifty-four, who

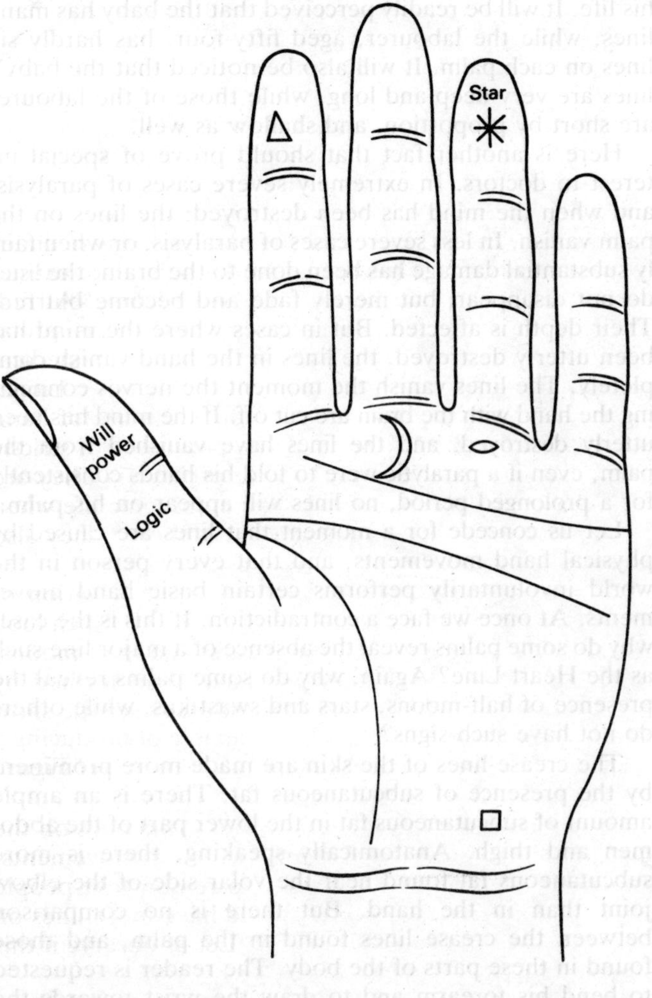

Figure 2-1 Which hand movements can produce a Star in this position?

has been doing manual labour for the last thirty years of his life. It will be readily perceived that the baby has many lines, while the labourer, aged fifty-four, has hardly six lines on each palm. It will also be noticed that the baby's lines are very deep and long, while those of the labourer are short by proportion, and shallow as well.

Here is another fact that should prove of special interest to doctors. In extremely severe cases of paralysis, and when the mind has been destroyed, the lines on the palm vanish. In less severe cases of paralysis, or when fairly substantial damage has been done to the brain, the lines do not disappear, but merely fade and become blurred. Their depth is affected. But in cases where the mind has been utterly destroyed, the lines in the hand vanish completely. The lines vanish the moment the nerves connecting the hand with the brain are cut off. If the mind has been utterly destroyed, and the lines have vanished from the palm, even if a paralytic were to fold his hands consistently for a prolonged period, no lines will appear on his palm.

Let us concede for a moment that lines are caused by physical hand movements, and that every person in the world involuntarily performs certain basic hand movements. At once we face a contradiction. If this is the case, why do some palms reveal the absence of a major line such as the Heart Line? Again, why do some palms reveal the presence of half-moons, stars and swastikas, while others do not have such signs?

The crease lines of the skin are made more prominent by the presence of subcutaneous fat. There is an ample amount of subcutaneous fat in the lower part of the abdomen and thigh. Anatomically speaking, there is more subcutaneous fat found near the volar side of the elbow joint than in the hand. But there is no comparison between the crease lines found in the palm, and those found in these parts of the body. The reader is requested to bend his forearm and to draw the wrist towards the shoulders. At once, a crease line of the elbow joint in the volar side will be seen very distinctly. But now the reader is requested to straighten his arm and to observe the position and formation of the crease lines. They have either disappeared, or almost completely disappeared. This can be repeated with other crease lines of the body, and the results will be similar. Now, the reader is requested to bend his fingers over the palm. The crease lines of the palm will be clearly seen, together with folds on the palm's surface. Now if the hand is straightened, the folds will disappear, but the crease lines are as deeply and clearly traced as before! Clearly, there is a substantial difference between the crease lines present, for example, near the volar side of the elbow joint, and those found in the palm. Any analogy between the crease lines of the palm and those found on other parts of the body is wrong.

Let us suppose that acid has been dropped on both palms. In such a case, the skin will be destroyed. But later, when the injury has healed, it will be found that the lines in both palms have assumed their original positions. What is even more significant is the fact that the lines on both palms will have the same depth and length as they had before. Had the lines been formed by mere physical hand movements, this could not be the case.

The hand is the servant of the mind. It reflects the workings of the brain. Let us now consider in detail the intimate connection between the brain and the hand.

Take for example, a person who is both deaf and dumb. Under these circumstances, the mind expresses itself through the hands. All the emotions and thoughts of the unfortunate person are also expressed by the hands. A sophisticated individual with these infirmities has a fine textured skin. This reflects the refined thinking of such a person, whereas a person with a coarse, crude mind would have a skin with a coarse texture. Such a texture reflects the lack of grace in such a personality.

Hand analysts have always regarded the thumb as reflecting the will power of the individual. The top phalange of the thumb reflects the will power. Figure 2-1 shows the sub-divisions of the thumb. The thumb is divided into two parts: the top phalange shows will power, while the lower phalange reflects logic.

With this as background knowledge, let us now consider a few examples. An adult idiot would have a thumb which is small, weak, and misshaped. The thumb would tend to droop towards the palm. This person's will power is seriously afflicted. A baby of a few months would have its thumb either in its mouth or hidden inside its closed palm. At this stage of its existence, the baby has no will power. Let us now consider the case of a person who is sleeping or on the point of death. The thumb is deprived of its power, and closes in towards the palm. In the case of the person who is on the point of death, this shows that the will to continue living has been broken. Again, the will has been affected.

The relevant conclusions can now be drawn from the illustrations given above, where the thumb was either abnormal in shape, in position, or both. And in all the cases given, the will power was either dormant, or sadly deficient and afflicted. The connection between the thumb and the will is thus readily discerned.

Doctors know that there is a thumb-centre in the brain. If this part of the brain and the thumb are dissected anatomically, it will be seen that there is a direct nerve-connection between these two parts of the body.

The reader should seize the opportunity to observe the pose and carriage of the hands of a group of people walking, standing, or sitting. Each pair of hands will have a different pose. Why should this be so? The explanation is that each individual is having his or her own private thoughts, and the hands have taken on the pose and carriage reflecting the secret thoughts of the individual. The hand analyst can learn a good deal about the true character of an individual merely by observing the habitual pose and carriage of his hands.

It is clear that the lines are not formed by hand movements. So where do the lines come from? Lines come from the MIND. It has been proved that lines change in accordance with changes in the mental attitude of the subject, when these changes are great enough to alter temperament and other characteristics. It has also been proved that lines respond to changes in health and constitution, that they show mental strength, and reveal details in the life of the subject when certain events have produced a powerful impression on his mind. Therefore, we can say with conviction that the lines in the hand are the direct reflection of the subject's mind, and that the mind produces, controls or alters them. The past and present is revealed by the conscious mind; the future by the subconscious mind. Doctors tell us that every part of the body has a specific function. It is therefore hard to believe that Nature created the lines in the hands for the amusement of the subject, or for mere decoration. Hand analysts have studied the lines in the hands for thousands of years, and empirical evidence, based on minute observation of millions of hands, has decisively proved that the lines on the hands have specific meanings. As hand analysts, we do not know exactly how this science works. Perhaps, when large numbers of doctors take up a serious investigation of this science they will be able to explain certain things which are not clear to us now. At best, up till today, only a working hypothesis as to how the science works can be offered.

Let us now study the anatomical structure of the hands. The hands are the most sensitive and versatile part of the body. They have roughly a third of the body's five million tiny sensory receptors, which register pain, heat, pressure, among various other types of information. In fact, certain fingers are so sensitive that several cases have come to light of people who can see with their hands. One case was that of Gusztau Arvai, a fifty-five year old Hungarian office worker. Watched by doctors, he was blindfolded, and yet he was able to read newspapers by moving his fingers several inches above the print. He said that he sensed in the nape of his neck images seen through his fingers.

There are innumerable corpuscles in the palm, called Pacinian, after Dr. Filipo Pacine (1812–1883), an Italian doctor, who discovered them. Meissner talks of these corpuscles.* He proved that these corpuscles were found in the finger-tips and the lines of the hand, and that they could not be found below the wrist. He further showed that they are capable of certain vibrations or crepitations. He asserted that these crepitations and vibrations ceased the moment life left the body. He further said that he had counted in the uppermost phalange of the volar surface of the forefinger of a full-grown man, one hundred and eight corpuscles, and about four hundred papillae (sensitive cells) in a square inch.

Medical scientists have now proved that each brain cell radiates some kind of electrical energy or force. They have recorded this electrical energy or force on graphs. So, there is definitely some kind of current radiating from the brain to other parts of the body. The palmar surface, however, receives more of this current than other parts of the body. This is because there are more nerve fibres here than in any other section of the body.

We are now in a position to present a working hypothesis as to the rationale of this science.

The mind is made up of a bundle of thoughts. The brain is the servant of the mind. The mind expresses itself through a physical organ — the brain. The thoughts, from

* Meissner, *Anatomy and Physiology of the Hand*, cited in Cheiro, *Palmistry for All*, Herbert Jenkins, London, 1966, p.15.

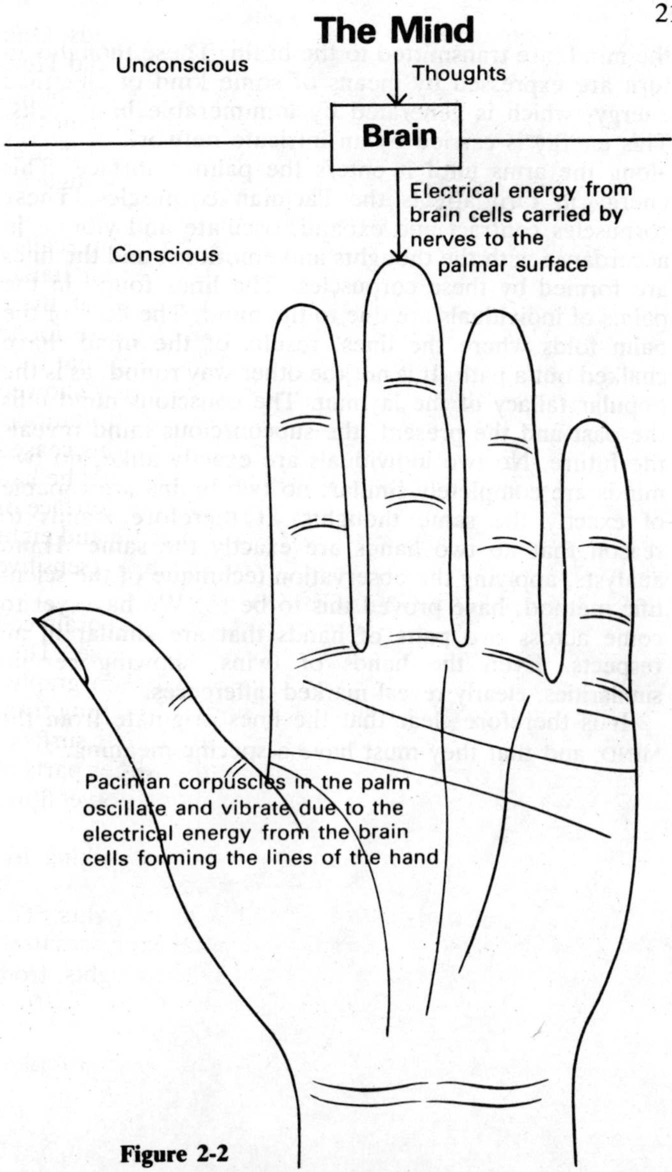
The Mind
Unconscious
Thoughts
Brain
Electrical energy from brain cells carried by nerves to the palmar surface
Conscious
Pacinian corpuscles in the palm oscillate and vibrate due to the electrical energy from the brain cells forming the lines of the hand

Figure 2-2

the mind, are transmitted to the brain. These thoughts in turn are expressed by means of some kind of electrical energy, which is generated by innumerable brain cells. This energy is carried by an intricate network of nerves along the arms until it enters the palmar surface. This energy in turn affects the Pacinian corpuscles. These corpuscles contract and expand, oscillate and vibrate in accordance with the thoughts and emotions, and the lines are formed by these corpuscles. The lines found in the palms of individuals are due to the mind. The flesh of the palm folds where the lines, results of the mind, have chalked out a path. It is not the other way round, as is the popular fallacy of the layman. The conscious mind tells the past and the present; the subconscious mind reveals the future. No two individuals are exactly alike, no two minds are completely similar, no two brains are capable of exactly the same thoughts. It therefore stands to reason that no two hands are exactly the same. Hand analysts, applying the observation technique of the scientific method, have proved this to be so. We have yet to come across two pairs of hands that are similar in all respects. Even the hands of twins, showing certain similarities, clearly reveal marked differences.

It is therefore clear that the lines originate from the MIND, and that they must have a specific meaning.

Chapter Three

The History of the Science. How to Become an Accomplished Hand Analyst

The Hindus were the originators of the science, which has now spread all over the world. The sages of India practised *Angavidyah,* which means the 'Science of the Body'. The earliest references to this science can be found in the *Ramayana,* the world-famous Indian epic poem. The *Mahabaratha* which is an equally renowned Indian epic, also has many descriptions of hands. Indian mythology says that *Samudra*, the Sea-God, started this science. That is why hand analysis is called *Hasthasamudrika Shastra*, or the Science and Knowledge of Hand Analysis. Amongst the old masters of this science of hand reading are the Indian sages Nandi, Narada, Garga, Parashara, Prahlada, Varamihira, Mahadeva and Kartikeya.

Indian hand analysis is very closely linked with astrology and philosophy. The ultimate aim of hand analysis, according to the Indian school of thought, is for the individual to achieve moral upliftment and perfection. The Law of *Karma* is significant in this context. It applies to Indian hand analysis as well as to Indian astrology. Certain profound Western thinkers have started taking this Karmic Law seriously. As you sow, so you reap. Cause and effect apply in the moral sphere as well, not merely in the physical world. Action and reaction, even in the moral sphere, are equal and opposite. We reap the effects of what we did in our previous life or lives. For every cause, whether major or minor, there has to be an effect. The major events shown in the hands have to take place. Certain adjustments can be made, as the lines can change according to the influence of positive thinking, intelligent redirection of efforts, the wearing of specially selected astrological gems and the worship of the nine planets, *Navagraha*, in the Hindu temple. This doctrine of truth will surprise those who believe that Man is complete master of his fate. Such a belief is certainly not held by Hindus.

Edgar Cayce, the great American medical clairvoyant, believed in the Law of *Karma* and in the truth of Reincarnation. This is primarily a book on hand analysis, not on *Karma* and Reincarnation, but for the sceptic who wishes to have very detailed information on these topics, I should refer him to some books which deal with these in depth, so that he can go through them and make up his or her own mind independently!

The following are authorities on *Karma* and Reincarnation:

Abhedananda, Swami. *Reincarnation,* Ramakrishna Vedanta Math, Calcutta, 1968.

Besant, Annie: *Reincarnation,* Theosophical Publishing House, Madras, 10th Ed., 1972.

Cerminara, Gina: *Many Mansions,* Signet Book Publications, New York, 1950.

Cerminara, Gina: *Many Lives, Many Loves,* Signet Book Publications, New York, 1963.

Dhammananda, K. Sri: *Do You Believe in Rebirth?* Buddhist Missionary Society, Kuala Lumpur, 1973.

Gunaratna, V.F: *Rebirth Explained,* Buddhist Publication Society, Ceylon, 1971.

Hodson, Geoffrey: *Reincarnation, Fact or Fallacy?* Theosophical Publishing House, Madras, 1970.

Longley, Noel: *Edgar Cayce on Reincarnation,* Warner Paperback Library Publication, New York, 1975.

Nyanatiloka Mahathera: *Karma and Rebirth,* Buddhist Publication Society, Ceylon, 1971.

Raman, B.V.: *Astrology and Modern Thought,* Raman Publications, Bangalore, 1965. Chapter two on 'Astrology and Karma' is significant.

Satprakashananda, Swami: *How Is a Man Reborn?,* Advaita Ashrama, Calcutta, 1975.

Sivananda Swami: *What Becomes of the Soul After Death?* The Divine Life Society, Shivanandanagar, U.P. Himalayas, India, 1972.

Story, Francis: *The Case for Rebirth,* Buddhist Publication Society, Kandy, 1973.

Vivekananda, Swami: *Life After Death,* Advaita Ashrama, Calcutta, 1975.

In reality, the lines in the hands reflect the effects of past *Karma,* which means the effects of deeds or misdeeds done in the past life or lives. But this is wrongly referred to as solely hereditary influences by those who have not made a deep study of this profound philosophy.

Taking the present life alone into context, there is such a concept as fate. But taking the previous lives into consideration as well, and thus having a more comprehensive picture, there is complete free will. What the individual has to experience now is the result of the free will exercised in a previous life or lives. The effects of these have to be experienced, in this birth. For every cause there has to be an effect — that is an inexorable law. But once these effects have been experienced and past *Karma* has been wiped out, the individual is again totally free to use his free will. So paradoxically, there is fate and also free will. Viewed in the limited context of this birth alone, it is true to say that fate and free will can co-exist happily, or practise *détente* to some extent.

But highly elevated souls like Buddha, Christ, Guru Nanak — such people can escape the iron grip of fate.

The Western concept of hand analysis is different. The

majority of Western hand analysts do not believe in *Karma*, Reincarnation or Fate. For them, only free will exists. Western hand analysis has done very good work on the medical and psychological aspects of this science. The western approach is that the individual, by strong will power, can change any line in the hand for the better. But my research has not borne this out.

The Western world has produced some eminent hand analysts. Among these have been D'Arpentigny, Adolph-Desbarrolles, William Benham, Noel Jaquin and Mrs. Katherine St. Hill. Among these, the most scientific of the lot was probably William Benham. Cheiro, a well-known western hand analyst, went to India twice and studied the finer aspects of the science with Indian masters. All these well-known hand analysts have been instrumental in giving hand analysis the dignity of a science. William Benham was an American, and his approach to the science was ruthlessly logical and entirely scientific. He did not lay any stress on the intuitive aspect of hand analysis. A real master of hand analysis will be proficient in both the Western and Indian systems of hand analysis.

Hand analysis is a science, as well as an art. It is an applied science. 'Know Thyself' is the foundation on which this science is built. By knowing oneself deeply it is possible to strengthen the character immeasurably. After all, character is destiny. But to understand character, the hand analyst must have a thorough knowledge of all branches of this science, and especially of psychological hand analysis. Those who are prejudiced against hand analysis should not erroneously jump to the conclusion that hand analysis is cheap psychology, merely because there is an aspect to it which is very deep and reliable. This aspect is psychological hand analysis. Hand analysis is certainly not psychology, but a general knowledge of psychology will make the hand analyst an even better practitioner, especially when dealing with certain aspects of psychological hand analysis, such as extrovert and introvert tendencies.

The hand analyst must be a keen observer of human nature. He should have a good background of general knowledge. Also, the mind of the practitioner must be calm, impartial, and ruthlessly logical. A good hand analyst will be well versed in the science of logic.

To be really brilliant as a hand analyst it is necessary for the serious practitioner to have a deep, thorough knowledge of the science itself. The knowledge of the theory of hand analysis must be profound. Therefore a vast theoretical knowledge of every intricate aspect of scientific hand analysis is a must.

But theory alone is not enough. This theory has to be applied — and so the eager student will analyse thousands of hands. As a schoolboy, I used to stop people in the streets of Penang, Malaysia, and politely request them to show their hands to me! It is necessary for the beginner to explain that he is a student of the science. No major predictions should be made until the student is proficient in the science. The beginner in hand analysis must take great care not to alarm those willing to show him their hands for the sake of research. The beginner must be frank enough to admit that he is learning. In this way, even if predictions of an adverse nature are made, the subject, knowing that this is the analysis of a beginner, will not be unduly alarmed.

So the master of hand analysis must have vast theoretical knowledge, as well as profound practical experience. The beginner must seize the opportunity to study every pair of hands that come his way. After all, practice makes perfect.

Through scientific hand analysis, it is possible to be a good hand analyst. But to be really brilliant, and to give astounding predictions, it is also necessary to have highly advanced intuitive faculties. Then only will the results be truly spectacular. This is a most vital point.

How does one develop intuition? This divine faculty is acquired through regular meditation. The serious student can practise TM or transcendental meditation. Buddhist meditation is also excellent.

Let us see the difference between a hand analyst who relies only on scientific hand analysis, and one who has got intuition as well. Let us assume that on both hands there is a small break in the Vitality Line, with a descending line from the Saturn Mount touching the Vitality Line at the point of the break. In scientific hand analysis, this refers to the high probability of an accident. This is about all a practitioner, who relies on scientific hand analysis alone,, can say. But let us suppose that the hand analyst has got unsurpassed intuition as well. He will then tell the client that he will suffer an accident at a certain age and that this accident will be caused by a fall from a tree. This hand analyst, through scientific hand analysis, knows that the client will suffer an accident. But by using intuition as well, the hand analyst is able to go further, and inform the client as to how the accident will take place. This additional insight was certainly not gained from the palms, but through highly developed intuition. But the intuition had solid foundations. It was based on a thorough knowledge of scientific hand analysis. Intuition, to be reliable, must be based on a deep knowledge of scientific hand analysis. Otherwise, it is not intuition – it is merely inspired guesswork or pseudo-intuition.

According to the code of ethics of Indian hand analysis, a serious practitioner of this divine science should not drink alcohol or smoke. Alcohol kills intuition and destroys judgement. Stimulants of all kinds such as tea, coffee and drugs should be avoided like the plague. Other things being equal, a vegetarian has sharper intuition than a meat-eater. To be convinced of the benefits of a vegetarian diet, the reader is advised to study the subject of vegetarianism seriously, and with an open mind. Harry Benjamin, a noted authority on nature cure, has written a good book on vegetarianism.*

Since hand analysis is a divine science, the practitioner himself must have divine qualities, or be as pure as possible. There is an Indian saying that in order to make gold, one has to become gold in conduct and character. Therefore, in the Indian approach to hand analysis as well as to astrology, it is emphasised that the practitioner must be a person of high morals and exalted motives. Hand analysis is a science of depth, requiring sacrifice of a higher order. It is not meant for the weak-willed. Of course, readers who are merely interested in studying the science for interest's sake rather than for practice can ignore all these strict rules.

So, the serious practitioner must be simple in his personal habits, have a strong body and a strong mind, and be free of worry, undue excitement, etc. A straightforward, honest disposition is a must. The hand analyst must be truthful in giving his analysis to a client. This great science has been degraded by flatterers. If you merely tell the good points, this is not being very helpful to the client. The client does not pay money to be flattered. A hand analyst who merely gives good news is not a serious hand analyst, but a 'fortune-teller'. A true hand analyst will tell you not only your fortune, but also your misfortune! There is only one exception. The sages of India have said that the exact time or year of death should not be revealed to the client. Such knowledge may have disastrous psychological effects, especially on a sensitive client. So, if the client asks for his life-span, give an answer like this: 'According to the palms, your life span is between seventy and seventy-five. Hand analysts and astrologers, for obvious ethical reasons, are not allowed to reveal the exact year of death.'

Barring this point, the hand analyst must be totally

---

* Harry Benjamin, *Commonsense Vegetarianism,* Thorsons Publishers, Wellingborough, England, 1966.

honest and specific. Of course, you can always tell the truth in a pleasant way. It is perfectly possible to be tactful, and yet very honest. The two need not be incompatible.

If the client has something to say, listen to him. Your aim is to help the client, and answer the questions that he has in mind. Do not waste time arguing with prejudiced people. You should try to convince an open-minded sceptic that hand analysis is a real science, as well as a great art, but if the subject refuses to give you a fair hearing, either ignore him or give him a demonstration of hand analysis. Request that he show you his palms. Examine them carefully, and narrate some major events of the past that have occurred. Reveal the ages and years when these took place. Also, describe the events in some detail. A serious practitioner, having reached a high standard, can do this. Show the lines and mounts of the hands as this demonstration is taking place. If the subject is still not convinced, even though the narration of major events that have occurred has been accurate, precise, specific and in some detail, leave him alone. In some future birth, he will be ready to understand higher occultism. You can't win them all! But an open-minded sceptic will be impressed or convinced, especially when it is clear that this knowledge of the past could not possibly have been mere guesswork, or have been learnt from a third party. The demonstration, to be satisfactory, must always be in private. It should never be done when others are listening. Even if the hand analyst is absolutely correct, the client may deny the truth, due to embarrassment. From professional experience, it has been learnt that many sceptics underestimate the skill of a really good hand analyst. So, when their most cherished secrets are revealed, they are taken aback, and, human nature being what it is, their first impulse is to deny the truth.

The really good hand analyst will keep up to date with the latest research in all aspects of hand analysis. He himself will do a great deal of research. The ancient writings on hand analysis should be interpreted intelligently in the light of modern circumstances. The basic principles will be the same, but the precise interpretation may have to be different. For example, a certain hand feature may, according to the sages of India, show that the subject will be a king. Now, kings were common in ancient India, but they are a rare commodity these days! So, in the modern context, the same feature would mean that the subject will be a rich and powerful person.

A hand analyst should, therefore, base his analysis on the cultural background of the subject. The circumstances of the subject have to be clearly understood before an intelligent analysis can be given. So *Kala* (Time), *Desha* (country) and *Varthamona* (present and existing circumstances) have to be deeply considered when the hands are being analysed.

Let us take a concrete example. A triangle on the Fate Line means good fortune, sudden wealth, unexpected gains, etc. Let us assume that this feature is found on the hands of a humble clerk, and that this sign does not refer to gain through speculation. So the triangle may mean that the clerk has been given arrears by the government, and that the arrears amount to say, one thousand two hundred Malaysian dollars. But let us assume that the same sign is seen on the hand of an oil tycoon from Saudi Arabia. In this case the triangle could mean that the lucky subject has pushed through a very successful oil deal and is the richer by three million Malaysian dollars! Also the entire hand has to be analysed carefully. Do not make the mistake of budding amateurs who pick out one sign, and start commenting on it! That is the surest way of giving hand analysis a bad name. Hand analysis is a comprehensive science, just like chess. All features of the hands must be studied in detail, and a final judgement arrived at only then. Every mount, every line, the texture of the skin, the flexibility of the hands and their consistency, the colour of the palms, the influence of one mount on another mount, of one line on another line – all these must be minutely studied, and then only should a decision be reached.

Always take handprints – this is a must for the beginner. With handprints, you can study the hands at leisure. You have a permanent record. The serious student should build up a library of thousands of hand prints. As soon as the prints have been taken, they should be labelled. The subject's full name, address, date of birth, place of birth, and time of birth should be recorded on the prints. The date when the hand analyst took the prints should also be noted.

There are other points to be borne in mind. A good hand analyst should have a powerful memory. There are thousands of lines that criss-cross the palms of subjects. A really good hand analyst will have a deep interest in the science, and be dedicated to it.

It is perfectly possible to be a master of hand analysis if the serious student gathers vast experience by analysing innumerable hands. Preferably, the number of hands analysed should run into thousands. A really competent hand analyst will have an advanced sense of intuition as well, to complement the scientific aspect of hand analysis. Experience in this science will contribute to sharpening the intuition. Potentially, every person in the world has intuitive faculties. These are merely awaiting development. Also, the real master will arrive at a sound judgement based on independent thought. He should never allow himself to be influenced by the judgements of other hand analysts, no matter how competent or renowned they be. This is because even the most brilliant hand analysts can sometimes make mistakes. After all, hand analysis is a perfect, divine science practised by mortals, not by gods or goddesses.

So, the serious student of hand analysis will concentrate deeply on this science. Concentration, deep and powerful, is the key to success in any walk of life. Hand analysis is no exception.

To develop the powers of intuition, one should practise yoga, and regular meditation. Breathing exercises, preferably yogic ones, will also calm the mind. A calm mind will doubtless promote the unfolding of intuition. But both the yoga exercises and meditation should only be practised under expert tuition. This point cannot be emphasised too strongly. Otherwise, the consequences can be dangerous for the over-enthusiastic student. Rome was not built in a day.

There is one yoga *asana* or posture that is excellent for developing intuition and promoting a good memory. This is the shoulder stand or *Sarvanganasa* as it is called in Sanskrit. Regular practice of this pose will build a strong memory and the practitioner will be able to remember many important combinations of hand analysis. But please do it only under expert guidance.

Hand analysis can be divided into analytical and intuitive aspects.

Analytical scientific hand analysis is that aspect whereby the scientific laws of hand analysis are applied in a systematic manner. A lot of practical experience is required in this case.

As regards intuitive hand analysis, the technique is different. The highly intuitive practitioner gets a certain aspect through a flash of intuition. No reasoning or analysis is involved here. The practitioner simply knows. This faculty of advanced intuition is very necessary for a hand analyst or an astrologer. But as explained earlier, the genuine practitioner will use intuition sparingly. The bulk of the analysis should always be based on scientific hand analysis. If percentages are to be given, let us say he should use 97 per cent scientific hand analysis and 3 per cent intuition. Real intuition *never* contradicts the findings of scientific hand analysis – it always complements it. Hence genuine intuition never contradicts the scientific aspect of the science. So the truly great hand analyst has a profound knowledge of the scientific theory of hand analysis, and also has unsurpassed intuition as a support. In this way, really brilliant and astounding predictions can be made.

Intuition is different from clairvoyance, telepathy, etc. It is superior to these psychic powers. But should a hand analyst also have the psychic power of clairvoyance, then the predictions will be even more remarkable. So intuition is preferable any time to clairvoyance. But there have been some gifted hand analysts who not only were very learned in scientific hand analysis, but also possessed the gift of clairvoyance as well as strong intuition. This has made them among the top hand analysts in the world.

The Indian belief is that intuition can be developed by meditating in a safe manner. Purity of heart, noble motives and a life of self-discipline also aid in developing intuition. Gifted hand analysts have a Line of Intuition on their palms. This gives them the power to predict with uncanny accuracy. But the heartening point is that this Line of Intuition can be developed by the serious student. Of course this requires sacrifice, and the earnest student must meditate regularly and lead a pure life.

Let us now examine certain very important principles of this study. Both the hands have to be examined very carefully. It is a great error to examine one hand only. Such a mistake is proof of the charlatan or the ignorant amateur. One hand shows the inherited tendencies, while the other shows the actual development of the subject. For women, the right hand is always the inherited hand. It is the left hand which is the active, operational hand in their case. It is the active, operational hand that reveals the past, present and future of the female subject. So the future of a woman has to be analysed from her left hand. This is a fact and I have conducted thousands of experiments on this point. At first I was very sceptical, but the evidence of empirical research cannot be ignored. The sages of India have stated categorically that in the art of prediction it is the left palm of a woman that should be studied very minutely. Scientific research has simply proved them to be correct. This is a most profound and important secret of hand analysis. I have been criticized for saying that it is the left hand that is operative for women. But there may be some psychological difference between the sexes that has so far eluded the scrutiny of the psychologists. This difference may account for the fact that in women the vital current flows in and out more strongly through the left palms. Perhaps, in future, when more psychologists study hand analysis seriously, it will become crystal clear why the left palms of women have to be studied in revealing their futures. However, as stated earlier, both the hands have to be scrutinized very carefully. In the case of men, if the man writes with the right hand, it is the right hand that will reveal the past, present and especially the future. But if the male writes with his left hand, it is this hand which will reveal the past, present and the future. So these very important points have to be borne in mind. One hand is the active hand, while the other is the passive hand.

Hand analysis is a mental science. So we are concerned with which hand the subject *writes* with. We are not worried as to whether the subject plays tennis, plays the piano, or does any other manual thing with a certain hand. The one and only criterion is with which hand the subject writes. This, in the case of a man, will give the clue as to which hand will reveal the past, present and the future. All else is irrelevant.

Often, doting parents are anxious to know the future of their children. In the case of children, the expert hand analyst will pay much more attention to the left hand.

This is because up to the age of thirteen years, the lines of the hands have not fully developed or matured. It is interesting to note that in Indian astrology, up to the same age of thirteen, the child is said to be dependent on the influence of his father's horoscope. So, in hand analysis, from the age of fourteen onwards, the lines become mature and relatively stable.

When doing a serious analysis, you should hold both the hands of the subject firmly. The subject should be seated directly opposite the practitioner. The subject and the practitioner should not sit side by side, or stand side by side. You should get into the right habit of analysing the palms by having the subject sit opposite you.

The analysis should be based solely on the evidence presented by the lines, mounts, texture, etc. Do not pay the slightest heed to any remarks made by the subject. The real hand analyst is objective in approach, and should not be influenced by any other factors. Also, the best results will be achieved when the analysis is given in strict privacy and in complete confidence. Hand analysis is a serious science, and a high code of ethics should be observed. There is no good reason for friends, relatives, and others wanting to be in the room, waiting to listen to what the hand analyst has to say regarding the subject. Besides, intuition tends to be disturbed if there is a third party in the room or office. The practitioner must tactfully but firmly explain the position to inquisitive members of the family or friends that they are not helping the practitioner to be at his best by insisting on being in the room. Just as normally, when a patient sees a doctor, it is in strict privacy and confidence, so also the serious practitioner should absolutely refuse to compromise on the ethics of hand analysis.

There should be clear light, so that the lines can be seen easily and readily. It is advisable to have the powerful light of a table lamp as an aid. An anglepoise table lamp is not only safe but most satisfactory for this purpose. With it, hands can be read accurately at night. In ancient India, it was advised that hands should be read during the day. But in those days, anglepoise table lamps were not available. Nowadays, we have various scientific devices to guarantee an adequate supply of light. So the objection to analysing hands at night is no longer valid.

Every feature of the hands should be studied in depth. The pose and carriage of the hands; the texture, colour, shape, proportion, thumb, fingers, nails, wrist, the lines, the mounts, consistency, flexibility – all these have to be analysed with care. Study each line minutely from its beginning to its termination. Consider the proportion and depth of the lines. The mounts in particular should be studied in the utmost detail. Amateurs are carried away by the fascination of the lines, and ignore the mounts. This is a grievous mistake. The mounts can overrule the lines; the lines cannot overrule the mounts. A practitioner who does not regard the mounts as the most important feature of the hand is no hand analyst. He is a rank amateur. The study of the mounts may not be as interesting as the revelations of the lines, but no really perceptive, accurate analysis can be done without a thorough study of the mounts. This is the biggest secret of hand analysis; ignoring the mounts will lead to constant error.

Also, use a powerful magnifying glass in studying the hands. The magnifying glass should be big enough to cover most of the palm. The serious practitioner must get into the habit of using a magnifying glass.

The flexibility of the hands has to be studied. To do this, try bending the four fingers backwards, and find out how far back they can bend. Likewise, the thumb too should be bent backwards, and its flexibility studied. There are three types of 'bends' in the fingers and the thumb. These are the stiff, unbending type, the excessively bending type, and the moderately bending type. The flexibility of the fingers and thumbs will give a clear idea of the adaptable or inflexible nature of the subject.

Also, always note the length of each finger in comparison with the other three fingers. Each finger is normally divided into three parts. The top phalange is at the tip of the finger, while the lower phalange is near the base of the finger nearest to the corresponding mount. In between these two is the middle phalange. We should bend the thumb close to the side of the index finger, and observe where exactly the tip of the thumb touches the lower phalange of the index finger. The index finger is the first finger, or the Jupiter finger. In hand analysis, the thumb is not regarded as a finger. By such a method, the practitioner will understand the subject's will and logical faculties. This is because will and logic are shown in the thumb.

Likewise, the length of the index finger should be measured in comparison with the third finger. The third finger is the ring finger, or the finger of Sun or Apollo. The idea is to ascertain whether it is longer, shorter, or equal to the index finger. The fourth, small or little finger should also be measured against the third finger. You must observe whether the tip of the little finger is above or below the top crease of the ring finger. The little finger is also called the Mercury finger. As regards the middle finger, it is to be measured and compared with the palm proper. By 'palm proper' we mean the area between the base of the fingers and that above the wrist.

The importance of these techniques will be explained in subsequent chapters. These measurements and comparisons have to be made for both hands. But the most accurate results will be obtained from the active, operational hand. In the case of women, it is a simple straightforward matter, as the left hand is always the active, operational hand.

We must also note whether the hand is small or large, and which is greater, the length or the breadth. Any abnormality, such as double thumbs, or curved or twisted fingers, should be noted with care.

Chapter Four

The Map of the Hand. Signs and Marks of Scientific Hand Analysis

The major mounts and the lines of hand analysis will be given in this chapter. It is impossible to understand the basis of the science without a thorough knowledge of the significance of the mounts and lines of the hand. So the eager student should first understand the meanings of the mounts and lines, and then memorize their qualities. To be a good hand analyst, the student must understand the basic principles or laws of scientific hand analysis, but a certain amount of memory work is unavoidable, and even desirable.

The mounts are named after the planets that rule human destiny. Actually, there are nine planets, but in this elementary work on hand analysis we shall study seven planets. In Western hand analysis, only seven planets are considered, but in Indian hand analysis, the shadowy planets **RAHU** and **KETHU** also have their places in the palm. An American hand analyst, Dr. Benham, said that there was no good reason why the mounts of the hand were named after planets. Benham could not have committed a bigger error. His statement reveals that he was certainly not an astro-palmist or an astro-hand analyst. An astro-palmist is one who has a deep knowledge not only of hand analysis but also of astrology. That there is a very deep connection between astrology and hand analysis is indisputable.

Hand analysis is based on two aspects. These two aspects are cheirognomy and cheiromancy. Cheirognomy is the study of character through the shape and size of the hands. Cheiromancy is the study of the lines proper, and these lines will reveal the past, present and future with astounding accuracy to the really brilliant hand analyst. A mastery of both these aspects is a must if one desires to be a really good hand analyst. The study of the lines is more exciting, and many students are tempted to by-pass cheirognomy and head straight for cheiromancy. As stated earlier, this is a most serious mistake. It is vital to master cheirognomy first before the lines can be understood in depth.

The muscular pads that are found on the palm below the fingers are called the **Mounts.** They are not to be confused with calluses on the hand. The mounts reveal the passions and sentiments of the subject. In many cases, the mounts may be displaced. This means that one mount may encroach upon another mount. The mounts have been named after the planets for a very good reason: astrology and hand analysis, as stated earlier, are twin sciences.

There are nine mounts in the hand (see Figure 4-1). These are

- The Mount of Jupiter
- The Mount of Saturn
- The Mount of Apollo or the Sun
- The Mount of Mercury
- The Mount of Lower Mars or Negative Mars (Rahu)
- The Mount of Upper Mars or Positive Mars (Kethu)
- The Mount of Moon
- The Mount of Venus, and
- The Plain of Mars.

Let us consider the mounts one by one. The normal position of the **Mount of Jupiter** is below the base of the first finger, which is called the finger of Jupiter. On this

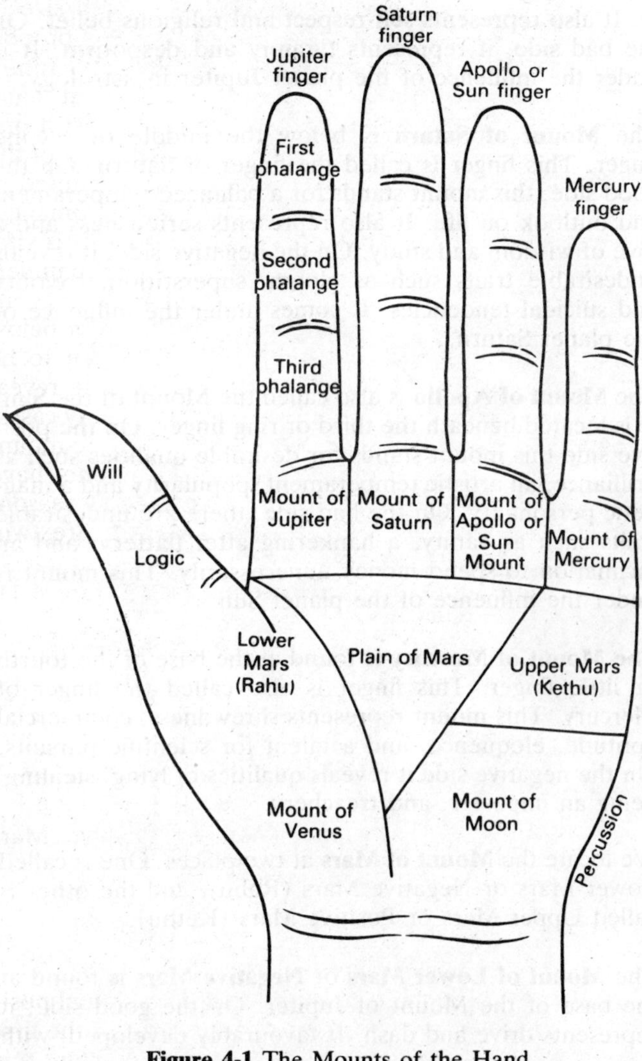

Figure 4-1 The Mounts of the Hand

mount the good side shows ambition, pride and authority. It also represents self-respect and religious belief. On the bad side, it represents tyranny and despotism. It is under the influence of the planet Jupiter in astrology.

The **Mount of Saturn** is below the middle or second finger. This finger is called the finger of Saturn. On the good side, this mount stands for a balanced temperament and outlook on life. It also represents seriousness and a love of wisdom and study. On the negative side, it reveals undesirable traits such as gloom, superstition, frivolity and suicidal tendencies. It comes under the influence of the planet Saturn.

The **Mount of Apollo** is also called the Mount of the Sun. It is located beneath the third or ring finger. On the positive side this mount stands for desirable qualities such as brilliance, an artistic temperament, popularity and a magnetic personality. On the bad side, there are undesirable traits such as vanity, a hankering after flattery, and an inclination to spend money unnecessarily. This mount is under the influence of the planet Sun.

The Mount of Mercury is found at the base of the fourth or little finger. This finger is also called the finger of Mercury. This mount represents shrewdness, commercial aptitude, eloquence, and a talent for scientific pursuits. On the negative side it reveals qualities of lying, stealing, being an imposter, and treachery.

We locate the **Mount of Mars** at two places. One is called Lower Mars or Negative Mars (Rahu), and the other is called Upper Mars or Positive Mars (Kethu).

The **Mount of Lower Mars** or **Negative Mars** is found at the base of the Mount of Jupiter. On the good side, it represents drive and dash. If favourably developed, with other good indications, such subjects are self-starters. Many dynamic marketing managers have a well-developed Mount of Lower Mars. On the undesirable side, it stands for an aggressive state of mind and a self-willed, obstinate personality.

The Mount of Upper Mars or **Positive Mars** is below the Mount of Mercury but above the upper Mount of the Moon. (Figure 4-5 will be helpful). On the positive side it stands for moral courage, endurance and fortitude. Women generally have a well-developed Mount of Upper Mars, as it is well known to psychologists that in general women have more moral courage than men. This applies to women of many races and nationalities.

The **Plain of Mars** is found in the centre of the palm. This is the area of struggle and action. On the bad side, it represents irritability and temper. Well-developed, it shows presence of mind.

The **Mount of Moon** is found under the upper Mount of Mars, and it extends to the wrist on the percussion or outer edge of the hand. On the favourable side it represents imagination, creative ability, idealism, love of travel and change. There is a master-weaver from Iran whose hands have a beautifully, proportionately-developed Moon Mount. On the bad side, there is excessive restlessness, superstition, a flighty nature, and a tendency towards lunacy. The Moon Mount comes under the influence of the planet Moon. The Latin word for Moon is luna, and from luna we get the word 'lunatic'.

The **Mount of Venus** is located at the base of the thumb, and it is enclosed within the Vitality Line. The desirable qualities of this mount are affection, love, sympathy, generosity, grace, sexual capacity, and a love of music.

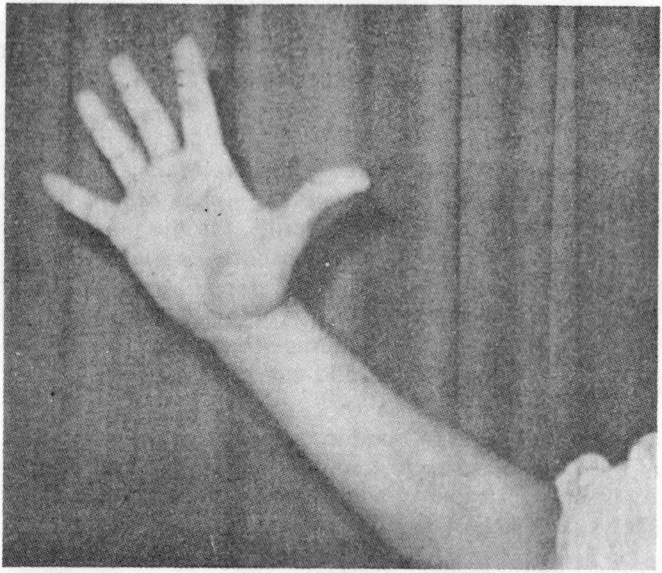

Figure 4-2 A photograph of an almost perfectly proportioned Mount of Venus.

A world-famous sitar player has very well-developed Mounts of Venus on both hands.

The undesirable qualities of the Mount of Venus are sensuality, lasciviousness, coldness, and a lack of the normal sex instinct. The Mount of Venus is under the influence of the planet Venus.

A Mount should not be flat or undeveloped. If it is, this reveals that it is a weak mount. Neither should the Mount be over-developed or over-elevated. This is a point that escapes the observation of many students of hand analysis. An over-developed mount is also bad, and represents evil qualities. A normal mount, and a good

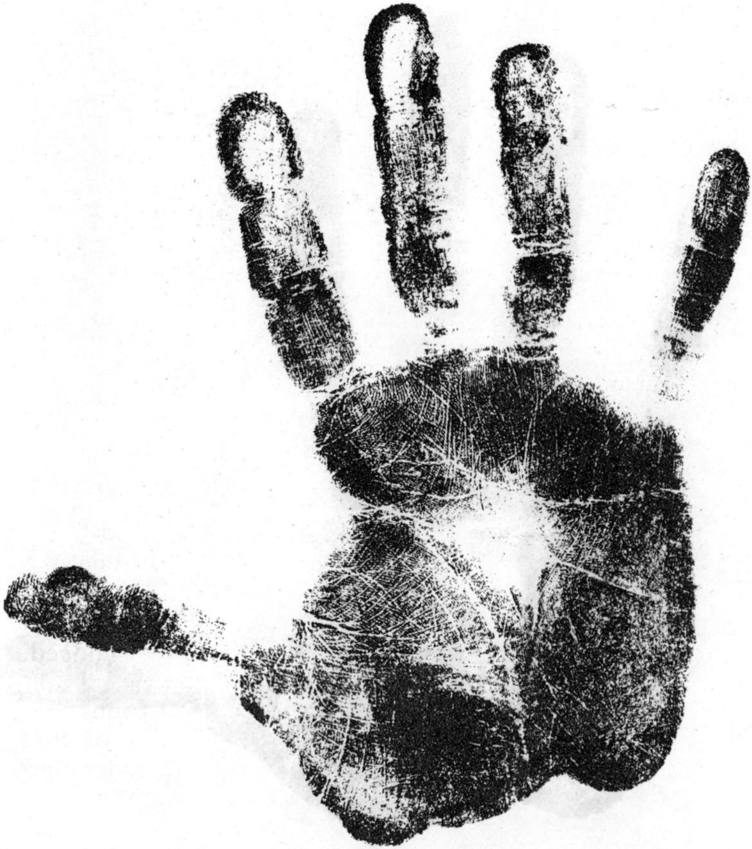

Figure 4-3 The right handprint of a famous musician. Note the well-developed Mount of Venus.

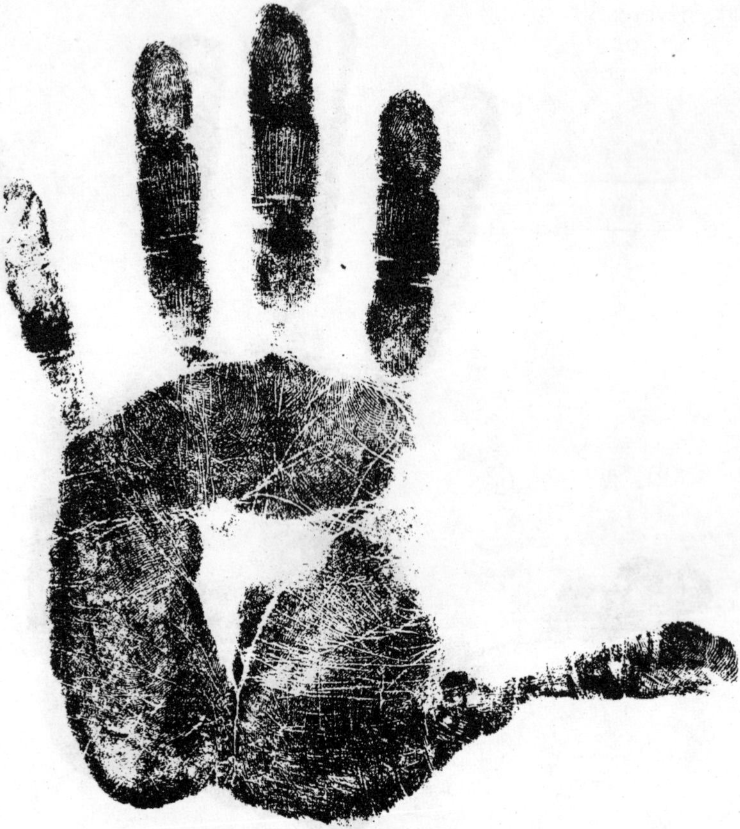

Figure 4-4 The left handprint of the same musician. Note that the Mount of Venus is equally well-developed on this hand.

one, is that which is normally developed. It should be raised in the hands, but not excessively. It should give the appearance of a mountain, but not look like Mount Everest!

For the sake of clarity, let us now tabulate the qualities, good and bad, of the mounts.

CHARACTERISTICS OF THE MOUNTS

Mount	Favourable	Unfavourable
(a) Jupiter	ambition, leadership, religious tendencies, self-respect, wisdom, ethical nature: seen in the hands of lawyers, judges, bankers, businessmen	inferiority complex, poor self-confidence, pessimism
(b) Saturn	serious nature, emotional balance, philosophical tendencies, love of mathematics and agriculture	melancholic tendencies, suicidal tendencies, criminal tendencies, accident-prone, rheumatism, death
(c) Mercury	quick sharp intellect, material success, business acumen, scientific bent of mind, effective communication, eloquence	cheat, liar, confidence trickster, poor communication with the opposite sex, sexual aberrations
(d) Sun or Apollo	magnetic personality, position, success, popularity, success in government service, gain from the govern-	scandal, disgrace, low education, loss in litigation, obstacles in life, failure in government service,

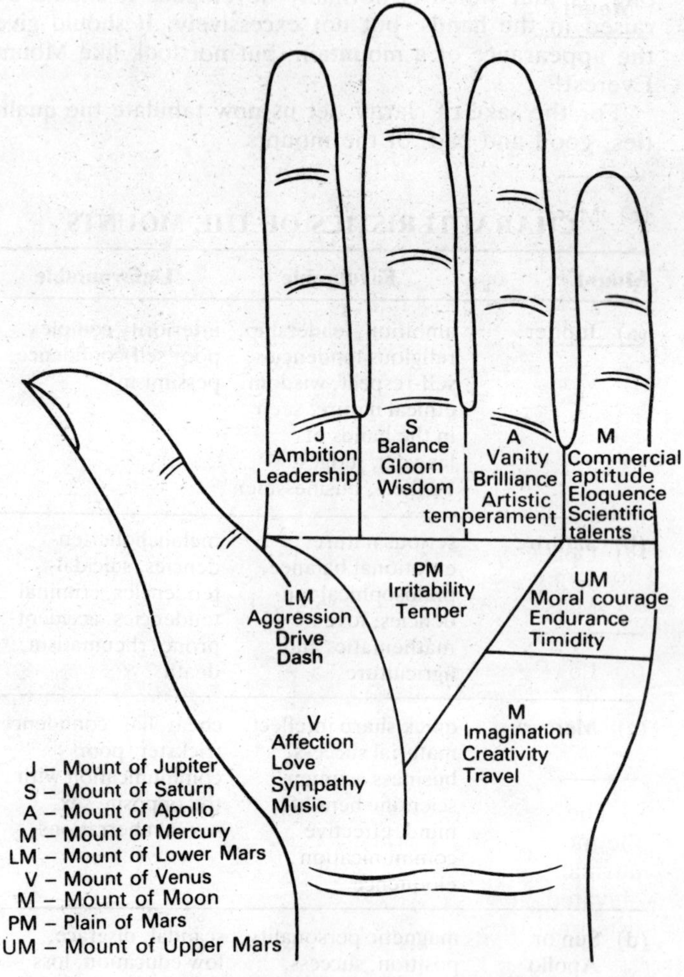

Figure 4-5 Good and Bad Qualities of the Mounts of the Hand

Mount	Favourable	Unfavourable
	ment, good relations with father, high educational qualifications	poor relations with the father
(e) Moon	imagination, poetic tendencies, love of water, love of travel, gain through liquids, creative ability	emotional, weak-minded, over-imaginative, lunacy, suffering from insomnia
(f) Venus	affectionate, lovable disposition, passionate, normal sex drive, love of music, dance	sensuous, over-passionate, immoral, excessive love of material pleasures and comfort
(g) Upper Mars or Positive Mars (Kethu)	moral courage. strong beliefs, resistance	vacillation, yielding nature
(h) Lower Mars or Negative Mars (Rahu)	strong personality, push and drive, adventurous, martial spirit	lazy, unimpressive personality, quarrelsome

The serious student *must* memorize the attributes of the mounts. The mount will show its good qualities if it is normally developed. But if it is depressed, flat or over-elevated, it will show some or all of the evil tendencies listed above.

Let us now have a brief look at the **Lines** of the hand. We shall deal with the lines in depth in later chapters.

The **Vitality Line** is wrongly called the 'Life Line' by amateur hand analysts. This line reveals the degree of vitality in the body, and whether it is basically physical or nervous. It records illnesses, worries and major changes in the subject's life. It also shows periods of good health. By itself, this line does *not* reveal the subject's life span. A long line does not necessarily bestow a long life. Nor does a short Vitality Line mean a premature death.

The **Head Line** is also called the **Line of Mentality.** It shows the intellectual calibre of the subject, as well as his type of mentality. Latent intellectual talents, if any, can be assessed by a thorough scrutiny of this line.

The **Heart Line** reveals the emotional attitude of the subject towards love and sex. This line also shows the physical strength and vitality of that most important organ of the human body — the heart.

The **Fate Line** is also called the **Line of Saturn.** This line shows the material prospects of the subject and his attitude towards his career. Major developments in material circumstances and career are reflected on this line. The Fate Line or Saturn Line comes under the influence of the planet Saturn.

The **Sun Line** is also called the **Line of Apollo.** This line shows the time when the subject feels that his talents are being recognised, and that important ambitions have been achieved. In other words, it reveals the period when 'sunshine' enters the life of the subject. This line comes under the influence of the planet Sun.

The **Line of Affection** refers to significant emotional involvements, *usually* with the opposite sex. It is wrongly called the Line of Marriage by ill-informed hand analysts.

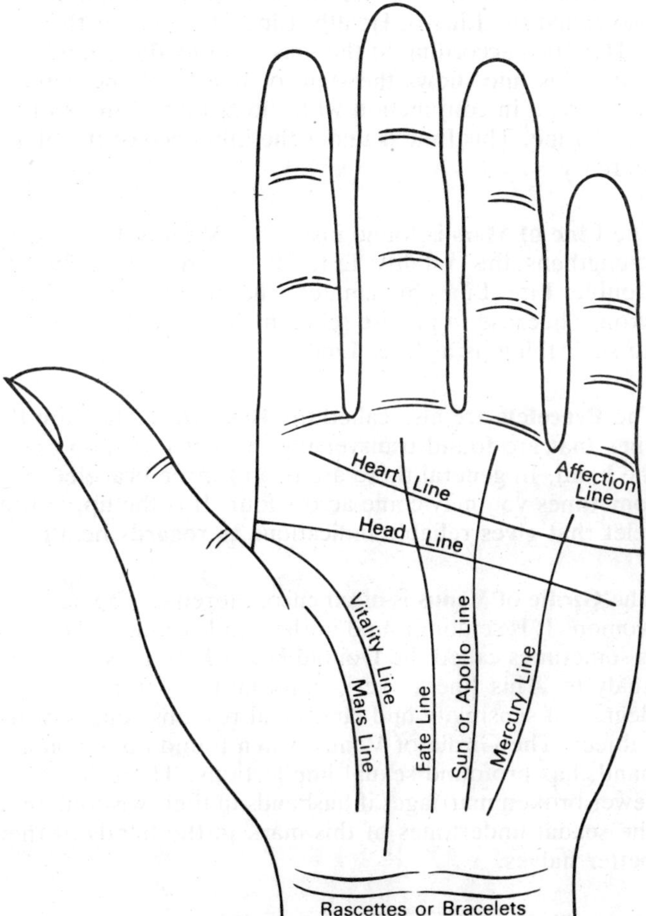

Figure 4-6 The Lines of the Hand

The **Line of Mercury** is referred to by various names. It is also called the Line of Health, Line of Liver, or the Line of Hepatica according to the bias of individual hand analysts. This line shows the state of health of the subject, and is read in conjunction with the Vitality Line and the Heart Line. This Line is under the influence of the planet Mercury.

The **Line of Mars** is found inside the Vitality Line, and it strengthens the Vitality Line. It is wrongly called the Double Life Line by amateur hand analysts. This is wrong, because in precise scientific hand analysis there is no such thing as a Life' Line.

The **Bracelets** are also called the **Rascettes.** They are the lines that are found transversing the wrist at the base of the hand. In general there are two to three bracelets, but sometimes you may come across four. It is the upper bracelet that gives reliable indications as regards health.

The **Girdle of Venus** is often encountered on the hands of women. It is seldom found in the hands of men. This line is sometimes called the Double Heart Line by some hand analysts. This line is very important, as it reveals the degree of sensitivity and emotional responsiveness of the subject. The Girdle of Venus, when found on a woman's hand, has profound sexual implications. There would be fewer broken marriages if husbands in their wisdom knew the sexual undertones of this mark in the hands of their better halves.

You will not often come across the **Ring of Solomon.** This is a semi-circular line found at the base of the index finger or Finger of Jupiter. This line shows a fondness for psychology and a potential talent in the field of occult sciences, such as hand analysis and astrology.

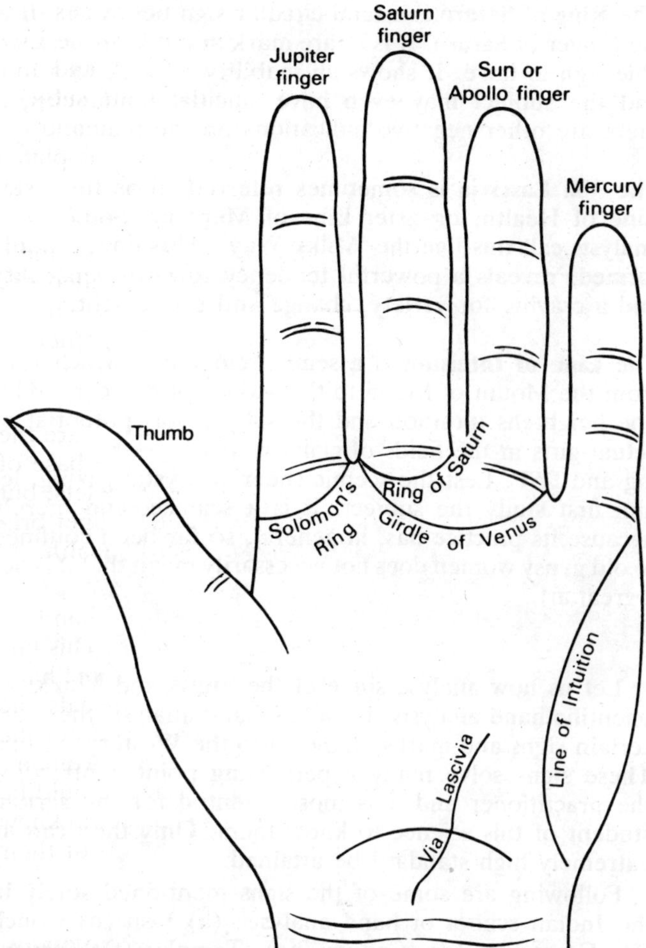

Figure 4-7 The Minor Lines of the Hand

The **Ring of Saturn** is a semi-circular sign below the middle Finger of Saturn. It is a rare mark and it is an undesirable sign to have. It shows an inability to stick to a job, and the subject may even have suicidal tendencies, if there are other negative indications on the hands.

The **Via Lascivia** is sometimes referred to as the sister Line of Health, or sister Line of Mercury. Some hand analysts call this line the 'Milky Way'. This line, if badly formed, reveals a powerful tendency towards sensuality and a craving for variety, change and excitement.

The **Line of Intuition** is a semi-circular line which runs from the Mount of Moon to the Mount of Mercury. This line heightens intuition and the subject has potential or actual gifts in the fields of clairvoyance, crystal-ball gazing and ESP. Lest the sceptic sneer at crystal gazing, let him first study the subject. It is a science, and merely because its practice has, in general, so far been confined to old gypsy women does not necessarily mean that it is not a great art.

Let us now analyse some of the **Signs** and **Marks** of scientific hand analysis. In Indian hand analysis there are certain signs and marks unknown to the Western system. These signs solve many a perplexing point confronting the practitioner and it is most essential for the serious student of this science to know them. Only then can an extremely high standard be attained.

Following are some of the signs mentioned solely in the Indian school oi hand analysis: (a) Fish (b) Conch (c) Crocodile (d) Canopy (e) Temple (f) Serpent (g) Pitcher (Pot) (h) Balance (i) Tree (j) Flag (k) Swastika (l) Line of 'Diksha' or Line of Renunciation (m) Lotus Flower (n) Moon (o) Sun (p) Bangle (q) Vagina (r) Human Face (s) Elephant (t) Horse (u) Club (v) Altar

(w) Arrow (x) Sword (Scimitar) (y) Chained Rascettes and (z) the Line of Bow.

It is interesting to note that these signs can be found in the palms of any race or nationality. For example, I have found the signs of temple, flag, conch, fish and serpent in the hands of Americans, Australians and Chinese.

Let us now consider some of the signs known to Western hand analysts.

The Island: This sign is a harbinger of misfortune, and denotes either a weakness or a loss. The island is made by the splitting of a line. The lower section of the area which has split then returns to the original line. In the palm, the island is always a defect. When a well-marked island is found on the Line of Mentality, the subject will experience mental strain and confusion for the duration of the island. On the Fate Line or Line of Saturn, the subject will be anxious, and perhaps experience financial loss or strain.

The Square: This is an auspicious indication and is generally regarded as a mark of protection. When, for example, the Vitality Line is broken, it shows danger to life and health. But if a square covers the break, it protects the subject from danger. The square is like a box which surrounds the danger-point. It does not allow the current to get out of the box without once again travelling through the normal channel. Hence the square, in a sense, localises the danger.

There is, however, one place where a square has an evil meaning. Should it be found near the Mount of Venus and touching the Vitality Line on the outside, it can mean imprisonment or detention.

A square on the Fate Line or Line of Saturn often refers to protection against difficulties in career or finan-

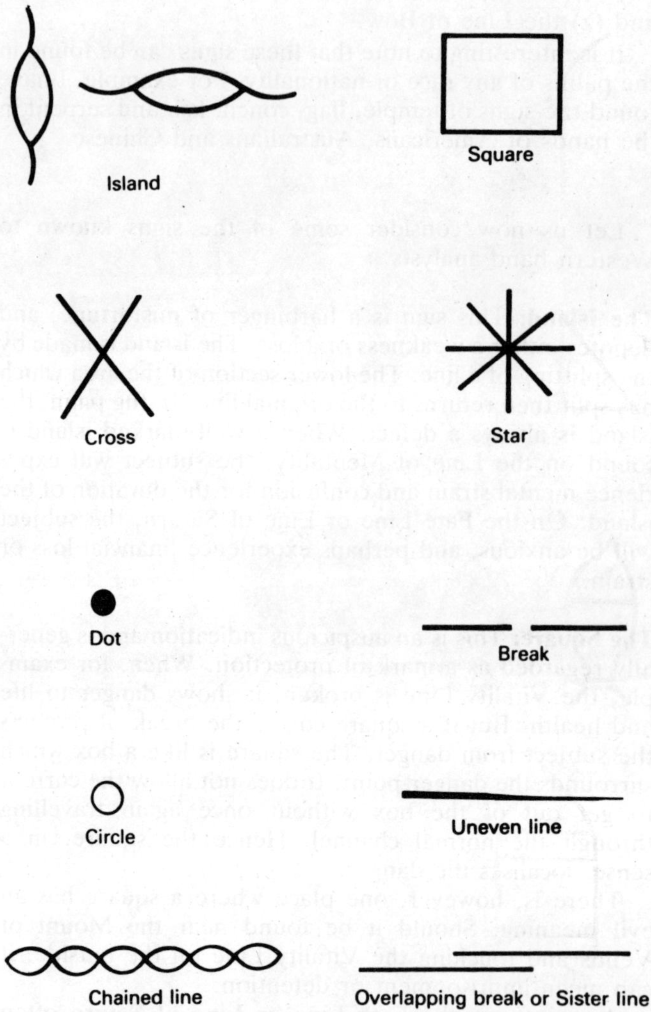

Figure 4-8(a) Some Signs and Marks of Scientific Hand Analysis

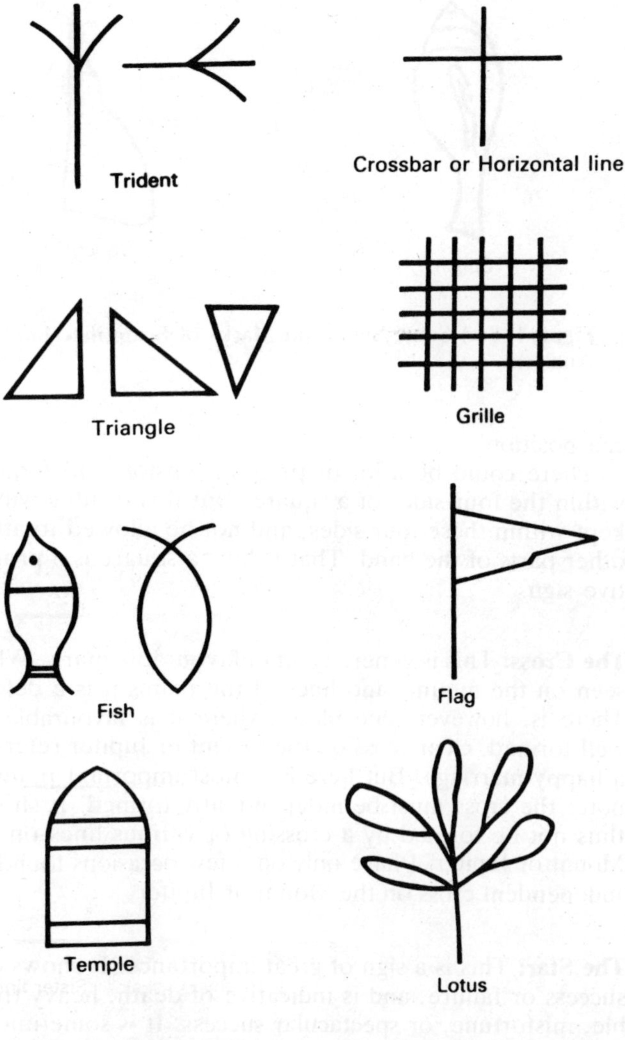

Figure 4-8(b) Some Signs and Marks of Scientific Hand Analysis

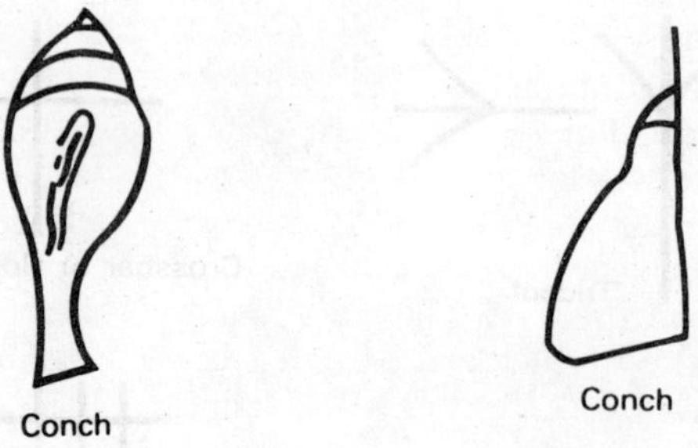

Figure 4-8(c) Some Signs and Marks of Scientific Hand Analysis

cial position.

There could be a lot of trouble, tension and ferment within the four sides of a square. But this trouble will be kept within these four sides, and not be allowed to affect other parts of the hand. That is how a square is a protective sign.

The Cross: This is generally an unfavourable mark. When seen on the mounts and lines of the palms it is a defect. There is, however, one place, where it is favourable. A well-formed, clear cross on the Mount of Jupiter refers to a happy marriage. But here is a most important point to note: the cross must be independently formed. It should thus not be formed by a crossing of various lines on the Mount of Jupiter. I have only on a few occasions found an independent cross on the Mount of Jupiter.

The Star: This is a sign of great importance. It shows our success or failure, and is indicative of death, heavy trouble, misfortune, or spectacular success. It is sometimes a brilliant indication, and sometimes an unfavourable one, depending entirely upon its location. A well-formed star on the Mount of Jupiter is auspicious. Should the Lines of Mentality, Fate and Sun also be well-formed, the subject will surely achieve honour and success in life.

The star thus either illuminates or destroys, in this science. It shows events over which we have little control. A star on the Fate Line shows some kind of catastrophe which the subject will experience. This could be some disaster in love, career or financial position.

The Dot: This is generally the sign of a temporary illness, often of nervous origin. The dot is always a defect. This is because it produces an obstruction to the smooth flow of the Vital Current through the palm. These dots can be black blue, red or yellow in colour. A dot on the Fate Line or Line of Saturn refers to a sudden set-back to the career of the subject. But a dot on the Vitality Line, if it is yellowish in colour, will suggest a bilious nature and an irritable temper.

The Grille: This mark is generally found on the mounts of the hand, and shows that the success of the subject will be hampered by a weakening of the qualities of the mount on which it is present. The grille forms a complicated network, and it is nearly impossible for the Vital Current to pass through it. The Current travels haphazardly through the lines of the grille. Should it finally escape the grille, it will be weak and diffused.

A grille on the Mount of Jupiter will spoil the good qualities of the mount. The subject will be arrogant, self-willed and pompous. I have often found grilles on the Mount of Jupiter of the palms of women clients.

The Break: In this case the Current or Vital Force going through the palm is interrupted and stopped in exactly the same manner as when a telegraph wire is cut. The wider the break, the more dangerous the indication. Thus a clear break in the Vitality Line will indicate either a serious illness or an accident. Always look for repair signs like a square, triangle, or sister line when you encounter a break in a line.

The Overlapping Break: This is a repair sign, and it is also called a sister line. Like the square, it is a sign of protection. Thus broken lines may be repaired when the broken ends overlap each other. So the overlapping break helps transmit the current or Vital Force from the broken end of the line to its regular channel. Let us assume that there is an overlapping break in the Vitality Line. This will mean that the subject will recover from a serious illness or accident.

Crossbars: These are horizontal lines closely grouped together. Crossbars are worse defects than grilles. This is because, with crossbars The Current or Vital Force is totally blocked and has no chance to escape except by overflowing the obstruction. To do this, it must first overflow into the surrounding areas. Crossbars will show the bad side of a mount, such as health defects, and they will also spoil the qualities of a line on the hand. So these marks adversely affect both the mounts and the lines of the hand.

The Chained Line: This formation is produced by the joining together of a number of links, forming a line which is vague, uneven, and shallow. This sort of line has a continuous series of obstructions. Thus a line so affected becomes weak in its operation. Let us assume that the Line of Mentality is chained. The subject will be vacillating, lacking in self-control, liable to headaches and other mental disturbances.

The Trident: This is always a favourable sign. It is often found on the upper part of a line. It is frequently seen at the end of the Lines of Saturn and Sun. A trident is also often seen on the Heart Line, and in this position it bestows wealth on the subject. In this position, the trident will be formed sideways, not upwards. The trident is certainly an excellent indication to have.

The Triangle: This too is always favourable if it is found in the palms. The triangle can refer to intellectual success or material gain. An independently formed triangle is the best formation. But even a triangle formed by a crossing of lines will show favourable effects to an appreciable degree. The clearer and better formed the triangle, the greater the benefits.

We will assume that the subject has a triangle on the Line of Saturn or Fate. In this context the triangle will mean protection of the subject's financial position from a crippling loss. But let us now assume that a triangle is seen on the Fate Line during a time when the subject is running a bright astrological period. The subject wants to know whether a major investment will be successful. Should there be a well-formed triangle on the Fate Line at the respective age, the subject will surely succeed handsomely in this investment.

The Uneven Line: The ideal line is even throughout, but seldom do we come across such a line. You will frequently meet uneven lines. In this case, the line will be deep in some areas, broad and shallow in others, and often fading away entirely. The part where the line is clear and deep will show a favourable period pertaining to the particular line. The period where the line is either broad, shallow, or fades away will be a bad one for the subject.

The Circle: This is a rare sign. Generally, this is an evil mark to have. It is only on the Mount of Sun or Apollo that it is a fortunate mark. In this position, it shows an unexpected rise in life. Eye specialists will be interested to know that a circle on the Line of Heart shows loss of sight.

Let us now study a few of the signs peculiar to the Indian system of hand analysis.

The Fish: A well-formed fish mark is always a boon to the subject. A clearly formed fish mark will show that the planet Jupiter is strong in the hands and horoscope of the subject. The subject will be financially strong, learned, good-hearted, and enjoy a post of authority. This mark also gives a philosophical bent of mind to the subject. It is excellent for a woman to have a clear, strong fish mark on her palms. If she is a housewife, it is a clear indication that her husband will rise materially in life. This will be all the more certain if the favourable, strong fish mark is found in the woman's right hand. This is because, in Indian hand analysis, the right hand reveals something of the material prospects of the husband. This only applies if the woman is fated to have only one marriage in this birth. In Indian hand analysis and astrology, the destiny of husband and wife are inter-related due to the *Karma* of their previous life or lives.

The fish mark can be found anywhere in the palm, but in general it is found near the wrist and frequently attached to the Vitality Line. The fish mark may or may not have an 'eye' mark to it. If the fish mark has the face pointing towards the wrist, the subject will rise in life in middle age. But if the face of the fish points towards the fingers, then the subject will be blessed with prosperity at an earlier age. Also, in this case, these blessings will, basically, last throughout life.

Let us assume that a married woman has a clear, strong fish mark on her palms. In this case she will not be childless if she keenly desires children. This should be of interest to gynaecologists. But the important point to note is that the fish mark must be clear and prominent.

The Temple: This is another rare sign. Great reformers and famous social workers have such a sign on their hands. Should the hand be materialistic, this sign bestows vast wealth on the subject. The temple mark shows that the subject will occupy a very high position in society.

The Conch: The subject having this sign will be learned, and could be a scholar. But if the subject has a materialistic hand, he will become a millionaire. The interpretation varies according to the type of hand and other features of the palms. I once saw a conch mark on the hands of a high official of a certain Asian country. Again, I saw it on the Mount of Mercury of a doctor who consulted me several times. He is extraordinarily brilliant as a physician, and will be world-famous within the next fifteen years. So far, up to the time of writing this chapter. I have seen the conch mark only three times over the past nine years.

The Lotus: This sign is called *Padma* in Sanskrit. It is a rare sign. A subject having this sign will be interested in divine pursuits. He will not show much interest in affairs of the world.

The Flag: The subject with this mark will be distinguished in society. He will possess strength of character and be capable of strong self-discipline. Prominent persons in society will have this favourable mark on their palms. The subject will have property transferred to him, will be strong financially, and will also enjoy peace of mind. A famous American author had this mark on his hand. A

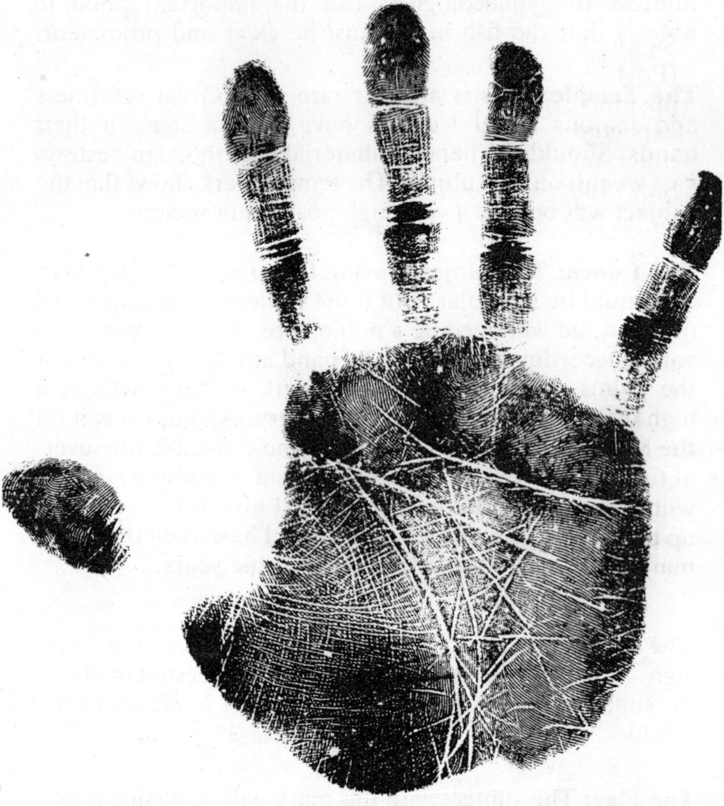

Figure 4-9 The right handprint of a Future Medical Genius. Notice the conch mark on the Mount of Mercury and the mark of the Temple in the centre of the palm. The doctor has an exceptionally brilliant academic record. He is destined to achieve world fame in medicine.

world-famous hand analyst has a prominent flag mark on the Mount of Upper Mars on his right hand. This hand analyst has an international clientele.

Signs of **Hill, Bangle, Vagina, Human Face,** or **Pitcher** (Pot): Any one of these signs will bestow a high political position on the subject. A prominent politician can be expected to have one of these signs on his hands. With other favourable marks such as good, strong Fate and Sun Lines, an ambitious politician can successfully aspire to be a minister in due course.

There are many other signs unique to Indian hand analysis. The ones I have discussed will suffice for an elementary work on the subject. Please do not be disappointed if you cannot locate signs such as the fish, trident, or star in your subject's hands. It takes years of practice to identify these signs surely and quickly. Also, some of the signs may not have the ideal shape as shown in the diagrams. But as long as the shape is substantially the same, the effects, favourable or adverse, will be felt. In identifying the signs and marks of scientific hand analysis, the golden rule is that practice makes perfect.

Chapter Five

The Classification of the Hands

By an accurate classification of his hands, the subject will be able to know, to a large degree, what makes him or her 'tick'. The subject will get a deep insight into the potentialities within his personality. Such knowledge is priceless. If knowledge is power, then foreknowledge is power par excellence. Also, an understanding of one's character is of great help in spiritual and mental development. Many people think that they know themselves, but they often do not have a deep insight into their inner natures. Hand analysis will help in this direction.

In the Indian concept of the universe, there are five elements. These are **Agni** (Fire), **Vaya** (Air), **Prithria** (Earth), **Jala** (Water) and **Akasha** (Ether). The Indians say that Man is a product of these five elements. In a man's make-up, one element may have a greater influence than the other four. Thus, often one of these elements will predominate in the human personality. In the Indian concept of hand classification, five planets are connected with these elements. These planets are Mars, symbolising fire, Mercury representing earth, Jupiter for ether, Venus for water, and Saturn for air. Here, once again, we see the intimate connection between astrology and hand analysis in the Indian concept of the occult sciences.

How do we know which element prevails most in the palms of the subject? For this, the hand analyst should see which of the mounts, Jupiter, Saturn, Mars, Mercury, or Venus, is most elevated in the hands. Generally, the mounts will be elevated, flat, depressed, or moderately elevated. The mount which is most elevated, representing the respective planet and its element type, will give the clue to the personality of the subject. Thus if Jupiter is the most elevated mount in the hands, then it is the planet Jupiter that has the predominant influence. Since Jupiter represents Ether, it is the Ether element that will strongly influence the subject. Thus the technique is simplicity itself: just see which of the five Mounts is the most elevated in the hands.

In the Indian concept of personality-types, there are also three types of personalities. These are known as the **Rajasik, Sattwik,** and **Tamasik** personality-types. This personality classification is followed in a highly specialised form of medicine, the Indian Ayurvedic medicine.

> The **Rajasik** personality is passionate, has desire, is active and has *Kamic* thoughts.
>
> The **Sattwik** type is religious, influenced by high ethics, pure has moral and spiritual feelings, and a calm mind.
>
> The **Tamasik** type is vulgar, indolent, moved by low ideals and has wicked tendencies.

Let us now, with this background knowledge, study the **Planets** and their personality types in the Indian method of hand classification.

Mars: When this mount is very elevated, we have a type called 'the Fire type'. Hence a fiery, aggressive personality is the result. This subject will be of the **Tamasik** type. He will be quick-tempered, very keen, brave, and the scourge of his enemies.

Mercury: When this mount is very bulging in the hands, the earthy qualities will prevail. This subject will be of the **Rajasik** type. He will be intellectual, learned, and of an independent nature. He will have many friends, and he will be very materialistic and practical by nature. He will be interested in money-making, trade, and commerce. It is interesting to note that in astrology the planet Mercury stands for intellect, trade, business instincts and commerce.

Jupiter: When this planet is highly elevated, the subject will be of the Ether type. This is because Jupiter represents Ether. The personality type will be that of the **Sattwik** category. The main characteristics of this personality-type will be kindness, wisdom, a calm, contented mind and mature judgement.

Venus: If this mount is very elevated, the subject will be influenced by the Water element. The personality-type will be **Rajasik.** The subject will be fond of the pleasures of the senses. Wine, women and song will be his battle cry. The subject will thus be pleasure-loving. Frequently this subject will be handsome, pretty, or good-looking.

Saturn: Should this mount be predominant, the subject will be moved by the Airy element. The personality-type will be **Tamasik.** The subject will have a body formation which is clumsy, unattractive, tall, bony, and the skin will lack lustre. Hence the physical appearance will not be particularly attractive. The subject will also be prone to diseases of the internal organs.

All you have to do now is to scrutinize both your palms very thoroughly and decide which mount is the most elevated. This highly elevated mount will give you a pretty good clue as to your personality-type. You will gain a fresh insight into the real 'you'. You do not have to tell them, but you can closely observe the palms of your friends the next time you see them, and then decide for yourself which element rules them. With incessant practice, you will soon be adept in deciding which element dominates your friends. This information should be especially useful to businessmen who wish to size up prospective clients.

The Indian system of classification of hands is logical, as it is based on the study of the mounts. The mounts represent each planet in turn. Of course a subject can have two elevated mounts, one being more elevated than the other, and in this case the classification of hands becomes more complex. But this book is meant for beginners. The Indian classification given here will be pretty accurate, and will still give you a good insight into your subject's character and potentialities. The assessment of a combination of two to three mounts is a very complex matter, requiring very sharp judgement and deep knowledge.

Let us now study the Western system of hand classification. While there are some differences of opinion among Western experts on this, the **Shape of the Hands** is very important. In the Western system, hands are classified into seven types. These are the (a) **Elementary** (b) **Square** (c) **Spatulate** (d) **Philosophic** (e) **Conic** or **Artistic** (f) **Psychic** and (g) **Mixed** types.

Let us first of all study (a) **The Elementary Type** (See Figure 5-1)

This type of hand has short fingers and the hand will have an awkward formation. Very few lines will be observed on either hand. The thumb, signifying intellect, will be badly formed. It will usually be short and poorly developed. Such a subject will be ruled largely by animal instincts. He or she will have a 'cave-man' mentality, and reason will take a back seat. Such subjects are well-suited to manual labour.

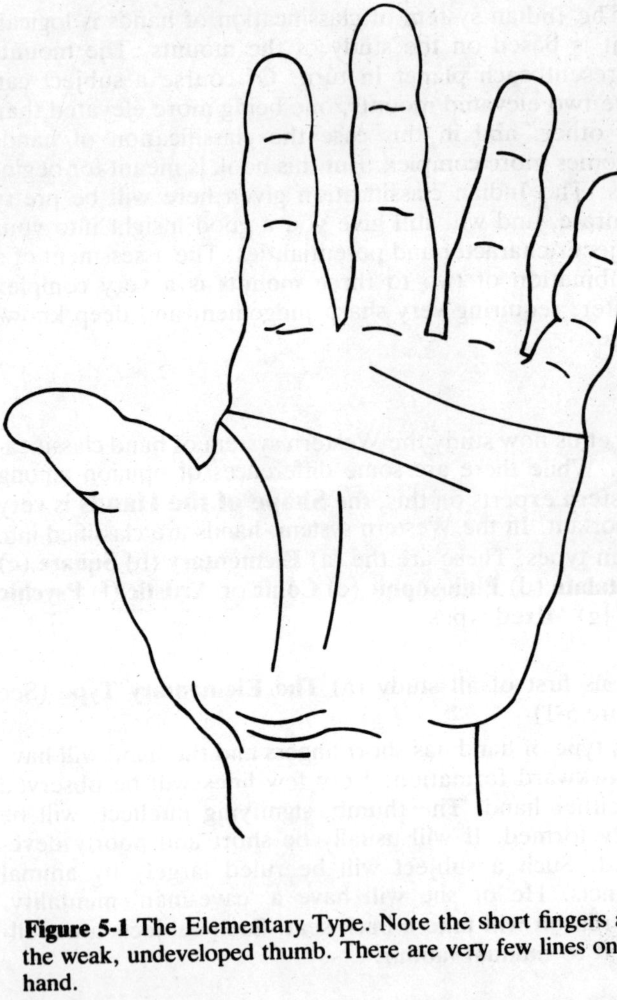

Figure 5-1 The Elementary Type. Note the short fingers and the weak, undeveloped thumb. There are very few lines on the hand.

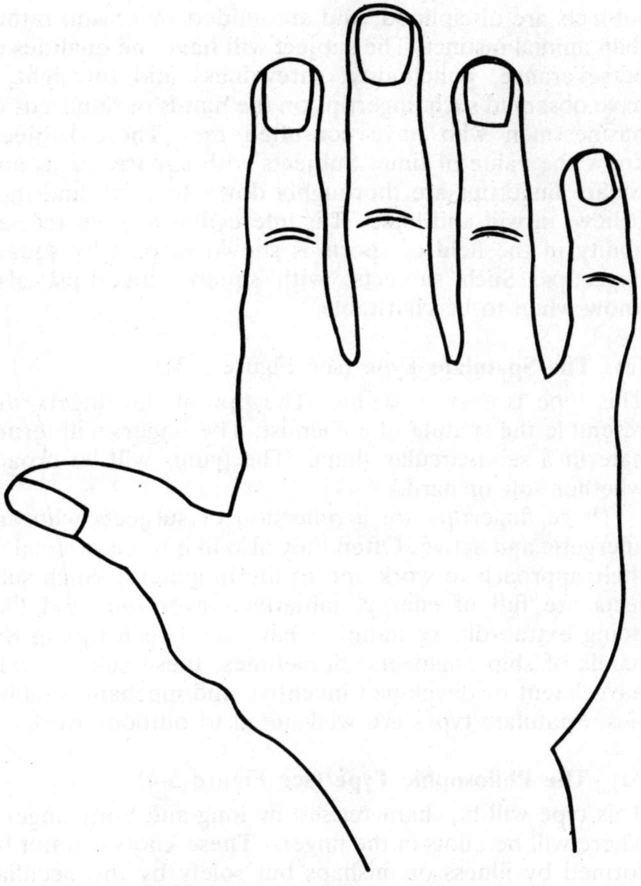

Figure 5-2 Square fingertips

(b) **The Square Type** (see Figure 5-2)

The palm will be more or less squarish in shape. The fingertips at the nail ends will also be quite squarish. Such subjects are disciplined, and are guided by reason rather than animal instinct. The subject will have the qualities of perseverance, punctuality, shrewdness and foresight. I have observed such fingertips on the hands of hundreds of businessmen who have consulted me. These subjects know the value of time. Subjects with square hands and square fingertips are thoroughly down to earth and they believe in will and logic. It is interesting to note that an ability in the field of sports is shown in part by square fingertips. Such subjects, with square fingertips, also know when to be charitable.

(c) **The Spatulate Type** (see Figure 5-3)

This type is easy to define. The tips of the fingers will resemble the spatula of a chemist. The fingers will terminate in a semi-circular shape. The palms will be broad, whether soft or hard.

These fingertips are a reflection of subjects who are energetic and active. Often they also like to be original in their approach to work and to life in general. Such subjects are full of energy, initiative, invention, and like doing extraordinary things. I have seen such tips in the hands of ship engineers. Sometimes, these subjects will have latent or developed inventive and mechanical abilities. Spatulate types are well-suited to outdoor work.

(d) **The Philosophic Type** (see Figure 5-4)

This type will be characterised by long and bony fingers. There will be knots in the fingers. These knots will not be formed by illness or mishaps but solely by the peculiar mental habits of the subject. Philosophers, yogis, and mystics have such hands. These subjects will prefer higher wisdom to a pot of gold. They are not fond of joining the rat race. Money is not their god, or the be-all and

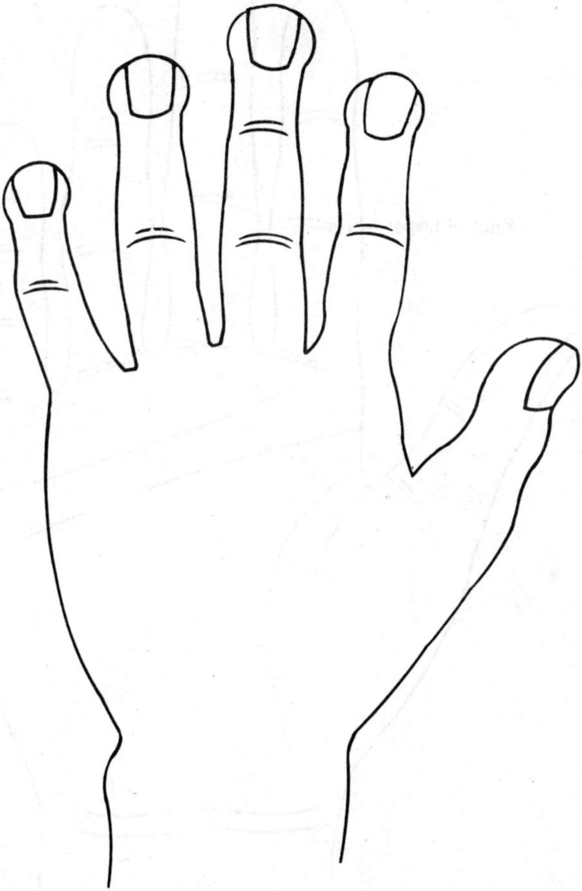

Figure 5-3 Spatulate fingertips

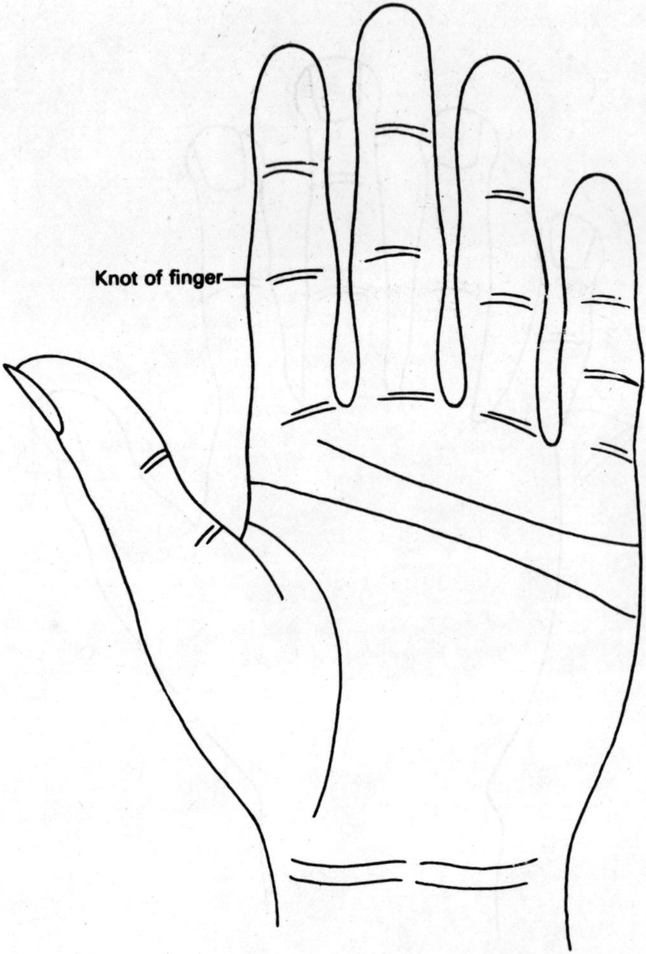

Figure 5-4 The Philosophic type of fingertips

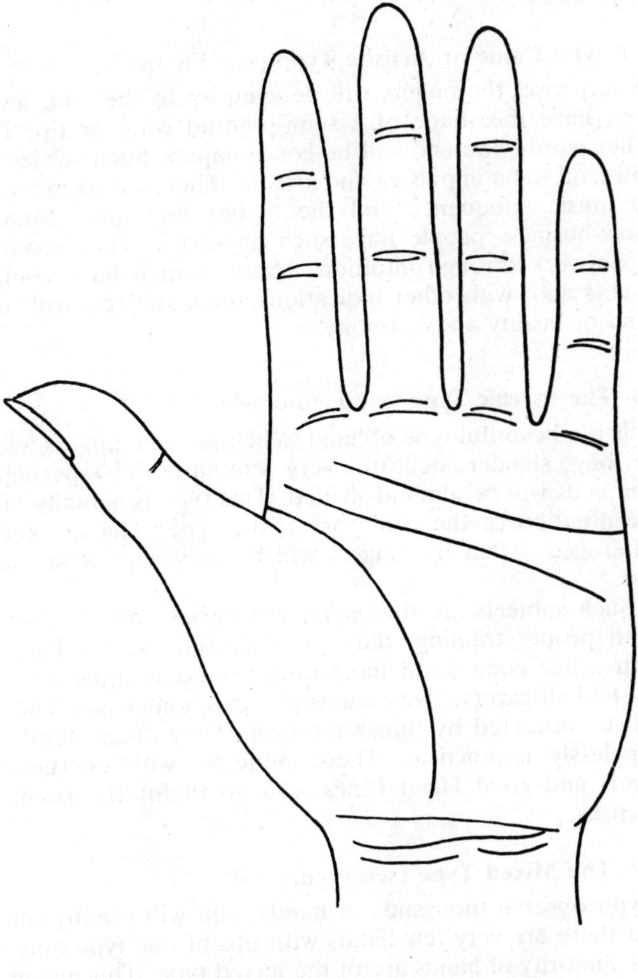

Figure 5-5 The Conic or Artistic type of fingertips

end-all in life. Many of the sages of India who discovered the laws of scientific hand analysis and astrology have had such hands.

(e) **The Conic** or **Artistic Type** (see Figure 5-5)
In this case, the fingers will be even up to the end, and then have the shape of a semi-pointed cone or tip. In other words, the end will be cone-shaped. Such subjects will tend to be impulsive and artistic. They will be moved by music, eloquence and the higher emotions. Many show-business people have such fingertips. These conic types work through intuition. Many women have conic fingers and, with other indications, such subjects will be fond of beauty and harmony.

(f) **The Psychic Type** (see Figure 5-6)
This is a beautiful type of hand to behold. The fingers will be long, slender, delicate, very feminine and tapering. The nails will be almond-shaped. This type is actually an accentuation of the conic or artistic type. The marked difference is that the fingers will be very narrow at the end.

Such subjects are dreamers, visionaries and idealists. With proper training, they could become seers. They, with other good hand indications, could become good crystal-ball gazers, clairvoyants and psychometrists. They will be attracted by things mystical. They are generally hopelessly impractical. These subjects, with energetic hands and good Head Lines, can go in for the occult sciences.

(g) **The Mixed Type** (see Figure 5-7)
If you observe thousands of hands, you will readily see that there are very few hands with tips of one type only. The majority of hands are of the mixed type. This means that one tip might be square, another conic, and yet

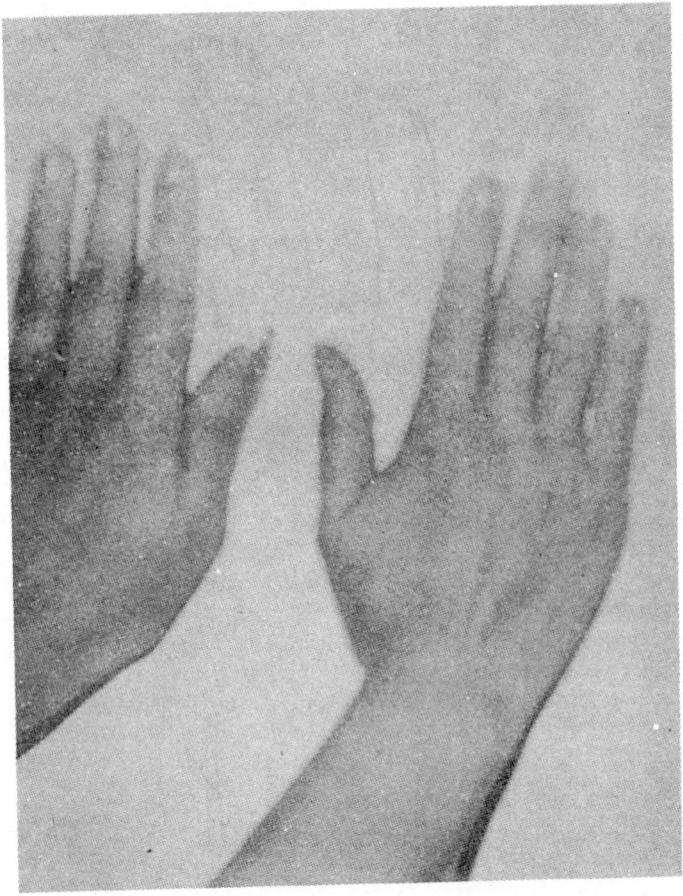

Figure 5-6 Psychic fingertips. Note the almond-shaped nails.

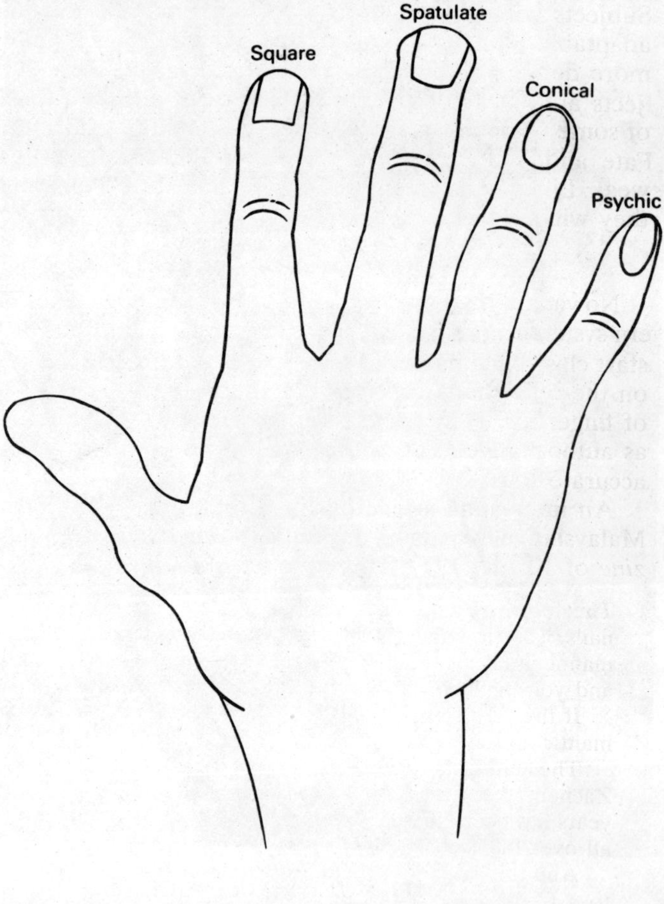

Figure 5-7 Mixed fingertips

another spatulate. Subjects with hands like these are frequently versatile and have various interests and talents. This is all the more certain if there is a small fork at the end of the Line of Mentality. This fork shows versatility. Subjects with mixed fingertips are generally flexible and adaptable to many different circumstances. This is all the more definite if their hands are also flexible. These subjects are 'Jacks of all trades'. They can also be masters of some, if they have good Lines of Mentality with strong Fate and Sun Lines. Otherwise, with mixed fingertips, weak Lines of Mentality and faint Fate and Sun Lines, they will be Jacks of all trades, and masters of none!

Nowadays, modern hand analysts who follow the Western system ignore the shape and size of the palm when they start classifying hands. A well-known Indian hand analyst on the other hand classifies hands according to the types of fingertips. If in doubt take the shape of the fingertips as authoritative. You will be right most of the time, and accurate too.

An interesting article by Jim Gibbins appeared in the Malaysian newspaper, the *Sunday Star's Parade Magazine* of 10 July 1977. He wrote·

> The future, friends, is in your hands. Well, your finger nails. Take a look at them. If they are cut in a squared-off manner that means that you are resolute and calculating and you ought to do very well in business.
>
> If they are rounded .... well, that means you are a romantic and a bit of a dreamer.
>
> The authority for these findings is Professor Daniel Zachen, the Czech sociologist, who over the past two years has been closely examining thousands of finger nails all over the world.
>
> And this week in Copenhagen he reported on his work to a Conference dedicated to *'physical manifestations of human proclivities.'*
>
> Said the professor: '93 per cent of the millionaires in

my survey had square finger nails — the squarer the nails the more powerful the tycoon. But 97 per cent of the poets, musicians and other artists I saw had pronounced rounded finger nails.'

And not a penny in the bank either!

The researches of the learned Professor Daniel Zachen bear out the truth of hand analysis in that square tips, with other good indications, reflect the successful businessman. But the learned professor, with due respect, mistakenly thinks that the squareness of the nails is due to the manner in which they are cut. The truth is that square tips are produced by a particular type of mind and thinking — practical, businesslike, shrewd — and these tips are produced by the way the Vital Current flows in and out of the fingertips. The MIND creates the shape of the fingertips!

Let us now study other aspects of hand classification. To summarise, we have learnt that the Western system classifies hand types into seven categories. The Indian system classifies the same into five categories, based purely on the mounts. Combine the two and you get the best of both worlds, and your diagnosis will be all the more keen and perceptive.

It is interesting to note that Cheiro, who was world famous during his time as a hand analyst and clairvoyant, speaks, in one of his works, of the hands of nations. He said that in northern Russia, Siberia, Iceland and Lapland, the primitive elementary type of hand is generally seen. This does not seem to agree with my research. I have studied the hands of clients from Iceland, and certainly they did not have the elementary type of hand. He also said that Swedes, Danes, Germans, Dutch, Englishmen and Scotsmen have square hands. They have a high regard for reason, logic, authority and the legal processes. There seems to be a fair amount of truth in this particular observation by Cheiro.

The Philosophic type of hand, according to Cheiro, is found generally among Easterners, and especially among the Indians, with their great emphasis on religion and philosophy. This again, according to my research, has more than a grain of truth in it.

The conic or artistic type of hand, according to Cheiro, may be found amongst Italians, Spaniards, French, Irish and Greeks. These people are artistic, romantic and poetic in their personality-types. My own observations have led me to the conclusion that many Filipinos also have conic tips. This is interesting, as it is well-known that many Filipinos have Spanish blood in them. Also, throughout the world the natives of the Philippines are renowned for music, song and dance.

Cheiro said that many Americans have spatulate hands; at least, their tips are generally spatulate. This observation seems to be valid even today. In fact among the white races, it is the Americans who seem to have spatulate fingertips more frequently than, say, the English, French, Germans, etc.

The psychic and mixed types can be found in any subject of any nationality. In other words, it is difficult even to make a broad classification of these types.

Let us now study other features of the hand in the classification of hand types. Let us have a look at the concept of the **Size of the Hand.** Incidentally, when the subject presents his hands for inspection, the expert hand analyst immediately tries to classify them. This procedure will give a valuable insight as to what makes the subject 'tick'.

Small Hands

The size of the hand should be in proportion to the size of the body. When the size of the hand is below average size, we call it a small hand. Subjects with small hands have the ability to grasp things quickly. They work through intuition. They will make fast decisions. They will be interested in grasping the main points of a problem. They will not have time for minor details. Subjects with small hands will have big ideas. They will desire to manage large organizations. They think big and plan big. It is interesting to note in this context that Napoleon Bonaparte, the great French dictator, had small hands. Certainly, his thinking was on a grand, sweeping scale.

Big Hands

This can be determined when the size of the hand is at least slightly larger than the average. Such subjects are interested in small details. They are fond of analysis. They will approach life with care, caution, and forethought. They will think a couple of moves ahead, just like expert chess players.

It is pertinent to note that in general, short and long fingers will show the characteristics of small and big hands respectively.

Even and Uneven Sets of Fingers

Noticing this is most useful when judging the ability to acquire wealth, as well as the character of the subject. To judge this, examine the lower creases of the four fingers of the hand. That means you ignore the thumb. The lower creases are the places where the beginnings of the fingers and the end of the palm proper meet. If these creases form a straight line, we then have an 'even' set of fingers. Should these not fall in a straight line, we have an 'uneven' set of fingers. The 'even' set of fingers give a well-balanced personality. The subject will have a good

Figure 5-8 Uneven set of fingers. The Mercury finger is low-set on the right hand.

sense of life's values. The 'uneven' set of fingers will show certain weaknesses pertaining to the respective fingers which are low-set.

Let us take a concrete example. Say for example, that the subject has an uneven set of fingers, and that only one finger is low-set. We shall assume that it is the little finger, or the Finger of Mercury. Now in astrology Mercury deals with money, wealth, business acumen, etc. So, a low-set Mercury finger will indicate some defect or handicap pertaining to money, wealth, business acumen, etc. Such a subject will therefore have to struggle against adverse financial circumstances for at least some part of his life. In the horoscope, it will be found that the planet Mercury will be correspondingly weak, or afflicted by evil aspects of a malefic planet. Should such a subject have other good marks, the subject will at some stage make money and be financially strong. But let us assume that the finger of Mercury is low-set, the Fate Line poor for most of its length, and the Sun Line tattered and battered. In such a case it is a certainty that this subject will have pressing financial problems for most of his life.

The Length and Breadth of the Palm

Firstly, we have to judge whether the palm is broad or narrow. So, let us study **the broad palm.** In this respect, the breadth of the palm will be greater than the length. If in doubt, use a six-inch ruler and measure. In scientific hand analysis, calculation plays an important role; mathematics has a definite place in this science. When we deal with the calculation of age in scientific hand analysis, it will become clear that mathematics is required before the times when events will occur can be pin-pointed ahead of time.

Let us continue with our study of the broad palm. A subject with broad palms will have ingenuity and will have the potential to achieve success in life. The circulation of blood in this subject will be strong and active. Such subjects have solid commonsense, which makes them successful in life.

The narrow palm is not so favourable. The subject will be selfish, unless there are compensating features. It is normally an undesirable feature.

The long palm will be longer than the fingers. Should the palm be shorter, then it is a short palm. Subjects with long palms will be thoughtful and go into detail in all they do. If the Line of Mentality is sloping towards the Moon Mount, then imagination will also be present.

The Flexibility of the Hands

The hand reflects the quality of the mind. Flexible hands show a flexible mind, stiff hands show a stiff mind.

Now let us assess this flexibility. How do we do this? Take the subject's hand in your left hand. With your right hand, press the subject's fingers backwards. Make sure that you do not break the fingers!

Subjects with **flexible hands** will have a good imagination. They could well have great material success. Subjects with flexible hands and thus flexible minds can accommodate other people and get along well in company. It is good to have flexible hands.

Let us now study **the stiff hand.** The fingers will bend back slightly. This reveals a stiff mind. Such subjects are rigid in their views. A tendency to be narrow-minded and to exert extreme care in money matters is shown. The entire personality will be unadaptable. A narrow quadrangle in the palm will show a tendency to be extra cautious in money matters. The quadrangle is the space between the Heart Line and the Line of Mentality. This space is the 'vision meter'. This subject will shun new ideas and will dress conservatively. Although these indications are largely accurate, there will naturally be exceptions, as in any other science.

If the Jupiter or index finger bends back a lot, the subject will be outspoken in nature. This outspoken nature will be confirmed by a wide space between the line of Mentality and Vitality. The subject will try out new ideas as well and be talkative.

The layman makes a mistake in thinking that the flexibility or stiffness of the hands is determined by manual labour or the occupation of the subject. Nothing could be further from the truth. Hand analysis is a science of the mind. The stiffness or flexibility of the hands is determined entirely by the mind that directs them.

The circulation of the blood determines the **Colour of the Hand.** The normal colour of the hand is rosy or pink. Any other colour will show that there is something wrong with the health or temperament of the subject. The colour of the hand can reflect the working of the cardio-vascular system of the body. It gives very valuable clues as regards health. This is so, regardless of the actual pigmentation of the skin. A healthy palm is rosy, whether it is that of a Tamil, a Chinese or a European!

The Pink Palm

On the predictive side, the colour of the palm is revealing. A pink colour will show good fortune. This palm reveals a happy nature and the subject will look on the bright side of life. Material prospects will be bright.

However, the palm will show that the subject has a tendency to suffer from blood pressure problems, especially if it is excessively red. A subject with a **red palm** will be under the influence of the planet Mars since in astrology Mars rules the colour red. Such subjects will view things seriously, whether it be in love, war or religion. The red palm is not a very good indication. But these subjects will be passionate by nature, and have robust personalities as well. The red palm will suggest certain conditions in excess.

The **yellow palm** will show a bilious nature. The subject will be melancholic and irritable by nature. He will suffer from an excess of bile in the body, which makes him irritable. The subject may also be prone to immoral sexual irregularities. He will be very much influenced by the planet Saturn, so we call this palm a Saturnian palm. For indications of immoral tendencies, we must also examine the Heart Line, Mount of Venus, and the Via Lascivia.

The White Palm

This is unfortunate. Such subjects will be cold and selfish. They will have very little sympathy for others. This whiteness is caused by an insufficient supply of red blood corpuscles in the body. These subjects will also be lethargic. With other bad indications, the white palm could show poverty.

Let us now study the **black palm.**

We must also study the race of the subject. If the palmist suspects that the blackness is due to an irregular or poor blood supply, then the black palm will have a meaning. However, among Southern Indians or Negroes, for example, we would expect the palm to be darker in colour. But if the blackness is not due to racial colour but to an irregular blood supply, then the black palm will have a distinct meaning.

Finally, let us study the **blue palm.**

Blueness of the palm will show that the subject suffers from poor blood circulation or heart weakness, especially so if there is a bluish tinge at the base of the nails. So the colour of the palm does give accurate indications of health and temperament.

The Texture of the Hands

This shows the coarseness or natural refinement of the subject. Here again the layman makes a mistake. The coarseness or refined nature of the subject's skin is not due to his occupation. Intellectuals can have a coarse texture to their skins, while a manual labourer can have a fine skin texture. When we study the texture of the skin, we study the back portion of the hand. Always examine both hands. The texture of the skin is determined by the quality of the mind. We must never examine one hand alone.

The Soft Hand

If the subject's hand has a fine or soft texture, the person will have a refined mind. Imagine the texture seen in the hands of a baby. Such a texture will be fine and delicate. An adult having such a texture will be refined and sensitive. This will be confirmed if the subject has many fine lines on both hands.

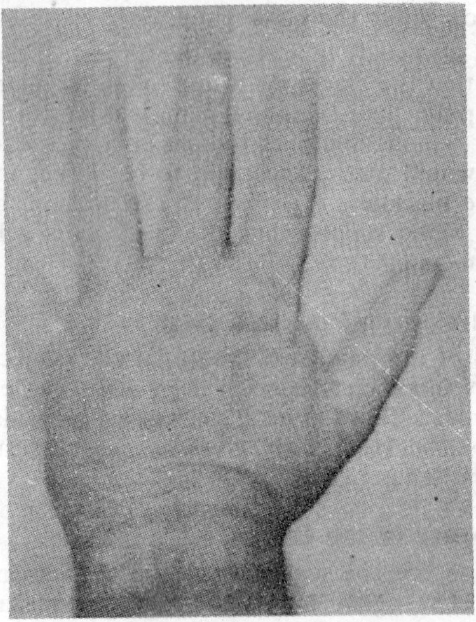

Figure 5-9 Note the coarse texture of the skin

The Coarse Hand

A coarse texture quite often goes with a robust constitution and a desire to work outdoors. Such a subject will be coarse in thinking, and tend to be aggressive in nature.

The Elastic-Textured Hand

We shall now examine a hand with an elastic skin texture. The texture of the skin will be neither fine nor coarse, but in between. Such a texture is often seen on the hands of lawyers, businessmen, and other active professionals. Such a texture is also called a 'medium texture'. Such a subject will be active, both physically as well as mentally.

'Sensitive Pads'

If you examine some hands you will find fleshy pads on the tips of the first phalanges of the fingers. These are called 'sensitive pads'. Such a subject will be careful not to hurt the feelings of others, and this is also a sure indication that the subject is most sensitive, and becomes upset even over trifles.

Chapter Six

The Study of the Thumb

There is an intimate connection between the thumbs and the brain. Doctors inform us that there is a 'thumb centre' in the brain. So the connection has a basis in physiology.

The thumb is vitally important in the study of the hand. Hand analysis and astrology are twin sciences. The thumb represents the *Lagna* or Ascendant (the sign rising in the eastern horizon at the time of birth). The Indian school of hand analysis which has gone into the study of the thumb in very great detail indeed places great emphasis on the importance of the thumb. The shape and size of the thumb strongly influence the character of the subject. Indian astrological experts also say that an individual's future can be analysed on the basis of the *Lagna* or Ascendant, and that from the thumb alone the *Lagna* and the person's whole life history can definitely be obtained. In the Indian study of the thumb, the colour, length, breadth, shape and the lines themselves of the thumb are very important features. Indian thumb experts say that the colour and length symbolize time and place. For example, when Aries is in the ascendant, a faint sign of a Ram can be seen on the first phalange of the thumb. In both Western and Indian astrology, Aries is symbolized by the figure of a ram. The Indian science of discovering destiny in the thumb is called *Ravana Samhitha*.

It is a fact that no two thumb imprints have been found to be exactly alike. The thumb therefore is a reliable symbol of a person's individuality. This fact is recognised by police and immigration authorities throughout the world. Therefore the thumb is like a unique, reliable, and individual seal. The very detailed Indian science of thumb analysis merits a book to itself, but for a start, let us analyse the Western system of thumb analysis.

The Western System

In Western classification, the thumb is divided into two sections. It is suggested that the reader flex the thumb towards the palm. The upper part or the top section of the thumb is called the Will phalange. The lower section is termed the Logic phalange. It is true to say that the thumb reflects inherited qualities. Besides, the way in which the environment affects character is also shown by the thumb. Let us now study the thumb according to various types.

The Stiff Thumb

Such a subject will have a will of iron. We can safely assume that certain strong-willed dictators and powerful world leaders had or have such thumbs. This type of thumb shows stubbornness and a certain lack of adaptability, but such a subject will be persevering, and have very strong powers of resistance. The subject with a stiff-necked, straight thumb will generally have good logical powers and will not allow himself or herself to be swayed by emotion. Such a subject will have a lot of common-sense and self-control. This will be all the more certain if there is a good Line of Mentality on the hand. However, it is not a desirable trait if the thumb is exceptionally stiff and so rigid that it will not bend in the slightest degree. Such a subject will have a mean nature. Let us now study the other types of thumbs.

The Supple Thumb

It is easy to identify such a thumb. This thumb will bend backwards without any trouble. These subjects will be adaptable, flexible, generous and may even have some artistic talents in their make-up. Also, they may be spendthrifts. This latter indication will be all the more certain if there are gaps between all the fingers when held close together. Because of their flexibility, these subjects will be very popular.

The Waisted Thumb

In this case, the second phalange will have a narrow appearance in the middle, and the thumb will resemble the waist of a slim woman. These subjects will be very tactful and make good diplomats. They will also make good salesmen. Frequently, they may be very intellectual by nature. These indications of a razor-sharp intellect will be confirmed by good Lines of Mentality on both hands, as well as by good Mounts of Mercury, Jupiter and Moon.

We now turn to the **Clubbed Thumb**

This is an interesting thumb. The first phalange will be very heavy, thick and bulbous. The second phalange, too, will be very thick. These subjects are moved by animal forces and show great obstinacy. If there are other bad indications, this shows that they may be brutal and violent in action. Of all the thumbs this is by far the most dangerous. It is wrongly called the "murderer's thumb", for, combined with other features of the hand which are favourable, the subject may not display brutal or violent tendencies. In scientific hand analysis, we must always study the entire hand. It is a great mistake to jump to conclusions on the basis of one sign alone, no matter how negative or positive this sign may be.

Let us now analyse the **Long Thumb**

Such a thumb will give the subject a favourable ability to think out and execute ideas. These subjects will be individualistic by temperament and possess sound powers of

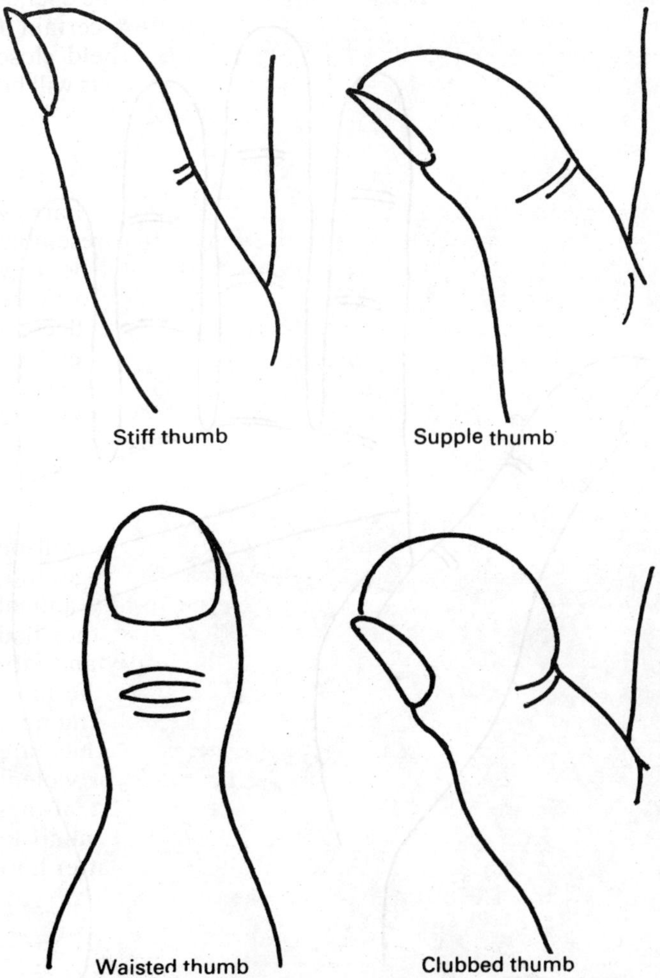

Figure 6-1 The different kinds of Thumbs: (a) the Stiff thumb (b) the Supple thumb (c) the Waisted thumb (d) the Clubbed thumb

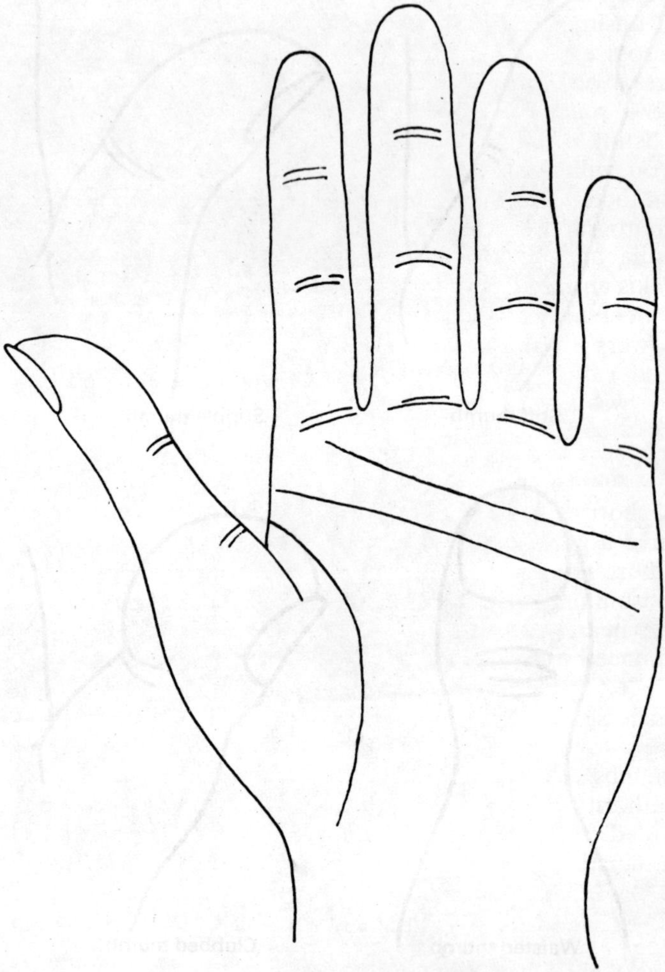

Figure 6-2 The Long Thumb

reasoning and will power. They can succeed in the fields of business, politics or science. Sometimes we may come across exceptionally long thumbs. This subject will possess a very good intelligence and a will of iron. There will be a remarkable ability to influence people as well as existing situations. Observe the thumbs of world leaders. You will notice that those who are regarded as strong characters will have exceptionally long thumbs. Look at photographs showing the thumbs of Indira Gandhi of India and Zulkifli Ali Bhutto, the former president of Pakis'an. Subjects with extremely long thumbs can handle almost every situation. These subjects display natural powers of leadership. Napoleon the First, the great leader of France, had very long thumbs. Incidentally, he too was a great believer in hand analysis.

We shall now study the **Small Thumb**

A short or small thumb is unfavourable. This subject will have a grasshopper mind and shift from one idea to the other. The character will also be weak and the powers of reasoning relatively immature. Such subjects are ruled by the heart, not the head. These subjects are easily influenced and they will not have strong powers of resistance. People with such characteristics cannot become leaders. You must search the Line of Mentality for defects to confirm these indications. Subjects with short thumbs will find it difficult to hold positions of power and authority. These people can be stubborn and yet weak-willed. A subject with a short thumb may suddenly become stubborn for no good reason whatsoever.

We shall now study thumbs from a different angle. We can have **low-set** and **high-set** thumbs. The diagrams will make the classification clear.

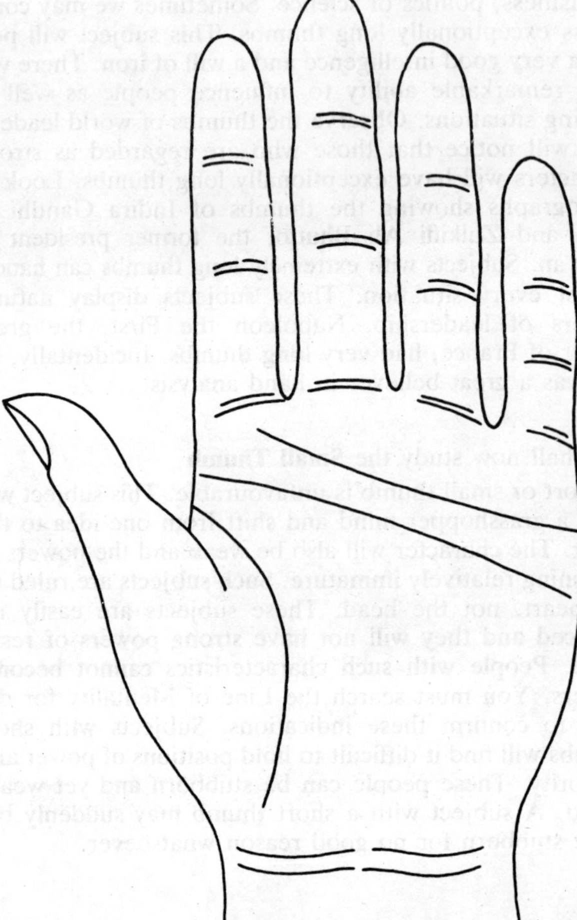

Figure 6-3 The Small Thumb

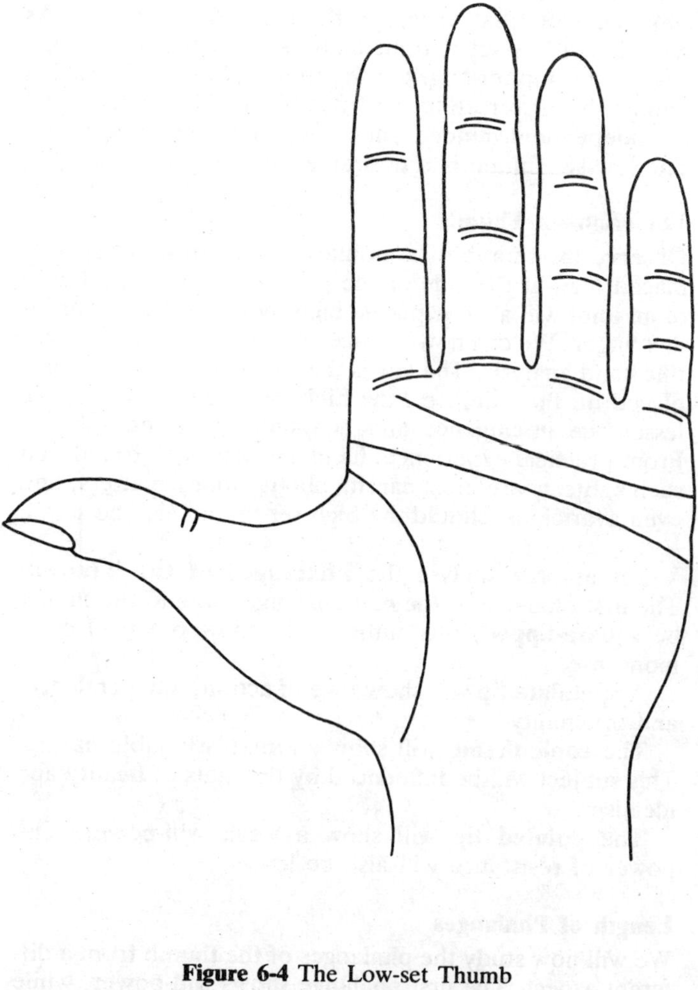

Figure 6-4 The Low-set Thumb

The Low-set Thumb

We judge the low-set or high-set thumb by the gap formed along the side of the thumb from the base of the Jupiter finger (first finger) to the base of the thumb. As regards the low-set thumb, there is a wide gap from the base of the Jupiter finger to the root of the thumb. Such a thumb shows versatility and flexibility. The subject will be independent-minded and have a distinct personality. The low-set thumb is a desirable thumb to possess.

The High-set Thumb

Observe the thumb of a monkey. You will find that it is placed high at the side of the paw. Likewise, the thumb of an idiot will also be placed high, near the Jupiter or index finger. We can now deduce an important law of scientific hand analysis. The law is that the higher the thumb is placed on the side, i.e., the higher-set the thumb is, the lesser the intelligence and adaptability of the subject. From practical experience, hand analysts have found that such subjects are most careful about money matters, and even avaricious, should the high-set thumb also be small.

Let us now analyse the **Phalanges of the Thumb.** The first phalange is the nail phalange. Should the thumb be **square-tipped,** this subject will show practical commonsense.

A **spatulate tip** will show love of action, independence, and originality.

The **conic thumb** will show an impressionable nature. This subject will be influenced by thoughts of beauty and idealism.

The **pointed tip** will show a weak will-power. The power of resistance will also be low.

Length of Phalanges

We will now study the phalanges of the thumb from a different aspect. The first phalange shows will-power, while

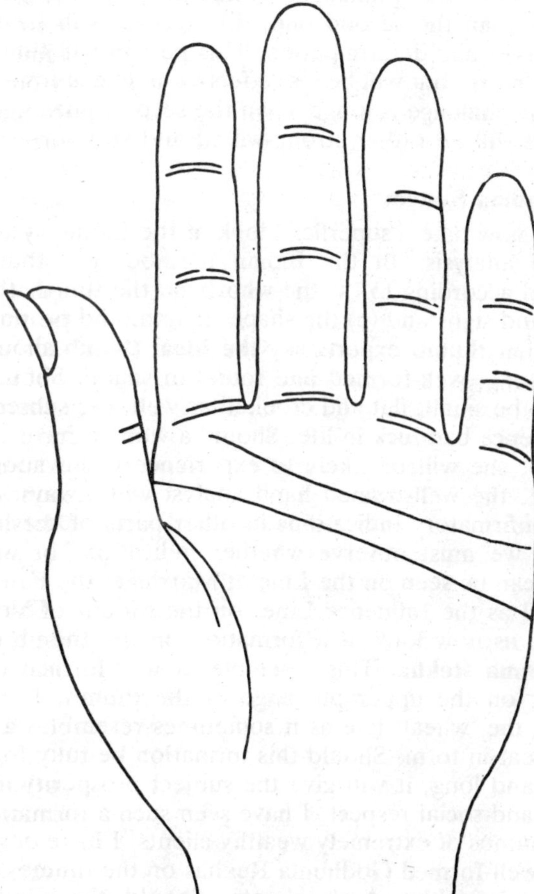

Figure 6-5 The High-set Thumb

the second phalange shows reasoning and logical powers. Should the first phalange, symbolizing will-power, be shorter than the second one, this subject will have less will-power and determination. This person will think and reason more, but will be less effective in execution. But if the first phalange is longer than the second phalange, the subject will be rather strong-willed and stubborn.

The Indian System

Let us now take a superficial look at the Indian system of thumb analysis. In the Indian method, the thumb is studied according to (a) the whorls on the thumb (b) the lines and signs and (c) the shape, length, and proportion.

Indian thumb experts say **the ideal thumb** should be high, long, well-formed and round in shape. Should the thumb be small, flat and crooked as well, the subject will experience bad luck in life. Should a woman have a wide thumb, she will be likely to experience widowhood. Of course, the well-trained hand analyst will always search for confirmatory indications in other parts of the hands. Thus, we must observe whether indications of widowhood can be seen on the Line of Marriage, the Fate Line as well as the Influence Lines on the Mount of Venus.

Let us now look at a formation on the thumb called **Godhuma Rekha.** This resembles a well-formed ear of barley on the upper phalange of the thumb. It is also called the 'wheat' line as it sometimes resembles a grain of wheat in form. Should this formation be fully formed, clear and long, it will give the subject prosperity in life, fame and social respect. I have seen such a formation on the thumbs of extremely wealthy clients. I have observed very well-formed Godhuma Rekhas on the thumbs of extremely wealthy Arab clients. Should the Godhuma Rekha be cut into two by any line, the subject will attain prosperity in the later part of life. To find out the years and ages, the Fate and Sun Lines must be examined minutely.

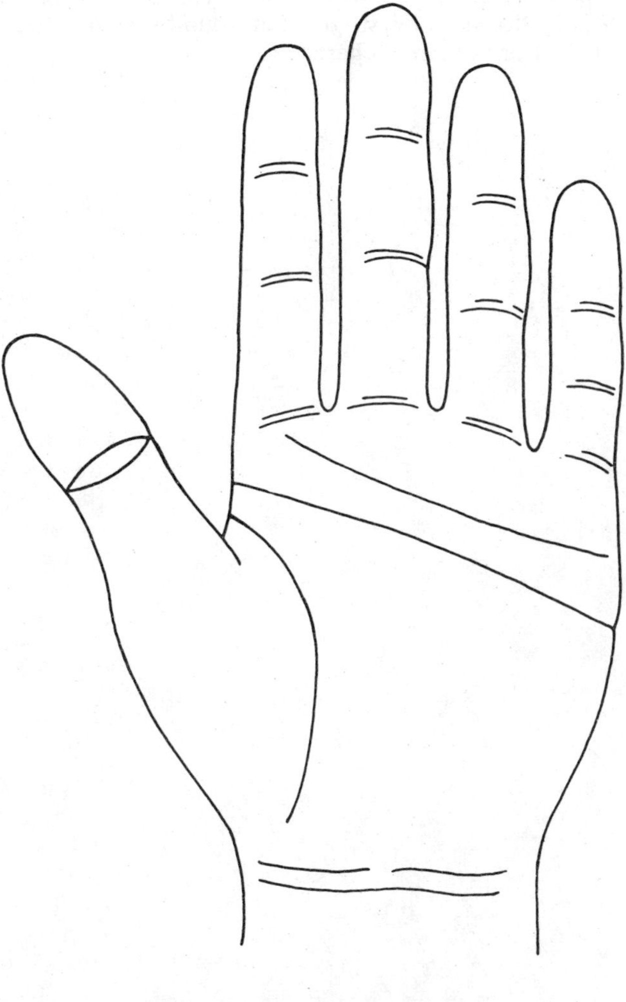

Figure 6-6 The Godhuma Rekha

Study your thumbs carefully. Are they low-set, high-set, short or long? Be honest with yourself. A careful ruthlessly honest analysis of your thumbs will reveal a great deal of your real character.

Chapter Seven

Your Character and Vocational Aptitude as Revealed by Your Fingers. The Nails Reveal Health and Temperament

We shall now study the fingers in some detail. Each finger is normally divided into three phalanges. Please have a look at the diagrams. The first phalange is the topmost phalange, the one furthest away from the base of the finger. The second phalange is found in the centre. The third phalange is located nearest the base of the finger. What is the purpose of studying the phalanges of the fingers? The answer is that they give accurate indications of vocational aptitude, as well as reliable indications of the real character of the subject.

Let us now analyse the **Phalanges,** one by one. The first phalange deals with the mental world. The second phalange represents the abstract. The last or third phalange represents the material world.

(a) **Longest First or Top Phalanges**

Have a look at the top phalanges of the fingers of both hands. Should they be the longest, it means that the mental world will rule. You will be inclined towards idealism. Such subjects are most suited for academic or intellectual work. They will be inclined to intellectual occupations.

(b) **Longest Middle or Second Phalanges**

Should these be the longest and largest, the business side will prevail. The subject will have practical wisdom and

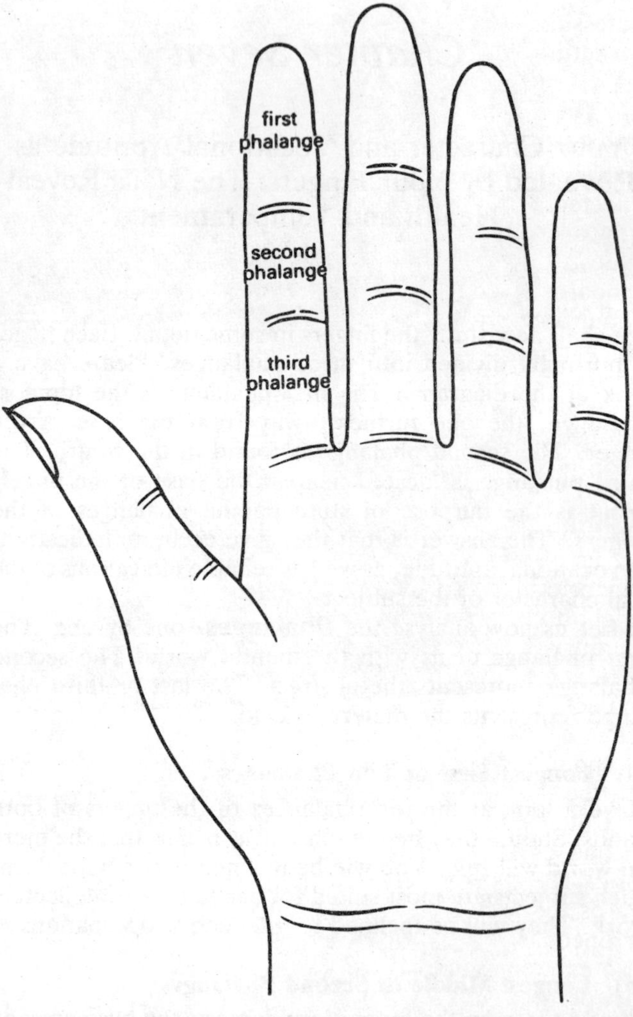

Figure 7-1 Longest First Phalanges

pursue commercial interests with vim and vigour. Many professionals such as doctors, businessmen, salesmen, and marketing executives have such phalanges.

(c) The Longest Third Phalanges

The third phalanges represent the baser world of hand analysis. Strong physical desires and animal instincts are reflected here. Subjects with long third phalanges will not show a keen interest in academic pursuits or high spiritual values. Simple living and high thinking will not be their standards. Such subjects may do well in agricultural labour and also in semi-skilled jobs — such as truck driving, garbage collecting, etc. The general idea is that the job they do should be a routine one. These subjects are generally big eaters. As long as their physical needs are gratified regularly, these subjects will be amiable in disposition.

Inclination of the Fingers

Let us now study the inclination of the fingers. Should a finger not be erect, but incline to some extent towards its neighbouring finger, it will absorb the characteristics of the finger towards which it inclines. Should all the fingers curve at their tips towards the middle or Saturn finger, the subject will surely be of a secretive nature. He would make a good spy or secret service agent!

Should the first finger lean towards the second at the tip, the subject will tend to be rather slow in many things. The little finger and the third finger leaning towards the second or middle finger at the tip suggest a love of solitude. The middle or Saturn finger leaning at the tip towards the first or Jupiter finger will give the subject an erroneous approach to life's problems. Such a subject may also experience some public scandal during a bad planetary period. The ring or Sun finger whose tip leans towards the middle or Saturn finger suggests immoral tendencies — the word 'immoral' being, of course, considered in

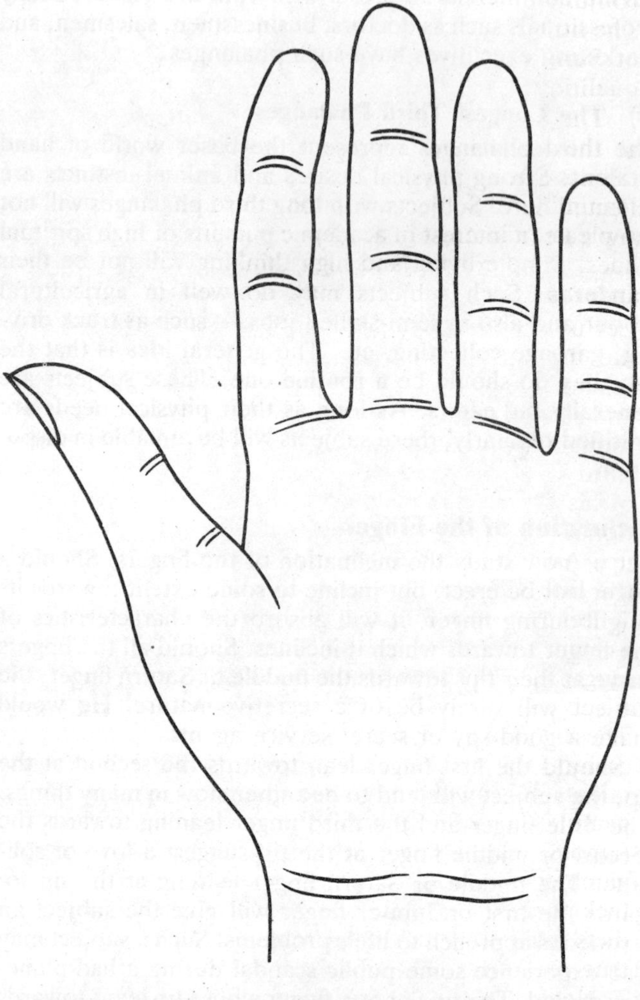

Figure 7-2 Inclination of Fingertips. The first is inclined towards the second.

conjunction with the cultural background of the subject. The little finger or Mercury finger leaning towards the ring or Sun finger reveals a subject with business and artistic qualities.

The third or Sun finger leaning towards the little finger at the tip produces a subject capable of using business talents to acquire wealth. The second or Saturn finger leaning towards the third or Sun finger at the tip produces a pleasure-loving disposition.

Intervals between the Fingers

Let us now study the meanings of the intervals between the fingers. To judge this, stretch out the fingers in a relaxed manner. Should there be a space between the first and second fingers, the subject will have independence of thought. An inter-space between the middle (Saturn) and third (Sun) fingers reveals a subject who is independent of his circumstances. Such a subject will have unconventional views and be reform-minded in his mental make-up. An inter-space between the third (ring or Sun) and the little fingers suggests freedom of action.

Let us consider a very interesting case. We shall assume that the third or ring finger is almost equal in length or just as long as the middle (Saturn) finger. Such a subject will love to gamble in various spheres in life. These gambling instincts which need not be limited to the casino, will reveal themselves according to the specific talents or interests of the subject. Thus a political gambler could have such fingers. In Malaysia, there is a famous casino at Genting Highlands. Compulsive gamblers sometimes consult the author before trying their luck there and I have observed that these gambling addicts invariably have long, prominent ring fingers. This is true regardless of their race or nationality.

Now close the fingers together. If they are so close together that not a single drop of water can escape through the fingers, such a subject will be miserly and selfish.

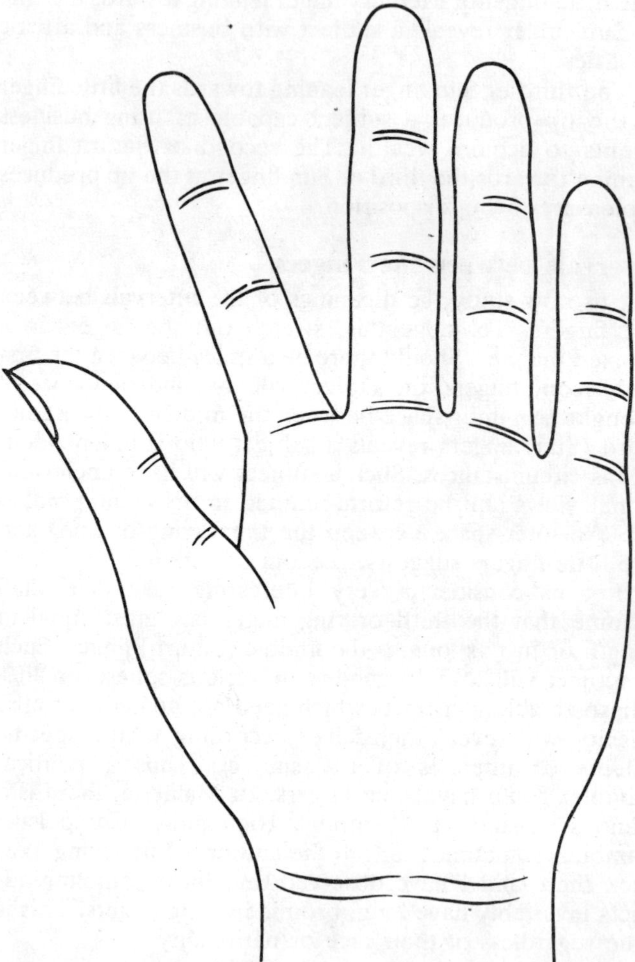

Figure 7-3 A wide gap between the first and second fingers

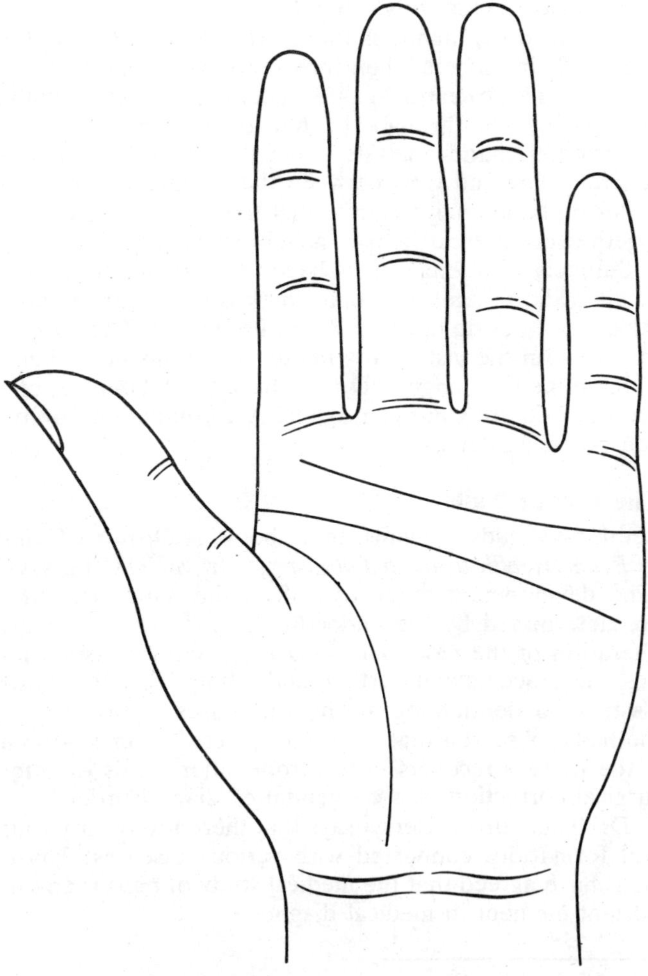

Figure 7-4 A hand with gambling tendencies. Note that the third finger is as long as the second.

With good mounts, strong Fate and Sun lines as well as materialistic hands, this subject will surely be rich.

On the other hand, if there are significant gaps between all the fingers when they are closed together, the subject will be extravagant. Speaking metaphorically, money will run through the fingers of such a subject. Experienced hand analysts know that very rich people generally have no gaps between their fingers. A famous writer on hand analysis wrote that fingers which are close together are a great help in acquiring wealth.

Subjects with long fingers have the patience to go into details. Short-fingered people think quickly, understand things fast, but do not like to go into details. They prefer to deal with the gist of any matter — details bore them.

Examine your fingers. Do you have the tendencies of a Scrooge? Or are you extravagant? Are you patient, or are you bored by details?

The Finger Nails

Let us now study the nails. In his book, *A Doctor's Guide to Better Health through Palmistry,*[1] Dr. Scheimann says, 'The development or growth of all the hand structures are determined by the endocrine glands. Therefore the alteration of the nail could indicate glandular disturbances.' Dr. Scheimann further adds that, 'Dr. V. Bardo Castello, a dermatologist who specialises in diseases of the nails, observed that nails and fingers become normal if the patient recovers either from tuberculosis or after surgical correction of a congenital cardiac disorder.'

Dr. Theodore J. Berry[2] says that there are twenty-four nail formations connected with various diseases. Physicians have agreed that the medical study of nails is an important element in medical diagnosis.

---

[1] Eugene Scheimann, *A Doctor's Guide to Better Health through Palmistry,* Parker Publishing Company, New York, 1960, p.43.

[2] Theodore Berry, cited in Scheimann, *op.cit.*, p.41.

The author personally knows doctors of medicine who have a close look at the nails of their patients before coming to a final conclusion as to their health. How much more will physicians know when they study the entire palm in medical hand analysis? Hand analysts for thousand of years have always known that the nails are accurate indicators of health and character.

Medical hand analysis is becoming gradually accepted in Western countries.

In 1977, an American lady told me that some American and European doctors practise medical palmistry. I was pleasantly surprised to learn that hand analysis, an ancient science and art, is now being widely used in Europe to diagnose diseases and with astonishing accuracy. It is even possible to do so years before the symptoms appear.

If my memory serves me right she mentioned that a certain Dr. Alexander Rodewald at the University of Munich had claimed that by scrutinizing the patterns and creases of a new-born baby's hand and foot-prints, he is able to diagnose a broad spectrum of congenital defects, with an unbelievable over 90% accuracy. It seems that Dr. Rodewald can predict with over 75% accuracy a new born baby's chances of developing diabetes, heart disease, cancer, leukemia and mental diseases.

The American client further surprised me pleasantly by saying that medical hand analysis is fast becoming an important diagnostic discipline for thousands of medical practitioners in Germany and the rest of Europe. One interesting fact that she revealed to me was that many German clinics, not having their own hand analysis experts, actually sent prints to Dr. Rodewald and his colleagues.

It seems that the use of scientific hand analysis in medical diagnosis is also endorsed by Dr. Daniel Stowens, an American doctor at St. Luke's Hospital in Ithica, New York. Apparently, Dr. Stowens has analysed thousands of handprints over the last two decades and according to my American friend Dr. Stowens feels that medical hand analysis will be significant in the early detection of primary tendencies towards cancer or diabetes. It seems that this learned doctor himself has diagnosed mongolism, schizophrenia and leukemia with remarkable accuracy.

It is therefore becoming clear that at least some doctors are beginning to take scientific hand analysis — or dermatoglyphics as they prefer to call it — seriously. The new name does not perturb hand analysts of the traditional school. After all, a rose by any other name smells just as sweet!

The nails play a very important part in medical hand analysis. Indications of ill health and disease are shown accurately in the palm proper, but a good scientific hand analyst will always study the nails most minutely when analysing the health aspect of the subject. It is a fact that the nails appear when the foetus is approximately three months old. Doctors know that some diseases hinder the development of the nails. Thus the development of the index finger nail or Jupiter (first) finger nail is arrested by diseases of the liver. The development of the middle finger nail or Saturn finger nail is obstructed by intestinal fever. It is a medical truth that all diseases that impede the development of the thumb nail also arrest the development of the remaining finger nails.

In studying nails, the hand analyst will see that we have various types of nails. There are long nails, short nails, broad nails and narrow nails. We shall now study the different types of nails in some detail.

Long Nails

The length of a nail is calculated up to the point where it is in contact with the flesh. Any part of the nail beyond or beneath the flesh must be totally disregarded. Those with long nails tend to have weak health. Generally, they tend

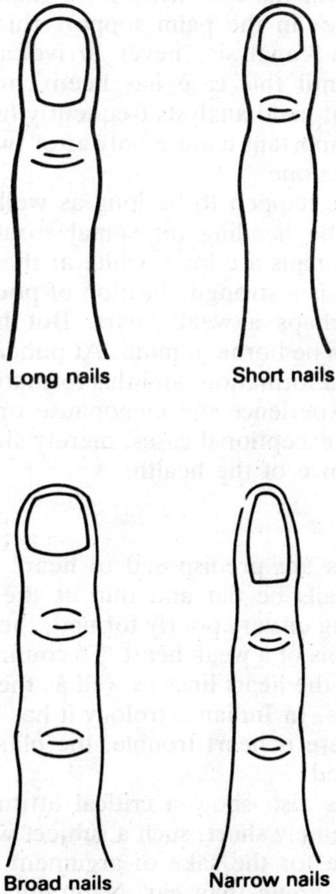

Figure 7-5

to have diseases affecting the upper section of the human anatomy. There could be a weakness of the lungs and the chest. But the golden rule to achieve outstanding accuracy in medical hand analysis is to make sure that the palm and lines in the palm support this judgement. In scientific hand analysis, never arrive at an important judgement until this case has been confirmed at least once. Brilliant hand analysts frequently find that they can confirm an important feature only after two or three readings, let alone one.

If the nails happen to be long as well as curved, this subject will be heading for spinal trouble in the near future. If the nails are long, white at the top, and bluish at the base it is a strong indication of poor blood circulation and perhaps a weak heart. But here two points should always be borne in mind. At puberty, women tend to have such a formation, and this formation is again seen when they experience the menopause or change of life. So these are exceptional cases, merely showing a temporary disturbance of the health.

Short Nails

Such subjects are predisposed to heart trouble. Should such short nails be flat and thin at the base, with the moons missing or very poorly formed, they are very accurate indications of a weak heart. To confirm this accurately, scrutinize the heart lines as well as the Mounts of Sun of both hands. In Indian astrology it has been found that whenever there is heart trouble, the planet Sun is malefically involved.

Short nails also show a critical attitude. Should the nails be extremely short, such a subject will be very critical and argue for the sake of argument. These subjects would rather argue than eat. Naturally, such extremely short nails would be undesirable on the hands of a prospective mother-in-law or spouse!

Fairly often, I have seen short nails on the fingertips of

lawyers. With other good indications, subjects with short nails will do well as lawyers, especially in the art of advocacy. These people are also very good critics and shine as literary critics. This is all right as long as the critical faculties do not result in personal attacks or nagging.

Almond-shaped Nails

There are nails which are shaped like **almonds** although these are generally found in the long nail category. These will show lack of energy, and the subject will tend to have a happy-go-lucky attitude towards life.

Then we have **Broad Nails.** In this case, the nails have more width than length. Broad nails are suggestive of good health and physical energy. An individual with such nails will also tend to be broad-minded in outlook. He will also believe in positive thinking and have a sunny disposition.

Narrow Nails

These are undesirable for they suggest poor health. Subjects with narrow nails live on nervous energy. Physical energy will be decidedly in short supply. It is common to find such subjects having a weak will.

Should the nails be long, curved and also narrow, the subject will be prone to asthma or bronchial difficulties. Examine the Quadrangle for confirmatory indications (the Quadrangle is the space or width between the Heart and Head Lines). When the Quadrangle or space is narrow, the subject will be prone to asthma or some other kind of breathing difficulties.

Others

Occasionally, you may find nails which are V-shaped. These are sure indications of trouble with the throat.

A predisposition to paralysis is indicated when the nails are short, shaped like triangles, besides being flat and thin.

Really healthy nails are pink in colour, transparent, not brittle, and of normal length. The moons will also be well-formed, clear and neither too long nor too short. The lucky person with such nails will enjoy good health and be optimistic as well.

You may often find nails with a cluster of white spots on them. This suggests that the subject has been over-exerting himself and living on nervous energy. The medical hand analyst should suggest that these people slow down and rest their strained nerves.

It is a bad feature if the nails are brittle and split. This suggests of a tendency towards rheumatism or gout.

The well-balanced nail will be neither too long nor too short. In scientific hand analysis, as in many other disciplines, extremes of development are undesirable features. A balanced harmonious development is what we look for.

Study your nails very thoroughly indeed, and regularly as well. They will give you accurate, valuable clues to your health and temperament. A regular, thorough observation of the nails will play an important part in preventive medicine in the future. A careful, ruthlessly honest analysis of your fingers will reveal a great deal of your real character.

Chapter Eight

How to Calculate the Time for Future Events in Hand Analysis. The Correct Way to Take Handprints for Scientific Hand Analysis

Calculating age is the most difficult part of scientific hand analysis. This is what separates the men from the boys. Every science has its limitations, and what follows are the limitations of the science of hand analysis: (a) there is no one hundred per cent correct system of telling, from the palms alone, the sex of children or the number of children, (b) the exact date or month of an event cannot be predicted, (c) it is not possible to get information about the future of children, uncles, aunts, grandfathers, etc., from the hand analysis of one subject and (d) the outcome of horse races, winning the lottery or cross-word puzzles, and the recovery of stolen articles cannot be analysed from the hand.

Dr. Benham, the American hand analyst, in his book *The Laws of Scientific Hand Reading,*[1] says that 'up to this time, there has not been discovered any way of positively telling from the hand the present age of the subject. There is no marking on the hands which will, independent of everything else, indicate this'. This is not quite correct. The celebrated astro-palmist, Mihira in his remarkable book, *Astro-Palmistry,*[2] reveals very deep an-

---

[1] William G. Benham, *The Laws of Scientific Hand Reading*, D.B. Taraporevala Sons, Bombay, 1968, p.379.

[2] Mihira, *Astro-Palmistry*, Calcutta, 1930, pp.42-68.

cient secrets of Indian astro-palmistry, whereby the age of the subject can be calculated correctly. Not only can the age be calculated but the month of birth can also be found by calculating the position of the planets in the hand.

Astro-palmistry combines astrology and palmistry (hand analysis). Let us be content with fairly accurate ways of calculating the ages when events will occur in the future for you. I have found that Cheiro's 'System of Seven' gives good and accurate results in age calculations for future events. Using hand analysis alone, at most the year when an event will take place can be revealed. It is not possible to tell the day or the month when a future event will occur. My friend, Mr. Jagjit Singh, is a keen student of hand analysis and astrology and a firm believer in these sciences. He put the difficulties of reckoning date and time in hand analysis in a witty manner by making this comment: 'If a hand analyst can predict an event to within two years either way, before or after the times when the events will occur in reality, he is good and knows his job. If he can predict to within one year either way, the hand analyst is brilliant. If the hand analyst can pinpoint the exact year when events will take place, all the time or most of the time, he is next to God Himself.' There is more than a grain of truth in this sharp observation.

An honest hand analyst will always inform his client that the timing of events will be approximate, and that a grace period of one or two years, either way, may be necessary, Thus, if a hand analyst says that the subject will get a promotion at the age of thirty-nine, the promotion may occur when the subject is thirty-eight, or forty. This is the way an honest hand analyst will express his prediction: '*Around* the age of thirty-nine, I see that you will probably get a promotion in your career.'

How to Calculate Age on the Hand

We shall take the normal life span of a subject as being seventy years. Many insurance companies in Western countries also regard this as the normal life span of a person. In hand analysis, there are advanced methods of working out the ages for future events beyond the age of seventy. We shall not, however, go into such advanced techniques in this book, which is meant largely for the layman.

Please follow all the diagrams on age calculation closely. The ages should be calculated for both hands. Normally, it is sufficient if ages are worked out on the Vitality and Fate Lines. The Vitality Line starts from above the thumb and ends near the wrist. Take the beginning of this line as representing zero years of age. This part will be under the first (index) finger on the outer edge of the Mount of Jupiter. In the centre of the Vitality Line, make an arrow mark as shown in the diagram. This will represent the age of thirty-five. The area where the line ends near the wrist represents the age of seventy. Next, subdivide the line between the ages of zero to thirty-five. Mark this with a small crossbar on the line itself. This will then work out to about the twenty-eighth year of age. Now subdivide the line from the thirty-fifth to the seventieth year. The centre mark, marked with a crossbar or a dot, will represent the age of about fifty-two. Now study the line between the ages of zero—twenty-eight. The centre part should be marked as representing the eighteenth year for the subjects. Do likewise for the line below the age of thirty-five. Between the ages of thirty-five to fifty-two, the centre mark will represent approximately the forty-fourth year of the subject's life. Between the ages of fifty-two to seventy, the central mark will show the age of approximately sixty-two. Should the Vitality Line be short and stop at, for example, the age of thirty-five, you must imagine that it continues up till the age of seventy, and continue marking as if the line had really been shown

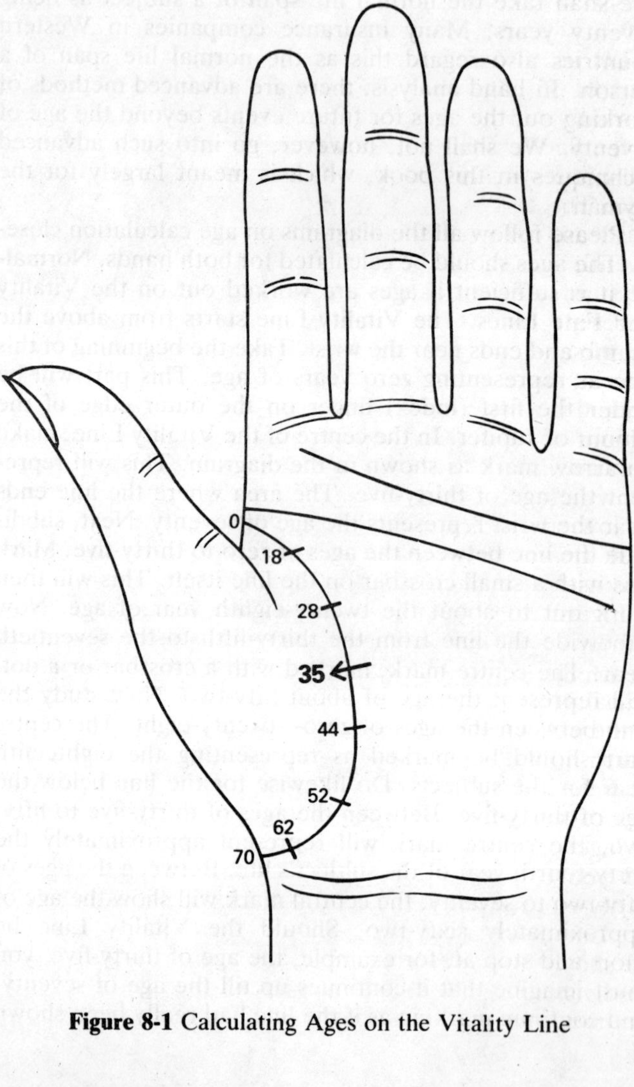

Figure 8-1 Calculating Ages on the Vitality Line

up till that age. After all, a short Vitality Line (the so-called Life Line), even if shown to be short on both hands, does not necessarily mean a short life.

Let us now work out the ages for the Fate Line or the Line of Saturn. The Fate Line starts from the wrist and normally travels upwards to the base of the middle finger or the Saturn finger. Bend the palm towards you and you will notice two to four Rascettes (Bracelets) at the wrist area. The first Rascette is the one at the junction of the wrist, and where the palm proper ends. Mark this as the seventh year of the subject. Please note that in this case, the start of the Fate Line from the first Rascette does not represent zero-year or the first year of existence, but the age of seven years. Why this should be, I am at a loss to explain. But kindly follow the instructions, test this method in at least three hundred cases, and you will find, to your utter surprise, that this method works in actual practice. The 'Why?' can be left for further research to throw light on this matter.

Now study the junction of the Fate and Head Lines. Mark this as showing the age of thirty-five, on the Fate Line itself. My technique is to draw a line, A-A as shown in Figure 8-2. A-A is drawn from approximately the bottom of the Mount of Lower Mars to the centre of the Mount of Mercury. By actually drawing this line on the palm, you will get a clearer picture of age calculations on the palms of the subjects. The bottom of the middle or Saturn finger will represent the seventieth year of age on the Fate Line. Now start subdividing the ages from the ages of seven till thirty-five. The centre mark will show the age of approximately twenty-one. Subdivide again, and you can easily work out the ages of fourteen and twenty-eight respectively. Now subdivide the ages on the Fate Line from thirty-five to seventy. The first subdivision will show the age of fifty-two, while subsequent further sub-divisions will work out to the ages of forty-four and sixty-two respectively. Should the Fate Line stop short

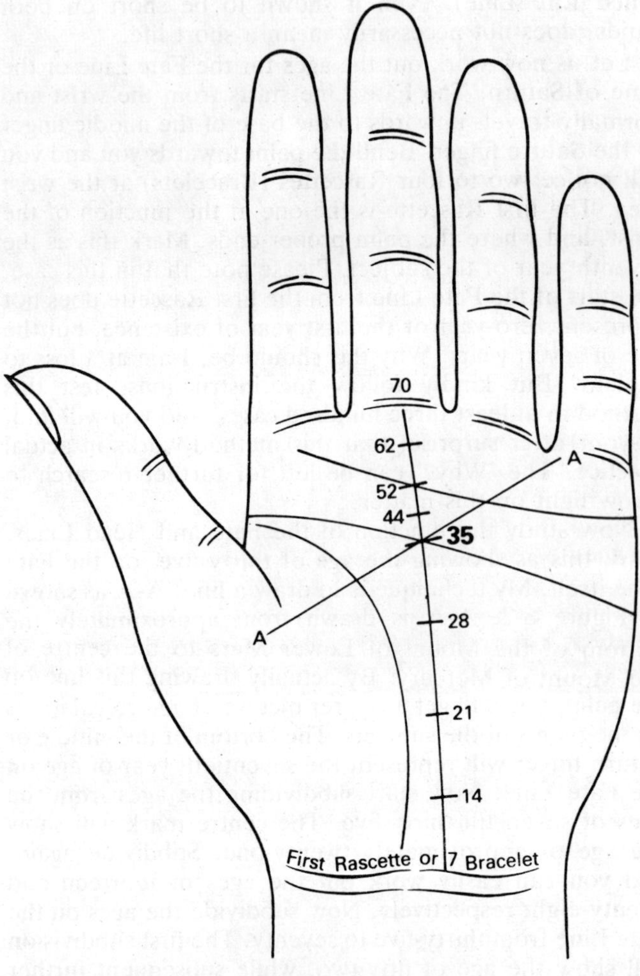

Figure 8-2 Calculating Ages on the Fate Line or the Line of Saturn

and not travel up to the bottom of the second finger, you must draw an imaginary Fate Line in your mind's eye up to the age of seventy. With practice, it is not actually necessary to draw the imaginary extension of the Fate and Vitality Lines on the palm itself. Even further subdivisions can be worked out, as shown in Figure 8-2. For working out the ages on the Fate Line, it is very useful indeed to use an accurate six inch ruler.

For an expert hand analyst, it is not necessary to actually work out the ages on the Sun Line, or Line of Apollo as it is also called. The Sun Line normally runs parallel to the Fate Line. Ages on the Sun Line can be read from the Fate Line itself. Of course, the events occurring on both lines at the same ages may be entirely different. Sometimes, it may be necessary to work out the ages on the Line of Mentality. The start of this line under the Jupiter Mount will show the age of zero-year. The end of the Line of Mentality on the percussion or outer edge of the palm will show the seventieth year of the subject. Most Lines of Mentality will not reach the edge of the percussion. In this case, you must imagine that the line has really reached the percussion itself. Generally, the meeting point of the Fate Line and the Line of Mentality will represent the age of thirty-five on both lines. Such is the case when the Fate Line heads in the direction of the Saturn or middle finger throughout its course.

Through experience and much practice, it is possible to work out the ages when events will occur on the Fate Line, Sun Line, and Line of Mentality. A more minute subdivision of ages can be done according to Figure 8-3 in this chapter. Please study the diagram carefully, for it is self-explanatory.

For the beginner especially, it is always best to check events that have occurred to the subject in the past. In this way, you can find out whether the system of calculating ages on the hand is correct or not. Let us assume that the subject is thirty-six years old. You observe a well-

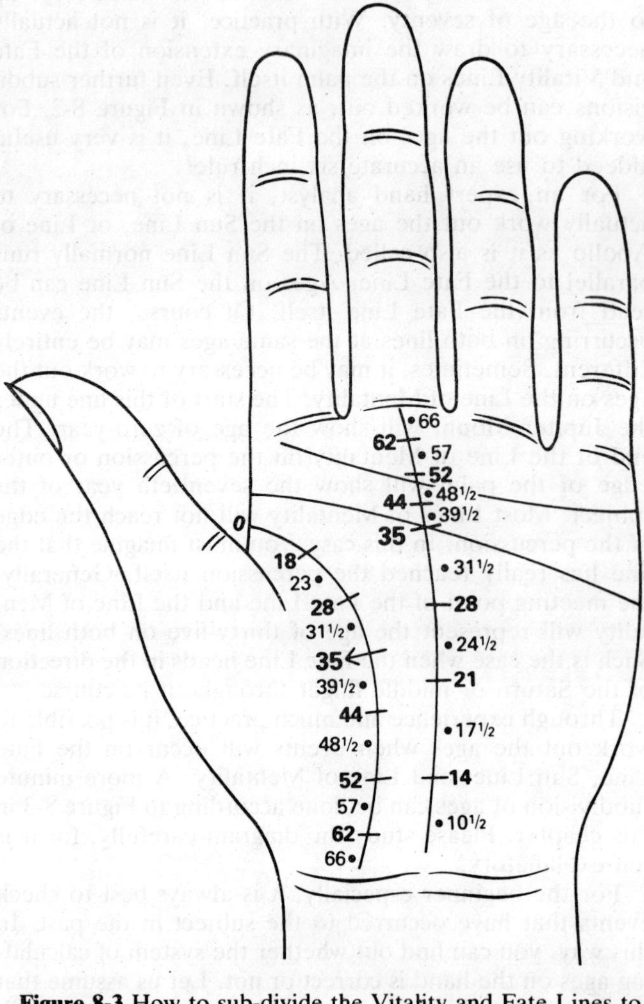

Figure 8-3 How to sub-divide the Vitality and Fate Lines to pinpoint the Ages

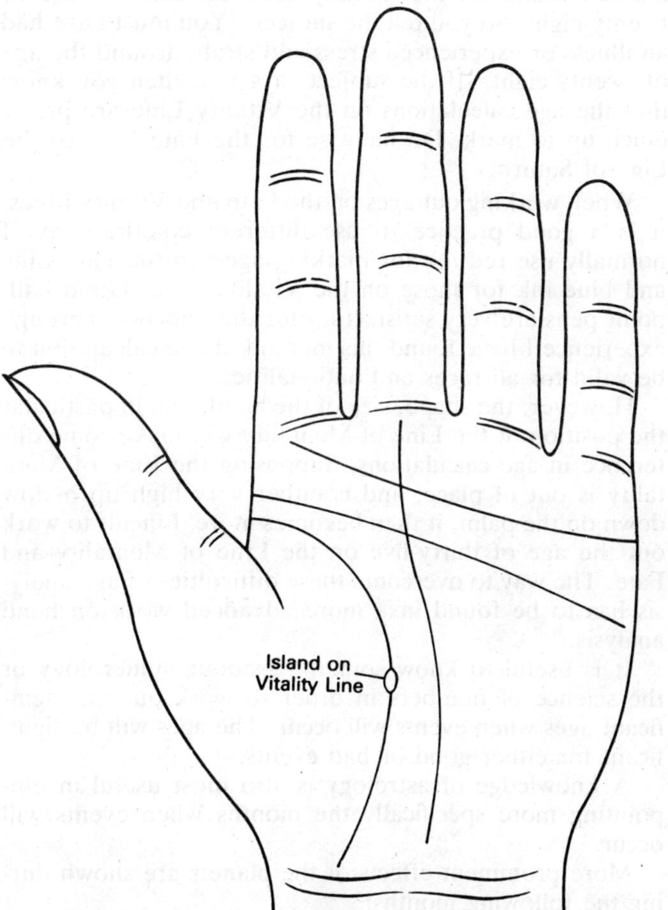

Figure 8-4 The Island on the Vitality Line shows some delicacy of health at about the age of 35. Study the figure showing calculation of ages on the Vitality Line.

marked island on the Vitality Line around the age of twenty-eight. So you tell the subject, 'You must have had an illness or experienced stress and strain around the age of twenty-eight.' If the subject says yes, then you know that the age calculations on the Vitality Line are pretty much up to mark. Do likewise for the Fate Line or the Line of Saturn.

When working out ages on the Fate and Vitality Lines, it is a good practice to use different coloured ink. I normally use red ink for marking ages on the Fate Line and blue ink for those on the Vitality Line. Good ball-point pens are very satisfactory for this process. Through experience I have found this method of age calculation to be valid for all races and nationalities.

However, the shape, size of the hand, and in particular the position of the Line of Mentality will make some difference in age calculations. Supposing the Line of Mentality is out of place, and is either very high up or low down on the palm: it then becomes more difficult to work out the age of thirty-five on the Line of Mentality and Fate. The way to overcome these difficulties of age analysis has to be found in a more advanced work on hand analysis.

It is useful to know something about numerology or the science of numbers in order to work out the significant ages when events will occur The ages will be significant for either good or bad events.

A knowledge of astrology is also most useful in pinpointing more specifically the months when events will occur.

More prominent effects of the planets are shown during the following months:

Sun – 16 August – 16 September
Moon – 15 July – 15 August
Mars – 13 April – 13 May
15 November – 16 December

Mercury	–	15 June – 15 July
		16 September – 16 October
Jupiter	–	16 December – 14 January
		12 March – 12 April
Venus	–	14 May – 14 June
		16 October – 14 November
Saturn	–	14 January – 12 March

How do you use this knowledge in scientific hand analysis? Let us assume a client has a most favourable Jupiter Mount. This mount will be centrally placed; it will be pink in colour and have favourable marks on it, such as a prominent vertical line, star, triangle or a clear Solomon's Ring. Also, remember that Jupiter is the strongest or leading mount on the hand. Now supposing the Fate Line or Sun Line shows that in 1978 the subject will have an advance in his career or some other favourable event. The hand analyst can then tell the client that there could be a promotion or other favourable event between 12 March and 12 April, or between 16 December and 14 January.

Likewise, you can work out the times during certain months when favourable events will occur for the client if the mounts representing the planets are favourable and well represented in the palms. In general, for any mount to be strong and favourable, it should be clearly raised on the hand, but not overmuch. As regards the upper mounts, Jupiter, Saturn, Sun and Mercury, ideally they should be centrally placed beneath the corresponding fingers. For all mounts, whether upper or lower, favourable signs and marks such as a pink colour, triangles and vertical lines, should be found on them. Remember that the star can be an unfavourable sign on some mounts.

Astrology and Time and Events

Let us now, with the aid of astrology, go on to a more detailed study of time and events. If Jupiter is strong and

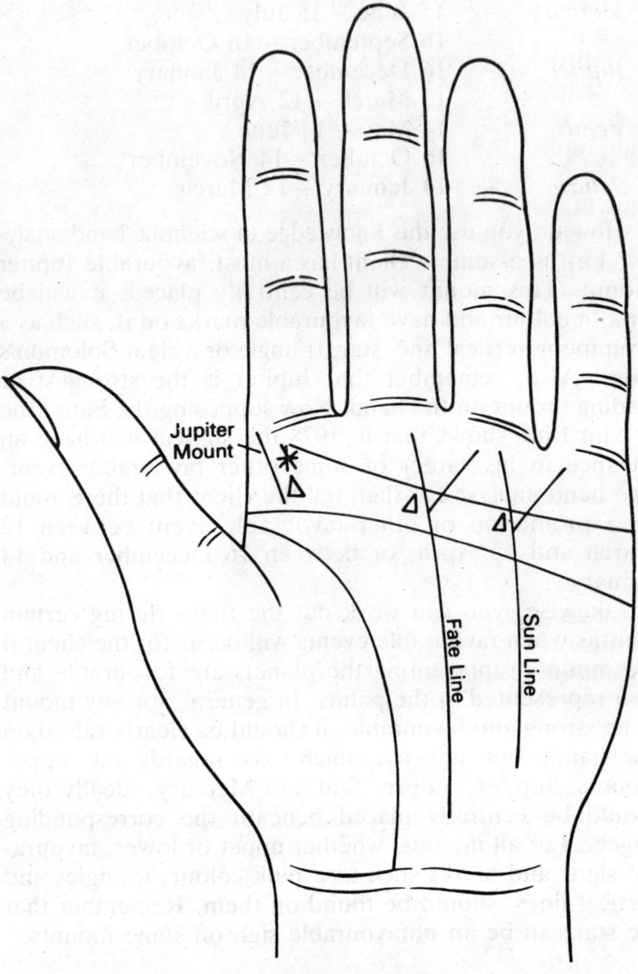

Figure 8-5 Diagram showing a strong Jupiter Mount. Note the Ascending Lines and Triangles around the age of 42 showing favourable events and success at that age.

marked with favourable lines and signs, the ages of sixteen to twenty-two, thirty-six to forty-two, and from the fifty-fifth year onwards, will be eventful, successful and constructive. A vertical line on the Jupiter Mount is called the Line of Jupiter, or Jupiter Line. It may rise on the Jupiter Mount itself, from the Vitality Line heading towards the Mount of Jupiter, or from the Head Line. If this Line of Jupiter is strong and well-marked, the subject will achieve success before the age of forty-two. Also, in general, the subject's forty-second year will be favourable as regards marriage, money, material prospects, education, etc. If a couple is biologically capable of having children, they will be blessed with a child or a son before the age of forty-two. The other condition is that the Jupiter Mounts for both husband and wife should be strong and favourable.

If the Mount of Venus is strong and favourable on the hands, the following ages will show success: twenty-two to twenty-seven, and more specifically, the ages of twenty-two, twenty-three and twenty-six. Career and life in general will be stabilized around the age of twenty-six. Success in love, and even in marriage, will stand a good chance of occurring around the age of twenty-six. Should the planet Mars be well placed on the hand, the subject will experience a favourable turn of events between the ages of twenty-nine and thirty-one. High intellectual development or academic successes will be likely to take place around these ages.

The planet Mercury is considered to be well placed in the hand if the Mercury Mount is centrally located, elevated and with favourable signs such as a vertical line and triangle on it. The Mercury finger will also be long and well-formed. Under these conditions the thirty-second year of the subject will be eventful and favourable.

If the Saturn Mount is strong and the Fate Line is well-marked as well, the subject's career will shine after the age of thirty-five. In astrology, the ages of thirty-six to forty-three, are ruled by Saturn. On the other hand, if Saturn is badly placed in the hand — e.g., if it is over-elevated, grilled, criss-crossed with bad moles, or has crossbars, etc., on it — the subject will experience misfortune during these ages. But with a favourable Saturn Mount and a strong, deep Fate Line, the thirty-eighth and fortieth years respectively will bring luck and success to the subject. Also, should the Fate Line together with a favourable Saturn Mount be present, the forty-fifth, forty-sixth and forty-seventh years of life will show a turn for the better in the career of the subject.

Finally, let us look at the Sun Line. If the Sun Mount is unfavourable, e.g. if there is an unfavourable mark on the Heart Line near the Sun Mount area or on the Sun Mount itself at about the age of forty-five, the subject may have either heart or eye trouble at that age. This is easy to understand, as in medical astrology the planet Sun rules the eyes and heart. Unfavourable marks on the Heart Line on the Sun Mount area could be a grille, mole, dot, bad crossbar, and crosses.

Let us assume that the Mount of Jupiter is very strong and favourable on the hand. We now know that the forty-second year of the subject should be favourable. So examine the Fate and Sun Lines on the hands, and see whether there are favourable marks on these lines at the age of about forty-two. Such favourable lines could be ascending branches from the Fate and Sun Lines, triangles on these lines, and the lines themselves becoming clearer and deeper. If these signs are present, then you know that the case is confirmed. In scientific hand analysis always confirm an event at least once, if not two or three times. This is the way to be scientific and accurate. By applying the techniques revealed here, with patience and incessant practice, you will improve rapidly in pinpointing the years and ages when events took place in the past, what events are taking place now, and which events will occur in the future. Nothing shatters the scepticism of a cynic so much as the ability of a competent hand analyst to reveal the years and ages when major events occurred in the past, and to describe them in specific detail as well. Of course, the events of the past can be described accurately and specifically from handprints alone.

A mastery of calculating ages can only be achieved by the sweat of one's brow. You have to put your shoulder to the wheel.

Taking Good Handprints

Now let us learn how to take good handprints.

The best way for the student of Scientific Hand Analysis to study the science is to take handprints. These prints should be filed immediately for future reference. Once you have clear handprints, you can study them at leisure. After incessant practice, a time will come when you can study the palms 'live'. This means that you hold the hands of the subject and study their various features. But if this is not possible, it is strongly recommended that palmprints be taken regularly. Study the diagrams showing the method of taking handprints.[3]

This is the technique of taking clear handprints: Take a thumb impression pad. This is the sort of pad used by immigration officers when taking thumb prints, and consists of a sheet of glass, a roller, and black finger-print ink. Squeeze a bit of the ink on the glass sheet. Take the roller and spread the ink on it. Having done this, spread the roller on the hand itself. Ink the sides, the thumb, fingers, as well as the spaces between the fingers. Do not ink the back of the hand as well in your enthusiasm! You must also ink the Bracelets or Rascettes (normally two to four) found below the wrist.

Next, take a large sheet of white paper. This paper should not be too thick. Spread out the inked hand and

---

[3] These diagrams have been adapted from Fred, Gettings, *The Book of the Hand*, Hamlyn House, London, 1970, pp.18-19.

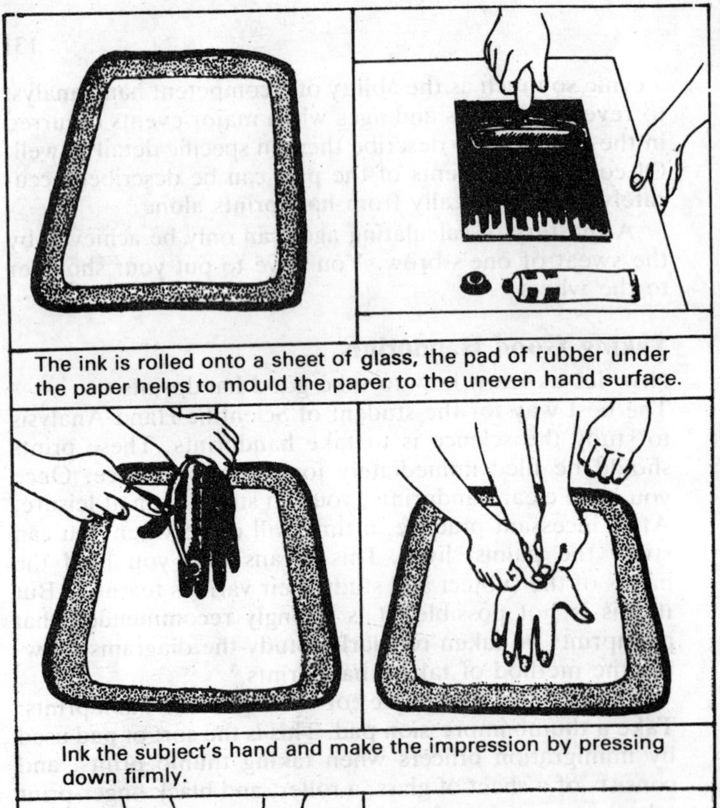

Figure 8-6 How to Make a Print

place it firmly on the white paper. Now do not move the inked hand. With your other hand, press the back of the hand. Also, be sure to press the knuckles at the back of the hand.

Now lift the hand upwards clear of the sheet of paper. You should have a clear impression of the hand. Do not use too much ink, or else the print will be too dark. You can ink the thumbs and the bracelets separately if these do not come out clearly in the handprints, and you can do likewise for the percussion, or outer edge of the hand. Information about love affairs and marriages is read on the percussion, in the area between the Heart Line and the base of the little or Mercury finger, so it is useful to ink this area separately, if necessary. Carry out the same procedure with the other hand.

You should take several prints, at least three of each hand. It is most important that the prints should be clear. The common mistake is either to use too little ink or too much. The above method is the best for taking clear prints. However, there is one small problem. The hands really get dirty! A worried friend may ask you whether the ink will come off or if he's been branded for life with black ink! You can assure him that he or she is not a victim of the science of hand analysis; vigorous washing with soap will remove the ink completely. It is best to use a little bit of kerosene oil as well – this will make the hand spotlessly clean in a short while.

In case of emergency, you will find it pretty useful to make do with good quality lipstick for inking the hands! However, the snag about lipstick is that the prints tend to fade with the passage of time.

Having inked the hands, immediately make notes on the following points:

- Full name
- Real date of birth
- Approximate time of birth, if known
- Indicate whether there was summer-time, double

summer-time, or daylight saving at the time of birth
- Place of birth
- Country of birth
- Which hand is used for writing
- Which are the good mounts and bad ones on both hands
- The texture of the skin
- The shape, size and colour of the nails
- The colour of each palm
- Detailed notes of any unusual lines and features, etc., of both hands.
- The date the prints were taken

Strictly speaking, for scientific hand analysis alone, it is not even necessary to know the first four points although this information is necessary for an astrologer. But, like good chess players, let us think ahead. You may become interested in the science of astrology, learn to draw horoscopes, and interpret them correctly. You will then be in a position to counter-check the findings on the palm by casting a horoscope. This is because astrology and scientific hand analysis are twin and sister sciences. In theory, astrology and scientific hand analysis should agree a hundred per cent. In practice, any analysis of hands tallies almost completely with the analysis of the best astrologers. Many people are fond of consulting both hand analysts and astrologers. They obviously believe, and quite rightly so, in getting the best of both worlds.

Chapter Nine

The So-Called Life Line Reveals Your Vitality

There is no such thing as a 'Life Line'. The 'Life Line' is correctly called the Vitality Line by expert hand analysts. In January 1975 there appeared an article in a Malaysian newspaper called *The Star*. This article appeared under the heading 'Doctor's Thumbs Down to Palm Reading'. Two British doctors had found out on examining the 'Life Lines' of corpses that they should have been alive! In other words, they found no connection between the 'Life Line' and the life spans of these subjects. So the learned doctors concluded that hand analysis is so much mumbo-jumbo. My reply, which appeared in the 17 January 1975 issue of the same paper, is given below:

> It is a grave misconception on the part of doctors to believe that the length of the Life Line, by itself, reflects longevity. It is therefore incorrect for them to imply that palmistry is no science, because their 'tests' and 'experiments' have shown no correlation between the Life Line and the longevity of the subject. This is a classic instance of a little knowledge being dangerous and misleading.
>
> The Life Line, strictly speaking, is called the Line of Vitality by masters of palmistry. Dr. Benham, himself a medical doctor and a palmist, says the 'Life Line' (Vitality Line) indicates the health of the subject during the various periods of life, his physical strength in general, and whether he lives during each period on his nervous force or relies on poor muscular robustness. Amateur palmists, by wrongly labelling this line the 'Life Line', give a wrong conception of its attributes and functions. In scientific hand analysis, longevity is assessed by the Vitality

Line, the Heart Line, Head Line, the Rascettes on the wrist, the thumbs as well as the length of the little finger.

Palmistry is a profound, exact science, and its claims should be scientifically investigated by well-informed scientists, not by those with a superficial knowledge of this applied science.

Some leading palmists have been medical doctors. The works of Dr. Benham, Dr. Spier, Dr. Charlotte Wolff and Dr. Eugene Scheimann are well known in the world of hand analysis.

Some of the most brilliant minds, like Aristotle, Hermanes. Pliny and Paracelsus, practised the science. Dr. Albert Einstein asserted that chirology (palmistry) may be one of the vital sciences of the future. Dr. Eugene Scheimann has written a good book entitled *A Doctor's Guide to Better Health through Palmistry*.

Palmistry is ... taught at university level in India. Lines come from the MIND, and the subconscious mind reveals the Future, as well as latent talents.

The time will come when palmistry and astrology will play a significant role in alleviating the sufferings of mankind.

A combination of modern medicine, medical palmistry, medical astrology, Chinese medicine, homeopathy, and Indian Ayurvedic medicine would be a boon to promoting health and happiness.

Doctors and scientists should carry out a serious investigation of this great science, preferably under the guidance of highly competent hand analysts. They will find that there is much more to it than meets the eye.

I made two mistakes in this article. Hand analysis is *not* an *exact* science. Even medicine is not an exact science. Recently, I learnt that some leading mathematicians do not regard even mathematics as an exact science. However, scientific hand analysis is a *reliable* science, as well as a great art.

The other mistake I made was in leaving out nature cure or naturopathy as one of the most effective forms of medicine that will be practised in the future.

From the foregoing it will be clear that the Life Line has got nothing or precious little to do with the life span of the subject. An incompetent 'hand analyst' once wrongly labelled this line the 'Life Line', and the mind of the layman has been seduced since then into the wrong impression that the 'Life Line' by itself reflects the life span which the subject is destined to enjoy in this birth. From now on, we shall correctly call this line the Vitality Line.

The Vitality Line

The Vitality Line normally starts just below the Mount of Jupiter and goes round the Mount of Venus. If the Vitality Lines on both hands are long, deep, perfectly flawless and a healthy pink in colour, then the subject will enjoy a good life span. But there are some very important features to be borne in mind. Such Vitality Lines must at the same time also be free of crosses, breaks, stars, and any irregularities such as fading away for any considerable length. Only then, with all these very important points being observed, can a good hand analyst promise the subject a long life on this planet.

A **break** is an unfavourable indication. It reveals danger to the health or life of the subject. But if there is an overlapping break, the subject will overcome this crisis. The golden rule is to always look for repair signs, such as sister lines and squares, when encountering breaks in this line. A break in both hands is more serious than if there is a break in only one hand. A **star** either on the Vitality Line or near it is ominous: it threatens sudden death or an 'explosion' in health matters. A **cross** at the end of this line also signifies a sudden death. **Small bars** cutting the line indicate worries and strains on the nervous system.

An **island** on the Vitality Line, especially if well-formed, reveals a problem with the health. The serious-

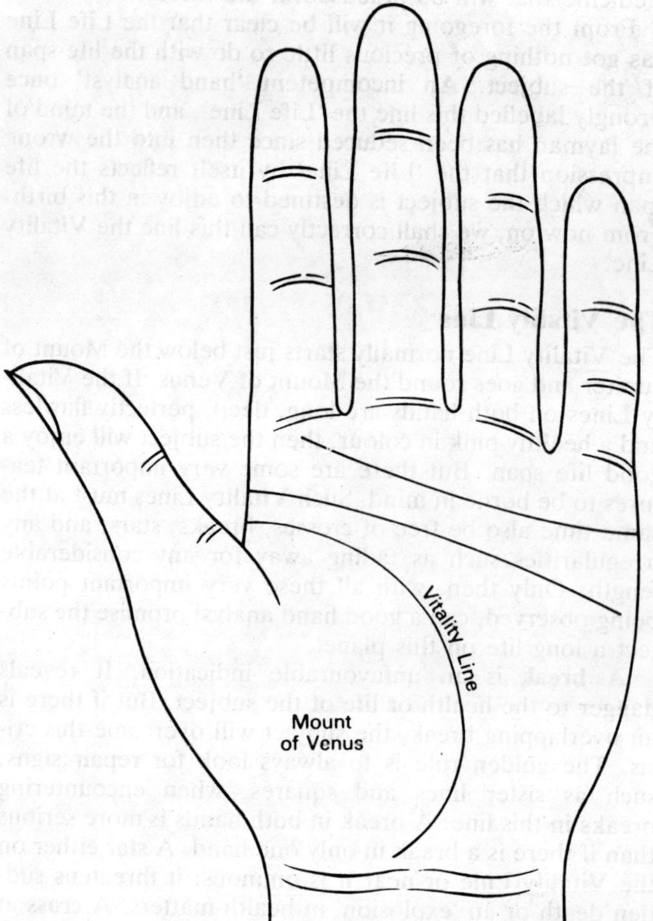

Figure 9-1 A good, long, well-formed Vitality Line going round the Mount of Venus

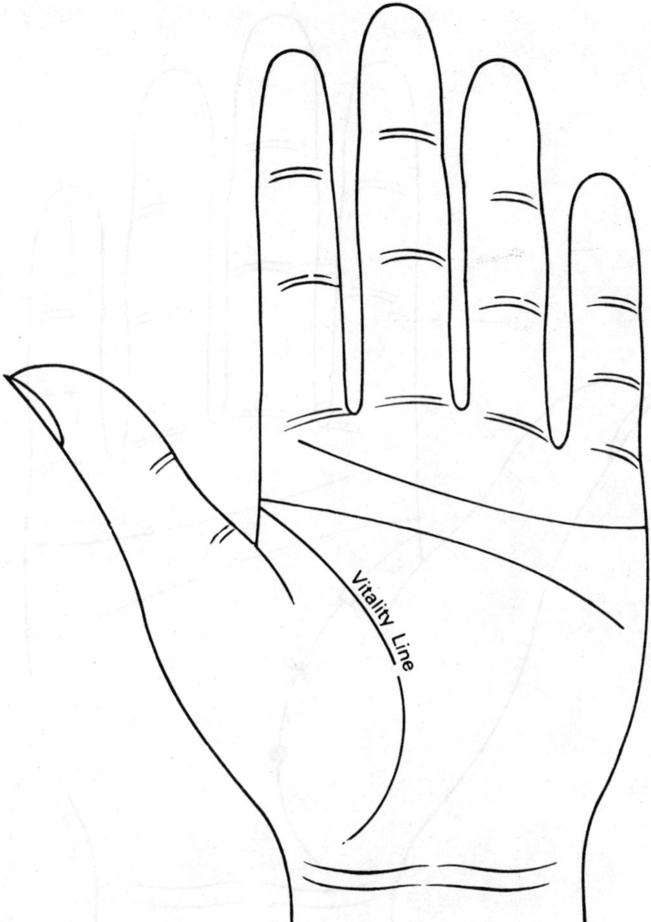

Figure 9-2 A Break in the Vitality Line

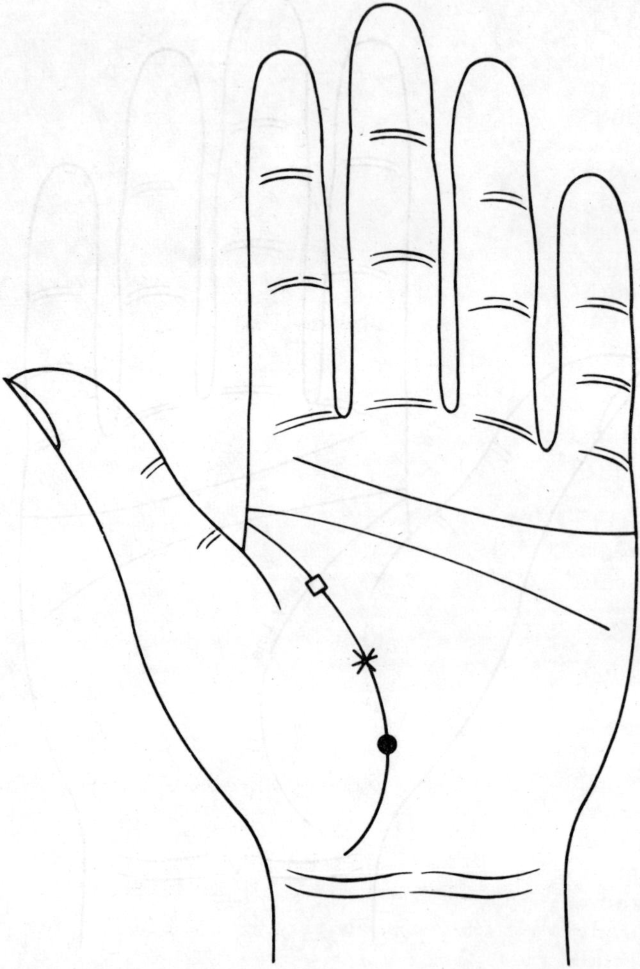

Figure 9-3 Examples of a Square, Star and Dot on the Vitality Line. The Square is a favourable sign.

ness, length and duration of the problem will depend on the size and colour of the island. The island shows that there is a health problem but it does not reveal what the actual disease with which the subject will be troubled is. The real disease which will afflict the subject can be deduced by studying other lines and features of the hand, such as the Heart Line, Line of Mentality, Health (Mercury) Line, and the Mounts of the hand. By itself the island does not refer to accidents, although it can reveal the health effects of an accident. So, basically, an island on the Vitality Line refers to disease, illness, or stress and strain on the nervous system.

Squares on the Vitality Line are signs of protection. A good Vitality Line will be long, strong, deep and clear-cut. Such a line shows vim and vigour. A Vitality Line that is fading, deep in some places yet fading at others, and marred by islands, crossbars, dots, stars and breaks, is unfavourable.

All **ascending lines** that leave the Vitality Line and head for the Mounts and the base of the fingers are highly favourable. These lines are called 'lines of ambition and success'. Thus an ascending line heading for the Mount of Jupiter, and preferably ending on this mount itself, can indicate a successful marriage or some significant achievement in the subject's life or career. For the favourable effects to be total, such ascending lines must be long, deep and free of defects such as islands, crossbars or any sign of fading, throughout their course.

Similarly, favourable ascending lines can leave the Vitality Line and turn upwards in the direction of the Mounts of Saturn, Sun and Mercury. It is always excellent to have many of these lines. The more of these, the more opportunities the subject will have to come up in life. Let us assume that a subject has many of these ascending lines. The last and most flawless ascending line will represent the age up to which the subject will achieve success without too much strife. In other words, this last

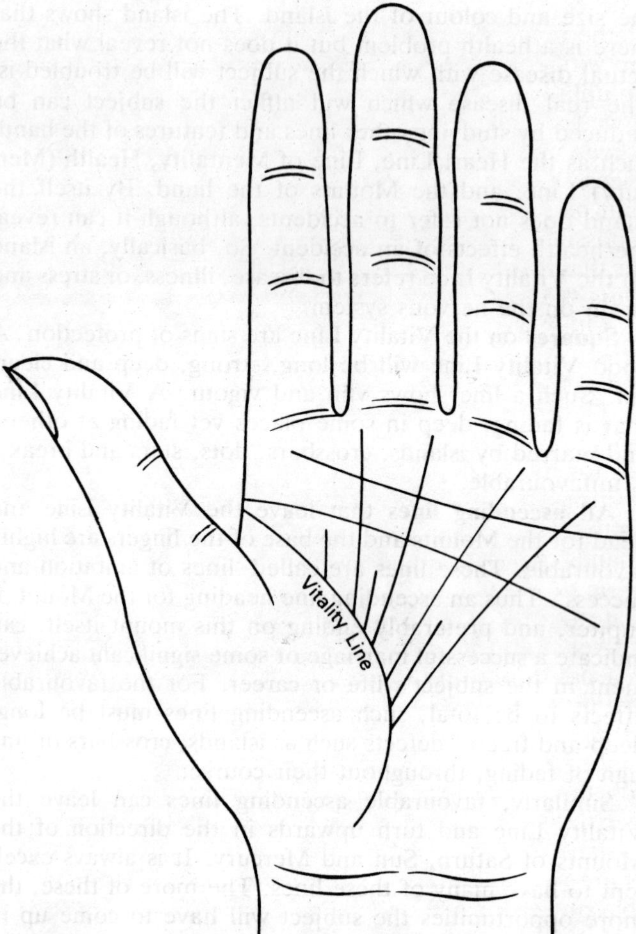

Figure 9-4 Long and short Ascending Lines rising from the Vitality Line.

ascending line will show the time up to which the subject can be creative and be at the pinnacle of success. After this, the subject can still be successful, but success will come with greater struggle. From then on it will be more of an uphill task. Nature intends us to be aware of this, so that we can make maximum use of this creative period of our lives in order to achieve the best success possible.

Please remember that the Vitality Line starts from the Mount of Jupiter and goes downwards towards the wrist. It is possible that subjects with many ascending lines have more than the usual share of good fortune.

Dots on the Vitality Line reveal some illness or accident. Other indications on the hand will give an accurate clue as to the type of illness.

Indications of **travel** can also be seen on the Vitality Line. Occasionally, you will come across hands where the Vitality Line turns away from the Mount of Venus and heads for the Mount of Moon. A subject with such a line will strongly desire to travel frequently, or even to migrate to foreign countries. Such a line is often seen on the hands of businessmen who travel very frequently, and also on the hands of professional men who want to migrate to other countries.

Travel is also shown by lines leaving the Vitality Line and heading downwards towards the Mount of Moon. Sometimes these **travel lines** leave the Vitality Line and go straight, horizontally, towards the centre of the hand, but more usually these travel lines head downwards towards the Mount of Moon. The longer the line, the longer the journey, or at least the more significant it will be. Islands, crosses, crossbars or stars on these travel lines are unfavourable indications. Such marks are undesirable anywhere on these travel lines. In these days of hijackings and other air disasters, anyone with such marks is advised to think twice before travelling, because the journey may end in either failure, disappointment or danger.

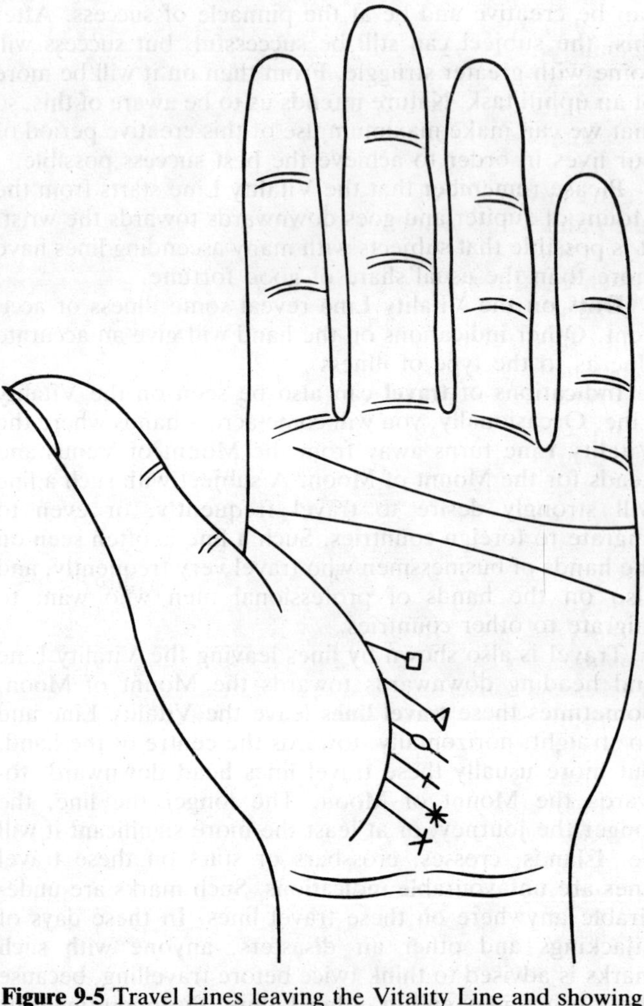

Figure 9-5 Travel Lines leaving the Vitality Line and showing the Square, Triangle, Island, Crossbar, Star and Cross formations on them.

On the other hand, when a travel line ends in a triangle, the journey will be successful, either spiritually, intellectually, or materially.

The age at which a journey takes place is calculated on the Vitality Line, at the point where the travel line leaves the Vitality Line.

The subject will be much more likely to travel if the palms are also elastic and firm at the same time. Should the palm be soft, or worse still, flabby, the probability of travel will decrease — especially if the palm is flabby, in which case the subject will not have the energy to make preparations for travel. Such a subject may travel mentally, or have a burning desire to travel, but will not necessarily *actually* travel. This is perfectly in accordance with the basic truth of scientific hand analysis which teaches that the lines on the hands reflect the workings of the subject's mind and psychology.

These lines which leave the Vitality Line and head for the Moon Mount need not always refer to overseas journeys. Sometimes they can refer to a change of house in the same town, or to a transfer from one town to another in the same country. In such case, these limited movements must be very important to the subject at that particular time. Psychologically, it is as if the subject had travelled overseas, even though the travel line merely referred to a transfer from one town to another in the same country. But in general these travel lines, especially if they are long, do show travel overseas.

Thus, to be really accurate, these lines could be called **Lines of Movement.** I prefer to call them Lines of Movement, since the movement need not always be to another country. In some cases such lines have been seen on the hands of officers in government service who had been transferred from one town to another.

So, to recapitulate, let us not believe wrongly that a short 'Life Line' necessarily means a short life, or that a long 'Life Line' promises a number of years amounting to the Biblical three score and ten!

This misconception has caused needless anxiety in the minds of people with potential prospects who would otherwise be most willing to consult an expert hand analyst. A few years ago, I had a lady client who seemed very troubled. On close questioning, she told me that some amateur had told her that she would have a short life and that she would ascend to heaven in one or two years' time. She was hardly twenty-four years of age at the time of consultation. After a thorough examination of her palms I was able to inform her with honesty and professional integrity that her life span was certainly beyond sixty. No doubt her Vitality Line (Life Line) was short in one hand, but there were other features of the hands which promised her a reasonably long life-span. This true incident illustrates the damage that can be done both to subjects as well as to scientific hand analysis by quacks and ill-informed amateurs.

Chapter Ten

The Line of Mentality Shows Your Mental Attitude towards Life

The **Line of Mentality** is frequently called the **Line of Head** or the **Head Line.** This line does not refer to the condition of the head! It shows most accurately the mentality of the subject — the quality of intelligence, the type of mentality, the power of mental concentration, and the capacity of the subject to exercise self-control. Therefore, we can easily perceive that this line should more accurately be termed the Line of Mentality.

Because of its ability to reveal so much about the workings of the MIND, many hand analysts quite rightly call this the most important line on the hand. But it must be emphasized straightaway that general intelligence and mentality should NOT be assessed from this line alone. We must study certain mounts of the hand thoroughly to get a true picture of the mental calibre of the subject. Three important mounts must always be considered at the same time: these are the Mount of Jupiter, Mount of Mercury, and Mount of Moon. All these mounts should be well-developed without being over-elevated. Certainly, these mounts should not be flat or depressed on the hand. Jupiter stands for wisdom, Mercury for sharpness of the intellect and quick thinking, while the Mount of Moon stands for imagination. It is therefore easy to see why these three mounts must also be considered in assessing the intelligence and mental calibre of the subject.

This very important point is only known to very

advanced students of the science of hand analysis. Again, this aspect reveals that scientific hand analysis is a science of *combination* of several features of the hand. For assessing the degree of education attainable by the subject, the Sun Mount and the Sun (Apollo) Line must also be thoroughly studied. It is possible for a subject to be brilliant without having a high standard of education. So, strictly speaking, for assessing intelligence *alone,* the following features have to be studied:

- the Line of Mentality
- the Mount of Jupiter
- the Mount of Mercury and
- the Mount of Moon

The Line of Mentality will reveal to a significant degree the potential the subject has for achieving success, happiness, intellectual development and material wealth. It is a truism that intelligence alone is not good enough for success in life. We must also look to other features of both hands which show an ability for hard work and perseverance. Psychologists will be interested to know that scientific hand analysis can specifically aid modern psychology in assessing the potential for success of the subject.

Carl Jung, the world famous psychologist, was a staunch supporter of astrology and hand analysis. On 6 September 1947 he wrote to Professor B.V. Raman, a world famous Indian astrologer and editor of the *Astrological Magazine.* Here is an excerpt from his letter:

> ... Since you want to know my opinion about astrology, I can tell you that I have been interested in this particular activity of the human mind since more than thirty years. As I am a psychologist, I am chiefly interested in the particular light the horoscope sheds on certain complications in the character. In cases of difficult psychological diagnosis, I usually get a horoscope in order to have a further point of view from an entirely different angle. I must say that I very often found that the astrological data elucidat-

ed certain points which I otherwise would have been unable to understand. From such experiences I formed the opinion that astrology is of particular interest to the psychologist, since it contains a sort of psychological experience which we call 'projected' — this means that we find the psychological facts as it were in the constellations. This originally gave rise to the idea that these factors derive from the stars, whereas they are merely in a relation of synchronicity with them. I admit that this is a very curious fact which throws a peculiar light on the structure of the human mind.

What I miss in astrological literature is chiefly the statistical method by which certain fundamental facts could be scientifically established.[1]

Professor Jung's complaint about insufficient statistics to establish a case for astrology is now out of date. He was certainly one of the most brilliant minds of the twentieth century in the field of psychology. This eminent scientist's personal experiences with astrology are of immense significance to supporters of astrology. This is because Jung's opinions are not coloured by the colossal misconceptions and prejudices against astrology which seem to be the trademark of many modern scientists. An in-depth psychological diagnosis can be drawn from a correctly interpreted horoscope; since astrology and hand analysis are twin or sister sciences, the findings of the hands and the horoscope as regards psychological diagnosis will agree to a significant degree.

Origin of the Line of Mentality

The Line of Mentality is thus one of the important features of the hand as regards the psychological pattern of the subject. Normally the Line of Mentality starts at the base of the Mount of Jupiter and crosses the palm in a horizontal manner. The ideal Line of Mentality should be

Raman, B.V, *op.cit.* p.147.

long, deep, well-formed and a healthy pink in colour. It should be neither too broad nor too thin. A long line reveals the ability to absorb ideas. However, if the line is long, but broad, it is no longer so favourable. A broad line indicates that the Current is diffused and scattered while making its way along the line. The subject with a long but broad Line of Mentality will understand many things, but only to a superficial degree — his thinking will tend to be shallow. The case will be confirmed if the Mounts of Jupiter, Mercury and Moon are either undeveloped or depressed. Empirical evidence has proved that those with thick or broad Lines of Mentality fight shy of intellectual occupations, and are much more attracted to an active outdoor life. If the line is short it means that the subject will understand a limited number of topics. Should a child have a short Line of Mentality, a well-informed teacher or parent should encourage the child to repeat his lessons.

The Line of Mentality may be joined to the Vitality Line. This shows that the subject is careful and sensitive by nature. Should this tied formation continue for a long distance, it is very unfavourable and reveals a nature that is exceptionally sensitive and self-conscious. The subject will also suffer from an inferiority complex. I have seen this frequently on hands of subjects who depend too much on parents, relatives or friends for advice. Self-reliance will be lacking in such cases. The Line of Mentality is considered to be excessively tied if it leaves the Vitality Line only under the Mount of Saturn.

It is also unfavourable if the Line of Mentality rises from *inside* the Vitality Line, on the Mount of Lower Mars. When the Line of Mentality rises in such a manner, it comes under the very adverse influence of the planet Mars. In astrology Mars is a fiery, aggressive planet, and it gives its negative qualities to such a Line of Mentality. The subject will be badly lacking in real self-confidence, and will also be over-sensitive, aggressive and highly irrit-

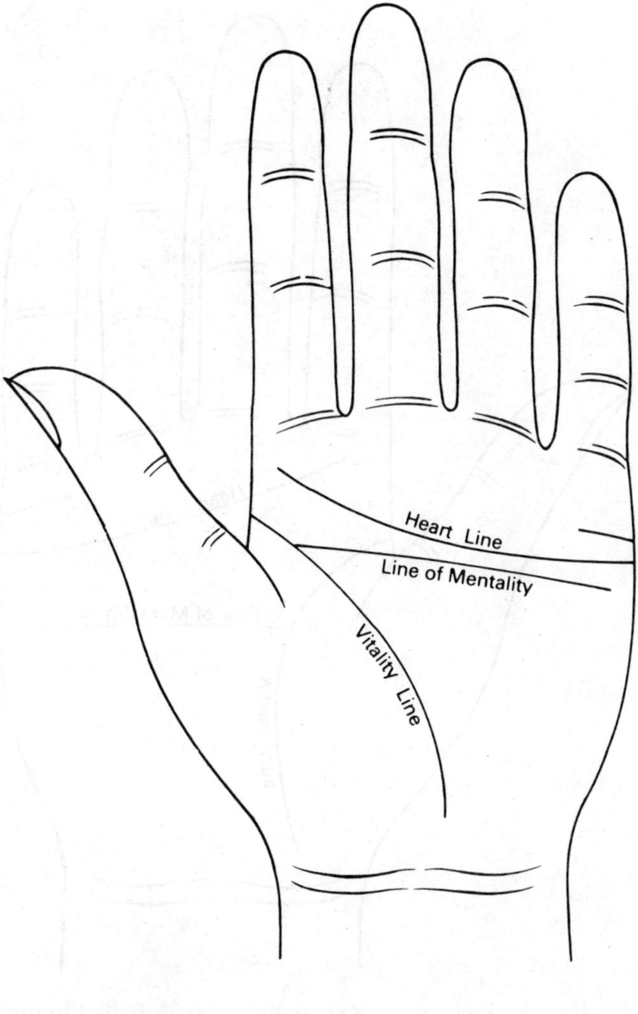

Figure 10-1 The Line of Mentality joined to the Vitality Line.

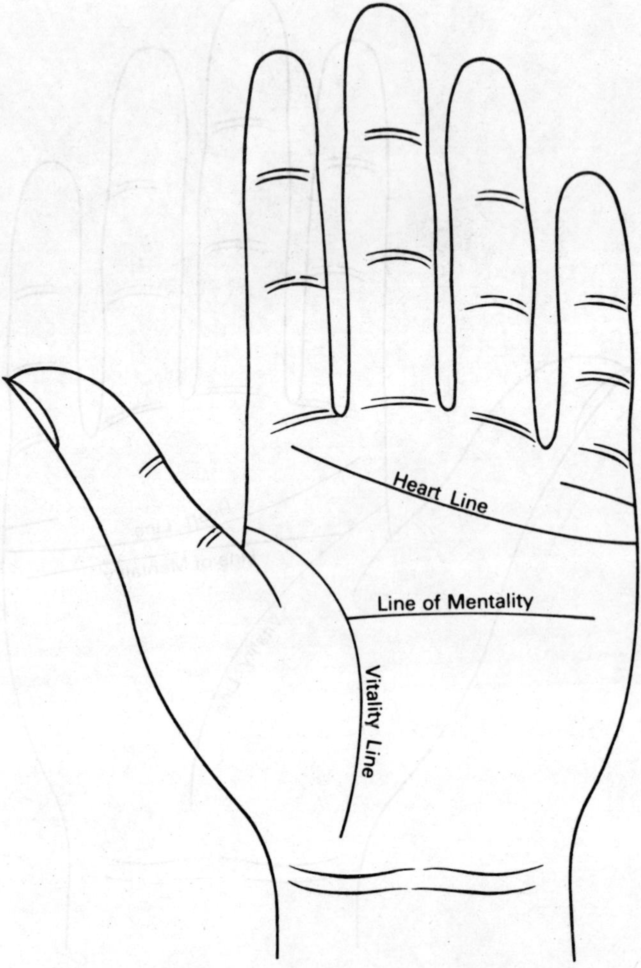

Figure 10-2 The Line of Mentality excessively tied to the Vitality Line.

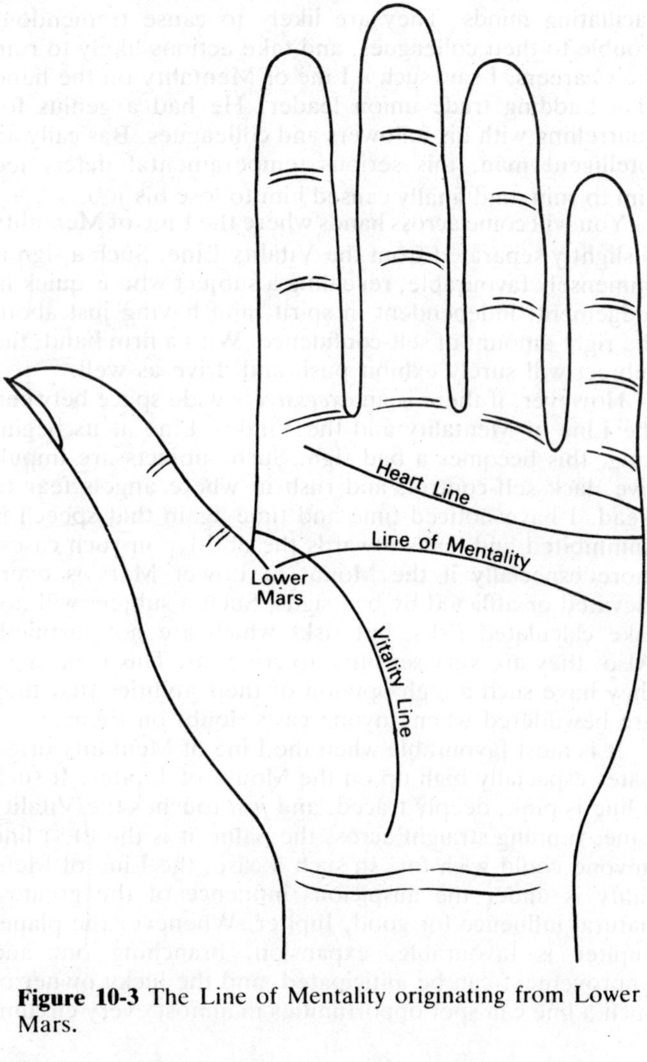

Figure 10-3 The Line of Mentality originating from Lower Mars.

able in temperament. These negative traits will be heightened if the thumb is weak. Such persons have shifting, vacillating minds. They are likely to cause tremendous trouble to their colleagues, and take actions likely to ruin their careers. I saw such a Line of Mentality on the hand of a budding trade union leader. He had a genius for quarrelling with his followers and colleagues. Basically an intelligent man, this serious temperamental defect led him to ruin, and finally caused him to lose his job.

You will come across hands where the Line of Mentality is slightly separated from the Vitality Line. Such a sign is immensely favourable, revealing a subject who is quick in judgement, independent in spirit, and having just about the right amount of self-confidence. With a firm hand, the subject will surely exhibit push and drive as well.

However, if there is an *excessively* wide space between the Line of Mentality and the Vitality Line at its beginning, this becomes a bad sign. Such subjects are impulsive, lack self-control, and rush in where angels fear to tread. I have noticed time and time again that speech is uninhibited and leans towards the abusive in such cases, more especially if the Mount of Lower Mars is over-elevated or afflicted by bad signs. Such a subject will not take calculated risks, but risks which are not justified. Also, they are very sensitive to criticism. This is because they have such a high opinion of their abilities that they are bewildered when anyone casts doubt on them.

It is most favourable when the Line of Mentality originates especially high up on the Mount of Jupiter. If such a line is pink, deeply traced, and *just* touches the Vitality Line, running straight across the palm, it is the BEST line anyone could wish for. In such a case, the Line of Mentality is under the auspicious influence of the greatest natural influence for good, Jupiter. Whenever the planet Jupiter is favourable, expansion, branching out and improvement can be anticipated, and the lucky owner of such a line can spot opportunities in almost every circum-

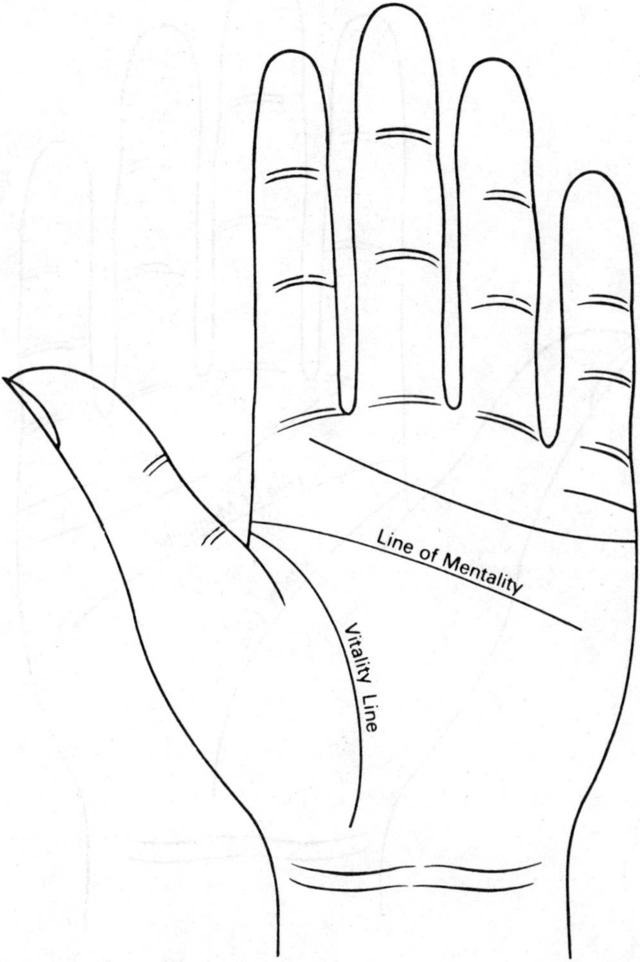

Figure 10-4 A moderate gap between the Line of Mentality and the Vitality Line.

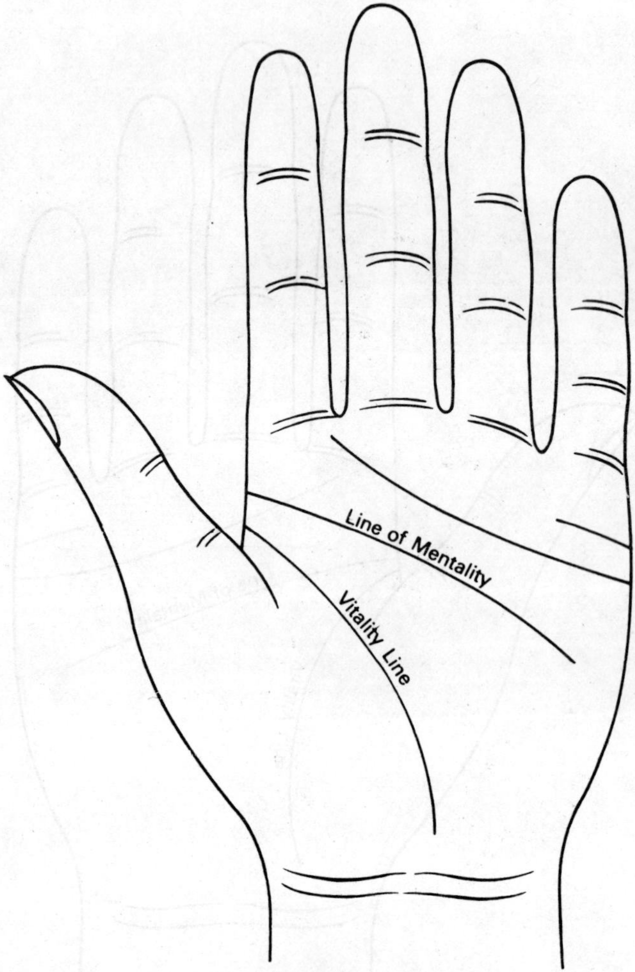

Figure 10-5 An excessively wide gap between the Line of Mentality and the Vitality Line.

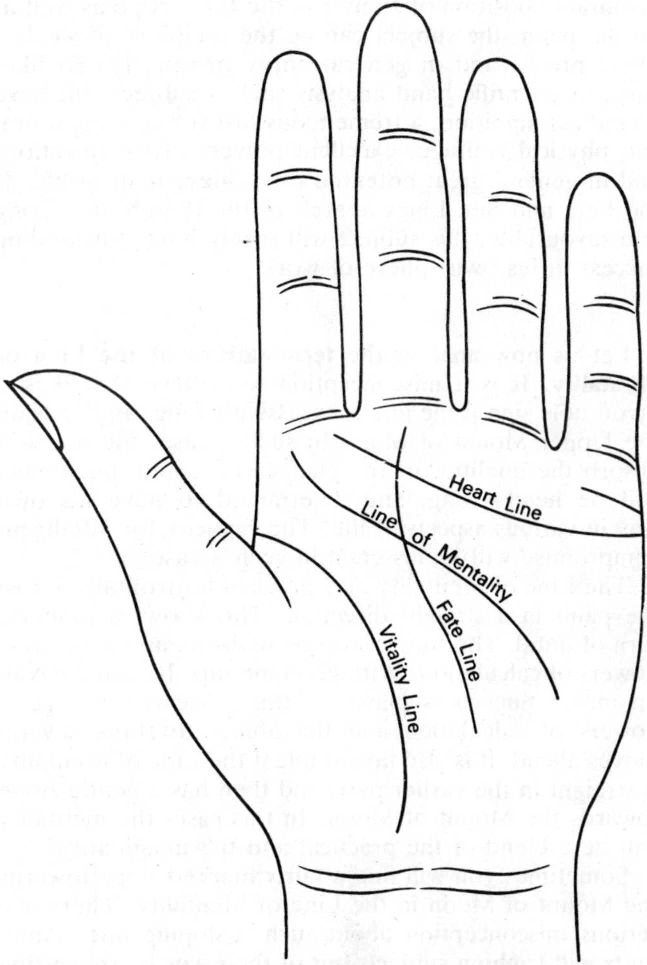

Figure 10-6 The Line of Mentality originating from the Mount of Jupiter.

stance. It is an open secret in astrology that through the favourable position of Jupiter in the horoscope as well as on the palm, the subject can be the recipient of wealth, titles, prizes, and in general enjoy prosperity. So likewise, in scientific hand analysis such a subject will have boundless ambition, a tremendous lust for success, moral and physical courage, excellent powers of organization, and in general great potential for achievement in life. If the Fate and Sun Lines as well as the thumb are strong and favourable, this subject will surely have outstanding success in his own sphere of work.

Let us now analyse the **terminations of the Line of Mentality.** It is a misconception to believe that it is a favourable sign if the line is excessively long, and ends on the Upper Mount of Mars. In such a case, the line will absorb the qualities of the planet Mars, and the subject will be head-strong, and determined to have his own way in various aspects of life. The capacity for intelligent compromise will be lessened in such a case.

The Line of Mentality may proceed horizontally across the palm in a straight direction. This shows a practical turn of mind. The subject will be realistic, and have good powers of calculation. With good mounts, he could develop into a fine chess player as this game requires good powers of calculation and the ability to think several moves ahead. It is also favourable if the Line of Mentality is straight in the earlier part, and then has a gentle slope towards the Mount of Moon. In this case, the mentality will be a blend of the practical and the imaginative.

Sometimes you will find a fairly marked slope towards the Mount of Moon in the Line of Mentality. There is a serious misconception about such a sloping line. Amateurs will frighten subjects out of their wits by suggesting that this reveals a tendency towards insanity or lunacy.

The Mount of Moon reflects imagination and the line

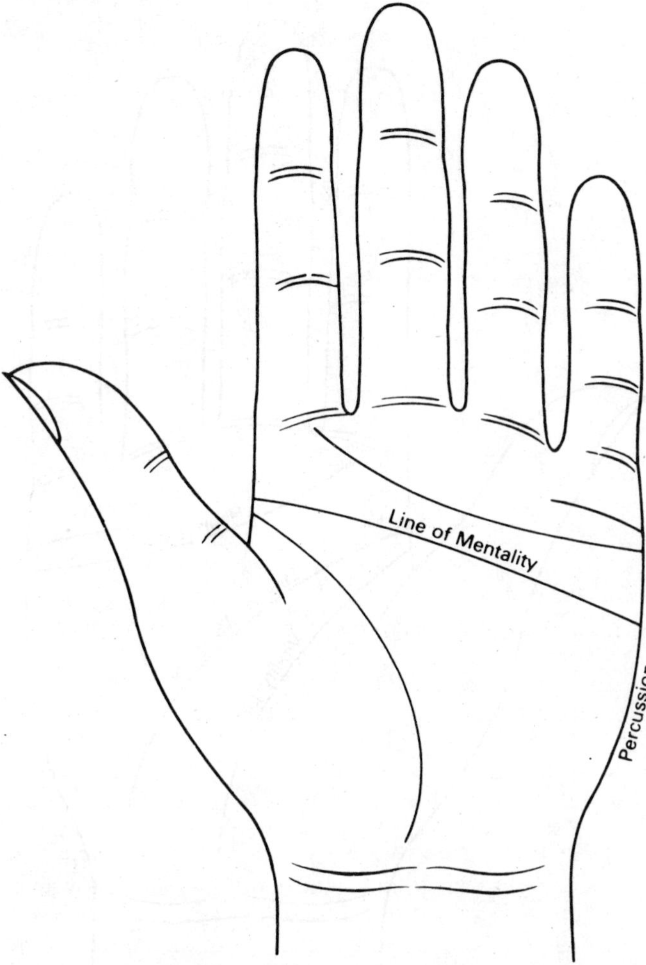

Figure 10-7 The Line of Mentality reaching the Percussion on the Mount of Upper Mars.

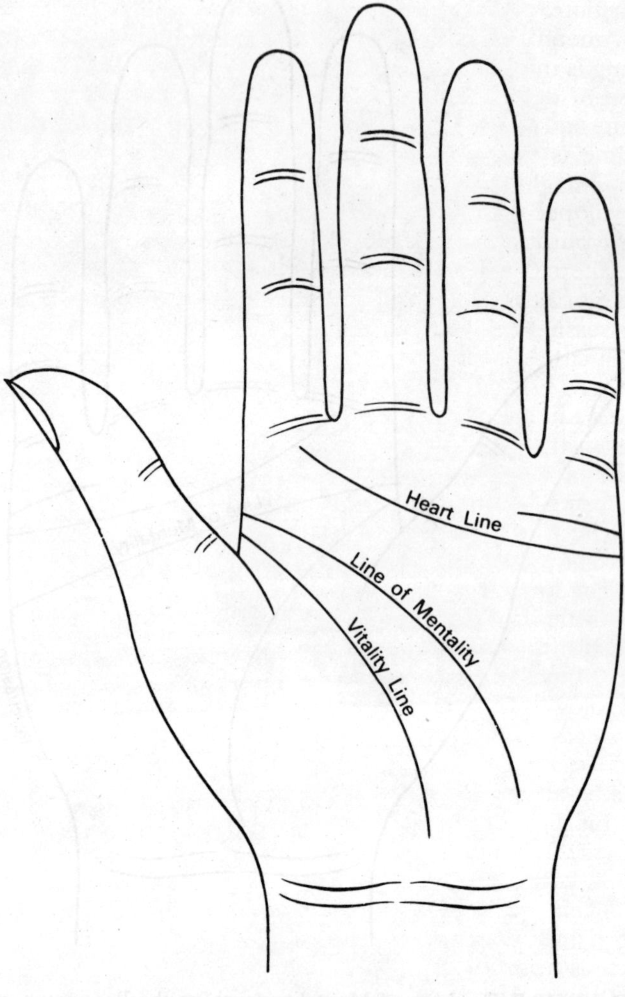

Figure 10-8 A sloping Line of Mentality.

being drawn towards this particular Mount reveals this attribute. Merely because a subject has imagination does not mean that he is likely to go round the bend! Everything is in order if such a line is long, clear, and above all, free of defects such as islands, breaks, a chained formation, and repeated crossbars. If this is the case, and such a line is free of such defects, the subject will possess a rich imagination, especially if the Mount of Moon is well-developed without being over-elevated. I have seen such a favourable Line of Mentality on the hands of writers, speakers, linguists and comedians. Such a long drooping Line of Mentality is dangerous only if it is weak, thin, and possessing serious defects such as islands and breaks. In such cases, especially if the palm is long and narrow, the subject will suffer from a flighty imagination as well as some kind of mental disorder. This analysis is so accurate that it may be advisable for psychologists to observe the Line of Mentality on the hands of patients believed to be suffering from mental disorders.

The Line of Mentality is sometimes found curving upwards towards the Mount of Mercury. In this case the line will be long. It is the course of the line under the base of the little finger, towards this finger itself, which will be the distinguishing feature. Such a formation means that the Mount of Mercury has pulled the line towards it. In astrology and hand analysis the planet Mercury deals with business, commerce, and money-making. This subject will be in deep love with money-making. *Money* will be the be-all and end-all of his life, and practically all aspects of his life will be weighed according to their financial worth. This is a mark which professional hand analysts often come across on the hands of businessmen.

Then, there is the Line of Mentality which is long, deep and clear, with a small fork at the end of it. A small fork is a very favourable termination, revealing a versatile mind with a union of the practical and the imaginative. The branch pointing downwards will show the

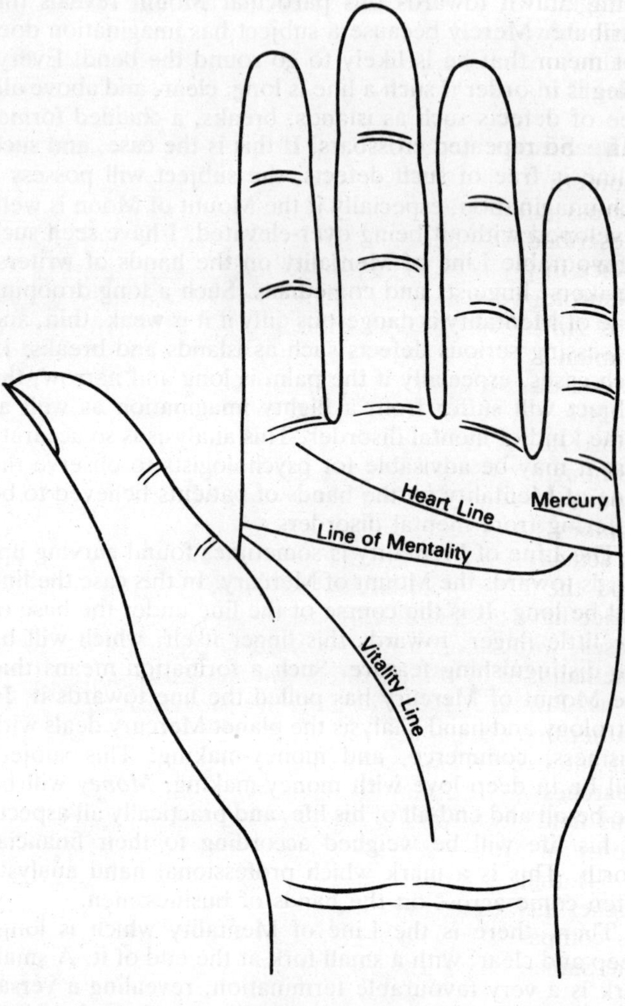

Figure 10-9 The Line of Mentality curving upwards under the Mount of Mercury.

imaginative aspect of the mind, while the straight part will show the practical aspect. This fork can be given full value only if the Line of Mentality is long, deep, and clear.

The Simian Line

Sometimes you will come across one straight line running across the palm. This is the transverse palmar crease described by doctors Pamela Davis and Victoria Smallpeice in their article 'Developmental Medicine and Child Neurology' on medical hand analysis in the 1963 issue of the *American Medical Journal.* This line is called the **Simian Line** by expert hand analysts. This is because it is found on the hands of chimpanzees.

It is not often that you will find such a line. It is even more rare to find such a line on both hands of a subject, although if you try hard enough and analyse many palms you will come across a few cases. At least two world famous statesmen have this line on their palms. This line is actually a joining together or fusion of the Line of Heart and the Line of Mentality. Doctors Davies and Smallpeice have associated this line, in a certain percentage of cases, with mongolism, but you will observe this line on the hands of extremely intelligent and strong-minded persons. Primarily this line has a psychological significance rather than, as has been suggested by the learned doctors, an intellectual one. The doctors have quoted the researches of Tunakan, a well-known Dutch specialist in this field, who, on examining 260 Turks, found an incidence of 3.5 per cent with this line.[2] Tunakan stated (in 1954) that Asian races in general show a considerably higher incidence, and quoted the example of the Chinese as compared to Dutchmen. I have, however, observed the Simian Line on the palms of various races and nation-

---

[2] Davies, Pamela A, and Smallpeice, Victoria, *op.cit.*, p.494.

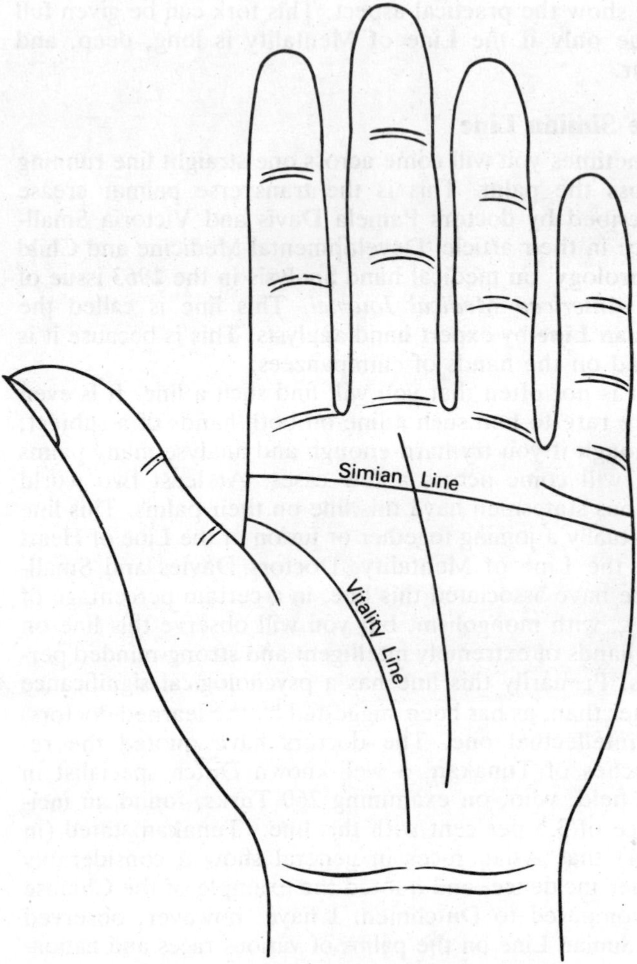

Figure 10-10 The Simian Line or the Transverse Palmar Crease is found where the Heart Line is normally located.

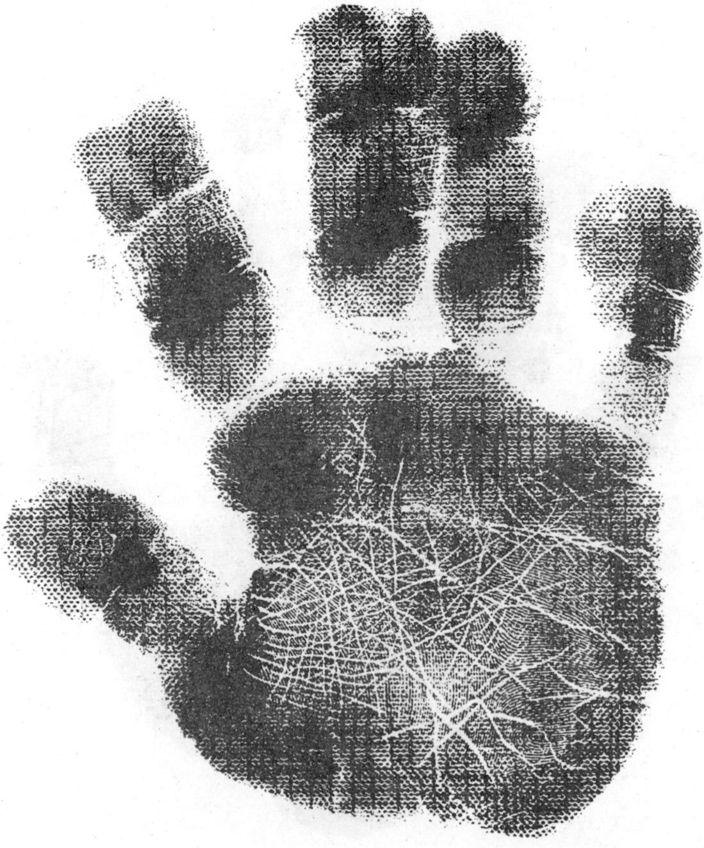

Figure 10-11 The right handprint of a Mongoloid. Notice the afflicted Line of Mentality and the awkward shape of the hand.

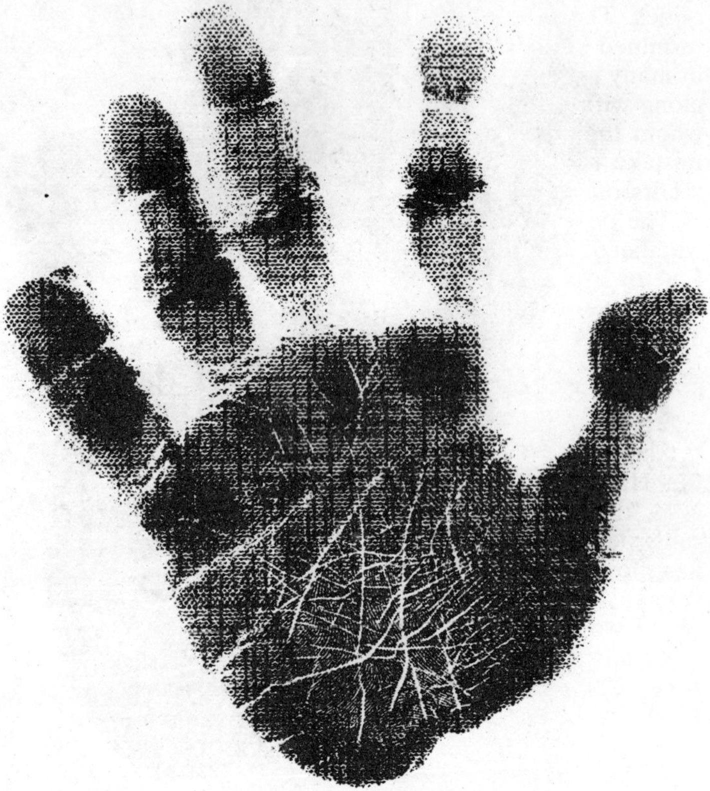

Figure 10-12 The left handprint of the same Mongoloid.

alities, and in my own research have not found the Chinese to have a higher incidence of the Simian Line than any other race. I have encountered this line on the palms of Dutchmen, Chinese, Malays, Indians and Americans, as well as on the palms of many others of different nationalities. This type of line reveals a subject with a very determined outlook, as well as someone who is an extremist in many spheres of life. These subjects find it hard to get along with others. They are dangerous not only to those whom they like, but to themselves as well. It is a grave mistake to take these people for granted, especially in affairs of the heart.

The position of the line should be noted to determine whether it is in the place normally occupied by the Heart Line or by the Line of Mentality. If it is in the place normally reserved for the Line of Mentality the subject will be strongly ruled by a most calculating mind. Such a subject will not do anything without an ulterior motive: even his acts of charity will be motivated by self-interest, enlightened or otherwise.

Should the line occupy the place normally reserved for the Heart Line, the interpretation is different. In this case, the emotional and sentimental aspect of the person's personality will have the upper hand. My research has shown that the Simian Line is an unfortunate sign for women of any race or nationality. Again and again I have found women who are unable to marry, or who suffer great misfortune in their love lives. I cannot agree with some Chinese hand analysts who say that this line is good, for even on the hands of some men who have achieved great material wealth I have often found that their married lives were wrecks.

Other Forms of the Line of Mentality

Occasionally you may find the Line of Mentality going upwards to touch the Heart Line. In this case, the Heart Line has pulled the Line of Mentality towards it. The sub-

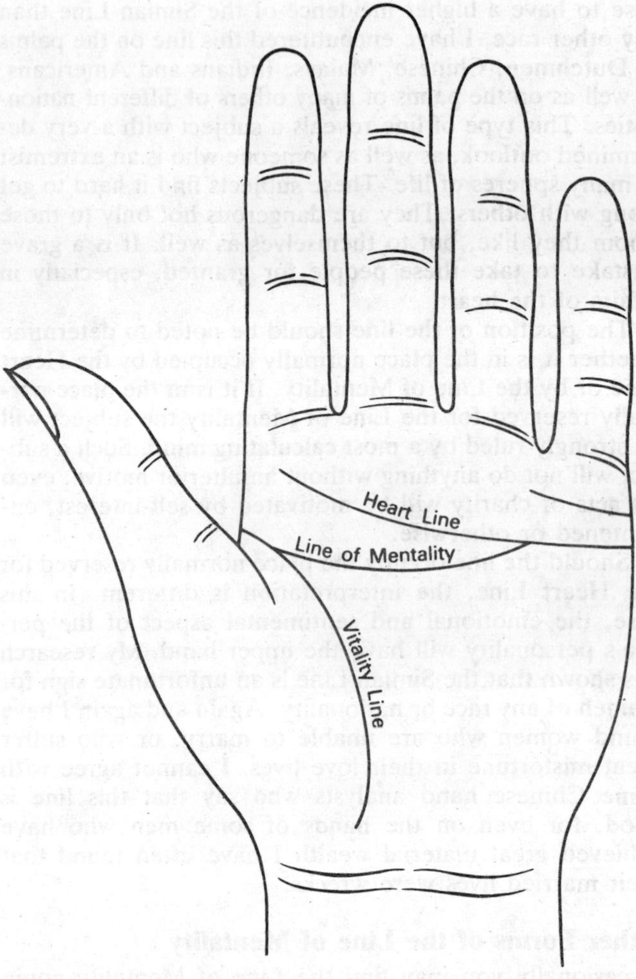

Figure 10-13 The Line of Mentality curving upwards to touch the Heart Line.

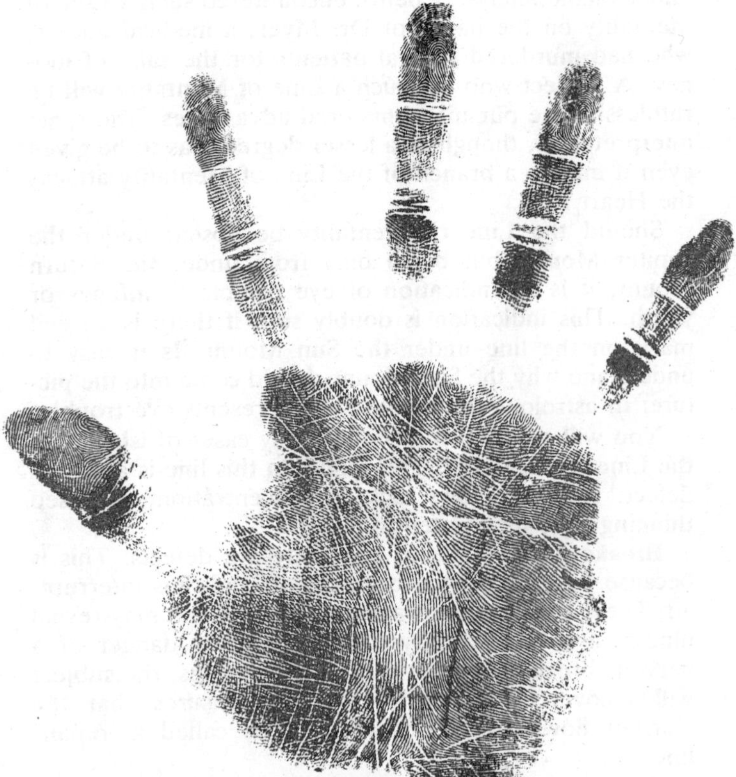

Figure 10-14 The right handprint of a doctor. The Line of Mentality bears a striking resemblance to that of Dr. Myer, the Chicago Poisoner.

ject will permit his feelings to get the better of his reason and judgement. With other bad indications, the subject with such a line will lose his mental bearings and allow himself to use criminal methods to make money. The famous hand analyst, Cheiro, encountered such a Line of Mentality on the hands of Dr. Myer, a medical doctor, who had murdered several patients for the sake of money. A subject who has such a Line of Mentality will be ruthless in the pursuit of material advantages. The same interpretation, though to a lesser degree, has to be given even if merely a branch of the Line of Mentality attacks the Heart Line.

Should the Line of Mentality be absent under the Jupiter Mount, but begin only from under the Saturn Mount, it is an indication of eye trouble in infancy or youth. This indication is doubly sure if there is an evil mark on the line under the Sun Mount. Is it easy to understand why the Sun Mount should come into the picture: in astrology the planet Sun represents eye trouble.

You will surely come across many cases of **islands** on the Line of Mentality. The island on this line is always a defect. It often shows lack of concentration, confused thinking, and mental tension.

Breaks on the Line of Mentality are defects. This is because the Current has been cut off and thus interrupted. These breaks are always undesirable, and may reveal illness, a physical injury to thc head, or danger of a nervous breakdown. But if the line overlaps, the subject will recover. The overlapping line ensures that the Current flows again, and hence it is called a 'repair' line.

A **square** on the line is also a repair agent. It boxes in the trouble, and thus prevents the negative Current from overflowing into other parts of the hand. If the break is covered by a Square, it means that the subject will escape either a threatened physical injury to the head or a nervous breakdown.

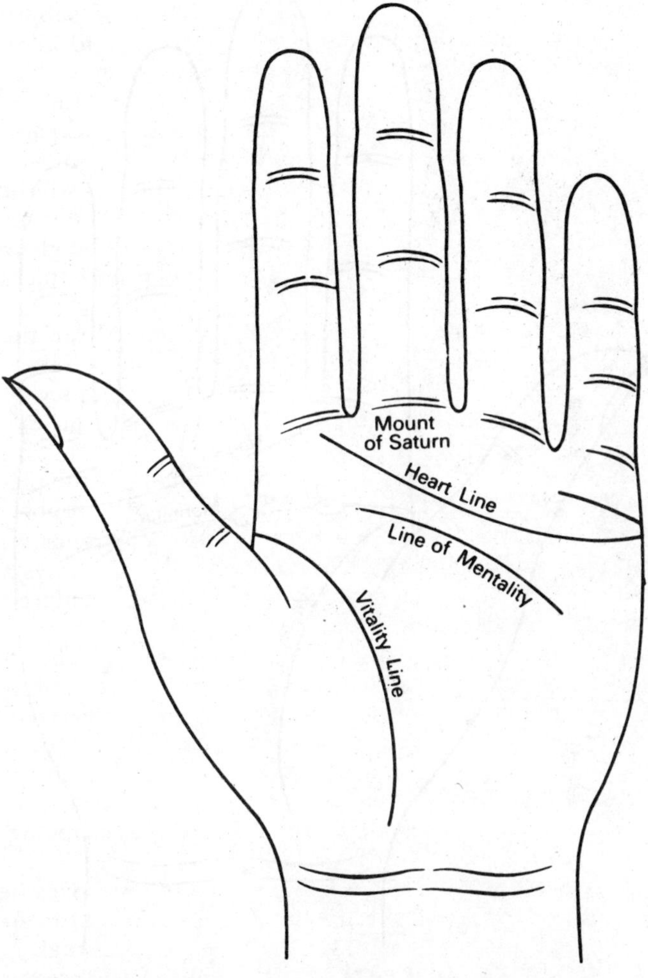

Figure 10-15 The Line of Mentality originating under the Mount of Saturn.

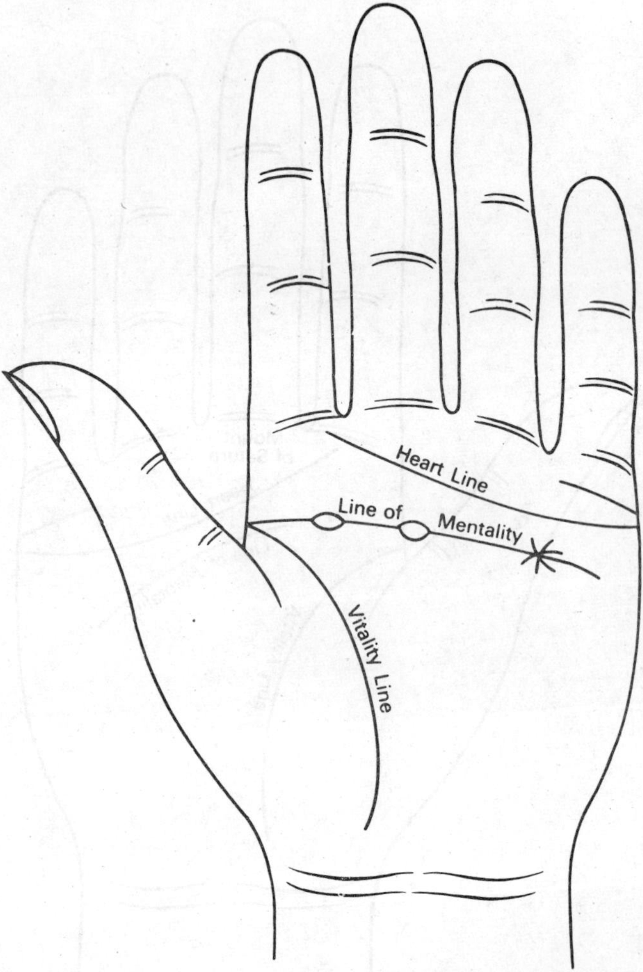

Figure 10-16 Islands on the Line of Mentality. Note the Star near the end of the line.

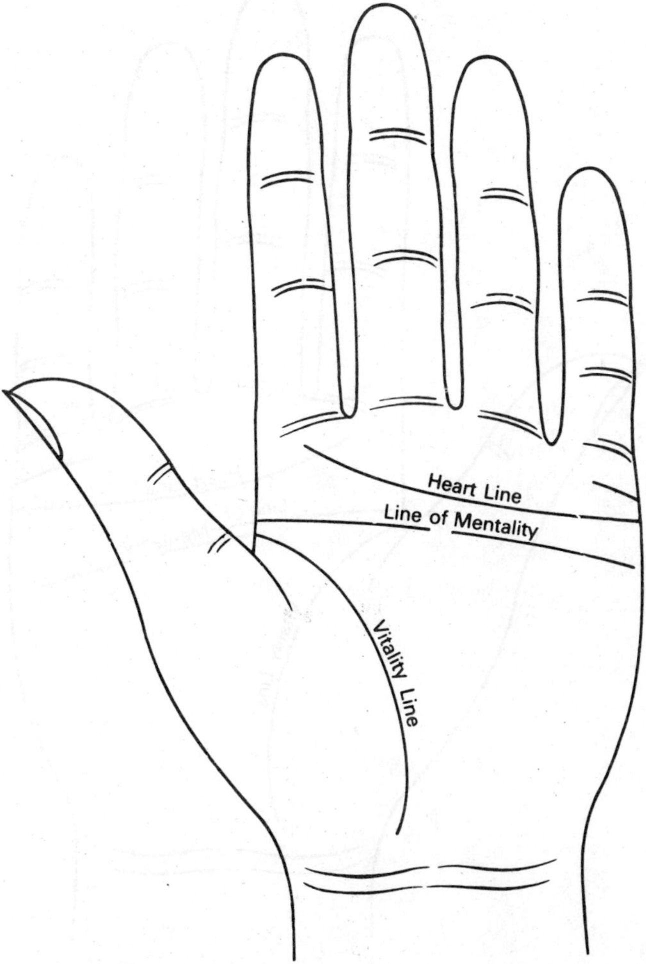

Figure 10-17 A Break in the Line of Mentality.

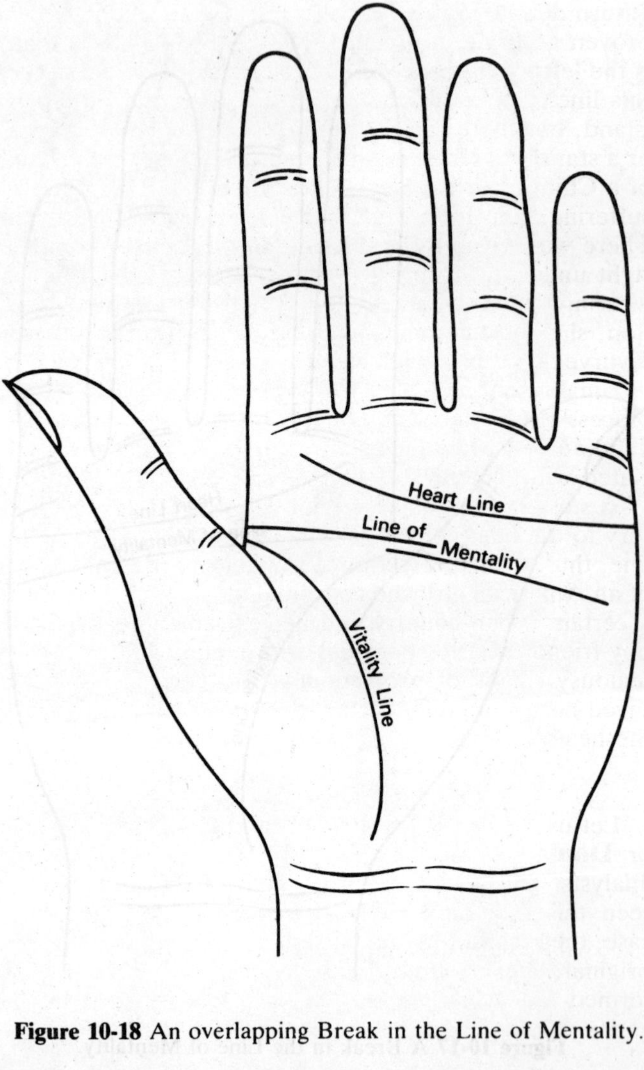

Figure 10-18 An overlapping Break in the Line of Mentality.

Defects on the Line of Mentality under the Mount of Saturn denote injuries to the leg. This indication has been proven accurate in practice. My research suggests that it is the left leg that is primarily affected by such a defect on this line. Generally, the defect will be in the form of an island, but there can be others, such as a break, a cross, or a star on the line. I confirmed such a case on the hands of a Chinese girl who consulted me in late 1977. She was suffering from foot drop, and her left leg was paralysed. There was a well-formed island on the Line of Mentality right under the Saturn Mount on her left hand. She was wearing braces when she consulted me. On my suggestion, she consulted an Indian physician practising Indian Ayurvedic herbal medicine. He gave her native Ayurvedic massages, and she was able to walk without the braces. From the standpoint of astrology and scientific hand analysis, it is important to note that Saturn is associated with lameness.

A **star** on the Line is an ominous sign. It denotes an injury to the head. Observe if there are repair signs on the line, thus giving protection. I saw this mark on the hands of an American girl who consulted me in 1977. She was in a certain Asian country and her extremely jealous local boy-friend tried to shoot her with a gun while in a fit of jealousy. Signs of protection at the corresponding age saved her from either certain death or a serious injury to the head.

Let us now consider **the Double Lines of Mentality** or **Double Head Lines** as it is called by some hand analysts. This is really a most rare sign, and so far I have seen this sign only about twenty-five times. In such a case, the second Line of Mentality will run parallel to the original line. If both lines are deeply marked, well-formed, and clearly traced, it is a sign of great intelligence. This is all the more certain if the Mounts of Jupiter, Mercury and Moon are well-formed on the hand. The subject, however, will have a double Mentality. He will be soft and tender at one moment, and hard and ruthless at the other. Undoubtedly, these people have what psychologists call a most complex personality. They are a real puzzle to most of their friends.

The Line of Mentality is called the 'Line of Mother' in Indian Hand Analysis. Definitely, Double Lines of Mentality shows some undue connection with the subject's mother. If the double lines are well-formed, the subject will be deeply attached to the mother, and/or vice-versa. This will be confirmed if the Mount of Moon is also elevated, preferably, on both hands, and has auspicious marks on it, such as triangles or vertical lines. In Indian Astrology, the Moon represents the mother. So it is easy to understand why the Mount of Moon must also be studied for indications of the subject's happiness from his mother. The Mount of Saturn also has a connection with the mother, and if this too is favourable, the case is triply confirmed! In my research I have found that the mother of the subject outlives the father if the subject has favourable Double Lines of Mentality. Strong and favourable Double Lines of Mentality together with other favourable indications reveal an accession to great wealth or power. But in such cases, these will be attained by virtue of the excellence of the subject's mind.

With favourable Double Lines of Mentality, the subject is often lacking in self-confidence in the earlier years of his life, but will develop self-confidence as the years go by.

However, Double Lines of Mentality are not favourable if they are badly formed, weak looking, and broken up at various places. In such a case, the subject will be very confused mentally, and have a split personality. I once saw three lines of Mentality on the hands of a traveller who consulted me in Penang. All three lines were badly formed, and the subject was certainly a badly

Figure 10-19 An example of Double Lines of Mentality.

mixed-up case!

Look at Figure 10-19 showing Double Lines of Mentality. Notice the short line in the print, ending beneath the Mount of Saturn. You will notice a long parallel line above it, heading for the Mount of Upper Mars, with a break beneath the Mount of Sun. The subject was the best student in an Arts subject at a certain prestigious university, and is now holding an extremely high position. From his schooldays he had a reputation for academic brilliance. He is most attached to his mother, who is still living, while his father passed away many years ago. He does not suffer fools gladly and has an irritable temperament. Notice the Double Lines of Mentality rising from Lower Mars to prove this point. He is also very stubborn and strong-willed, as shown by the formidable nature of the Double Lines of Mentality. This line is long, and has ended on the Mount of Upper Mars beneath the little finger. The thumb is strong, showing a strong will. However, from the Vitality Line there is a curved line heading for the Mount of Upper Mars, but not quite reaching it. This is the **Via Lascivia.** The subject has a fondness for liquor. Notice the sign of a fish found attached to the Vitality Line. The tail of the fish is formed by the Via Lascivia and the Fate Line, while the head of the fish is pointing downwards towards the wrist. The Double Head Lines are free of islands. It is a fact that this subject has excellent powers of concentration.

Let us study the **length** of the Line of Mentality. Look at Figure 10-21. Draw an imaginary line vertically across the palm from the space between the index and middle fingers. Let it touch the Line of Mentality. Draw two other imaginary lines, from between the second and third fingers as well as from the third and fourth fingers.

The Line of Mentality should at least enter Section B. It is rare to find a line shorter than this. Such a short line

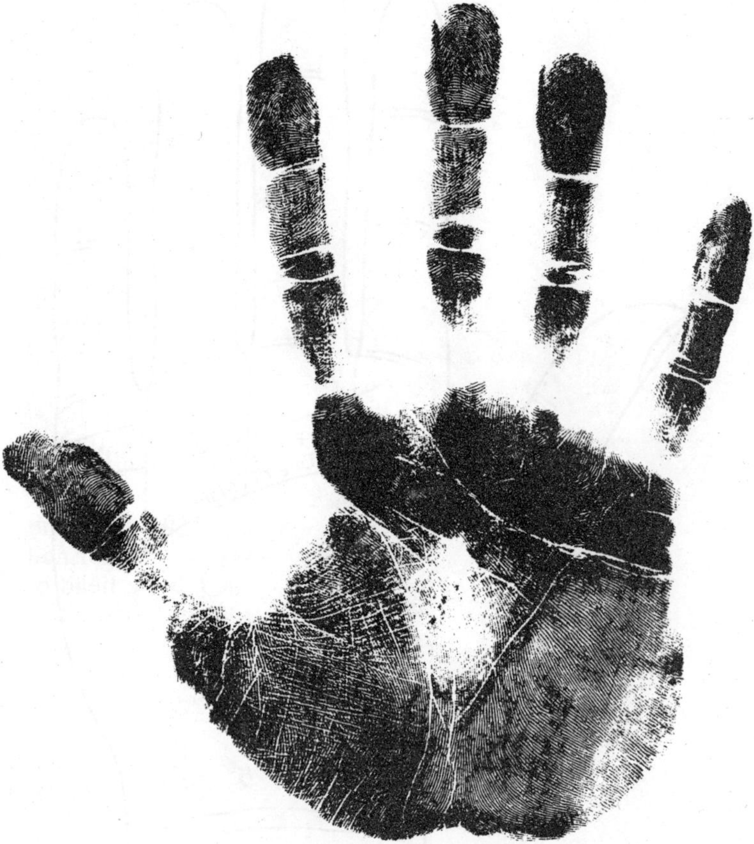

Figure 10-20 Another example of Double Lines of Mentality.

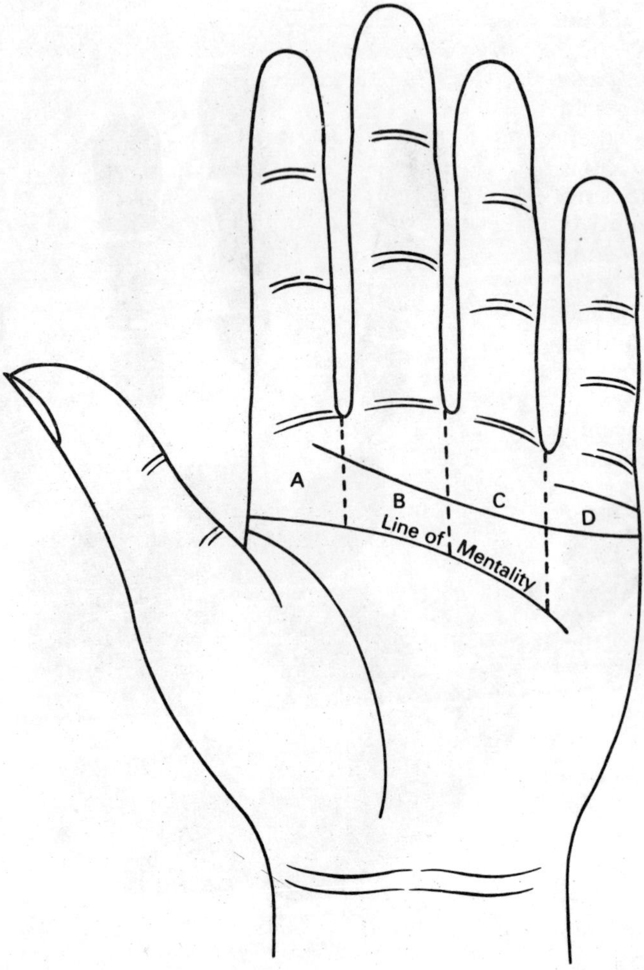

Figure 10-21 Assessing the length of the Line of Mentality.

will show a primitive intellect.

Should the line enter Section C, somewhere between B and C, it would show the normal length. When it crosses the mid-point between B and C, and the hand has other favourable indications as well, such a line shows an awakened mind. Should the line go beyond C and enter D, it is also a favourable indication, provided the line does not actually touch the percussion. Of course, bear in mind that the depth, clarity and colour of the line must be considered carefully.

Many aspects of the Line of Mentality can be studied. The main thing is to understand the principles of scientific hand analysis. You can then reason out various combinations affecting this line. A serious study of this line will be well worth your effort. You will understand your own psychology that much more, to your own permanent advantage.

Chapter Eleven

The Heart Line Reveals Accurately Your Capacity for Emotional Response

The **Heart Line** or the Line of Heart is another major line of the palm. For judging **longevity,** Indian hand analysts regard it as being more important than the Vitality Line or the so-called Life Line. This is entirely logical, as when life begins, the heart functions, and when life ends, the heart ceases to work. There is some controversy among eminent hand analysts as to the origin of this line. It need not be taken as an argument that hand analysis is not a science merely because there is some controversy over one or two of its aspects. After all, such controversies exist in other respected and accepted fields of science, such as medicine. It is worth noting that barring the controversy over the origin of the Heart Line or Mercury Line, there is very little controversy over other aspects of this science. So this is one of the few points over which there is dispute.

The Indian school of hand analysis generally considers the Heart Line as starting from the percussion under the little finger and crossing the palm in the direction of the Mount of Jupiter. My research, however, suggests that it actually starts from the area of the Mount of Jupiter, goes across the area below the four fingers, and ends in the percussion under the little finger. Dr. Benham, an eminent American hand analyst, also holds this point of view. Let us now analyse my reasons for stating why the Line must originate from the area of the first or Jupiter finger. High blood pressure and weakness of the heart is shown by islands on the Heart Line under the little finger. Now I have had clients who said that they developed high blood pressure only at the age of about forty. If we were to assume that the Heart Line starts under the little finger, then, by calculating age from this source, the subjects should have had high blood pressure much earlier, let's say around the age of about twenty. One does not have to be a lawyer to see that this contradicts what actually happened in the medical experience of the subject! But if we assume that the Heart Line starts under the Jupiter finger, then middle age and old age will be represented by the area of the line beneath the Mounts of Sun (Apollo) and Mercury (third and fourth fingers) respectively. This, therefore, makes much more sense than saying that the Heart Line starts from the Mount of Mercury or under the little finger.

The Heart Line in its normal condition runs under the four fingers across four mounts or planets. These are Jupiter, Saturn, Sun and Mercury. It is therefore easy to see why this line has assumed such a major role in Indian hand analysis. Understand fully the qualities and attributes of the planets Jupiter, Saturn, Sun and Mercury, and you will to a large degree be able to grasp the meaning of the Heart Line from a study of the hand.

The Heart Line reveals your attitude towards love, attraction and sexual matters. It also shows, with the most astonishing accuracy, the physical condition of that most vital organ of the body — the HEART. This is a sublime truth which eminent cardiologists of the world can only ignore to the detriment of patients under their care. I have examined the Heart Lines of hundreds of clients who have suffered heart attacks, and, without exception, their Heart Lines had been afflicted. There are many ways in which the Heart Line will reveal heart disease or some kind of heart trouble. In this elementary work we shall only consider the major ways in which physical heart weakness is shown by the Line of Heart.

The Heart Line must always be considered together with the **Mount of Venus.** Actually, the Heart Line reveals the more spiritual, uplifting concepts, such as love, duty, and moral responsibility. The Mount of Venus reveals the more ordinary emotions of sexual love, lust, and gregarious instincts in society. So a defect in the line may be compensated to some degree by a basically favourable Mount of Venus, and vice-versa. Let us assume that the Mount of Venus is over-elevated, red in colour and having criss-cross lines on it. This will show a tendency towards excessive sexual appetite and lasciviousness. But let us assume that the Heart Line is very favourable, and is long and deep. In such a case, the unfavourable effects of the Venus Mount will be subdued by the favourable Heart Line. This subject, while basically still having a very strong sexual appetite, will yet show tenderness and sympathy as well as loyalty to those women with whom he associates intimately. He will also, in such a case, be more selective in his choice of sexual partners. Even if the relationship ends, he will still have feelings of goodwill and sympathy for the former friend. So the golden rule when considering the Heart Line is always to study the Mount of Venus simultaneously. In this way you will stun the sceptic by describing the emotional and sexual make-up of the subject with surprising accuracy.

The Heart Line can start from various places. It can start low on the Mount of Jupiter, or higher up on the same Mount; from the base of the second finger, and high up on the base of the Mount of Saturn. In very exceptional cases it starts from the Mount of Sun.

Here is a very important rule. The Heart Line absorbs the qualities of both the mount from which it starts as well as the mount on which it ends. Having once grasped this rule, we will be in a position to work out which two mounts or planets influence the Heart Line to a major degree. Naturally, these two will be the mount from

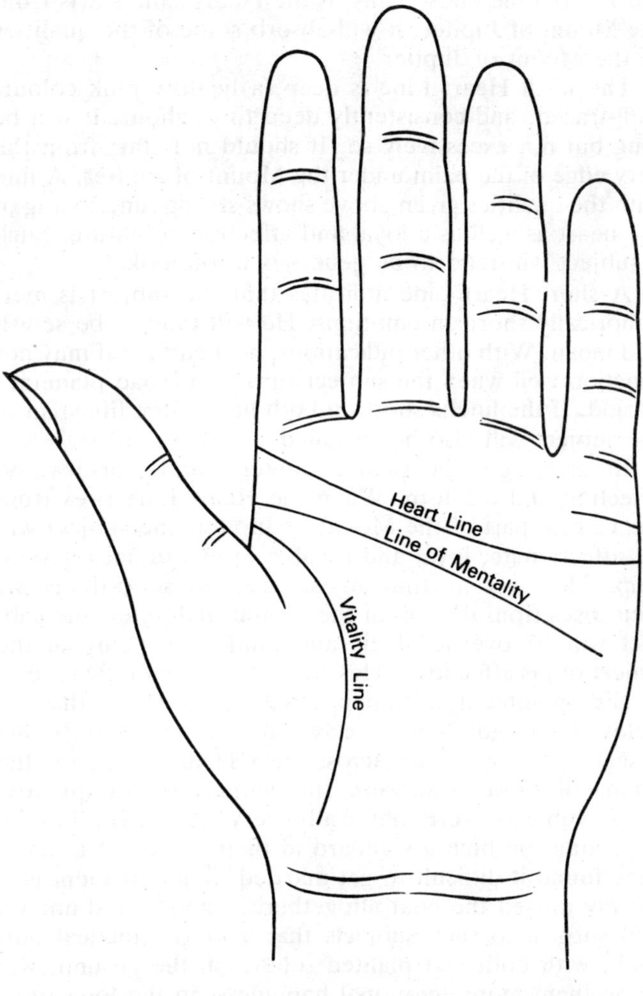

Figure 11-1 An excessively Long Heart Line.

which the Heart Line originates and the mount on which the Heart Line ends. Thus, if the Heart Line starts from the Mount of Jupiter, it will absorb some of the qualities of the Mount of Jupiter.

The ideal Heart Line is deep, a healthy pink colour, well-traced, and consistently deep throughout. It will be long but not excessively so. It should not start from the very edge of the palm under the Mount of Jupiter. A line with the qualities given above shows strong functioning of the heart as well as a loyal and affectionate nature. Such a subject will tend to be generous in outlook.

A short Heart Line indicates that the subject is metaphorically short on emotions. He will tend to be selfish and mean. With other indications, his heart itself may not function well when the subject runs into a bad planetary period. If the line is short on both hands, the life span of the subject will also be curtailed.

In astrology, the planet Jupiter stands for loyalty, affection and idealism. When the Heart Line rises from the central part of the Mount of Jupiter, the subject will be affectionate, loyal and reliable in emotional relationships. However, anything in excess is bad: so, if the Heart Line rises from the top of the Mount of Jupiter, the subject will be over-idealistic and think too highly of the object of his affections. This subject will generally tend to be disappointed if, as time progresses, he realises that the beloved has got feet of clay and not of gold! In my research I have come across such Heart Lines on the palms of those who were still unmarried. Frequently, these subjects were physically very attractive, but by expecting too high a standard in their choice of a mate, they found it difficult to get married. Some of them ultimately missed the boat altogether. A good hand analyst will suggest to such subjects that a more practical outlook, with both feet planted solidly on the ground, will bring them more emotional happiness, in the long run.

It is a defect should the Heart Line start from the edge

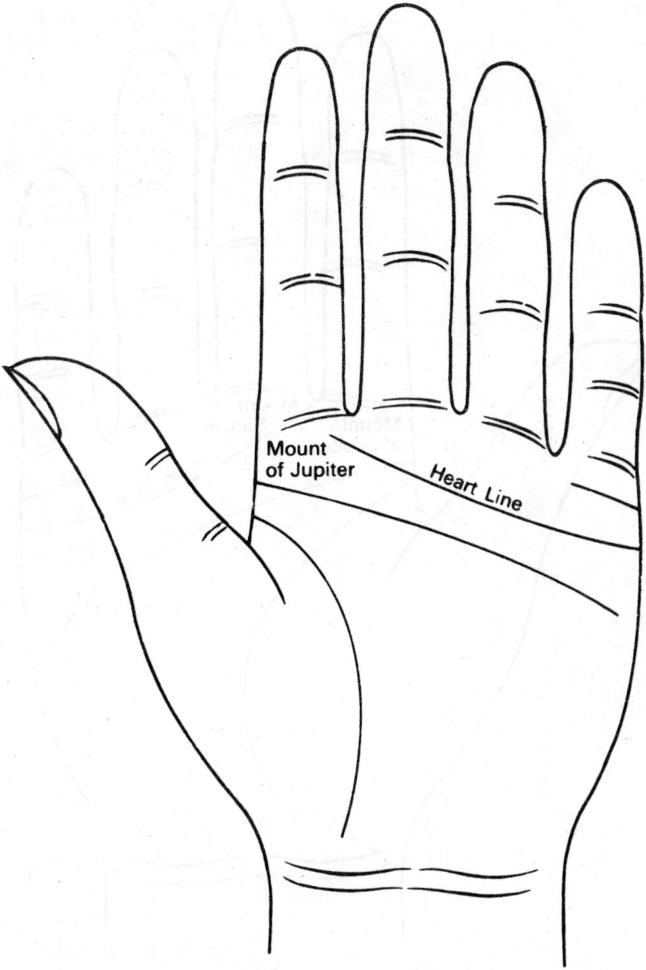

Figure 11-2 The Heart Line starting from the Mount of Jupiter.

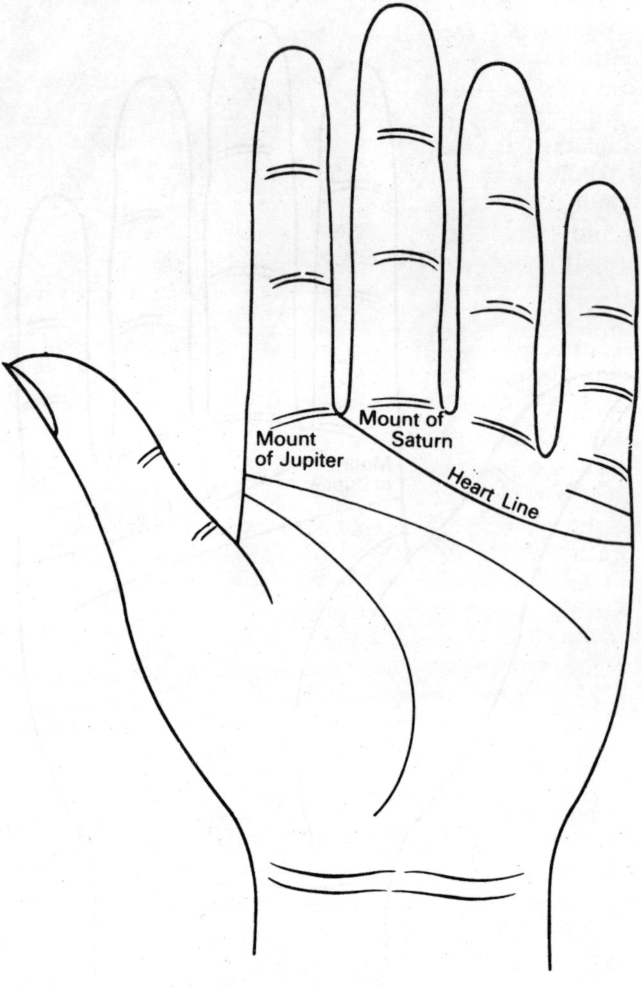

Figure 11-3 The Heart Line originating between the Jupiter and the Saturn Mounts.

of the Mount of Jupiter nearest to the thumb and run right across the palm to the end of the percussion under the little finger. This is a rare mark, and it shows a subject who is a perfectionist. Such a Heart Line shows an excess of love and devotion. A tyrannical, possessive disposition is indicated, and such a subject will be disillusioned in the course of time.

Then there is the Heart Line which rises between the first and second fingers (Jupiter and Saturn fingers). This is probably the best origin for the Heart Line. The sobriety of Saturn is combined with the wisdom of Jupiter. The subject will feel deeply, but will seldom make an outward show of affection in public. Nonetheless, his love will be deep, well-balanced and happy, and the faults of the beloved forgiven during the course of married life. These people are practical, make good friends, but they are not foolishly sentimental. It is not often that the expert hand analyst comes across such an origin of the Heart Line.

If the Heart Line begins from the Mount of Saturn, it is not a favourable sign. It must be remembered that in hand analysis Saturn is basically regarded as a malefic mount or planet. This is all the more so if the Mount of Saturn is over-exalted or depressed, with evil signs such as crosses, crossbars, grilles, moles, and dark spots or stars on it. The subject having such a Heart Line will tend more to be sensual than truly affectionate. These qualities will be exaggerated if the hand happens to be soft or flabby at the same time. Soft or flabby hands indicate a nature that is basically lazy and reluctant to do difficult physical or mental work. If the Mount of Venus is also highly developed, with bad marks on it (e.g., a red grille, several crossbars, moles, dark spots, criss-cross lines), then the subject will only care for self-satisfaction in sexual relations. You will find such Heart Lines in the hands of both men and women. These subjects will not allow any obstacle to stand in the way of their sexual fulfilment. Several men and women who are involved in

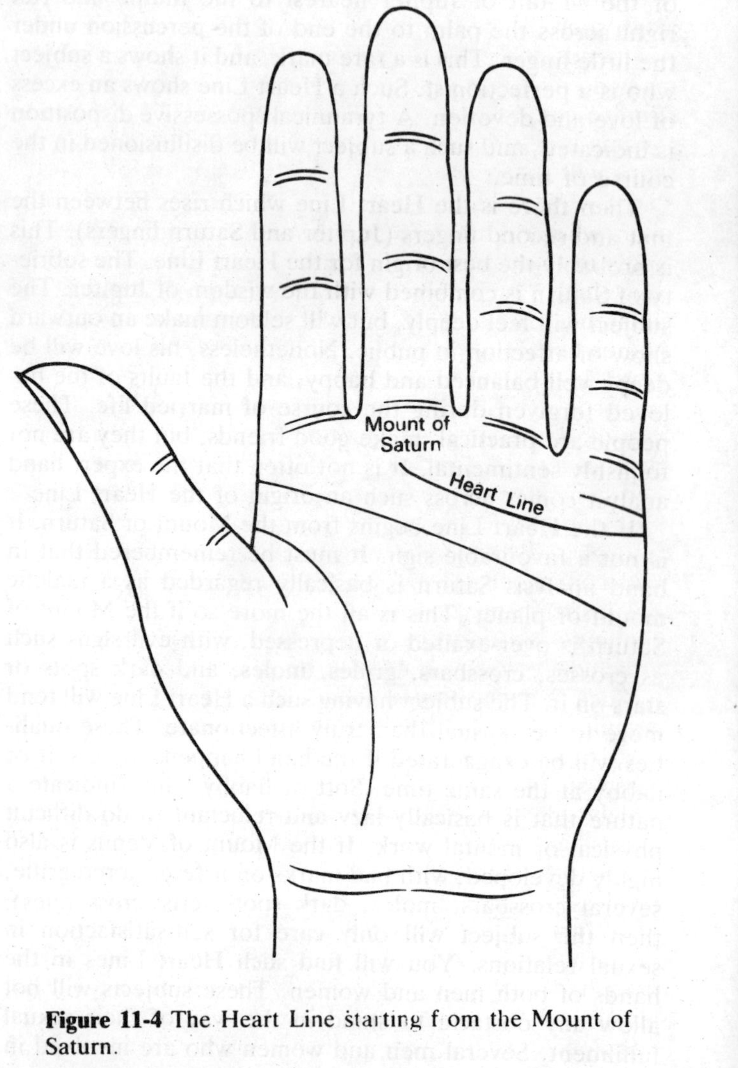

Figure 11-4 The Heart Line starting f om the Mount of Saturn.

extramarital affairs have such a Line of Heart. People with such Heart Lines are prone to using others for their own ends, and then discarding them ruthlessly. However, they do make expansive outward demonstrations of affection to cover up these undesirable traits. If the Mount of Venus is also badly formed and unfavourable, such persons will surely prove to be fair-weather friends.

I saw such a Heart Line on the hands of a prominent man who was charged with rape. He had several dark spots in the centre of his palm. His Mount of Venus was very high and badly formed. His defence counsel, an amateur hand analyst, informed me that the Mount of Venus had been higher before the accused was put in the court lockup, but, due to the immense worry of being imprisoned, it had shrunk slightly. Nonetheless, it was still a formidable Mount of Venus! I informed the defence counsel that the subject would be found guilty and convicted. On the same day the accused was found guilty and sentenced to five years' imprisonment. Later it transpired that this was not the first rape that the subject had committed. He had committed rape several times, but justice caught up with him at long last, when he was running a most adverse planetary period, as shown by the afflicted Line of Sun (Apollo) on his hands.

Such subjects, with Heart Lines beginning on the Mount of Saturn, often have a contempt for the opposite sex, but the expert hand analyst must not be surprised if these subjects state that his psychological diagnosis is widely off the mark! All these unfavourable qualities are intensified if the Heart Line rises high from the base of the Saturn or middle finger. Such subjects will be utterly ruthless in their emotional outlook.

A **fork** in the Heart Line on the Jupiter Mount is a favourable sign. It is a sign of fortune, especially if one branch of the fork runs between the first and second fingers. Such a subject will be materially prosperous, and emotionally well-balanced in the sphere of love.

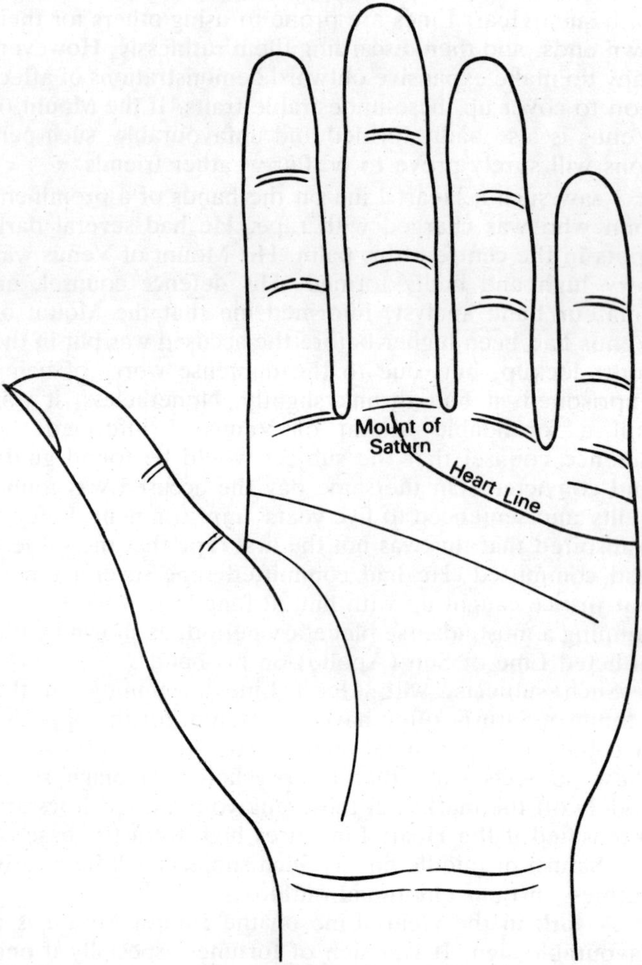

Figure 11-5 The Heart Line starting high on the Mount of Saturn.

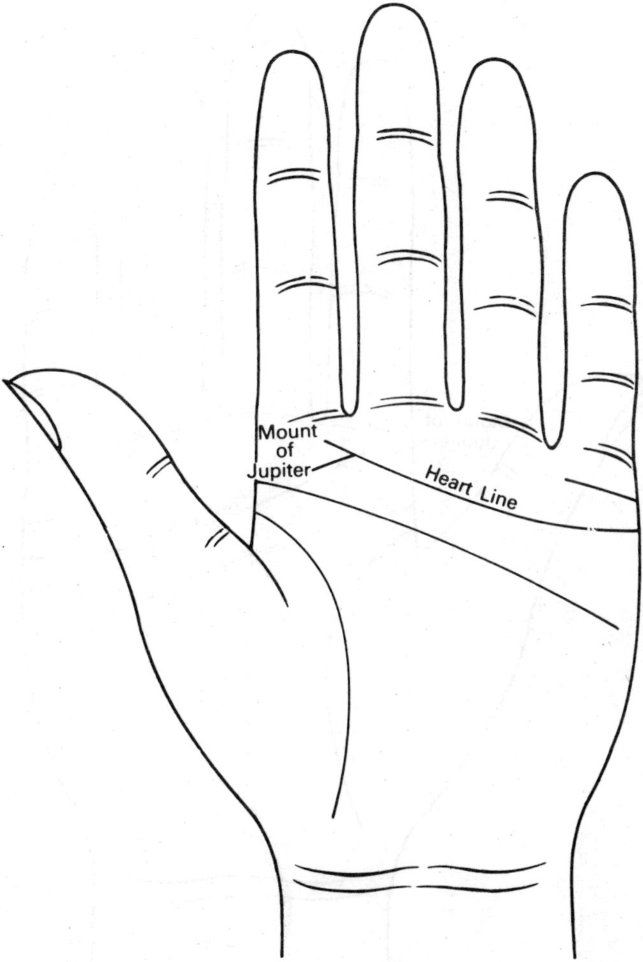

Figure 11-6 The Heart Line starting with a Fork on the Mount of Jupiter.

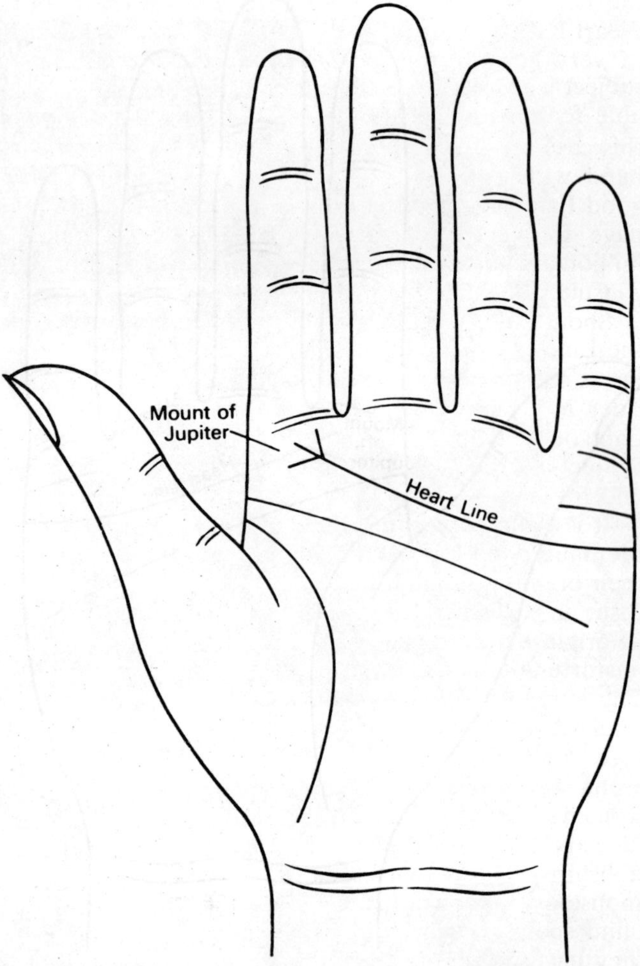

Figure 11-7 The Heart Line starting with a Trident on the Mount of Jupiter.

A **trident** on the Heart Line is a three-pronged fork at the beginning of the line. Should such a trident of the Heart Line be formed on the Mount of Jupiter, it is a sign of very good fortune. Frequently, it is a sign that the subject is or will be a millionaire, if there are other favourable features on the hand to complement this point. In this case the favourable features would be a materialistic hand with well-developed mounts below the fingers, a good Fate Line, and preferably a favourable Sun Line. I have frequently seen such a trident on the palms of millionaires of every nationality, when these clients have consulted me.

Should the Heart Line itself **curve downwards** to touch the Line of Mentality, it is an unfavourable indication as far as emotional happiness is concerned. We should consider it a cardinal rule that downward lines are *always* unfavourable in hand analysis. With such a sign, the subject will meet with major disappointments in affection and friendship.

It is even more unfortunate if the Heart Line, Line of Mentality, and Line of Vitality are all joined together at their origin, just under or on the Mount of Jupiter. In this case, an excessive current is being poured into one point of origin by three major lines. Such people are liable to misfortune either through physical accidents, or in love. The interpretation is most interesting if this combination refers to love. Such a subject will be accident-prone in love, and will be unable to learn from mistakes in that arena. I have found this mark more often on the hands of women than men. This mark shows some persistently defective judgement in connection with emotional relationships. These subjects will stick to an undeserving spouse or lover against their better judgement. There is a blind spot somewhere in their emotional make-up, and they have no real insight into the circumstances causing an unhappy emotional relationship. It is surprising to note that these subjects are often intelligent, highly

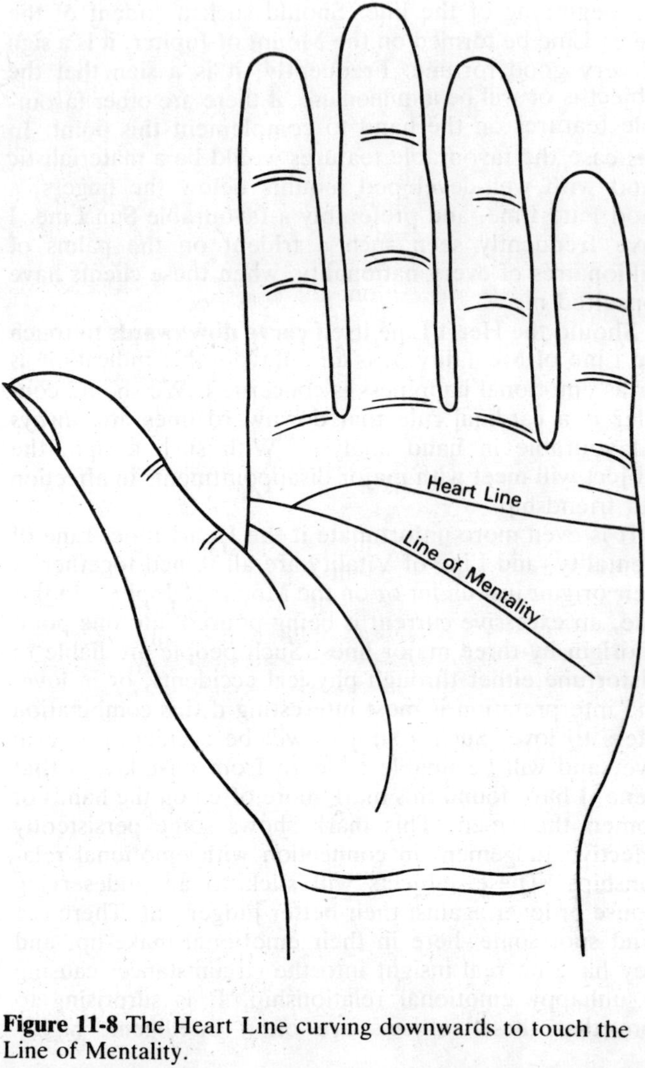

Figure 11-8 The Heart Line curving downwards to touch the Line of Mentality.

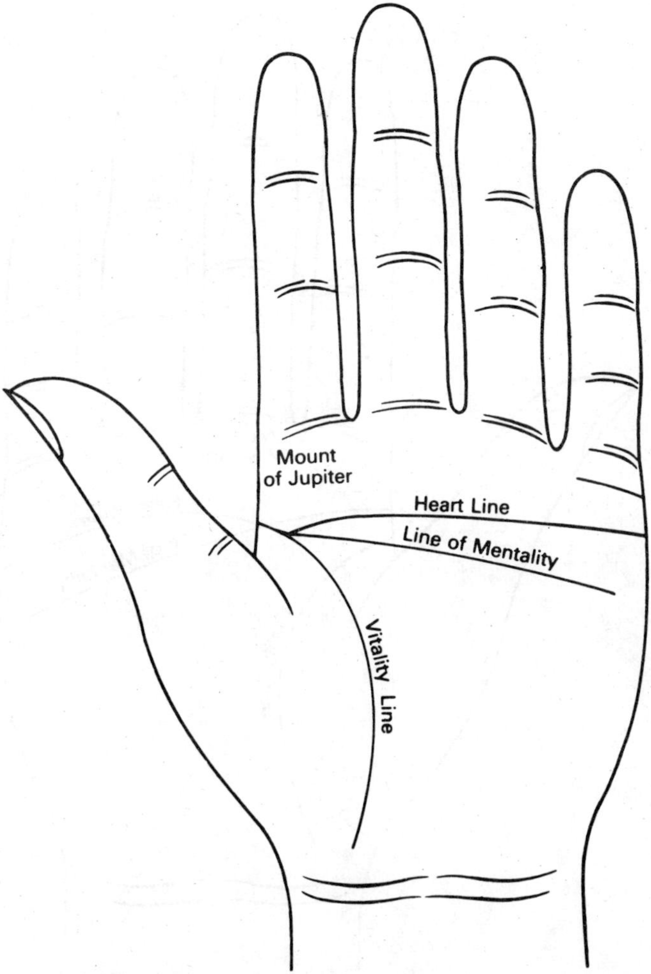

Figure 11-9 The Heart Line, Line of Mentality and the Vitality Line all joined together at the origin on the Mount of Jupiter.

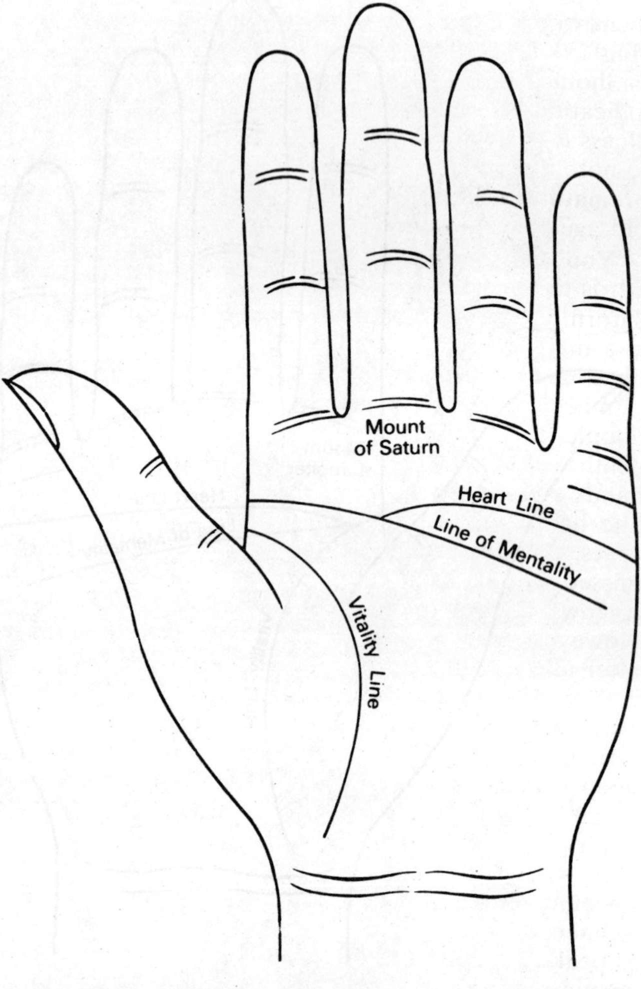

Figure 11-10 The Heart Line touching the Line of Mentality on the Mount of Saturn.

literate and capable of learning from experience in other spheres of life — yet these admirable qualities desert them when it comes to emotional matters. Truly, love is blind.

Should such a sign be found on both hands, the evil indications are intensified and sudden death, accident or illness is likely to take place. It is, however, very important to note that sudden death does not necessarily have to be premature death. Sudden death can take place at a ripe old age.

You will sometimes find a Heart Line curving downwards to touch the Line of Mentality under the Mount of Saturn. Please bear in mind again that Saturn is essentially a malefic mount in hand analysis and that descending lines are unfavourable. Such an unfortunate mark signifies an emotional calamity due to blindness in love. Should such a mark be found in both hands, sudden death will take place. I found such a mark on one of the hands of a lady client who consulted me many years ago. She had a relationship with a man for almost fourteen years, and she sacrificed a great deal for this love. She missed various chances of marriage, and to add to her sorrows, the boy-friend eventually married someone else However, as far as I know, she is still alive — the mark after all, was only on one hand.

You will often find a Heart Line which is **straight and horizontal,** or one which is curved from its origin to the termination. The long straight Heart Line reveals a very deep attachment to the family. The subject will be very much devoted to his father and mother, brothers and sisters. But such a Heart Line also shows a romantic, psychic attitude towards sex. In my experience, I have encountered such Heart Lines more often on the hands of women than men. These subjects require partners who appeal to them mentally and spiritually before their sexual urges become activated to a large degree. These people are content to hold hands, whisper sweet nothings

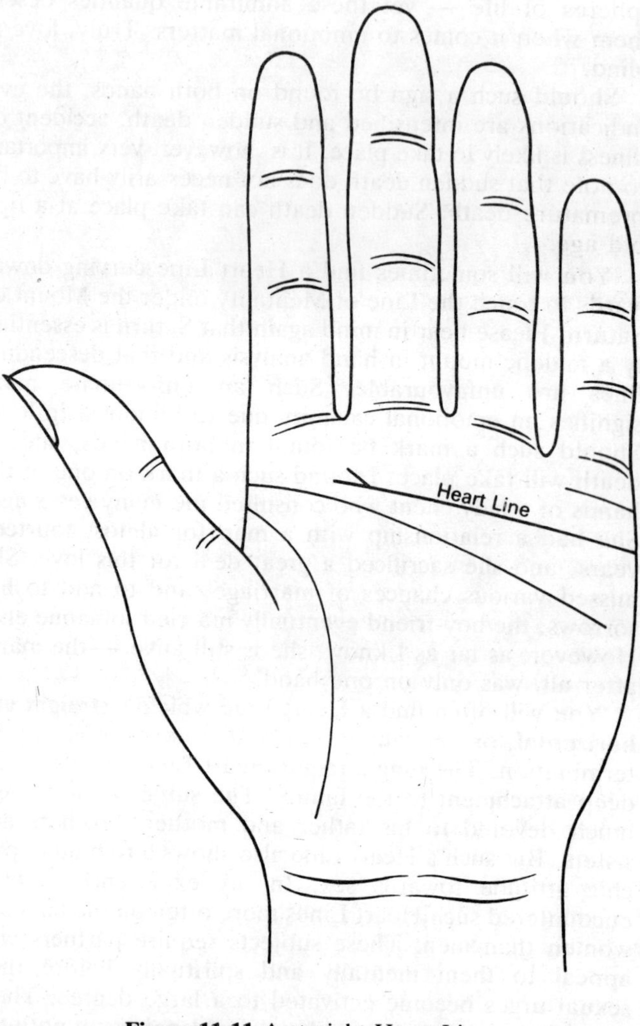

Figure 11-11 A straight Heart Line.

in the ears, or have such 'sweet nothings' whispered into their ears, and if such a romantic attitude does not ultimately lead to the physical aspect of love, they will not feel particularly deprived.

We must contrast this with the **strongly curved Heart Line.** This will reveal a vigorous, physical, sexual attitude towards the opposite sex. Psychologists inform us that the male is more easily aroused sexually than the female. This truth is backed up by the science of hand analysis, for you will find many more men than women having such a Heart Line. Men complain that it is very difficult to understand women. This is true, but at least a deeper understanding would be achieved by making use of the science of hand analysis to probe the minds of women. Then, there are women who have the same complaint about men. To even matters up, women, too, can use this science to achieve a better understanding with men in general.

You will often find **islands** on the Heart Line, especially under the mounts of Sun and Mercury. In Indian astrology the planet Sun represents the heart and eyes. An island on the Heart Line, under the Mount of Sun, if it refers to a physical defect, therefore shows a tendency towards heart and eye trouble. If the island is under the Mount of Mercury, heart straining could be due to financial or business worries.

Islands on the Heart Line can also refer to emotional sorrows in love and friendship. How then can we distinguish between emotional sorrow and health trouble as represented by the same sign on the Heart Line? The technique is actually very simple. When you encounter defects on the Heart Line, such as islands, breaks, stars, dots and moles, always consider the health aspect first. If the Vitality Line especially misbehaves at the age of the subject at the time of consultation, if the nails show signs of heart disease, and if the colour of the lines and the palm in general, as well as the nails is unfavourable, you can

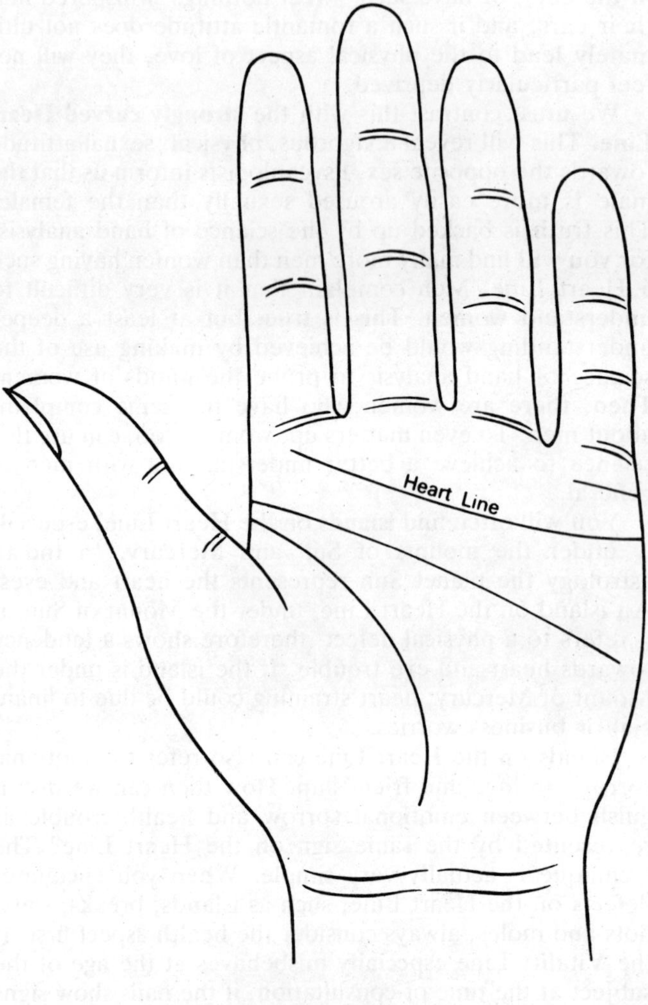

Figure 11-12 A curved Heart Line.

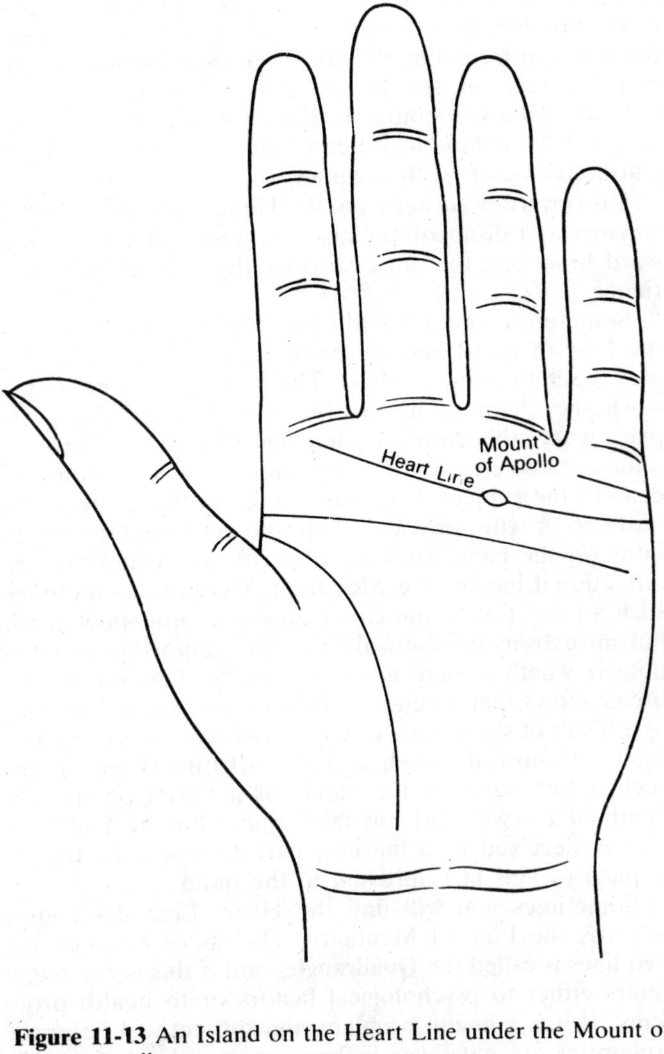

Figure 11-13 An Island on the Heart Line under the Mount of Sun or Apollo.

rest assured that a defect on the Heart Line will represent health trouble. If there are no such confirmatory indications of health trouble, then the logical deduction is that a major defect on the Heart Line refers to emotional sorrows and disappointment. Kindly follow this rule, and you will learn how to differentiate between health and emotional factors with accuracy.

Downward branches from the Heart Line indicate love sorrows and disappointments. The more of these downward branches, the more sorrows the subject will experience.

Sometimes, you will find a line going downwards from the Line of Heart and attacking the Fate Line. This line may touch the Line of Head. The important thing to note is whether there is a distinct break in the Fate Line at the place where this downward line has attacked it. This is an unfavourable sign and it represents the loss of someone dear to the subject. It can also refer to the death of the husband or wife, provided there are confirmatory indications on the hand, such as a line of widowhood on the Affection Line on the Mount of Mercury. Sometimes, such a formation of the Heart Line does not show death, but an extremely severe illness. The important point to note is whether there is a break in the Fate Line. This break shows that a new set of circumstances will develop as a result of the trauma or emotional sorrow represented by the downward branch of the Heart Line. I once found such a formation on the hands of a businessman. The death of his wife did not take place, but he had been cruelly deceived by a business partner whom he trusted implicitly. This fact hurt him to the quick.

Sometimes you will find the Heart Line descending towards the Line of Mentality. The space between the two lines is called the **Quadrangle,** and if this is narrow, it refers either to psychological factors or to health problems. If it is a health problem, the subject will be prone to fainting fits, hay fever, asthma, or some kind of trouble

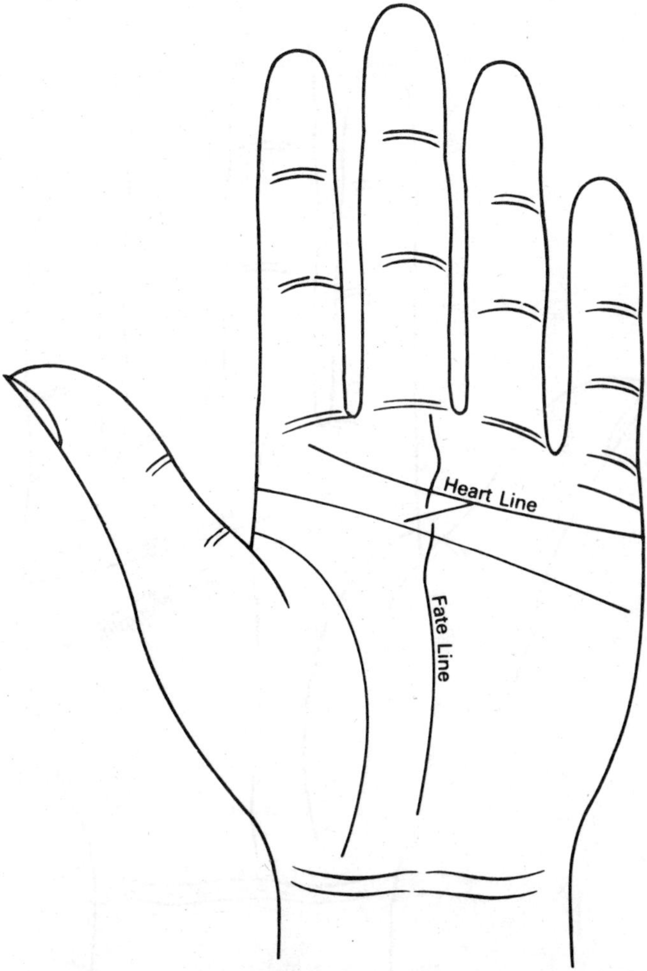

Figure 11-14 A descending branch of the Heart Line attacking and cutting the Fate Line. Notice the clear break in the Fate Line.

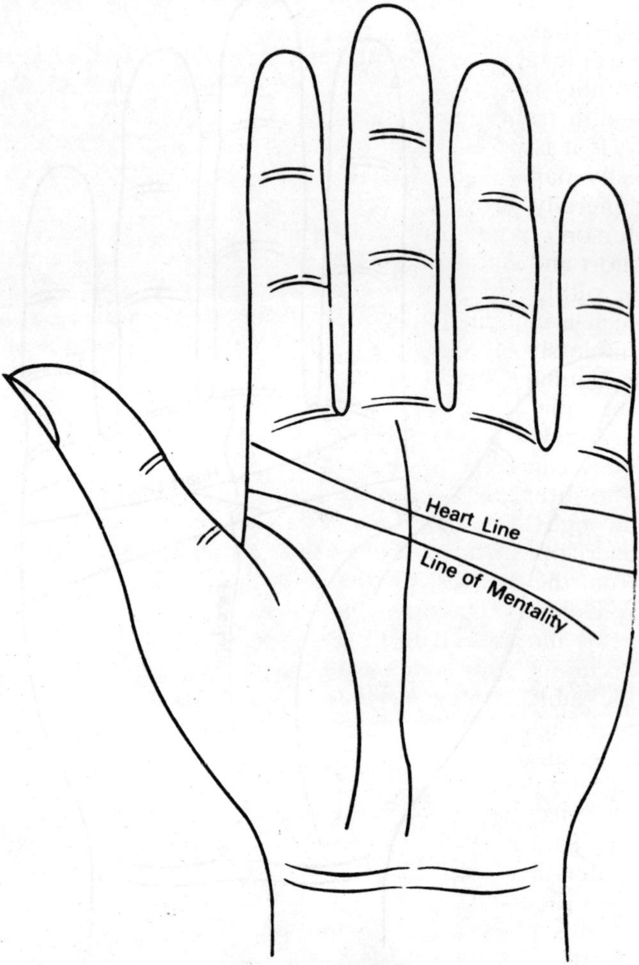

Figure 11-15 Example of a narrow Quadrangle — the width between the Heart Line and the Line of Mentality.

with the chest and lungs, such as pneumonia or bronchitis. I have found that the narrower the gap, the more chronic and serious the health problem. Observe the Vitality Line, nails, etc., for confirmatory indications of health trouble.

If it is not a health problem, this mark reveals a basically narrow-minded and selfish nature. This person is generally not capable of looking at things from the other person's point of view. Should the Heart Line also be short and start from the Mount of Saturn, this subject will be ruthless in matters of love and affection. I actually saw such a combination on the hands of a subject who was ruthlessly deceptive towards her parents in order to camouflage a secret love affair that had been going on for a couple of years.

Breaks on the Heart Line are always unfavourable. They can refer to health defects or emotional troubles. The break is a defect because the current, flowing through the Heart Line, suffers a short circuit. But an overlapping break shows that the subject will recover from the trouble, whether it be health or emotional.

Generally, a break under the Sun Mount refers to heart illnesses. It is all the more serious if such a break occurs in both hands at the same place. But rarely does the subject suffer a fatality if there is a break under the Sun finger on only one hand.

As has already been mentioned, Saturn is essentially a malefic planet in scientific hand analysis. Therefore, experience has shown that a break of the Heart Line under the Saturn finger is much more serious than a break under the Sun finger. In astrology, Saturn is connected with rheumatism, so it is easy to understand why a break at this place refers to trouble caused by a rheumatic heart.

The bad Jupiterian tends to overeat, and consequently suffers from that and indigestion. We can easily understand, therefore, why a break under the Jupiter finger

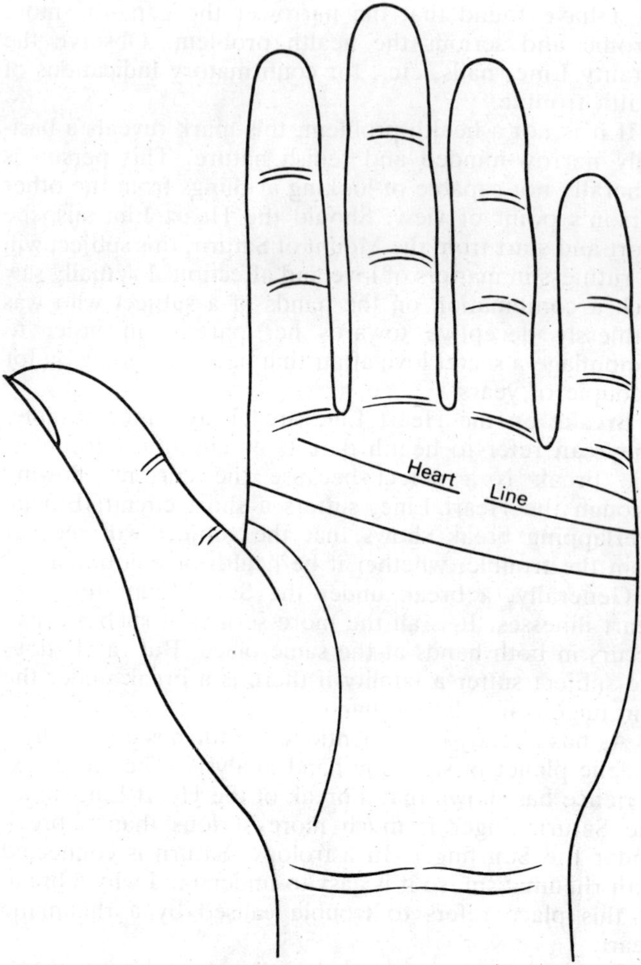

Figure 11-16 A Break on the Heart Line.

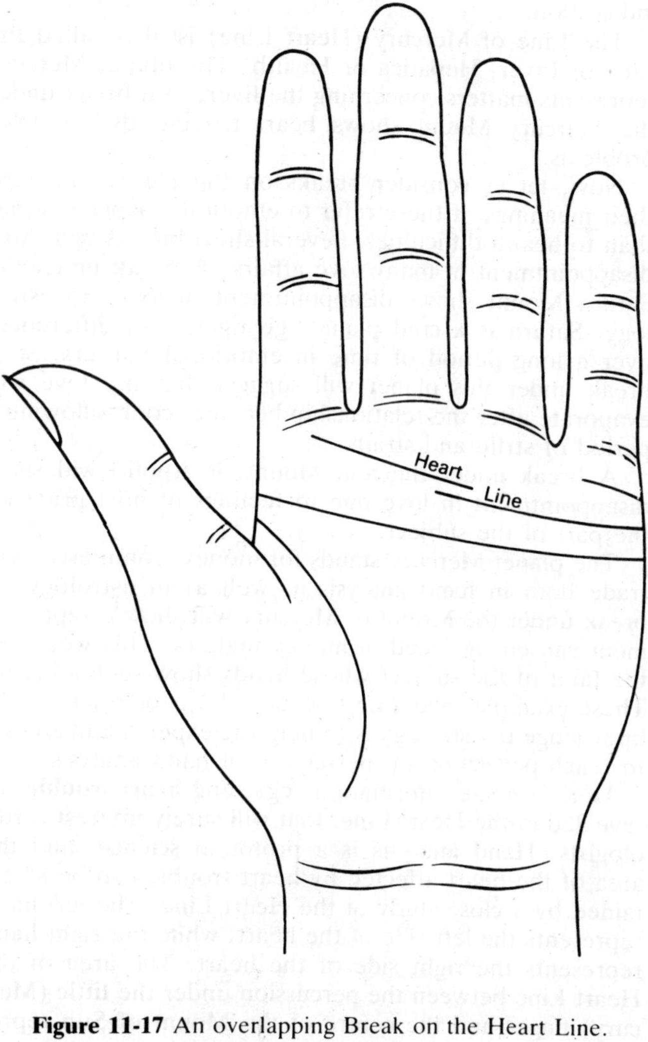

Figure 11-17 An overlapping Break on the Heart Line.

shows heart trouble caused by overeating and consequent indigestion.

The Line of Mercury (Heart Line) is also called the Line of Liver, Hepatica or Health. The planet Mercury represents matters concerning the liver, so a break under the Mercury Mount shows heart trouble due to liver problems.

Now, let us consider breaks on the Heart Line and their meanings, if these refer to emotional aspects rather than to health difficulties. Several short breaks will show disappointment in many love affairs. A break under the Saturn Mount shows disappointment in love. In astrology, Saturn is a cold planet, giving rise to differences over a long period of time in emotional matters. So a break under this planet will suggest that the love will evaporate after the relationship becomes cool following a period of strife and strain.

A break under the Sun Mount or Apollo will show disappointment in love due to feelings of hurt pride on the part of the subject.

The planet Mercury stands for money, commerce, and trade both in hand analysis as well as in astrology. A break under the Mount of Mercury will show disappointment caused by greed in money matters. This would be the fault of the subject whose hands show such a break. These examples illustrate how useful a good background knowledge of astrology is to help the expert hand analyst to reach perfection in the science of hand analysis.

Here is some information regarding **heart trouble,** as revealed in the Heart Line, that will surely interest cardiologists. Hand analysis is a profound science, and the area of the heart affected by heart trouble can be ascertained by a close study of the Heart Line. The left hand represents the left side of the heart, while the right hand represents the right side of the heart. The area of the Heart Line between the percussion under the little (Mercury) finger and the centre of the Mount of Sun repre-

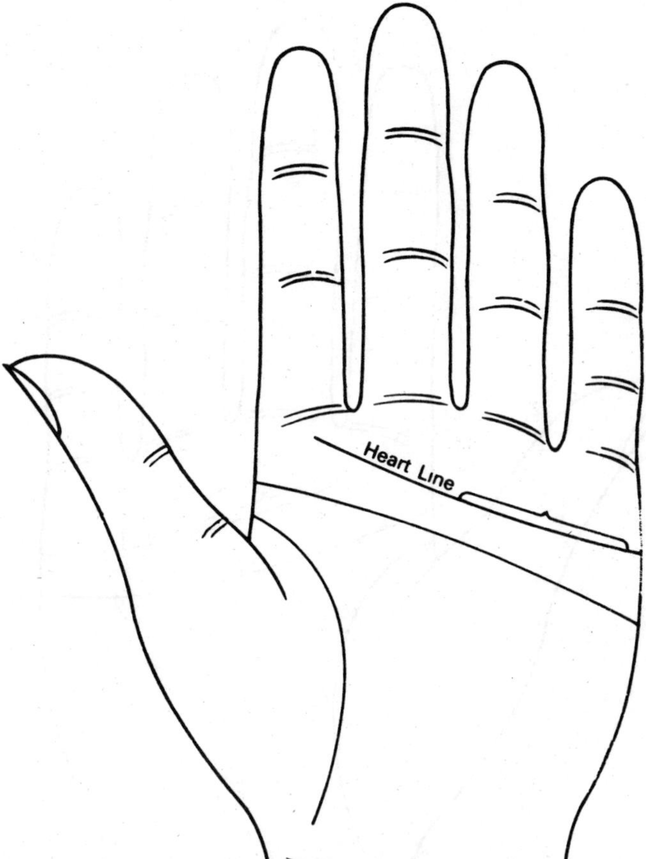

Figure 11-18 The marked area shows the myocardium of the heart on the Heart Line.

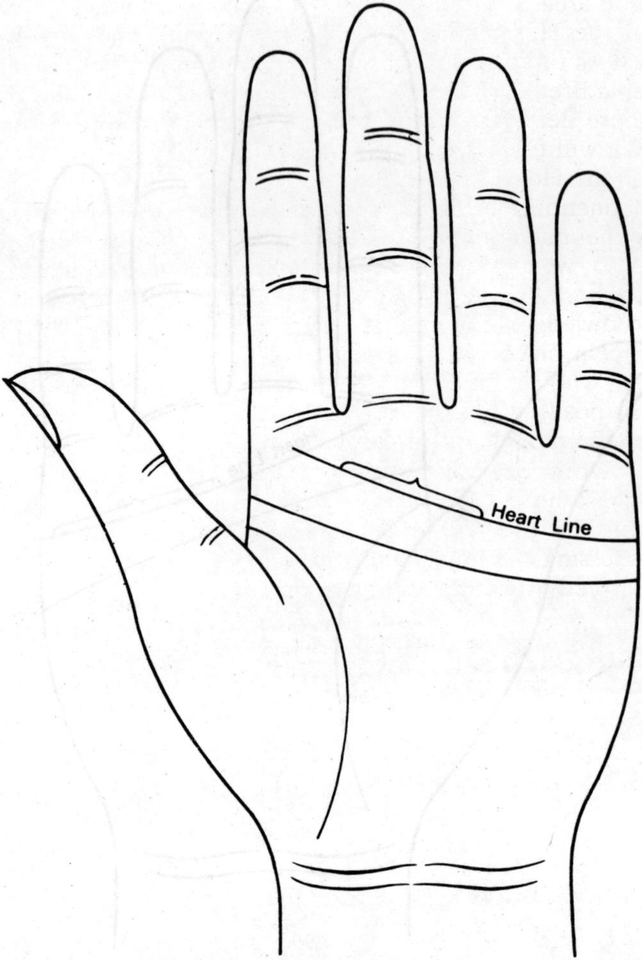

Figure 11-19 The marked area shows the valves of the heart as seen on the Heart Line.

sents the myocardium or the muscular wall of the heart. The area from the centre of the Mount of Sun to the end of the Heart Line on the Jupiter Mount symbolizes the valves of the heart. Let us suppose a subject has red dots or a break on the left hand on the Heart Line, and that these defects are shown just below the Mount of Saturn. We will further assume that no distinct defects are shown on the Heart Line on the right hand. It is now a very easy deduction that this subject will have heart trouble due to a rheumatic heart if the defects refer to health problems. Also, we can easily come to the conclusion that the valves of the left side of the heart will be affected. Since foreknowledge is power par excellence, and symptoms are shown on the hand several years in advance, a cardiologist who is also a competent hand analyst will be in a better position to practise preventive medicine for the sake of the patient's health.

Work out various combinations of the Heart Line. Please note again that it is very much more important to consider this line rather than the so-called 'Life' Line in assessing the life span of the subject. The Heart Line is correctly regarded as one of the major lines of the hand.

Chapter Twelve

The Fate Line or Line of Saturn Shows Your Psychological Attitude towards Work and Material Prospects

The **Fate Line** is also called the **Line of Destiny** as well as the **Line of Saturn.** It is referred to as the Line of Saturn because it is under the influence of the planet Saturn. This line reveals the material prospects of the subject to a significant degree. It accurately records changes in career and job position during the lifetime of the subject. Periods of financial brightness or dullness can be worked out by a close study of the line. Financial losses, specific set-backs in married life, and periods of worry and anxiety are all reflected in the structure of the line. By itself, the Fate Line does not give any health indications, but it most accurately shows the effect of good health or poor health upon the career of the subject.

The ideal Fate Line will be long, deep, clear and well-cut. Such a line will bestow favourable effects on the career of the subject. This type of line has got plenty of potential to brighten the material prospects and general success of the subject.

Origin of the Fate Line

The Fate Line or Line of Saturn can start from various places in the hand. It may start from the centre of the palm or the Plain of Mars as it is called in this science. In astrology Mars symbolizes strife, struggle and determined efforts. Such an origin means that the subject will really

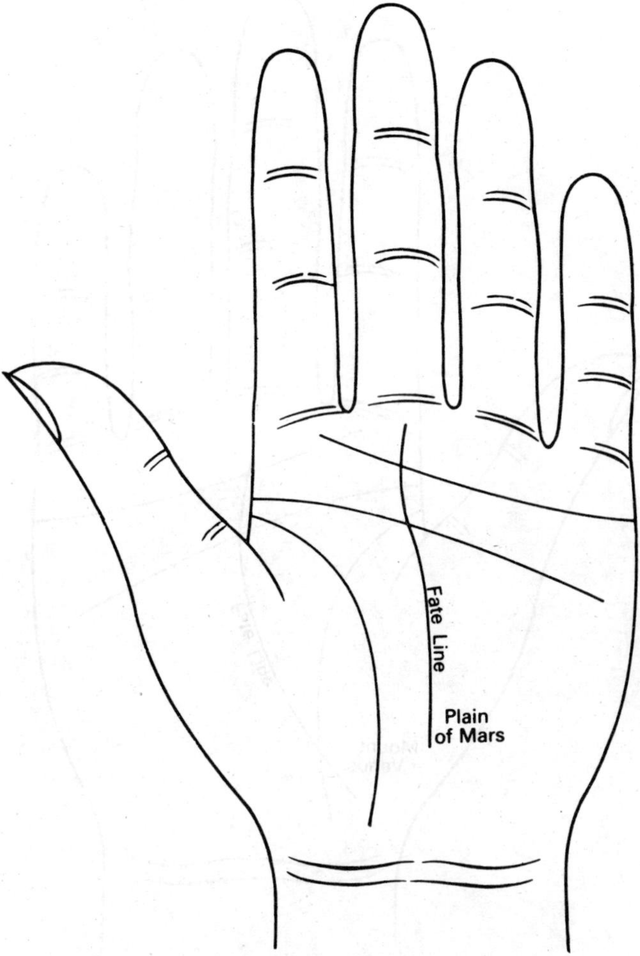

Figure 12-1 The Fate Line starting from the Plain of Mars

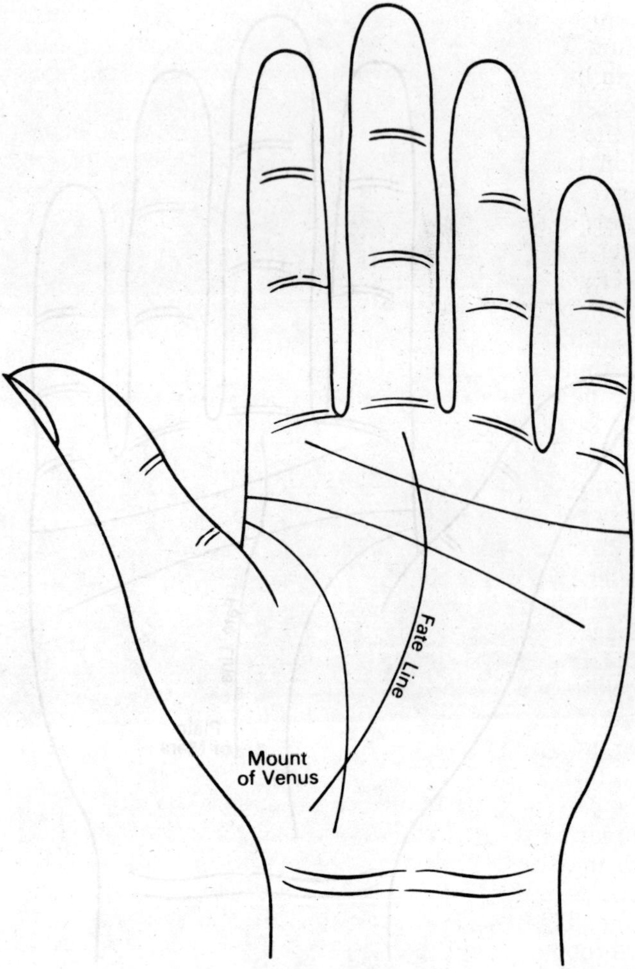

Figure 12-2 The Fate Line starting from inside the Mount of Venus

have to struggle very hard to achieve success in life. It will only be by "blood, sweat, toil and tears", to use Winston Churchill's famous phrase, that the subject's aims in life will be achieved. Mars and Saturn are malefic planets, hostile to each other. When the Fate Line starts from the Plain of Mars and ends on Saturn, there is a connection between Saturn and Mars in the career of the subject. Since Saturn and Mars are bitterly hostile to one another, it is easy to understand why such an origin shows a bitter struggle before success is achieved. Truly, such a subject will achieve success with practically no help from anyone.

In astrology, the planet Venus symbolizes, among other things, the family and relations of the subject. By family here, is meant the father, mother, brothers and sisters of the subject. You will sometimes find the Fate Line originating inside the Vitality Line, from the Mount of Venus. The life of such a subject will be strongly influenced by his family, and his career could be very strongly influenced by family members. It is observed through practical experience that such subjects will be very strongly attached to their families even after marriage.

The Fate Line can also have its origin from the first Bracelet or Rascette and travel straight up through the centre of the palm to end on the Mount of Saturn just under the second finger. With other favourable indications, this means that the subject will attain great heights in his career. It is a truth of hand analysis that a long, well-marked Fate Line shows that the subject is very much under the influence of fate.

You will often find the Fate Line rising from the Vitality Line. This means that the subject will be self-made and rise through personal merit. Most of the planning for his career will be done by the subject himself. In a few cases I have seen, such origins also mean that the subject initially secured help from family members.

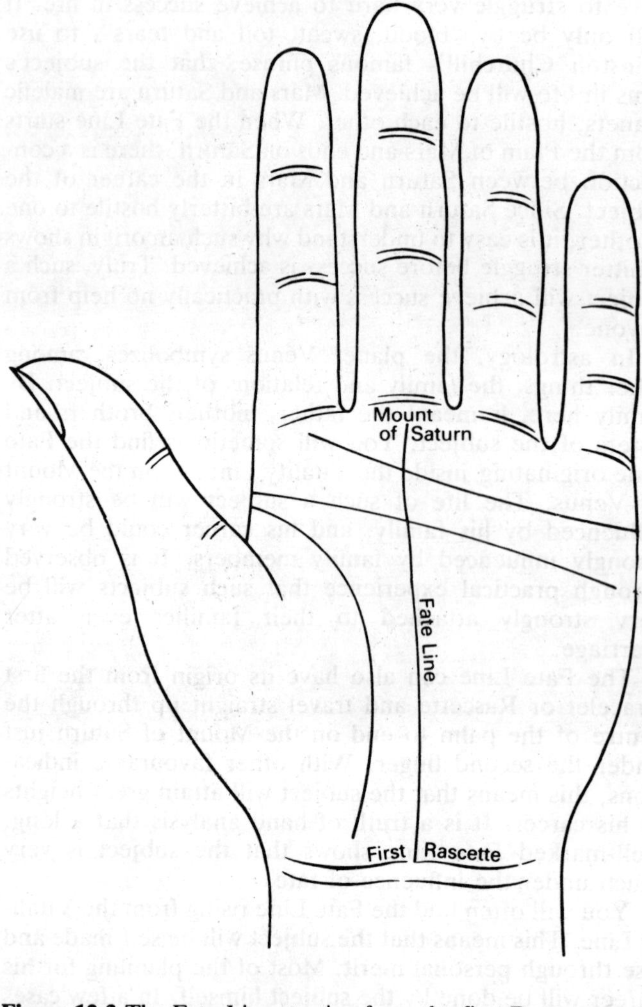

Figure 12-3 The Fate Line starting from the first Rascette and ending on the Mount of Saturn

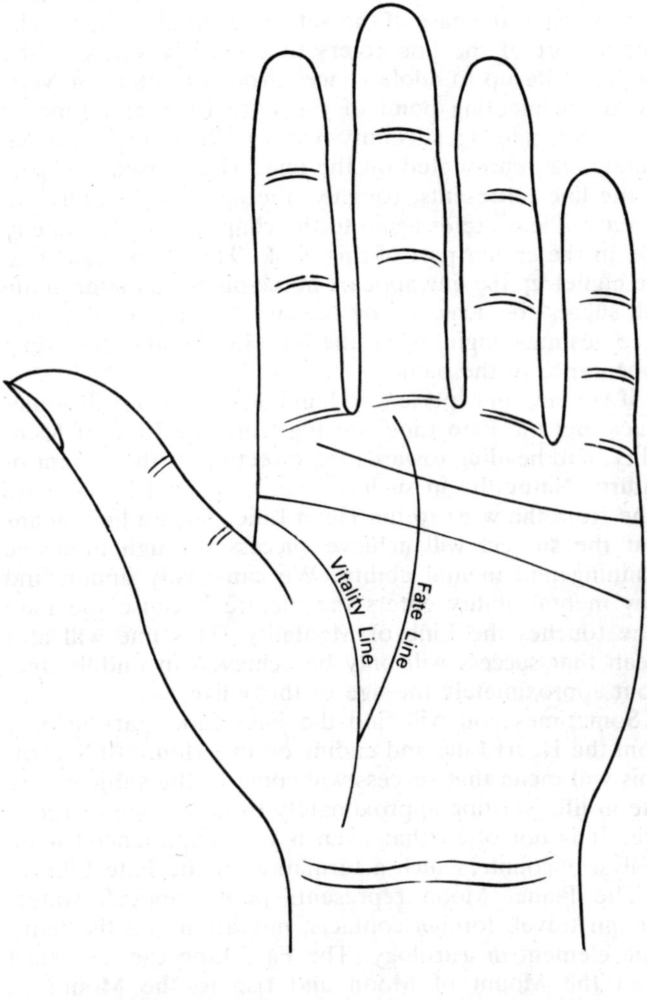

Figure 12-4 The Fate Line rising from the Vitality Line

The normal termination of the line is on the Mount of Saturn just at the base of the Saturn or middle finger. The earlier part of the line refers to the early years of the subject's life up to adolescence. From the plain of Mars up to the meeting point of the Fate Line and Line of Mentality, the ages twenty-one to thirty-five approximately are represented on the line. The subsequent part of the line represents, roughly, the ages of thirty-five to seventy. Please refer again to the chapter on age calculation in the earlier part of this book. The principle is that the higher up the line appears in the palm, the later in life will success be achieved by the subject. The career only becomes meaningful when the Fate Line makes a distinct appearance in the palm.

If you are an experienced hand analyst, you will sometimes find the Fate Line starting from the Line of Mentality, and heading towards the direction of the Mount of Saturn. Naturally, in such a case, there will be no Fate Line from the wrist to the Head Line. Such a line means that the subject will achieve success through intensive planning and mental ability. We can easily understand how mental ability enters the picture because the Fate Line touches the Line of Mentality. This line will also mean that success will only be achieved in middle age, from approximately the age of thirty-five.

Sometimes you will find the Fate Line starting only from the Heart Line and ending on the Mount of Saturn. This will mean that success will come to the subject very late in life, starting approximately from the age of forty-five. It is not often that even a very experienced hand analyst encounters such a formation of the Fate Line.

The Planet Moon represents public appeal, water, foreign travel, foreign contacts, migration and the feminine element in astrology. The Fate Line can also start from the Mount of Moon and rise to the Mount of Saturn. Such a subject can achieve success in a career that deals largely with the public. We hand analysts find such

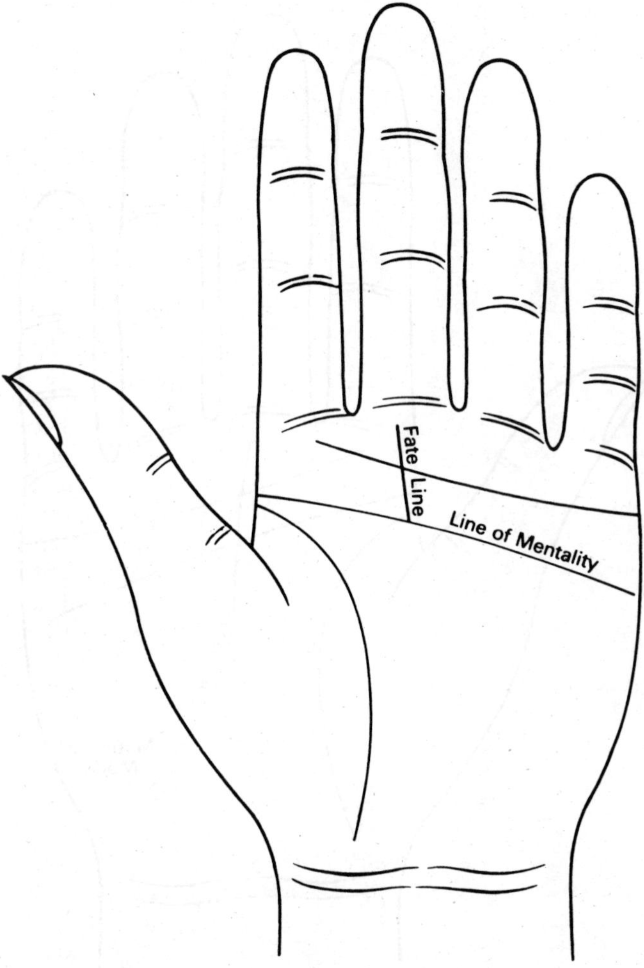

Figure 12-5 The Fate Line rising only from the Line of Mentality

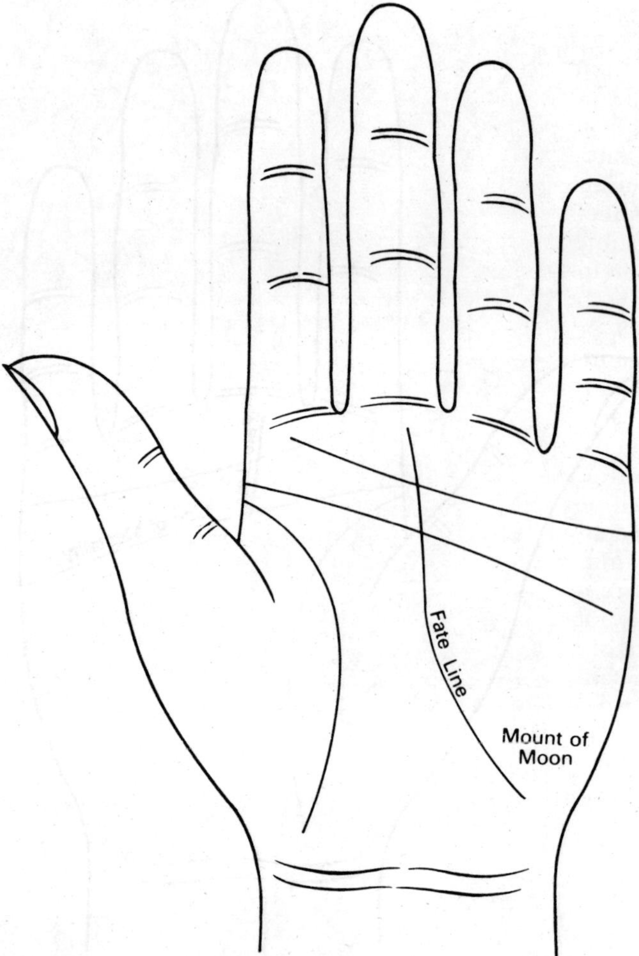

Figure 12-6 The Fate Line rising from the Mount of Moon

an origin of the Fate Line very often on the hands of doctors, lawyers, politicians, entertainers, hand analysts and astrologers. It will readily be perceived that these people owe their success to the approval and appreciation of the public. With such a line, the subject will get plenty of help from outside contacts and pretty often also from the opposite sex. If the Marriage Line or Line of Affection is favourable, the Mount of Venus is well-formed and free of defects, and the Fate Line is strong and well-marked, the subject with this formation will definitely get substantial help from his or her spouse. This help need not always be financial or material. It can also mean good, timely advice, or introduction and recommendation to influential parties.

The normal direction which the Fate Line takes is towards the second finger or the Mount of Saturn. The normal **termination of this Line** is also on the Mount of Saturn. But in some cases you will find the Fate Line terminating on the mounts of Jupiter, Sun, and Mercury respectively. However, even in such cases, the Fate Line will initially travel in the direction of the Saturn Mount before branching off towards these other mounts. Please take note of this principle, and you will not confuse the Line of Saturn or Fate with the Lines of Sun and Mercury respectively.

It is a grievous error on the part of amateurs to think that a **long Fate Line** promises a bright career and untold wealth for the lucky subject. A lot of subjects have been disillusioned by such well-meaning but ignorant amateurs. You will find, much to your surprise, that even beggars and bankrupts have long Fate Lines. I have examined the palms of several beggars along Jalan Tuanku Abdul Rahman, one of the main roads of Kuala Lumpur, (much to the amusement of onlookers!) and I have also examined the palms of beggars sitting in Kuala Lumpur's Central Market and found many among them with long Fate Lines. So, although the Fate Line can be long, in such cases there have to be reasons why such subjects are beggars. Invariably it will be noticed on the palms of these subjects that the mounts, especially the upper mounts of Jupiter, Saturn, Sun, and Mercury, will be flat or depressed; the palm will be dry, and unattractive to look at, the fingers will be poorly shaped, awkward looking, and not evenly set on the palm either.

A **broad Fate Line** is unfavourable as the Current travels through a shallow channel. Hence the energy flowing through the Fate Line will be diffused and not concentrated. I have observed in the hands of beggars that even though the Fate Line may be long, it is invariably thick and broad. So far, I have not even once come across a beggar with developed mounts, especially the upper ones, in the palms. Should a beggar have well-developed mounts, a long Fate Line, fingers evenly set on the palm and well-shaped as well, you can rest assured that this so-called 'beggar' has a healthy bank balance, with money stashed away, perhaps in Switzerland!

Sometimes the Fate Line or the Line of Saturn will begin with a **fork.** In such a case, one fork may start from the Mount of Venus. This could mean that the subject was adopted by a relation some time after birth, but occasionally such a fork can also represent an unhappy marriage for the parents of the subject. This sometimes results in litigation over the custody of the child. I have confirmed a few cases of this in my professional experience. I saw such a fork on the hands of a Chinese girl who consulted me in the latter part of 1977. Among the conservative Chinese of Malaysia, especially before the Second World War, there was a belief that daughters did not bring luck to the parents. Thinking that she would be a burden, the mother of my client had wanted to kill her daughter, my client, soon after her birth, but a kind relative took pity upon the girl and offered to bring her up. That is why my client lived long enough for me to tell her the prospects for her future. My client told me that her

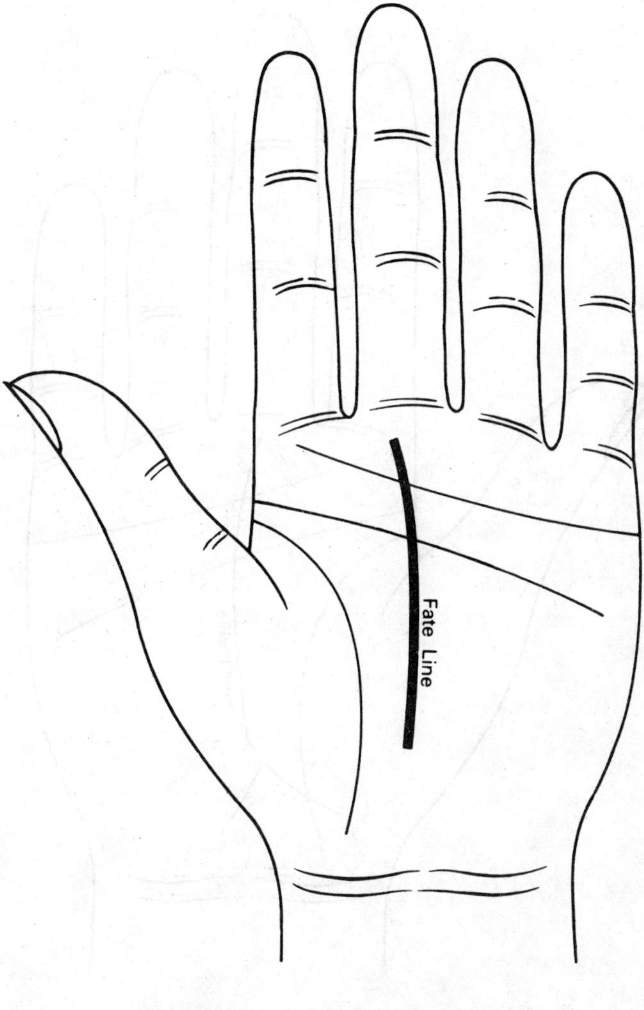

Figure 12-7 A broad Fate Line

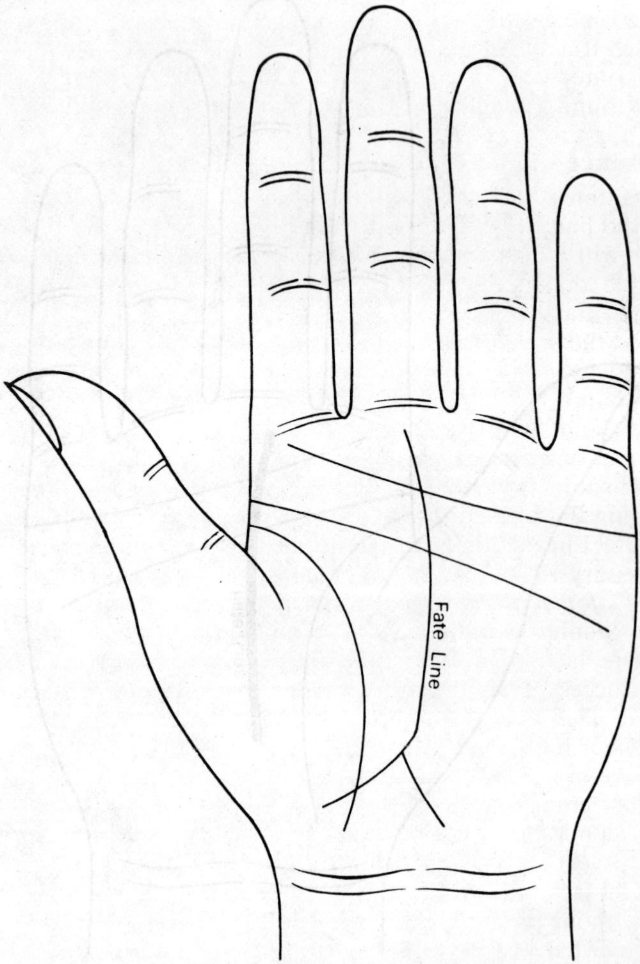

Figure 12-8 The Fate Line starting with a Fork

sister, too, had been adopted under the same circumstances. I showed the client how to interpret this fork of the Fate Line and requested her to examine her sister's palms to see if a similar mark was present on her hands. A few days later, my client telephoned to inform me that she had found a similar fork in the hands of her sister.

Absence of the Fate Line

Sometimes you will find that the Fate Line is missing on the hands. This certainly does not mean that the subject will not be a success in life — several wealthy people do not have Fate Lines on their hands. I have found that on the hands of wealthy people without Fate Lines the mounts of the hand were well-developed, the palm was broad, the hand showed a materialistic outlook, the thumb was strong, the fingers were evenly set on the palm, and there were favourable signs such as the fish, temple, and trident on the hand. This explained why these subjects were wealthy and successful, in spite of the missing Fate Line. To the expert hand analyst the lack of a Fate Line holds no mystery and he does not think it necessary to write a novel or detective story called *The Case of the Missing Fate Line* in the best tradition of Erle Stanley Gardner.

The lack of a Fate Line is only adverse for material success if there are no compensating features on the hand. The missing Fate Line means that the subject rises by sheer hard work and determination. Such men do not believe in luck or chance but in grabbing every opportunity that comes their way to achieve success in life. However, a missing Fate Line does show some major defect in the psychology of the subject — it tends to suggest a certain lack of direction in life. Should a multi-millionaire be without a Fate Line, it would mean that he does not know what to do with his wealth! In that sense, the missing Fate Line is a psychological handicap to the subject.

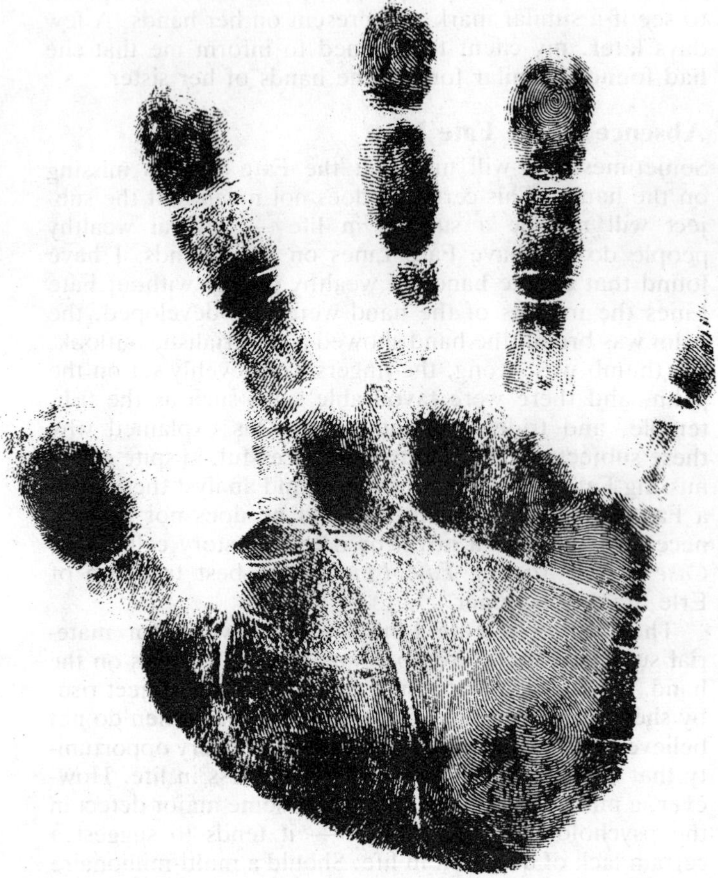

Figure 12-9 The handprint of a female aborigine in Malaysia. Notice the absence of the Fate Line.

Weak Fate Line

Please do not jump to the conclusion that if the Fate Line is weak, the subject will have a poor career or financial weakness at the particular age concerned. Should the mounts of the hand be well-developed and other features such as the Sun Line be favourable, the subject can still be rich and have a bright career. In such a case, a weak Fate Line at that particular age will represent some psychological frustration in the job, troubles in domestic life, or worries over health, etc. Something will definitely be wrong somewhere, but it would be a serious mistake to jump to the conclusion that the subject has hit rock bottom in career and bank balance just because the Fate Line is weak or missing at a particular point.

The **terminations** of the Fate Line are most important. The Fate Line may curve towards the mounts of Jupiter, Sun or Mercury, or it may end on the Mount of Saturn itself, this being the normal termination of the line. If it curves towards the Mount of Jupiter and ends on this mount, it is a most favourable marking. This is easy to understand as Jupiter is essentially a benefic planet and mount in hand analysis. From the age where it starts to curve towards the Jupiter Mount, the Fate Line reveals the subject becoming powerful, or pursuing a significant business career. The subject will attain the highest position that he is capable of, considering the environment and other relevant circumstances. This is a good marking for a politician to have, because a successful politician needs a good Mount of Jupiter.

Should the Fate Line curve towards the Sun Mount, the subject will achieve success in public life, money-making, or in some artistic field, such as art and painting. If the third phalange of the Sun finger is prominent as well, the subject will be successful in amassing money. Please remember that the planet Sun represents public life, crea-

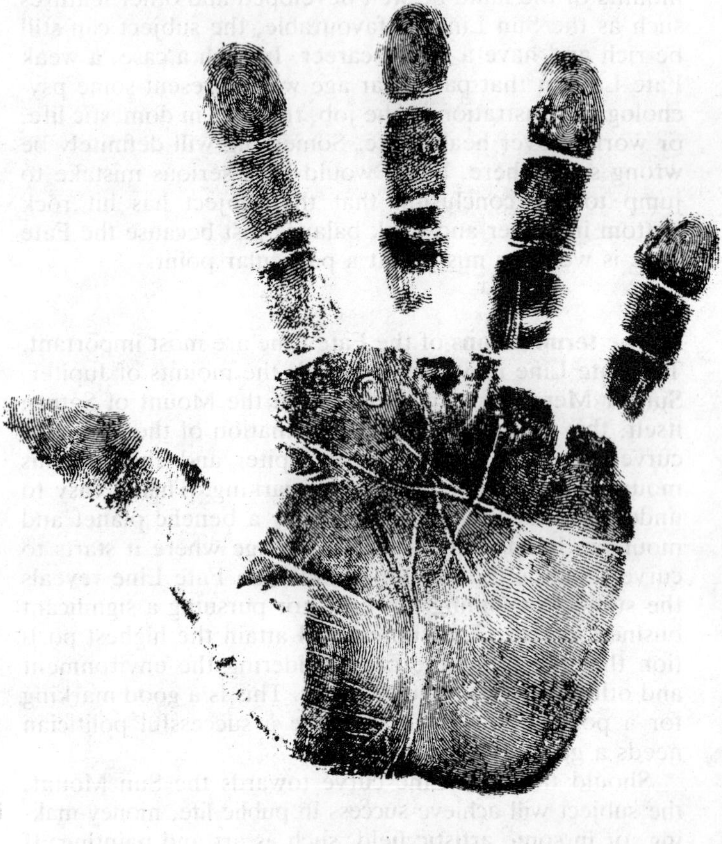

Figure 12-10 The handprint of a male aborigine in Malaysia. Notice the badly formed and shadowy Fate Line.

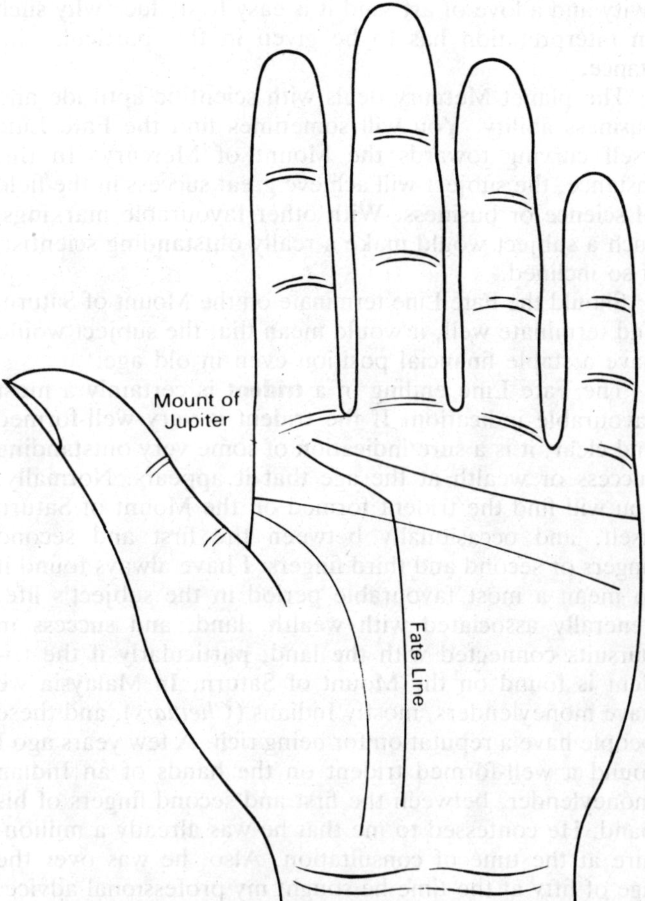

Figure 12-11 The Fate Line terminating on the Mount of Jupiter

tivity and a love of art, and it is easy to deduce why such an interpretation has to be given in this particular instance.

The planet Mercury deals with scientific aptitude and business ability. You will sometimes find the Fate Line itself curving towards the Mount of Mercury. In this instance, the subject will achieve great success in the field of science or business. With other favourable markings, such a subject would make a really outstanding scientist, if so inclined.

Should the Fate Line terminate on the Mount of Saturn, and terminate well, it would mean that the subject would have a stable financial position even in old age.

The Fate Line ending in a **trident** is certainly a most favourable indication. If the trident is very well-formed and clear, it is a sure indication of some very outstanding success or wealth at the age that it appears. Normally, you will find the trident formed on the Mount of Saturn itself, and occasionally between the first and second fingers or second and third fingers. I have always found it to mean a most favourable period in the subject's life, generally associated with wealth, land, and success in pursuits connected with the land, particularly if the trident is found on the Mount of Saturn. In Malaysia we have moneylenders, mostly Indians (*Chettiars*), and these people have a reputation for being rich. A few years ago I found a well-formed trident on the hands of an Indian moneylender, between the first and second fingers of his hand. He confessed to me that he was already a millionaire at the time of consultation. Also, he was over the age of fifty at the time he sought my professional advice.

All **upward branches** of the Fate Line are favourable. They show increased gains, promotion, or academic success, depending upon what the subject is doing. The longer, clearer and deeper these upward branches, the better for the subject. These branches should preferably be flawless.

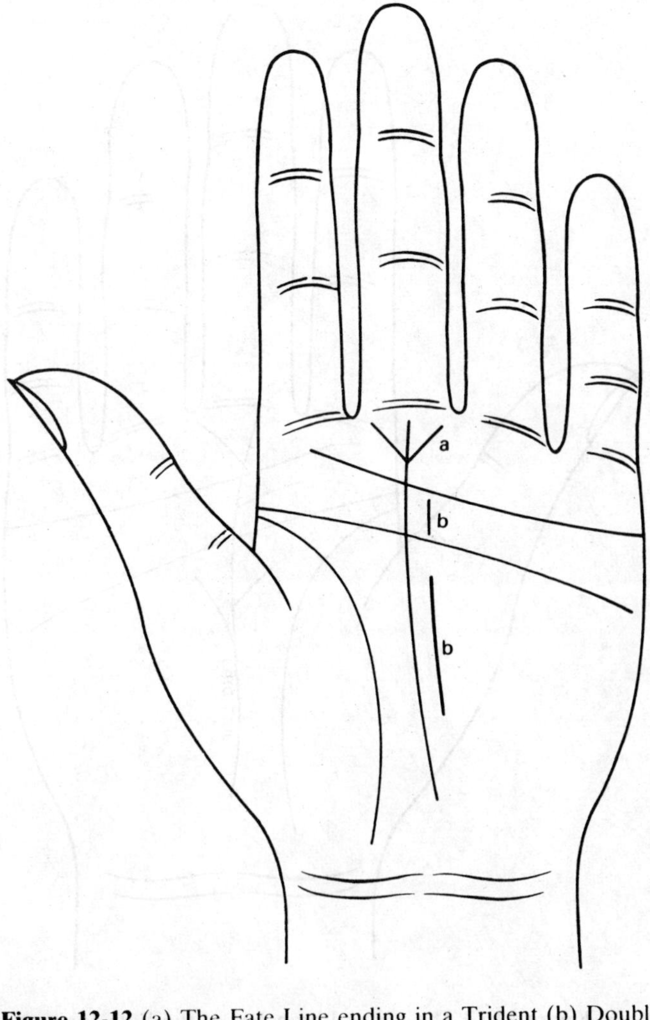

Figure 12-12 (a) The Fate Line ending in a Trident (b) Double Fate Lines

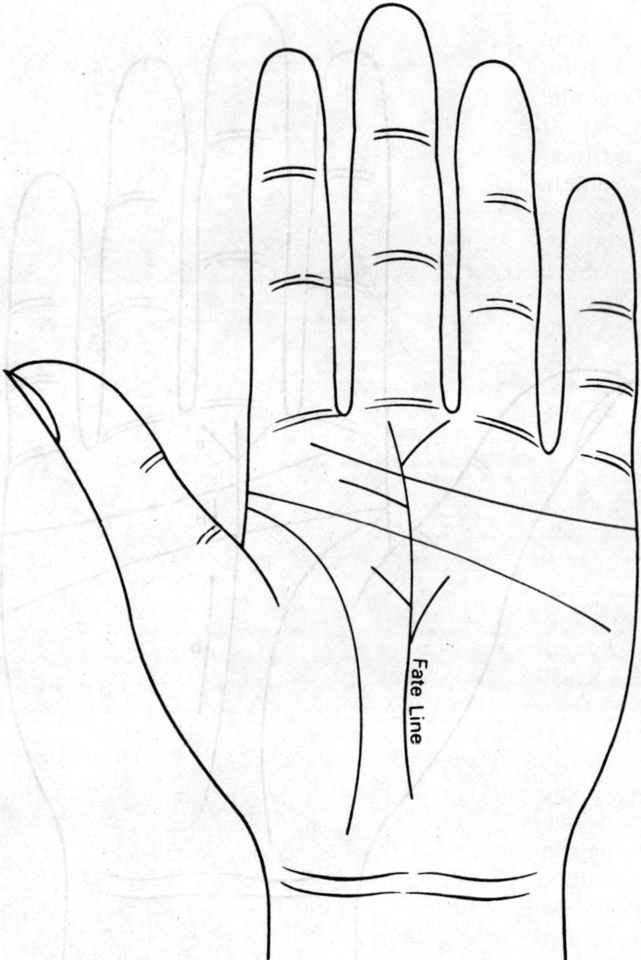

Figure 12-13 The upward branches of the Fate Line

You will occasionally encounter **double Fate Lines** (see Figure 12-12). A double Fate Line is always a strengthening factor, especially if both Fate Lines are long and well-formed. These double lines always refer to a strengthening of the career or financial position. I have found that if the double lines are long, flawless, and well-formed, this interpretation is astoundingly accurate. Sometimes they can refer to two jobs, two sources of income or dual responsibilities that the subject has to shoulder at the age that the double lines appear. However, I have not found this second interpretation to be correct in all cases.

You will often find **islands** on the Fate Line. After a deep study of thousands of islands on the hands of my clients, I can say with full confidence that the island always shows a period of anxiety that troubles the mind of the subject. Dr. Benham in his work *The Laws of Scientific Hand Reading*[1] states that an island on the Fate Line indicates a period of financial difficulty. This is largely true, and I have found many islands on the hands of businessmen who lost heavily in business ventures.

However, the island by itself does not necessarily refer to business losses or financial difficulties. Basically, it refers to a period when the subject cannot adjust himself to his environment, and experiences a period of mental worry, insecurity and vacillation. Please remember that the island is always a defect, but it needs vast experience and intuition to give the precise interpretation to the meaning of an island on the Fate Line.

An island on the Fate Line can also refer to an extra-marital affair, but with regard to this you must always, without exception, look for confirmatory indications on the Mount of Venus, the Heart Line, and the Line of Affection or the Marriage Line. Another confirmatory indication of such an event is an **Influence Line** coming

William G. Benham, *op.cit,* p.541

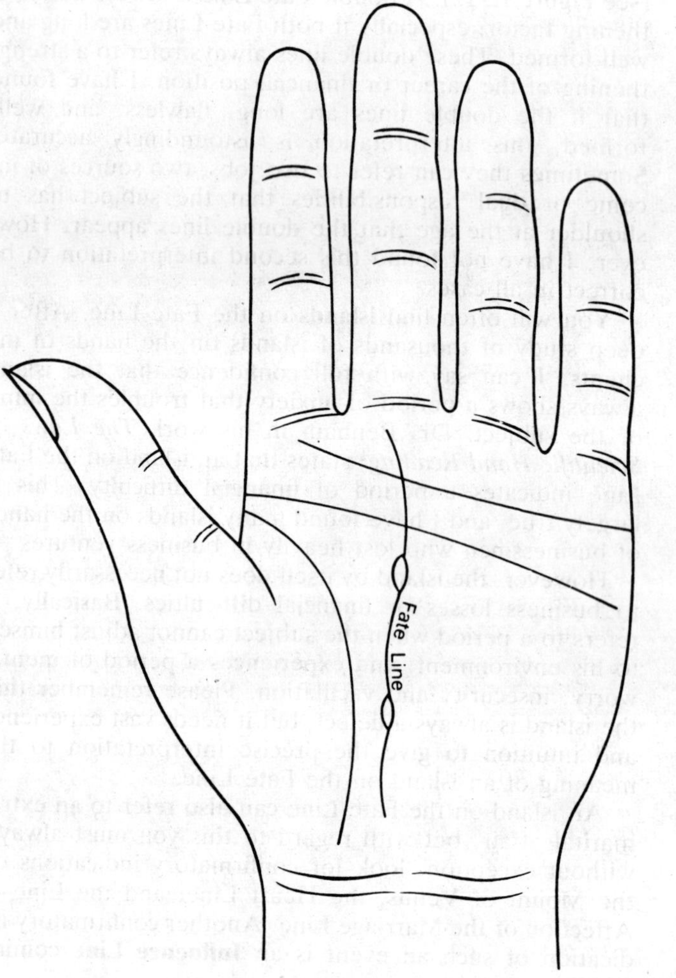

Figure 12-14 Islands on the Fate Line

from the Mount of Moon and joining the island on the Fate Line. In all seriousness, it takes a really experienced hand analyst to handle the island on the Fate Line if the interpretation is likely to refer to adultery. A little knowledge is extremely dangerous. If you find islands on the Fate Line in the palms of your spouse, lover, boyfriend or girlfriend as the case may be, please do not jump to any conclusion prematurely!

Here are all the interpretations I have, in my researches so far, found to be true with regard to **the island on the Fate Line:**

(a) always a period of mental anxiety
(b) financial losses
(c) no particular financial losses, but heavy financial commitments
(d) a period of anxiety caused especially by an emotional relationship, generally with someone of the opposite sex
(e) a most unhappy childhood, during the duration of the island — in this case, the island is found a little above the wrist, in the earlier stages of the Fate Line
(f) mental confusion as to the choice of a career
(g) inability on the part of the subject to adjust to a new environment, perhaps in a new country — this interpretation I found to be repeatedly correct in the hands of European and American women who had accompanied their husbands on transfer to other countries
(h) anxiety caused by an unwanted pregnancy, sometimes leading to an abortion or miscarriage.

The longer the island, the longer the duration of trouble; the more well-formed the island, the more acute the problem. Be on the lookout for islands, and learn how to interpret them correctly.

Crossbars cutting the Fate Line show some obstruction to the career of the subject. The longer, deeper and more

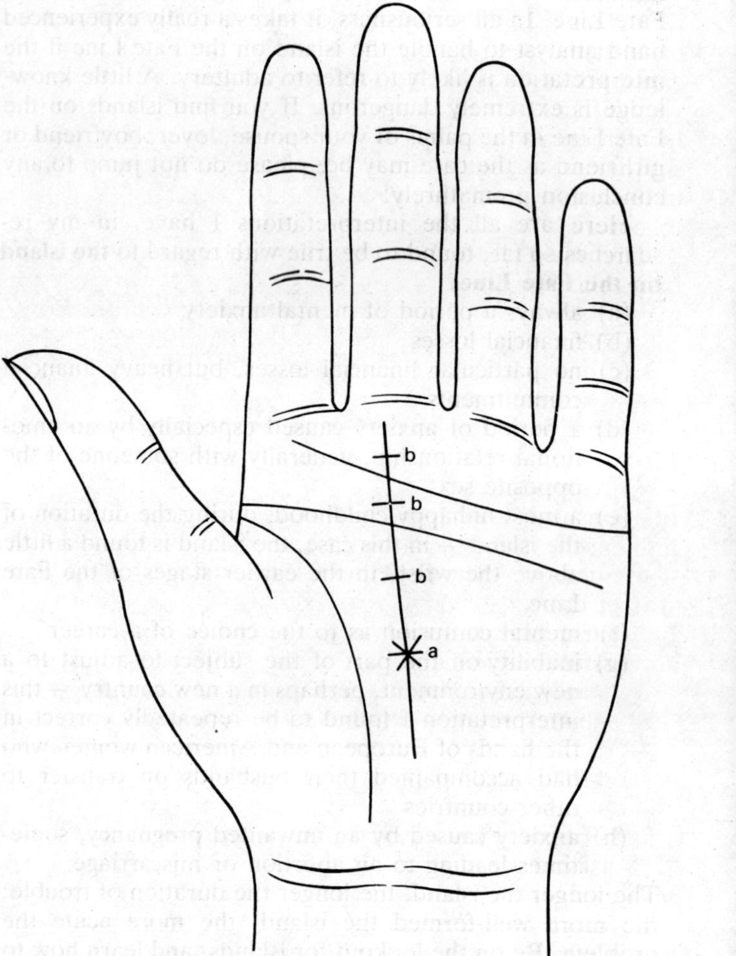

Figure 12-15 (a) Star on the Fate Line (b) Crossbars cutting the Fate Line

well-marked the crossbar, the more serious the obstruction. This obstruction need not necessarily refer to a setback in the subject's job or business. You will find such crossbars on the hands of women who are undergoing a very difficult period in their married life. In other cases I have found a crossbar to mean failure in an important examination, failure to get a promotion, disappointment in love, and defeat in a court case. Anyway, the principle to note is that the crossbar is always a defect.

The **square,** however, is a sign of protection and it helps the subject during a period of crisis. The subject may be saved from financial losses and difficulties in his job. There is an interesting interpretation found in the hands of various women, namely that a well-marked square in the Fate Line sometimes refers to an emotional relationship, and that this relationship continues to survive very much to the surprise of the woman emotionally involved in it. The woman would have expected the relationship to end, and yet because of the protective influence of the square on the Fate Line, the relationship continues. So, note that the square always shows some sort of danger to the subject, either physical or mental, but that the subject will be able to overcome this problem successfully.

A **star** on the Fate Line is always a sign of disaster. The subject is caught flat-footed, and taken by surprise, with the catastrophe beyond his control. Anyone with a well-marked star on the Fate Line will soon learn that there is such a thing as 'Fate' sometimes. Should it refer to loss of money, the subject will experience a real financial disaster at the age shown by the star.

Now, to the best of my knowledge, no hand analyst has yet given the following interpretation of the occurrence of a star on the Fate Line, that is that such a star refers to a catastrophe in love. I have confirmed this in a number of cases. The catastrophe occurs without warning and causes great mental anguish to the subject. In one case a client informed me that to the best of her knowledge she had been having a good and smooth relationship with the boyfriend, but he suddenly stopped phoning her, and made no attempt to contact her for several months; nor did he give any explanation for his strange behaviour. This certainly took her by surprise, and caused her mental agony.

It is an unfavourable sign if the **Fate Line is stopped by the Line of Mentality.** In this case, the progress of the Fate Line is arrested by the Line of Mentality. It is a principle of hand analysis that two main Lines should never clash, but both lines should proceed favourably to their natural termination. The Line of Mentality also refers to judgement, so such a formation means that the subject has made some blunder either in career or in finance. Whether the subject recovers or not will be seen by the subsequent structure and character of the Fate Line. I have confirmed one case where a woman client trusted her brothers and was deceived by them in money matters: instead of immediately withdrawing the money left to her by her husband on his death, she delayed, and with this gain of time, the brothers, by some foul means, secured the share due to her. In other cases the subject may have had to leave his job due to some major blunder on his part.

It is also unfavourable if the **Fate Line is stopped by the Heart Line.** The Line of Heart deals with emotions, and a Fate Line terminating at the Line of Heart shows that the subject will either suffer from heart weakness or make some wrong emotional decision. Both these interpretations are possible, so now we have to decide which interpretation will fit the subject. Examine the Vitality Line, the Health Line and the nails for health defects at the age the subject consults the hand analyst. If there are no confirmatory health defects, you can rest assured that this formation refers to some emotional sorrow or trouble due to unfortunate emotional involvements. In such a

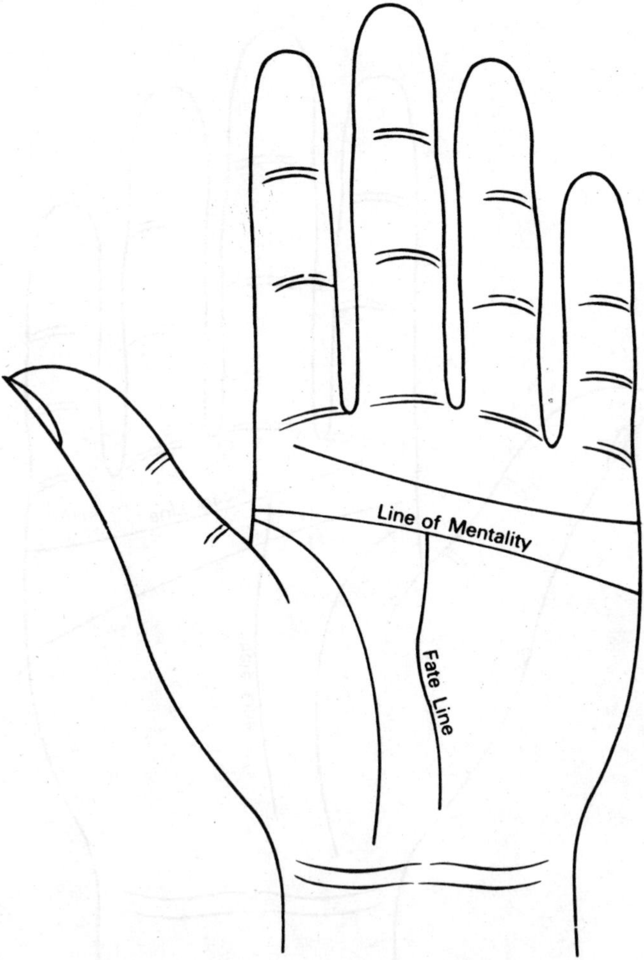

Figure 12-16 The Fate Line stopped by the Line of Mentality

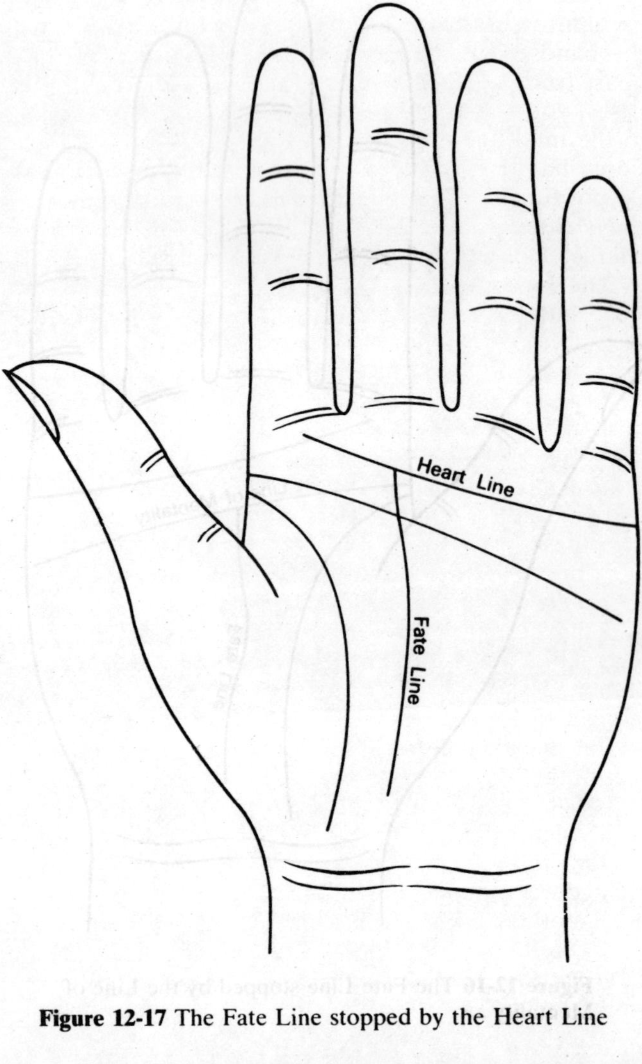

Figure 12-17 The Fate Line stopped by the Heart Line

case, the subject may have an unwise affair of the heart, be deceived by relatives, or in general carry out some immature emotional decision. You will often find this on the hands of men and women who have an affair of the heart from which they find it hard to withdraw. In most cases, you will find that the Fate Line is better developed in the inherited hand, as compared to the active, operational hand. This is not surprising as most people either do not fully develop the potential that is in them, or else they fritter away chances of improving in life by some character defect or by wasting their time on trifles.

The **Fate Line** and **the Sun Line** are sister lines, and they must be read together for an accurate diagnosis of the subject's material prospects. The Sun Line will compensate if the Fate Line is poor. Life will at least not be so hard for the subject if such is the case. However, if both the Fate Line and Sun Line are defective, at the same age, then the subject is really in trouble. On the other hand, if both are very well-formed, then the subject will run a very bright period in his career or in family happiness, or in both.

A **break** in the Fate Line or Line of Saturn is a serious defect. It means that the current has been short-circuited and that a major crisis has or will threaten the subject. The subject may lose his job, or be forced to give up his career. The longer the break, the longer it will take the subject to overcome the difficulty.

But an **overlapping break** is an entirely different matter. In this case, the new line starts before the old one has ended. Should the new line be well-formed, it is a welcome sign. The overlapping break reveals a change in career, job, or environment. It also reveals that this change was planned ahead of time, and that it was effected smoothly and with the minimum of friction. Please be very careful never to confuse a proper break in the Fate Line with an overlapping break. The overlapping break will definitely refer to some significant change in the life

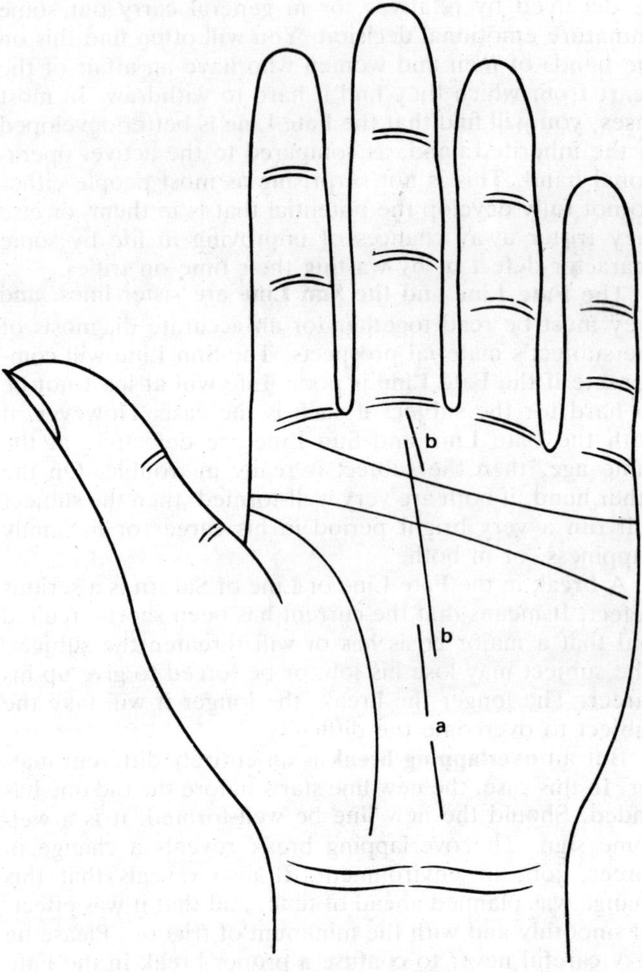

Figure 12-18 (a) a Break in the Fate Line (b) Overlapping Breaks in the Fate Line

of the subject, but only an experienced hand analyst can tell whether it is a change of country, a change in career, or merely a change of the subject's job. I have frequently seen breaks on the hands of my business clients when they changed companies.

A **wavy and twisted line** is an unfavourable line. Such a line is under the influence of the essentially malefic planet **Rahu.**[2] It means that the subject will be continuously changing in his outlook and fortune, and his material prospects will also fluctuate constantly. In Hindu astrology Rahu symbolizes snakes and danger from snakes or reptiles will be heightened if such a Fate Line ends in a fork like the mouth of a snake or serpent. This subject will have no peace of mind, and he will experience trouble of one kind or another. He will also have difficulty in having children, or even if there are children, they may prove to be troublesome to their parents. The bad effects of the wavy, twisted Fate Line will be minimized if there is a good Sun Line to compensate at the same age as the Fate Line is twisted.

Triangles on the Fate Line are always favourable features. They refer to a period of heightened success for the subject. Generally, a triangle refers to financial gains, expected or unexpected, as the case may be. The triangle need not necessarily be attached to the Fate Line. It can be beside the Line, on either side. The bigger and better marked the triangle, the better the effects. These are the various interpretations for a triangle on the Fate Line, which have been found to be true in practical experience:

(a) promotion
(b) passing an important examination
(c) sudden wealth (e.g., gaining on the stock market)
(d) in general, feeling happy with life, feeling creative

---

[2] In Indian astrology, **Rahu** represents the ascending node of the Moon, not an actual planet.

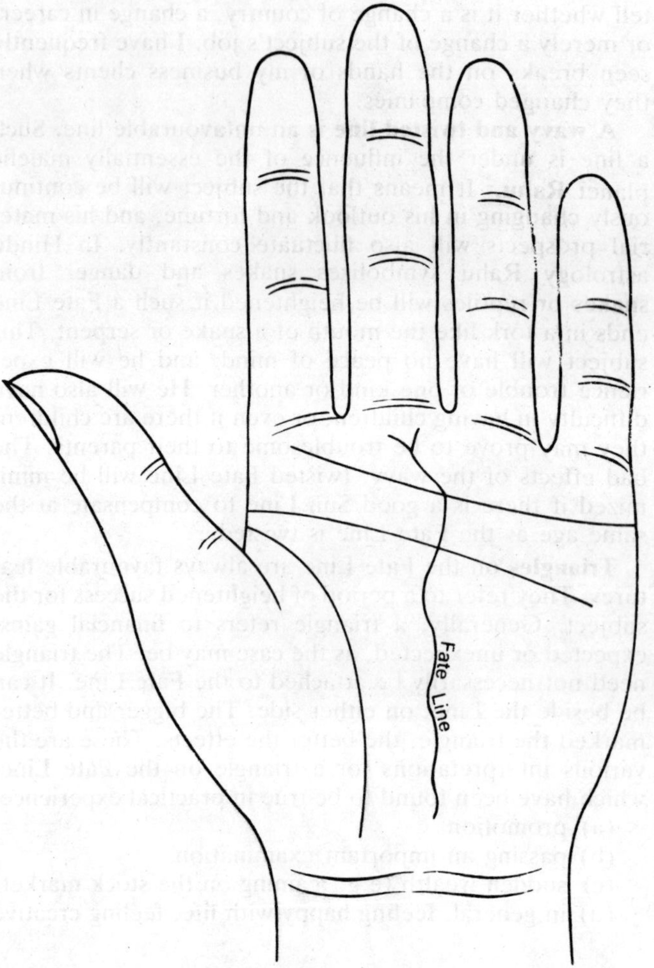

Figure 12-19 A wavy, twisted Fate Line ending like the mouth of a snake

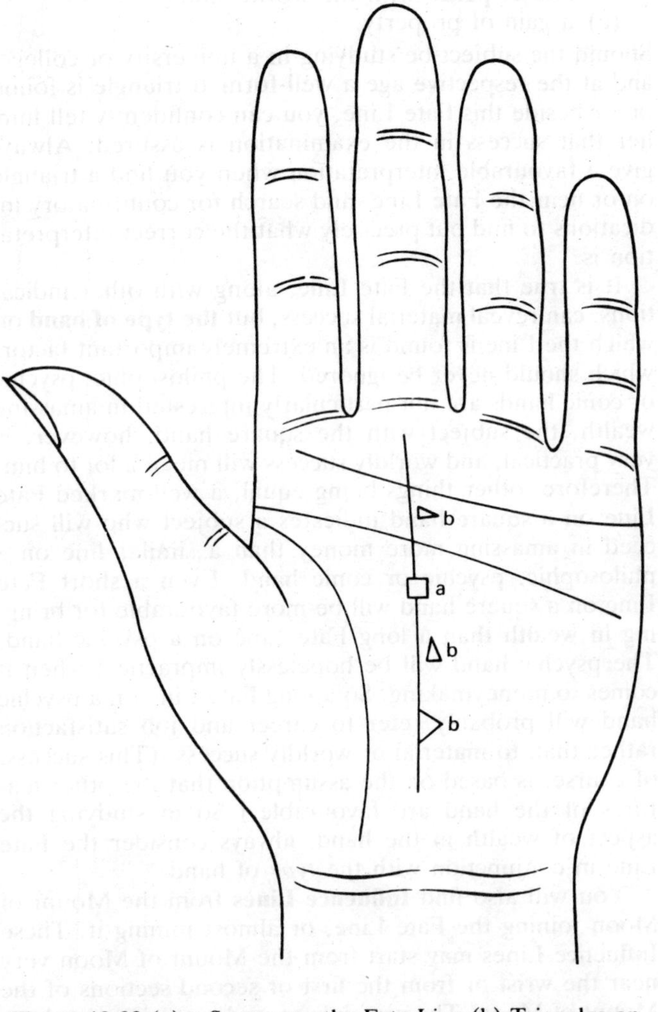

Figure 12-20 (a) a Square on the Fate Line (b) Triangles on and near the Fate Line

and at peace with the world, and

(e) a gain of property.

Should the subject be studying in a university or college, and at the respective age a well-formed triangle is found on or beside this Fate Line, you can confidently tell him her that success in the examination is assured. Always give a favourable interpretation when you find a triangle on or near the Fate Line, and search for confirmatory indications to find out precisely what the correct interpretation is.

It is true that the Fate Line, along with other indications, can reveal material success, but **the type of hand** on which the Line is found is an extremely important factor, which should never be ignored. The philosophic, psychic or conic hands are not particularly interested in amassing wealth; the subject with the square hand, however, is very practical, and worldly success will mean a lot to him. Therefore, other things being equal, a well-marked Fate Line on a square hand indicates a subject who will succeed in amassing more money than a similar line on a philosophic, psychic or conic hand. Even a short Fate Line on a square hand will be more favourable for bringing in wealth than a long Fate Line on a psychic hand. The psychic hand will be hopelessly impractical when it comes to moneymaking. So a long Fate Line on a psychic hand will probably refer to career and job satisfaction rather than to material or worldly success. (This success, of course, is based on the assumption that the other features of the hand are favourable.) So in studying the aspect of wealth in the hand, always consider the Fate Line in conjunction with the *type* of hand.

You will also find **Influence Lines** from the Mount of Moon joining the Fate Line, or almost joining it. These Influence Lines may start from the Mount of Moon very near the wrist or from the first or second sections of the Mount of Moon. The principle to understand about these Influence Lines is that some important influence has

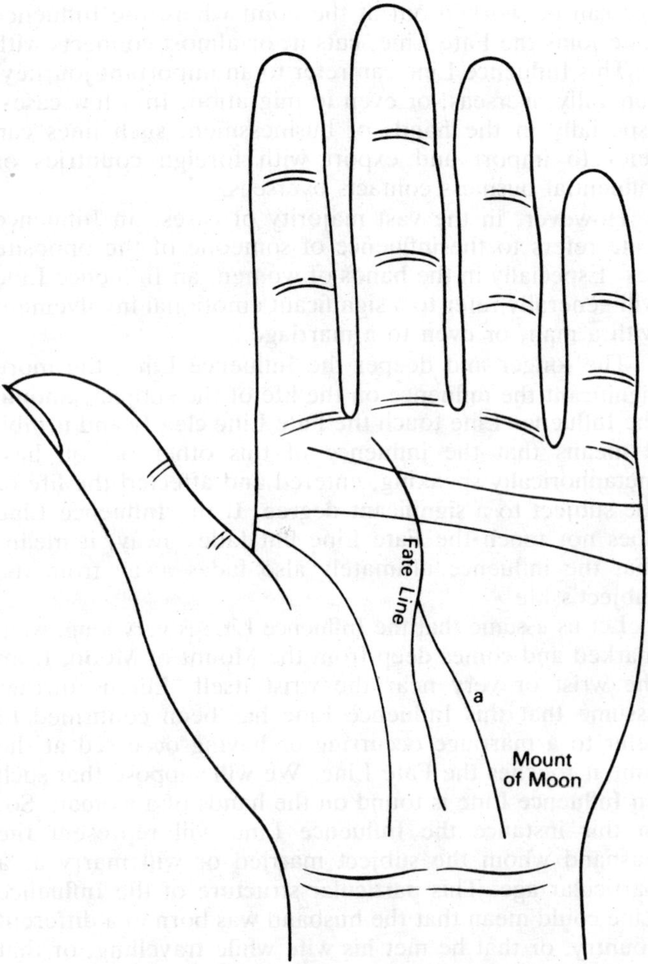

Figure 12-21 An Influence Line (a) coming deep from the Mount of Moon and touching the Fate Line

come into the life of the subject at a particular age. The age can be worked out at the point where the Influence Line joins the Fate Line, cuts it, or almost connects with it. This Influence Line can refer to an important journey, generally overseas, or even to migration. In a few cases, especially in the hands of businessmen, such lines can refer to import and export with foreign countries or influential business contacts overseas.

However, in the vast majority of cases, an Influence Line refers to the influence of someone of the opposite sex. Especially in the hands of women, an Influence Line will generally refer to a significant emotional involvement with a man, or even to a marriage.

The longer and deeper the Influence Line, the more significant the influence on the life of the subject. Should the Influence Line touch the Fate Line clearly and firmly, it means that the influence of this other person has, metaphorically speaking, entered and affected the life of the subject to a significant degree. If the Influence Line does not touch the Fate Line but fades away, it means that the influence ultimately also fades away from the subject's life.

Let us assume that the Influence Line is very long, well-marked and comes deep from the Mount of Moon, from the wrist or very near the wrist itself. Let us further assume that this Influence Line has been confirmed to refer to a marriage occurring or having occurred at the time it touches the Fate Line. We will suppose that such an Influence Line is found on the hands of a woman. So, in this instance the Influence Line will represent the husband whom the subject married or will marry at a particular age. This particular structure of the Influence Line could mean that the husband was born in a different country, or that he met his wife while travelling, or that he is of a different race or nationality. I have found in my research that if this Influence Line represented a husband of the same race, then the subject would have met him in a foreign country, or he was born in a foreign land. However, hand analysis reveals not only events, but the psychological attitude of the subject towards events and influences. In a few instances, the husband while courting the subject was living barely a hundred miles away and yet the subject confessed to me that she felt as if he were living in a foreign land. So, psychologically, the subject felt that her future husband was living very far away, although the distance was barely a hundred miles, and the separation of a mere hundred miles, before her marriage, was very painful to the subject.

It is unfortunate if the Influence Line cuts the Fate Line and heads in the direction of the Mount of Jupiter This means that, speaking metaphorically again, this influence has cut across the life of the subject. If it refers to love or an emotional relationship, it means that the influence has created a very unhappy impact on the subject's life at that particular age. The influence has, metaphorically, used the subject for ulterior motives. I have found this sign, repeatedly, on the hands of women who had been seduced and then discarded, or else had been seduced emotionally, or exploited for ulterior motives. At any rate, even if the man had honourable motives and was basically decent in his behaviour, yet the ultimate impact was painful to the subject. I have also found in my research that if this Influence Line is very well-marked and deeper than the Fate Line itself around the area of contact, then the influence, (referring, here, to a person) has a very strong personality and has mentally overpowered the subject. On the other hand, if the Influence Line is much weaker than the Fate Line, it means that the personality of the influence has been weaker than that of the subject.

Sometimes you will find an Influence Line rising from the Mount of Moon, but islanded at the beginning. This is a sure case of the influence having a very unhappy impact on the subject's life, particularly if the Influence Line cuts

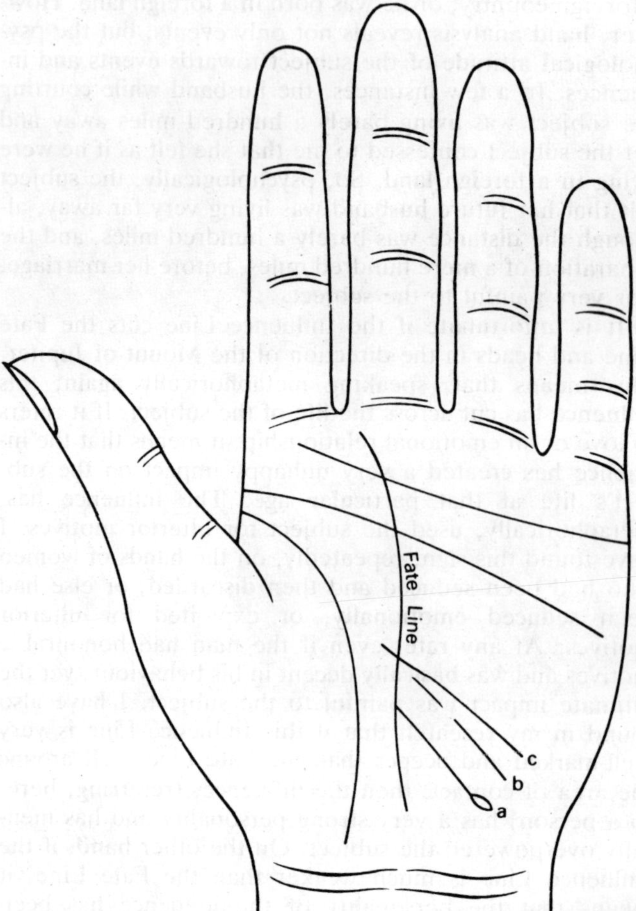

Figure 12-22 (a) an Influence Line islanded at the start (b) an Influence Line fading away from the Fate Line (c) an Influence Line cutting the Fate Line

the Fate Line as well. It could also mean that this particular influence has an unsavoury background. I once saw such a formation on the hands of a girl who later confessed to me that for some time she had not known that her lover was addicted to heroin. She had had a most traumatic relationship with him, and she wept repeatedly in my office while describing this experience. In another case, I found that such an islanded Influence Line represented a man who had a criminal record and the girl on whose hand I saw this mark did not have the faintest inkling of his past until the relationship had been firmly established.

Sometimes you will find the Influence Line neither cutting the Fate Line nor touching it, but running beside it. This means that the influence will affect the subject for the duration that this Influence Line runs parallel to the Fate Line. After that, it may fade away for some reason. If the Influence Line is staggered and repeatedly broken, it means that the subject has had an unstable relationship with this influence. This could be due to any number of reasons, such as having a poor emotional relationship, or being separated by distance or some other reason, from this influence.

You must work out the ages on the Fate Line according to the diagram and method described in an earlier chapter. The Fate Line is a line that will tell you a great deal about your psychological attitude towards work. The best harvest periods of your life are clearly revealed on your Fate Line. A close study of this line will tell you when to strike when the iron is hot. This information should be especially useful to businessmen who wish to make the greatest money while they are still alert and healthy. It would also be of use to students, because they will know when they can perform best in their academic studies. For example, if the subject is sitting for an impor-

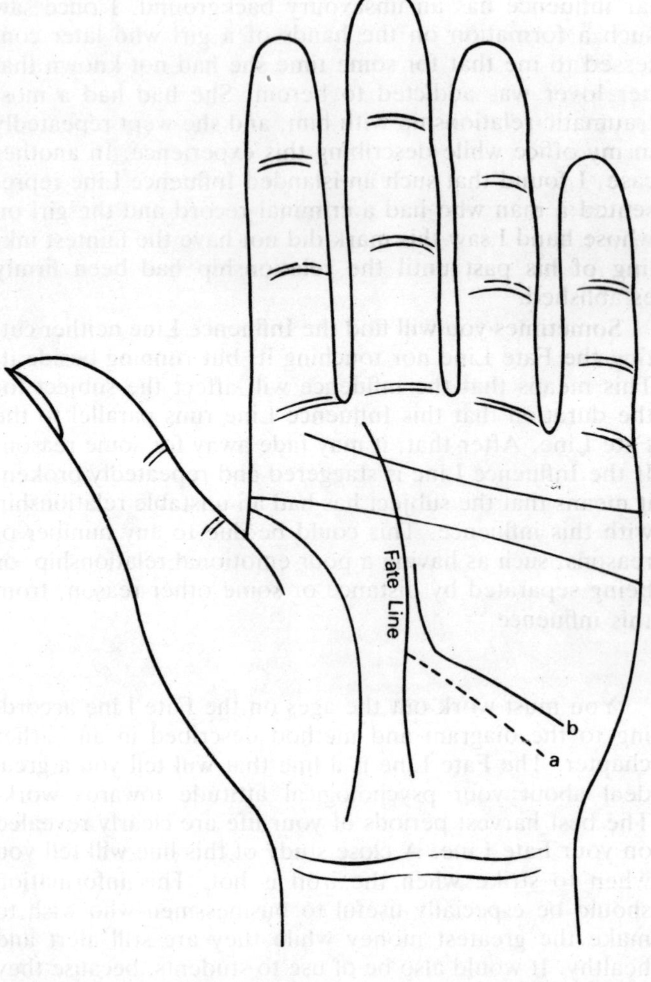

Figure 12-23 (a) a broken Influence Line (b) an Influence Line running beside the Fate Line

tant examination and there is a very well-marked triangle either on the Fate Line or beside it at the relevant age, it is a sure sign that he will do well in the examination. This should be a source of great encouragement to the subject and perhaps, by redoubling his efforts, he might do even better. In this case, the triangle on the Fate Line may become more distinct and better marked.

Work out the combinations of the Fate Line. They can run into literally thousands of combinations. The important thing is to grasp the principles of hand analysis, and learn how to apply them intelligently, with a scientific bent of mind, as well as with strong intuition. Scientific hand analysis alone is not sufficient. You must also have intuition, because mere calculation will fail at times, and because the language of the hand is truly a most complicated matter.

Chapter Thirteen

The Sun Line or Line of Apollo Reflects Your Latent Potential for Fame, Distinction and Success

The **Sun Line** is also called the **Line of Apollo.** Some noted hand analysts call it the Line of Capability, Success, or Brilliance. This line is under the influence of the planet Sun, which is why it is called the Sun Line.

The Sun Line is an important line in scientific hand analysis. It stands for honour, reputation, learning, education, artistic ability, and wealth. It should always be considered together with the Fate Line, and in fact, since in runs parallel, it can be called a sister line to the Fate Line. A weakness of the Fate Line can be compensated for by a good Sun Line. Thus the subject can be wealthy even if the Fate Line is absent, if he has a good Sun Line. There should, of course, be other confirmatory indications of wealth, besides the good Sun Line.

The Sun Line in actuality reflects the period when 'sunshine' metaphorically enters the life of the subject. In other words, it reflects the time when the subject receives recognition of his talents and ability in his own sphere of work. Finally, the Sun Line is also an accurate reflector of personal happiness, or the lack of it.

Amateur hand analysts regard a good Sun Line as always bestowing artistic gifts on the subject. The subject is misled into believing that he is potentially a writer, painter, or sculptor of fame — perhaps even a budding Leonardo da Vinci! This of course may confuse the client if he knows very well that, at a mature age, he can't even draw a decent apple or cat, and, to add insult to injury, he may not even have any artistic tendencies.

Properly speaking, a good Sun Line makes the subject capable in his own sphere of work. Thus, an artist will be talented in drawing, a hand analyst capable of making accurate predictions, while a businessman with a good Sun Line will have a reputation for being rich and successful in business ventures. Should a thief or robber have a good Sun Line, he will be no ordinary thief or robber, but one of distinction! Robin Hood must have had a really good Sun Line in his palms. Of course, it is possible for a subject with a good Sun Line to be interested in artistic ventures, although he himself may hardly be able to draw anything worthwhile, but please do not make the tragic mistake of thinking that a good Sun Line always bestows artistic abilities upon the 'lucky' subject. The golden rule to remember is that a favourable, well-marked Sun Line, together with other favourable indications, will certainly make the subject capable or talented in his own sphere of work, whatever that may be.

Should the Sun Line be prominent, deep, and favourable, it will reveal what is known as luck. Of course, according to the Indian theory of *Karma,* there is no such thing as luck: all so-called Luck has been earned by meritorious deeds in the subject's previous life or lives, and is merely a favourable effect of a previous set of circumstances, begun by the subject himself in a former existence. The casual observer thinks that due to some unfairness on the part of Nature or God, a certain individual seems to be given more opportunities for growth or improvement than other less fortunate mortals, but to one steeped in the hoary traditions of Indian philosophy and the theory of *Karma,* that is too easy and superficial an explanation. Even morally degraded subjects can have a well-marked Sun Line on their hands. The existence of a favourable Sun Line is no proof that the man has an upright and honourable character. Thus, a subject may have a long and deep Sun Line, but also a crooked Mercury finger, a short, twisted Jupiter finger, and a grille on the Mount of Mercury. A grille on the Mount of Mercury together with a crooked little finger reveals dishonest tendencies. A short, ill-formed Jupiter or first finger reveals a lack of basic self-respect. With such a combination, the subject will use his talent for evil purposes.

The Sun Line can begin from the wrist and travel vertically upwards across the hand to end on the Mount of Sun, under the third or ring finger.

The ideal Sun Line should be long, deep, well-marked, and preferably extend from the wrist straight up to the Mount of Sun. With other good indications, such a good Sun Line will promise fame, wealth, and success for the subject. However, the majority of us have misbehaved in our previous life or lives! That is why we find that very few people enjoy such a happy situation as possessing a well-formed Sun Line. It is true to say that no real success will come to the subject unless there is at least a fairly well-formed Sun Line on one or both hands.

Let us now study the **origins of this line.**

The Sun Line may start from the Vitality Line. This means that the subject will achieve distinction and success in life by his personal ability and efforts. Sometimes, with such a beginning the subject may achieve this success through initial help from relatives or family members. This interpretation is given because the Vitality Line is called the 'Line of Father' in Indian hand analysis, and because the Vitality Line is near the Mount of Venus. As we know, in hand analysis Venus represents the family.

This line may also start from inside the Vitality Line, on the Mount of Venus. Since Venus represents the family, such an origin heightens the influence of the family or relations. Such a formation therefore means that the

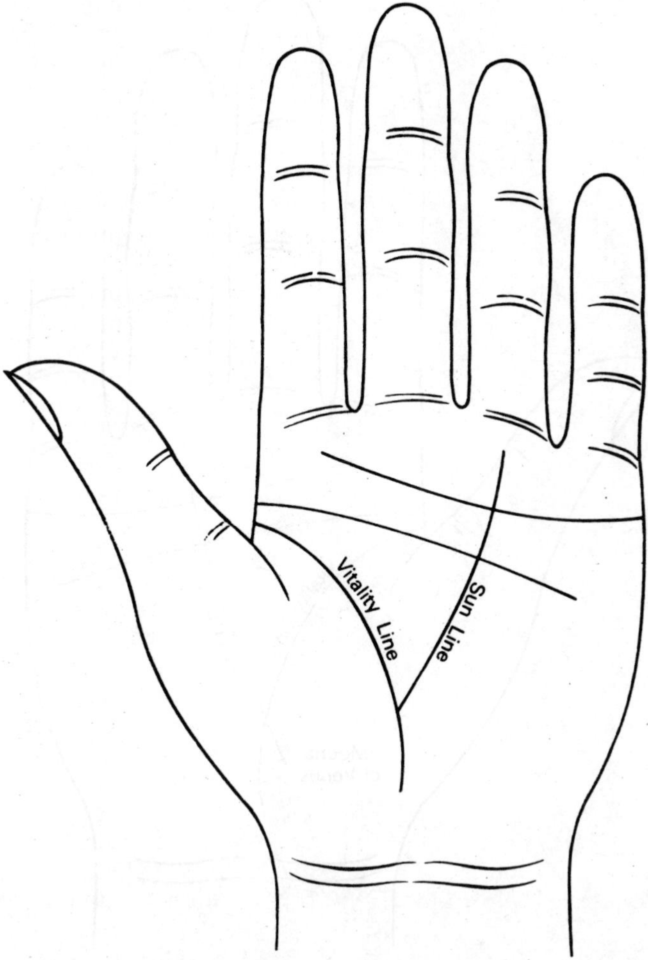

Figure 13-1 The Sun Line starting from the Vitality Line

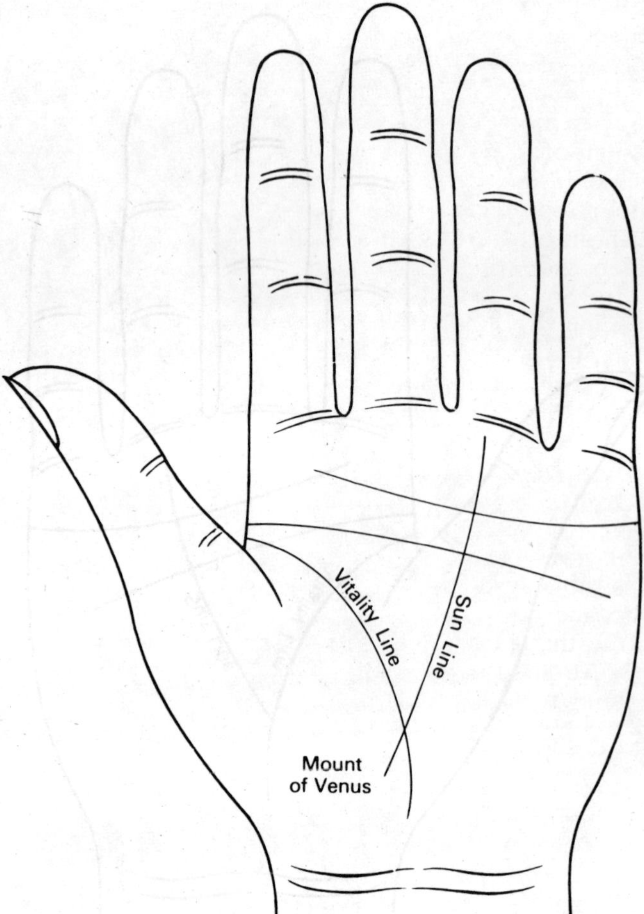

Figure 13-2 The Sun Line starting from inside the Vitality Line on the Mount of Venus

subject will be aided by relatives at the beginning of his career. Should this line later rise steadily towards the Mount of Sun, it means that this initial help will lay a good foundation for the future success of the subject.

It is most fortunate if the Sun Line starts from the Mount of Moon, and reaches the Mount of Sun in a well-marked, favourable formation. As we know, the satellite Moon represents foreign influence and imagination. With such an origin, the subject will get help more from outsiders than from his own family. This is understandable, as the Sun Line will now be fairly distant from the Vitality Line. The more distant this line is from the Vitality Line, the less the influence of the family or relatives. The subject in this case will get help from influential people, and perhaps their patronage as well.

A long, favourable Sun Line with an origin on the Mount of Moon will give personal magnetism to the subject. The subject will also have a good deal of sex appeal, especially if the Mount of Venus is well-formed, pink in colour, and elevated. In a fair number of cases, this subject will be aided in his career by someone of the opposite sex. Businessmen will be keenly interested to know that such a line also means that the subject can achieve great success in business with foreign countries. Should the subject be an employee of a company, he would achieve more success working for a foreign company.

Let us assume now that, with this formation, the Vitality Line has swerved away from the Mount of Venus and is headed towards the Mount of Moon. Also, that the Fate Line is strong and well-marked. With such a hand combination, the subject, having a well-formed Sun Line starting from the Mount of Moon, will find success in migrating to a foreign country. Also, by and large, the subject will achieve knowledge, success, or earn money through travels to other countries. Businessmen will be further interested to know that such a line can make them

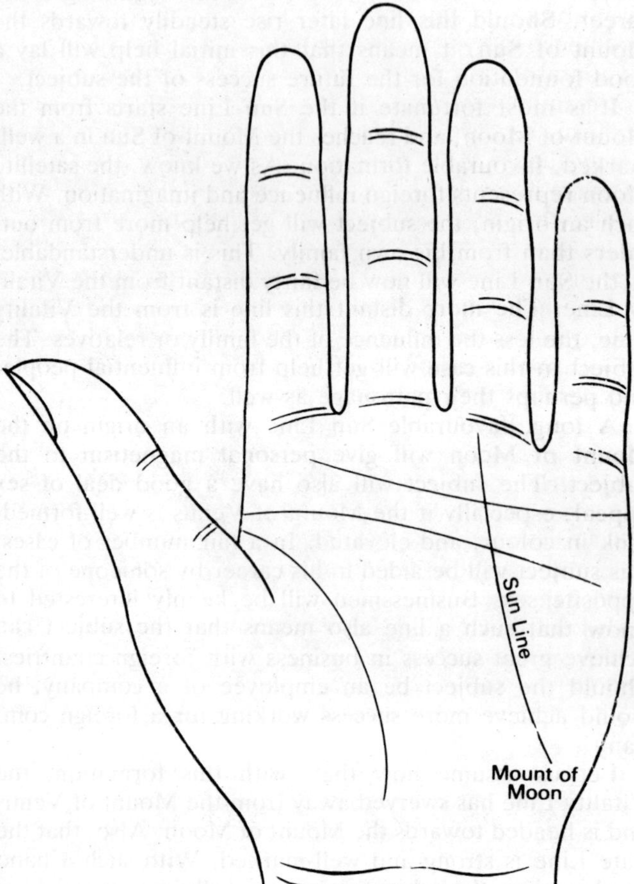

Figure 13-3 The Sun Line starting from the Mount of Moon

successful in the import and export trade.

Subjects with such a Sun Line have the ability to influence other people fairly easily. I once saw such a favourable Sun Line on the hands of a very prominent woman lawyer. She possessed considerable personal magnetism, and was clearly very intelligent. She told me jokingly that if she merely said 'Boo!', others would sit up to take notice of her words! If the Marriage Line is favourable, the Mount of Venus is well-formed and the Fate Line is strong and well-marked, the subject with this formation will definitely get substantial help from women, men, the husband or wife, as the case may be. This help need not always be financial or material; it can also mean good timely advice or introductions or recommendations to influential parties.

The Sun Line may also start from the Plain of Mars. As we know, the planet Mars is associated with struggle and strife in both hand analysis and astrology. This means that success will come to the subject after tremendous hard work, and without any significant aid from others. Should the subsequent nature of the Sun Line be favourable, the success will last a long time since a solid foundation will have been laid by the subject himself.

It is a favourable sign if the Sun Line starts from the Fate Line itself. The age of success, shown by such a Sun Line, has to be calculated on the Fate Line. Generally, in such cases, the Sun Line, starting from the Fate Line, heads in the direction of the Sun Mount under the third finger. Should this type of Sun Line be well-marked and long, it is certainly a most favourable mark. From that time, the subject's career will certainly be more successful and eventful, and success will enter his life The subject may even achieve happiness, or greater happiness, at that age. In many cases I have confirmed that a favourable opportunity presented itself to the subject, and he took advantage of it. Success could, therefore, come through what is termed 'Luck'. In a fair number of cases I found

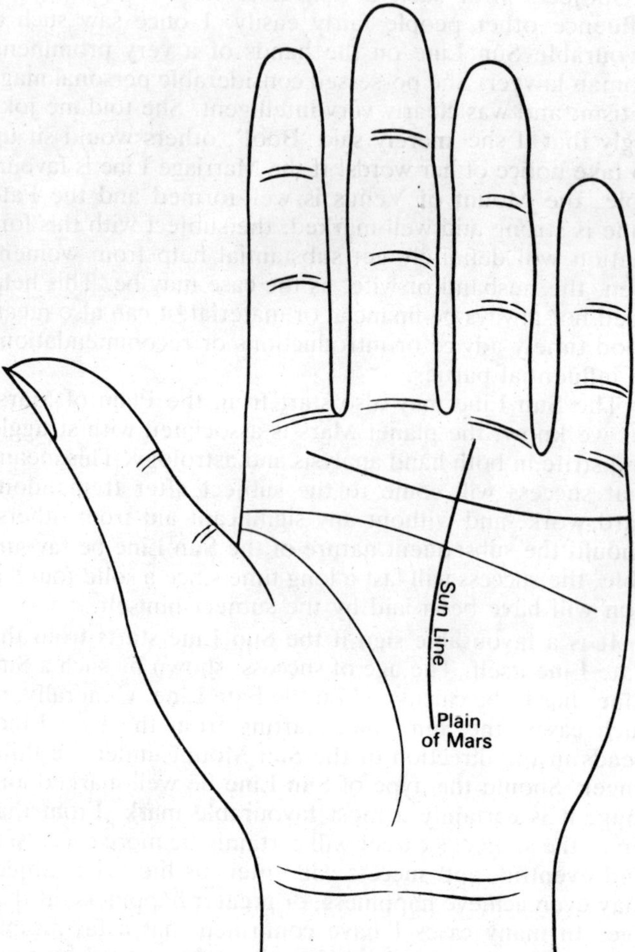

Figure 13-4 The Sun Line starting from the Plain of Mars

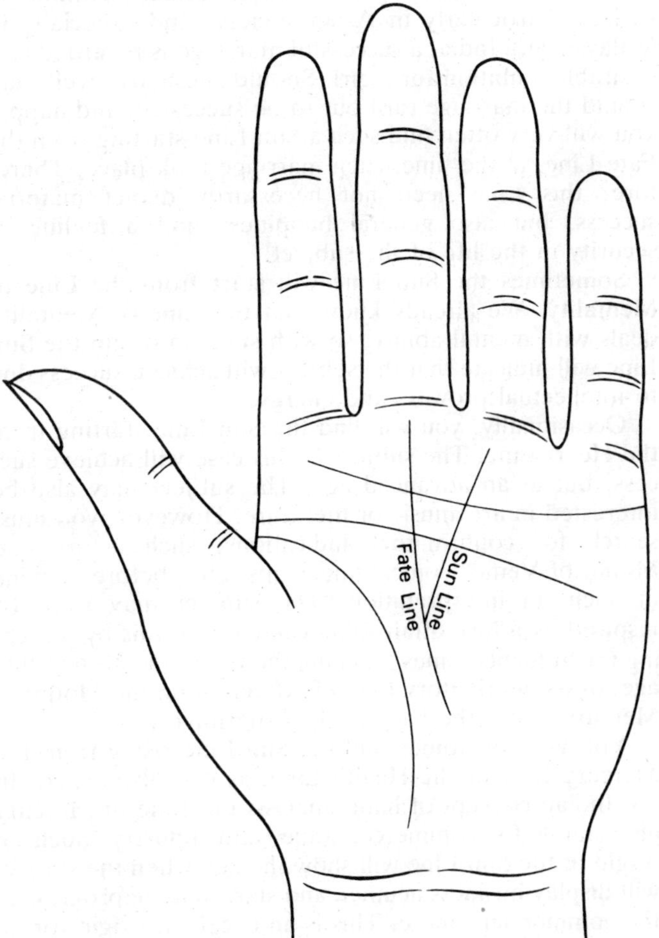

Figure 13-5 The Sun Line starting from the Fate Line

such lines on the hands of women who had married well to husbands holding good, distinguished positions in society. Particularly in Asian society, and especially in Malaysia and India, a successful marriage is regarded as a desirable ambition for a girl. Should she marry well, and should the marriage turn out to be successful and happy, you will very often find such a Sun Line starting from the Fate Line, at the time when marriage took place. Therefore, this Line need not necessarily depict material success, but also general happiness and a feeling of security in the life of the subject.

Sometimes the Sun Line will start from the Line of Mentality. We already know that the Line of Mentality deals with mental ability, so with such an origin the Sun Line will indicate that the subject will achieve success due to intellectual prowess and energy.

Occasionally, you will find the Sun Line starting from the Heart Line. The subject in this case will achieve success, but at an advanced age. The subject may also be interested in art, music or literature. However, you must search for confirmatory indications, such as a good Mount of Venus, conical finger-tips, etc., before arriving at such an interpretation. The subject may even be inspired by a love affair. You can confirm this by searching for Influence Lines touching the Fate Line at the same age, or a confirmatory Line of Affection on the Mount of Mercury under the base of the little finger.

You will sometimes find the Sun Line rising from the Mercury Line or the Health Line, as it is also called. In the Indian concept of hand analysis the Line of Mercury also stands for commerce, trade, and industry. Such an origin of the Sun Line will show the age when the subject will display business acumen and start making progress in the commercial sphere. This is an excellent origin for an ambitious businessman to have. Should the businessman be involved in a major financial enterprise, the indications are that the enterprise will be successful, if both the

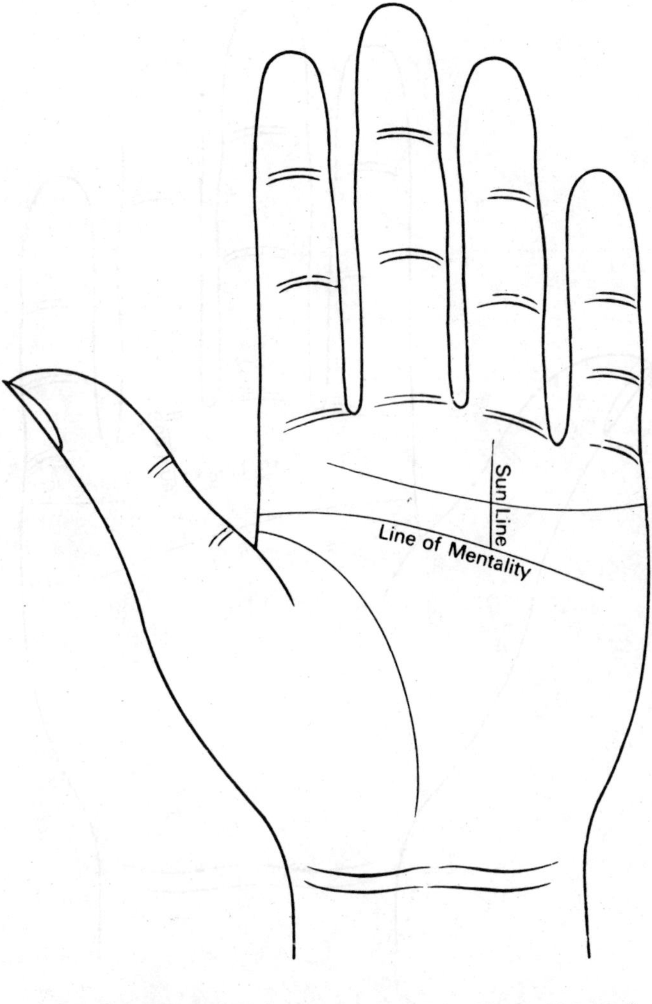

Figure 13-6 The Sun Line starting from the Line of Mentality

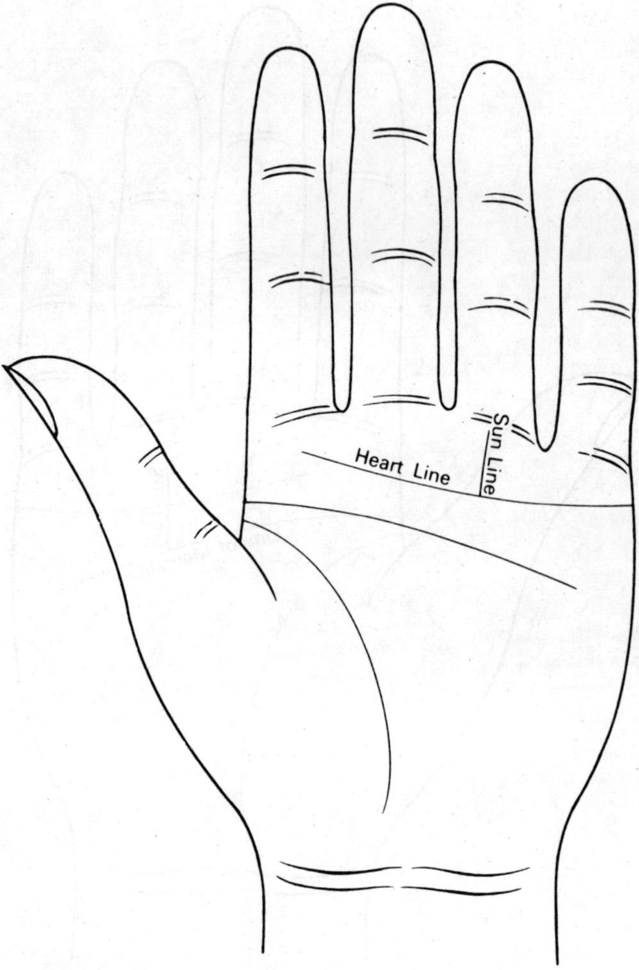

Figure 13-7 The Sun Line starting from the Heart Line

Sun and Health Lines are well-formed.

It is really rare to find a long deep Sun Line rising from the wrist, travelling up the palm, and ending on the Mount of Sun. If such a Sun Line is well-formed, the subject will definitely be 'lucky', and with other favourable indications, enjoy distinction, material wealth, and social status. The subject will have luck entering his life at a young age. Should the Line of Mentality be well-formed, the mounts of Sun, Mercury and Jupiter well-developed, undoubtedly the subject with such a line can or will go far in intellectual pursuits, and will possess an incisive mind. Such a subject is destined to make a mark in some field of work, and acquire both name and fame in the process. So far, at the time of writing, I can count on my fingertips the number of such Sun Lines that I have encountered in my professional practice. Sad to say, but true nevertheless, most of us have to struggle hard, or very hard, to achieve success in life. The 'lucky' owner of such a Sun Line will find numerous opportunities thrown in his path. It may not be necessary for him to create opportunities to progress in life.

The Mount of Upper Mars deals with moral courage and the ability to withstand competition. In some cases you will find the Sun Line starting from the Mount of Upper Mars and travelling up to the Mount of Sun. This means that the subject will achieve success through a strong fighting spirit, and although encountering competition, will undoubtedly achieve success, if this type of Sun Line is well-formed. Occasionally, with such a formation, I have found that the subject was interested in foreign business — for example, in dealing with the import and export trade. These subjects succeed very well in such a field of trade. I confirmed this on the hands of a man who told me that he was seriously thinking of expanding his business and going into foreign trade. Earlier, I had seen on his hand a well-formed Sun Line starting from Upper Mars, and had suggested to him then that he was proba-

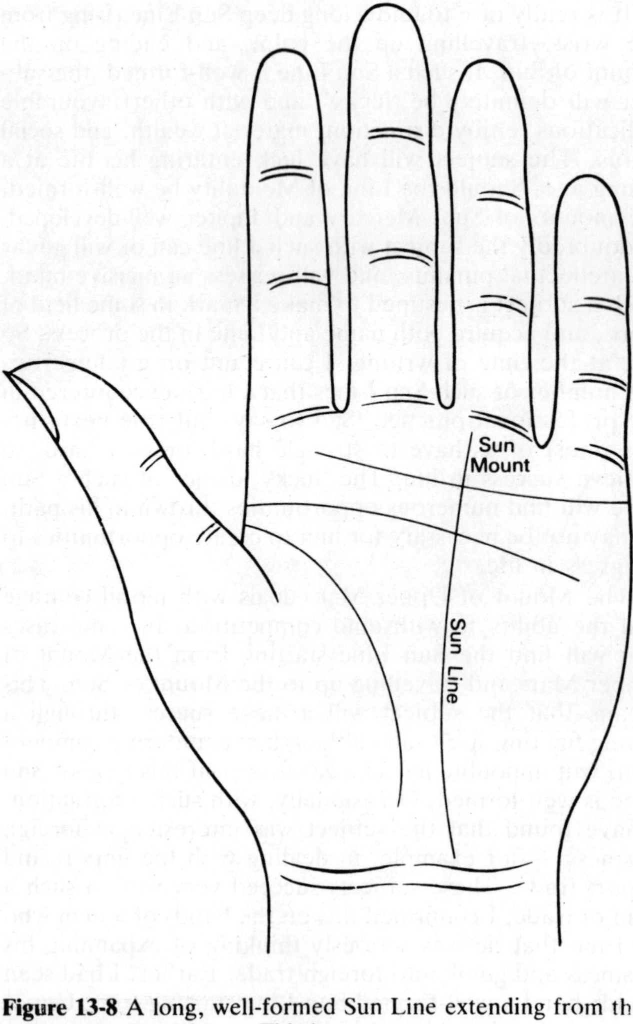

Figure 13-8 A long, well-formed Sun Line extending from the wrist to the Sun Mount. This is very rare.

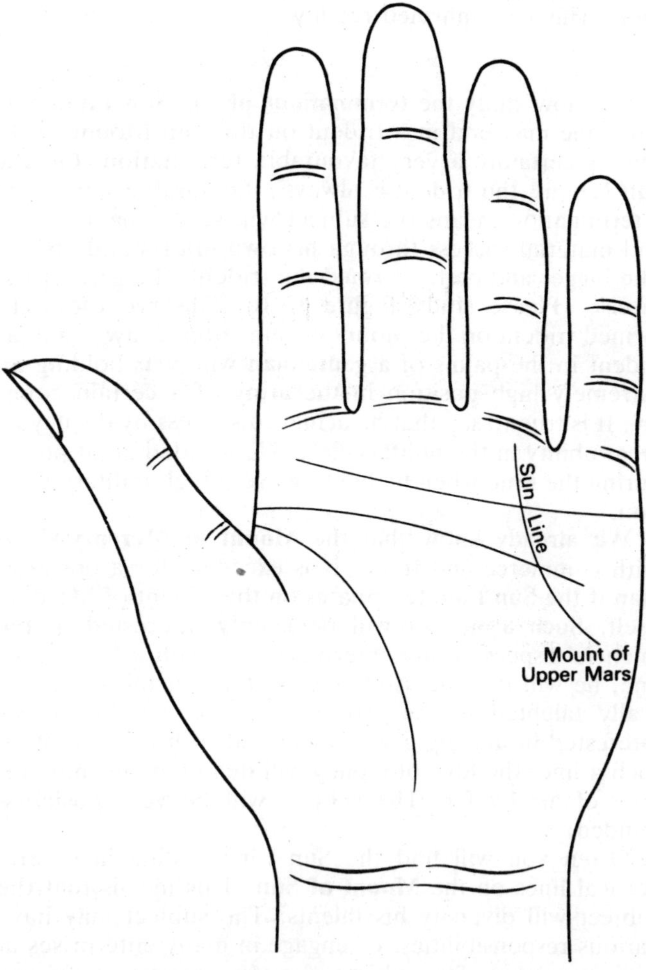

Figure 13-9 The Sun Line starting from the Mount of Upper Mars

bly thinking of starting some kind of foreign business soon. This he confirmed readily.

Let us now study the **terminations of the Sun Line.** The Sun Line may end in a trident on the Sun Mount itself. This is certainly a very favourable termination. On the Sun Mount, the trident is always a favourable sign. Such a termination means the subject will secure name, fame and material success through his own efforts and ability. The bigger and better formed the trident, the greater the success. Please study Figure 13-10. Observe the well-formed trident on the Mount of Sun. I once saw a similar trident in the palms of a gentleman who was holding an extremely high position in the army of a certain country. It is true to say that he achieved success by displaying great ability in the military field. He wielded great power during the time when he held this very high military position.

We already know that the **Mount of Mercury** deals with commerce and trade. It is excellent for a businessman if the Sun Line terminates on the Mount of Mercury itself. Such a subject will be keenly interested in the financial aspect of any enterprise, and with a favourable line, he will be successful as well. Even if the subject is really talented in the artistic field, he will be keenly interested in making good money out of his talent. With such a line, the love of money will definitely outshine his love of art by far. The subject will be very business-minded.

Often you will find the Sun Line ending in several vertical lines on the **Mount of Sun.** This means that the subject will diversify his talents. The subject may have various responsibilities, or engage in many enterprises at the same time. The subject may also tend to have too many public responsibilities. If there are too many of these vertical, parallel lines, the subject will meet with

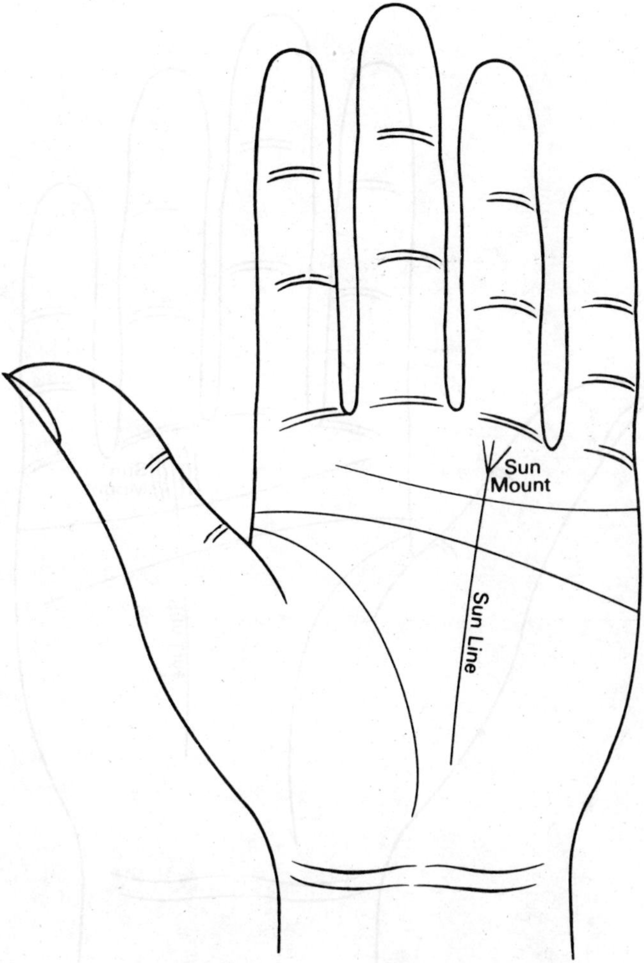

Figure 13-10 The Sun Line ending in a Trident on the Mount of the Sun

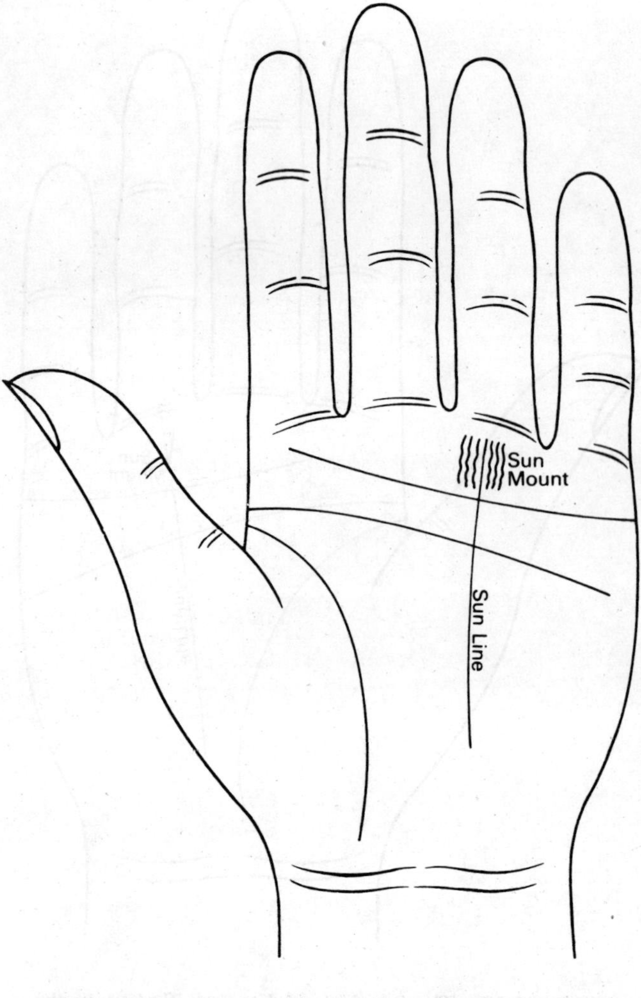

Figure 13-11 The Sun Line ending unfavourably in too many vertical lines on the Mount of the Sun

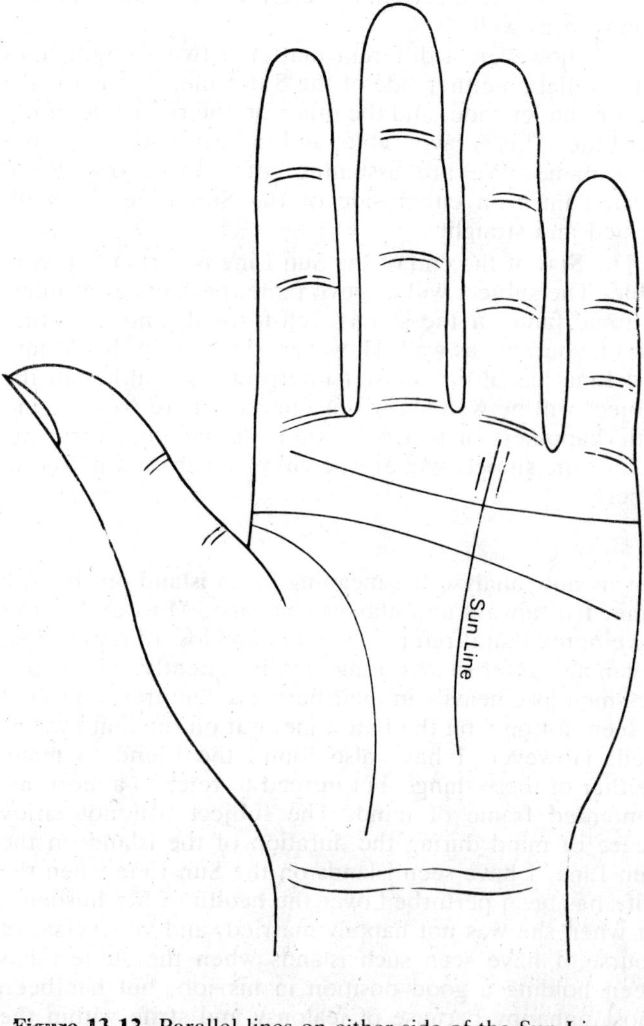

Figure 13 12 Parallel lines on either side of the Sun Line

failure in at least some enterprises or responsibilities. This is all the more certain if these lines are badly formed or curved as well.

It is, however, a different matter if two straight lines run parallel on either side of the Sun Line, that is to say, one on the left side, and the other on the right side of the Sun Line. This is favourable, and indicates success and a good name. We are assuming, of course, that these parallel lines on either side of the Sun Line are well-formed and straight.

The **Star** at the end of the Sun Line is certainly favourable. The subject will achieve fame, perhaps even international fame, if the star is well-formed, and the other lines favourable as well. However, the star on this Mount and Line has also a sinister interpretation: although the subject will be well-known or famous, there will be very little happiness or peace of mind. Perhaps the very success of the subject will arouse envy, anger, and hatred in others.

Let us now analyse the meaning of an **island** on the Sun Line. It is always an unfavourable sign. Most authorities have noted that it refers to scandal and loss of reputation. It can also refer to loss of money. Frequently, when businessmen lose heavily in their business ventures, an island is seen not only on the Fate Line, but on the Sun Line as well. However, I have also found the island to mean neither of these things, but instead to refer to a most discontented frame of mind. The subject will not enjoy peace of mind during the duration of the island on the Sun Line. I have seen islands on the Sun Line when the wife has been perturbed over the health of her husband, or when she was not happily married, and vice versa, of course. I have seen such islands when the subject has been holding a good position in his job, but has been most unhappy because of jealousy and strife within the

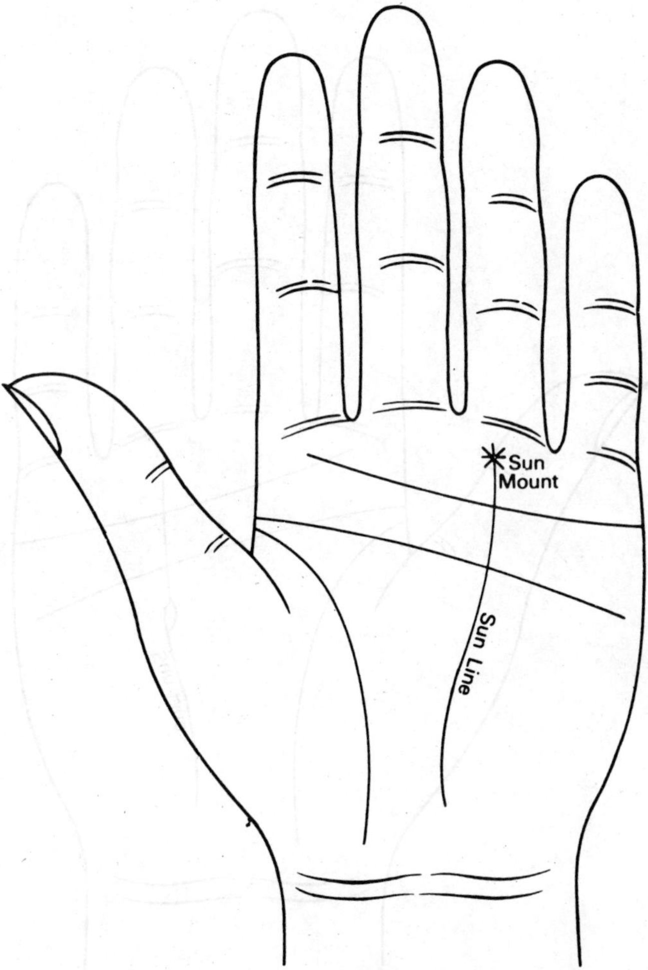

Figure 13-13 The Sun Line ending in a Star on the Mount of the Sun

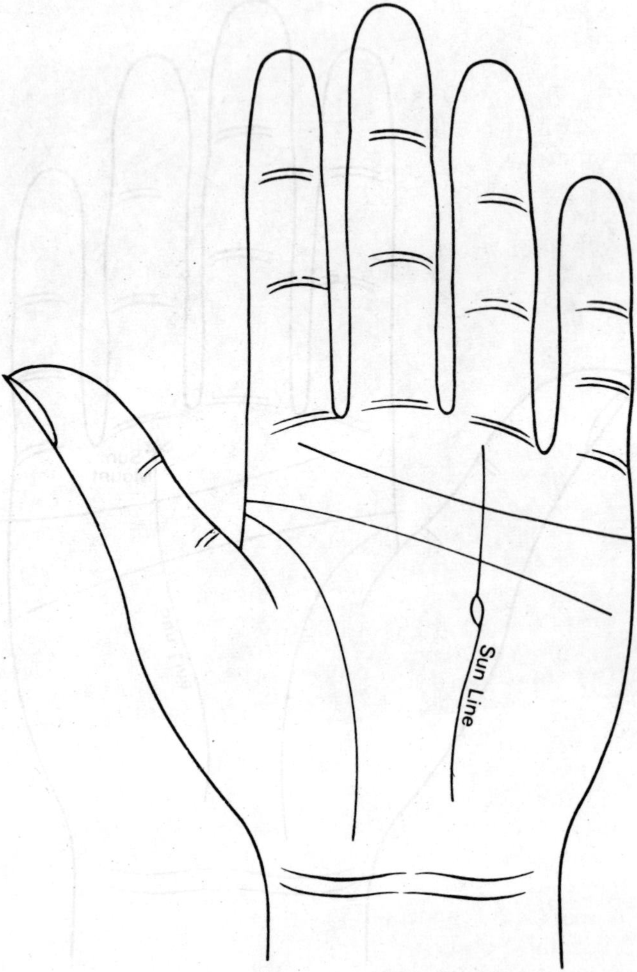

Figure 13-14 An Island on the Sun Line

organization that he works for. Actually, it is seldom that the interpretation of the island on the Sun Line refers to scandal or loss of reputation. Most of the time it refers either to loss of money, or a disturbed, discontented and worried frame of mind. I once saw an island on the Sun Line on the hands of a client who was selling sports equipment. He confessed that he was unhappy and worried, and said it was neither because of scandal nor loss of money, nor due to domestic strife. His children were not giving him any trouble or cause for anxiety either. But he had suffered a heart attack and was constantly worried and anxious about his health. This gave him a discontented mind most of the time. So we must not jump to the conclusion that an island on the Sun Line always refers to the loss of money or to danger of some kind of scandal.

Let us now consider **crossbars** cutting the Sun Line. In scientific hand analysis, crossbars are always bad, as they obstruct the Current that is heading towards the fingers. A crossbar cutting the Sun Line shows a check in the career of the subject. Especially on the hands of businessmen it can mean some severe competition or jealousy affecting the subject's career. Should the crossbar be thin and faintly marked, but the Sun Line deep and clear, the subject will be able to deal with this attack successfully. However, should the crossbar be long and very deep, and worse still, deeper than the Sun Line itself, then it is an ominous indication. Undoutedly, the attack on the subject's peace of mind and career will be heavy, and the subject should be warned to be very careful.

In the Indian concept of hand analysis, we interpret enemies from signs on the Mount of Upper Mars. You will sometimes find a crossbar starting from the Mount of Upper Mars, and cutting the Sun Line. This is a really bad mark, and indicates that some enemy will harm the prospects of the subject. The subject may lose money or honour due to this attack by an enemy. The longer and deeper the crossbar, the worse it is for the subject.

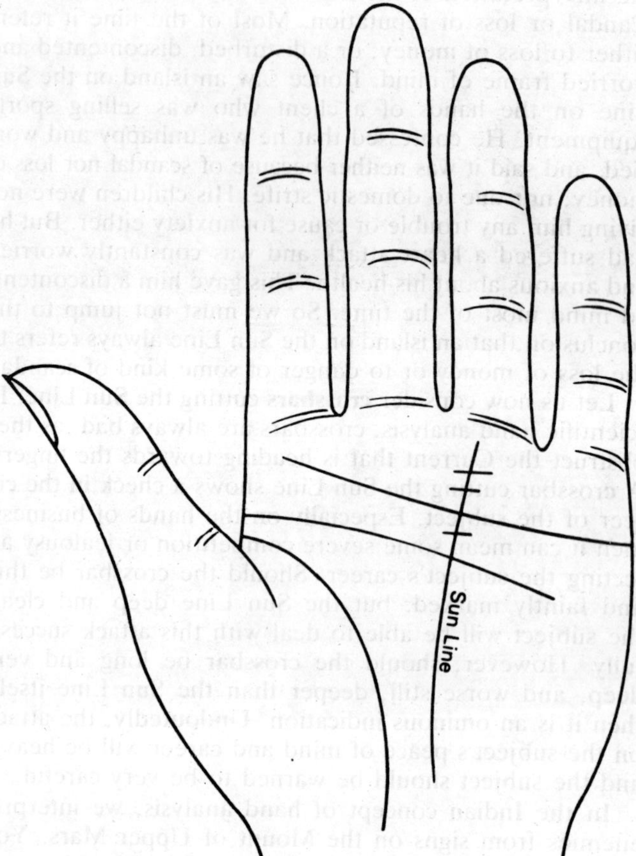

Figure 13-15 Crossbars cutting the Sun Line

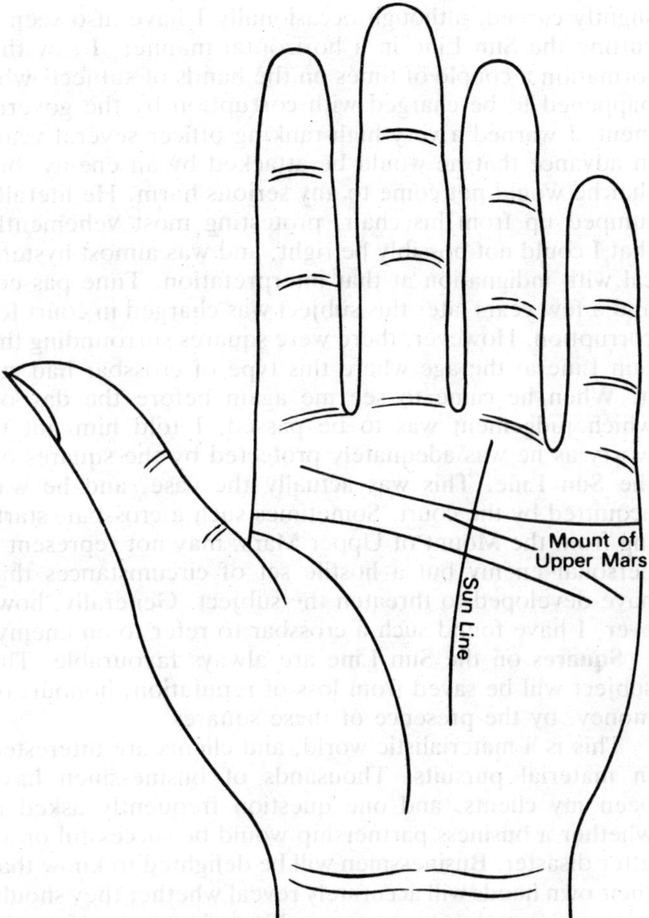

Figure 13-16 Crossbar or Influence Line from Upper Mars cutting the Sun Line. Such a line is dangerous. It shows personal enmity against the subject.

Generally, with such a formation, the crossbar will be slightly curved, although occasionally I have also seen it cutting the Sun Line in a horizontal manner. I saw this formation a couple of times on the hands of subjects who happened to be charged with corruption by the government. I warned a very high-ranking officer several years in advance that he would be attacked by an enemy, but that he would not come to any serious harm. He literally jumped up from his chair, protesting most vehemently that I could not possibly be right, and was almost hysterical with indignation at that interpretation. Time passed, and a few years later this subject was charged in court for corruption. However, there were squares surrounding the Sun Line at the age where this type of crossbar had cut it. When he came to see me again before the day on which judgement was to be passed, I told him not to worry as he was adequately protected by the squares on the Sun Line. This was actually the case, and he was acquitted by the court. Sometimes such a crossbar, starting from the Mount of Upper Mars, may not represent a personal enemy but a hostile set of circumstances that have developed to threaten the subject. Generally, however, I have found such a crossbar to refer to an enemy.

Squares on the Sun Line are always favourable. The subject will be saved from loss of reputation, honour, or money, by the presence of these squares.

This is a materialistic world, and clients are interested in material pursuits. Thousands of businessmen have been my clients, and one question frequently asked is whether a business partnership would be successful or an utter disaster. Businessmen will be delighted to know that their own hands will accurately reveal whether they should venture into a business partnership or keep away from it. Should a line travel upwards from the Line of Fate and merge into the Line of Sun, the subject can enter into a successful business partnership. However, should the same line cut the Sun Line, the business partnership will

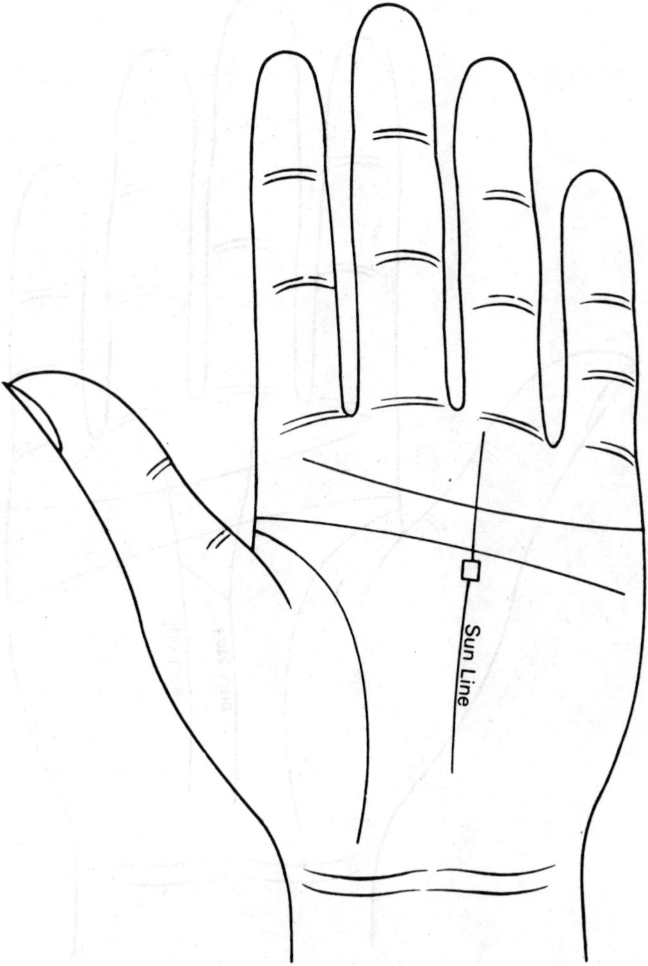

Figure 13-17 A Square protecting the Sun Line. The Square is a sign of preservation.

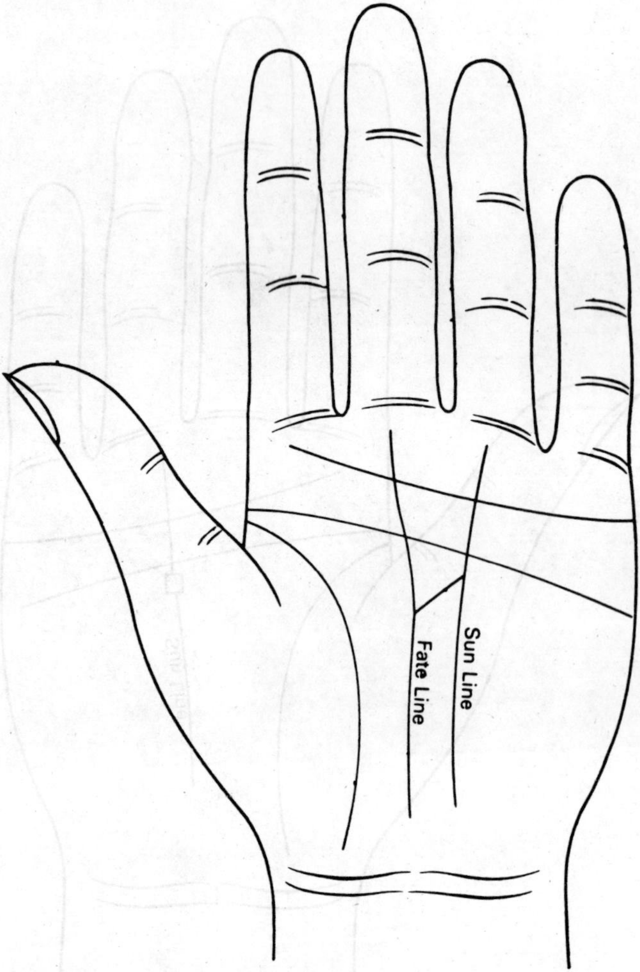

Figure 13-18 An Ascending Line from the Fate Line touching the Sun Line. This is favourable for a happy and successful business partnership.

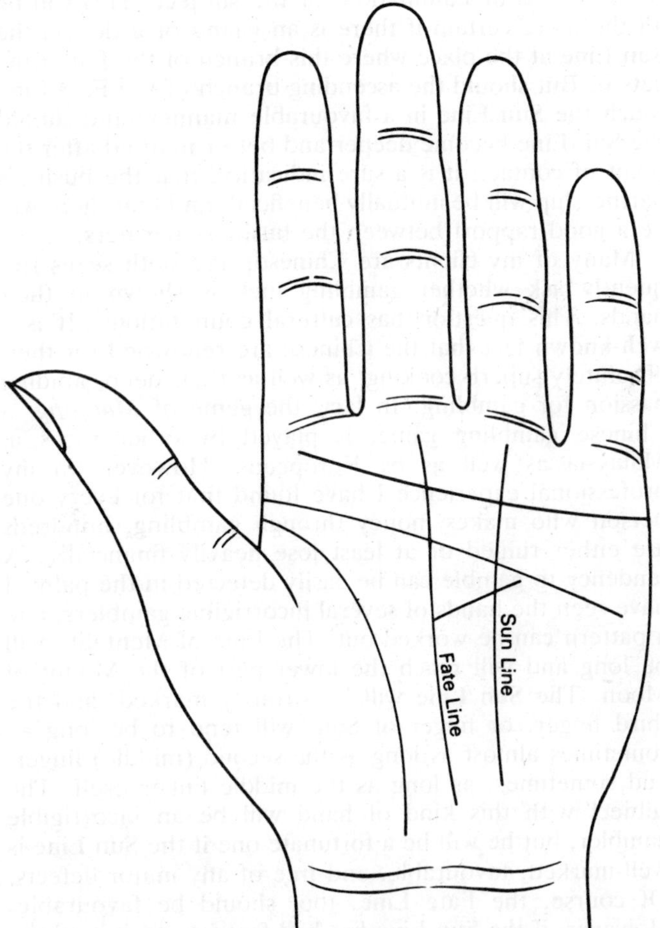

Figure 13-19 An Ascending Line from the Fate Line cutting the Sun Line. It is dangerous to have a business partnership with such a mark on the hand.

result in loss or humiliation for the subject. This will be all the more certain if there is an island or a dot on the Sun Line at the place where this branch of the Fate Line cuts it. But should the ascending branch of the Fate Line touch the Sun Line in a favourable manner, and should the Sun Line become deeper and better marked after the point of contact, it is a sure indication that the business partnership will be mutually beneficial, and that there will be a good rapport between the business partners.

Many of my clients are Chinese, and both sexes frequently ask whether gambling luck is shown in their hands. This question has cultural connotations. It is a well-known fact that the Chinese are renowned for their absolutely superb cooking, as well as their deep, abiding passion for gambling. In fact, the game of *Mahjong,* a Chinese gambling game, is played by other races in Malaysia as well as by Europeans. However, in my professional experience I have found that for every one person who makes money through gambling, hundreds are either ruined or at least lose heavily financially. A tendency to gamble can be easily detected in the palm. I have seen the hands of several incorrigible gamblers, and a pattern can be worked out. The Line of Mentality will be long and will reach the lower part of the Mount of Moon. The Sun Line will be strongly marked, and the third finger, or finger of Sun, will tend to be long — sometimes almost as long as the second (middle) finger, and sometimes, as long as the middle finger itself. The subject with this kind of hand will be an incorrigible gambler, but he will be a fortunate one if the Sun Line is well-marked, favourable, and free of any major defects. Of course, the Fate Line, too, should be favourable. However, if the Sun Line has bad features on it, and the Fate Line also shows defects, then surely the subject will lose heavily in speculation and gambling. The hand analyst could suggest that such a subject join some organization which might help cure him of this terrible affliction.

Sometimes a subject with a gambler's hand may not be interested in gambling for money, but may have strong gambling instincts in a different sphere. For example, a famous leader of a certain country who had a long Sun finger was known as a political gambler. However, he burnt his fingers when he miscalculated, and was eventually deprived of his office because of a historic scandal. So if you see such a combination, and the subject tells you that he is not interested in gambling for money, question him closely and examine his palms. Try to determine whether he is a gambler in other spheres of life.

It is a very interesting sign if there is an **island** at the beginning of the Sun Line. This means that the subject will engage in a secret love affair. Should the subsequent Sun Line be well-formed, this affair of the heart will help the subject in his career. Thus the interpretation could be that he is attached to an influential or wealthy member of the opposite sex, or vice versa.

Clients sometimes ask whether they will inherit something from their parents or some rich relative. Should a line start from the Mount of Venus, travel up the palm, and run parallel to the Sun Line, the subject will get a legacy from a relative. How do we come to such an interpretation? It is very simple. As we already know, the Mount of Venus stands for the relatives and family of the subject. So such a line, starting from the Mount of Venus and going upwards, is a favourable line. It is a law of hand analysis that all upward lines are favourable. Such an origin from the Mount of Venus will therefore suggest some contact with a family member or relative. However, should a similar line, instead of running parallel to the Sun Line, cut it, then financial loss will occur to the subject. It is also a law of hand analysis that one line should not cut another. In this latter case, the loss will be caused by the relative in question, whoever that may be.

Often clients will go to a hand analyst to find out the outcome of a lawsuit. In fact, there is a famous lawyer in

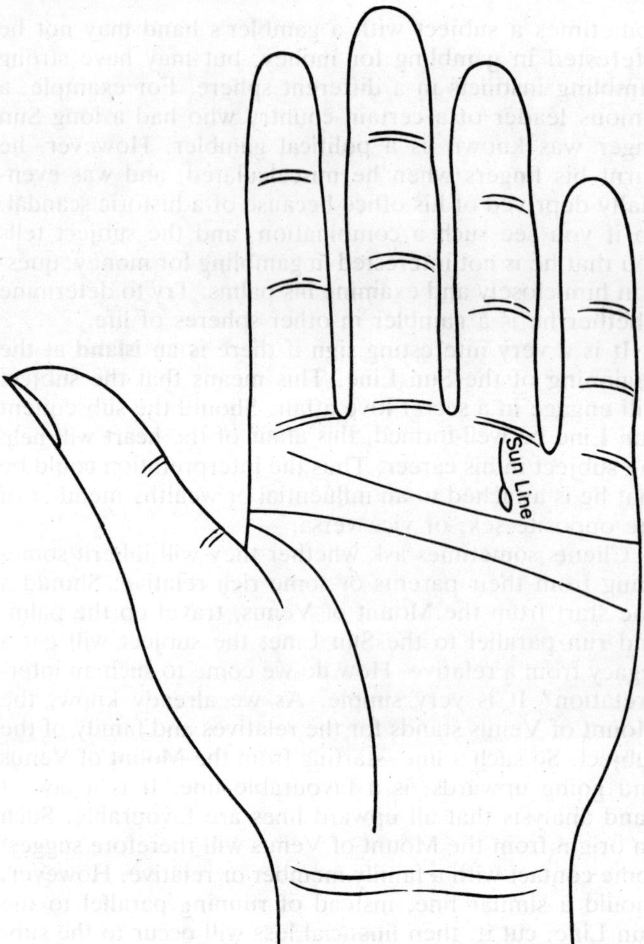

Figure 13-20 An Island at the beginning of the Sun Line shows that the subject may indulge in a secret affair of the heart.

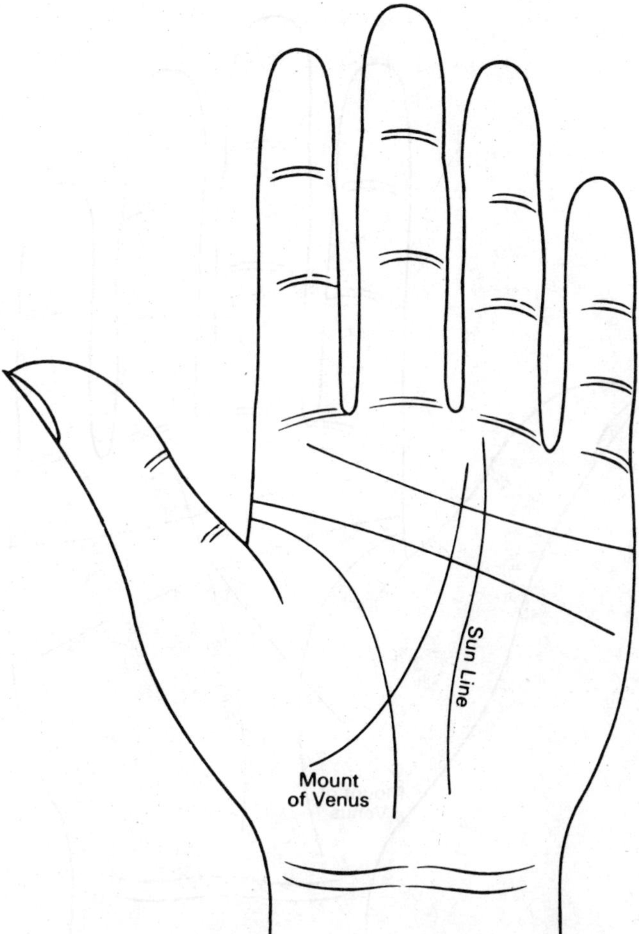

Figure 13-21 An Ascending Line from the Mount of Venus running parallel to the Sun Line. This shows that the subject may get a legacy from a relative.

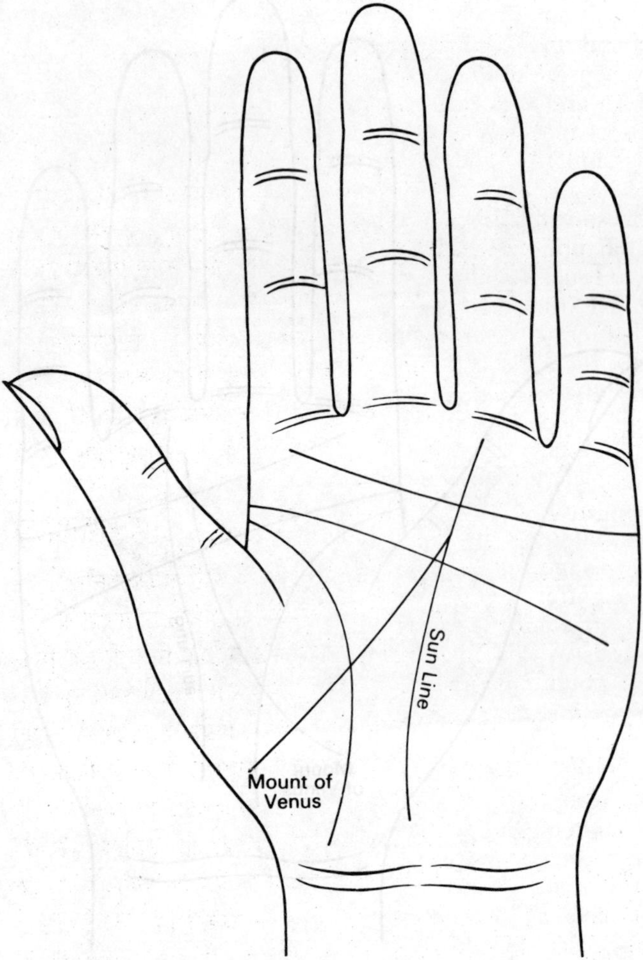

Figure 13-22 An Ascending Line from the Mount of Venus touching the Sun Line shows that money may come to the subject from his own family or relatives.

Malaysia who believes implicitly in the sciences of hand analysis and astrology. He sometimes consults professional hand analysts and astrologers to find out the outcome of a sensational legal suit for one of his important clients. There are indications on the hand which show that the subject may be involved in a lawsuit with a relative. Let us assume that there is an upward branch from the Vitality Line. Let us now suppose that there is an Influence Line starting from the Mount of Venus, cutting this particular upward branch of the Vitality Line, and carrying on to touch the Sun Line. This will reveal a lawsuit with a relative, but since this Influence Line has just touched the Sun Line, the subject will win the suit. This success will be all the more certain if there is a triangle beside the Sun Line at the point of contact, or on the Sun Line itself. However, if the same Influence Line with the same combination cuts the Sun Line, then the subject will lose the case. Even the most brilliant lawyer in the world will not be able to save the subject, who will probably suffer a financial loss. This financial loss will be confirmed if there is an island on the Sun Line just at the point of contact, or just after it. It is a perfectly feasible proposition that in time to come, lawyers with a good knowledge of hand analysis will be able to predict the outcome of a case for their potential clients.

One important point must always be borne in mind. A **hollow palm** will reduce, or in extreme cases, will nullify the effects of a good Sun Line. The hollow section is normally found in the area of the centre of the palm, called the **Plain of Mars.** Such a hollow palm will show a certain lack of push and drive, a lack of resistance, and the subject with allow himself to be pushed around by others. He will have a tendency to accept defeat meekly and be easily discouraged, will tend to indulge in negative thinking, and constantly harbour pessimistic thoughts. Is it any wonder then that eminent hand analysts have said that the effect of a good Sun Line is substantially reduced if

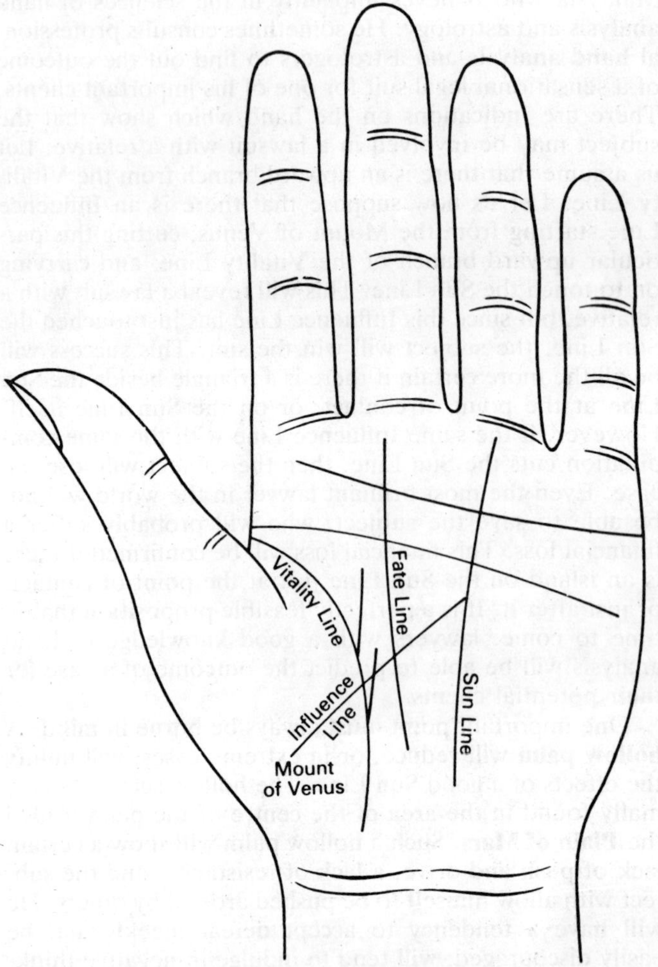

Figure 13-23 An Influence Line from the Mount of Venus cutting an ascending branch of the Vitality Line and touching the Sun Line. This shows success in a lawsuit with a relative.

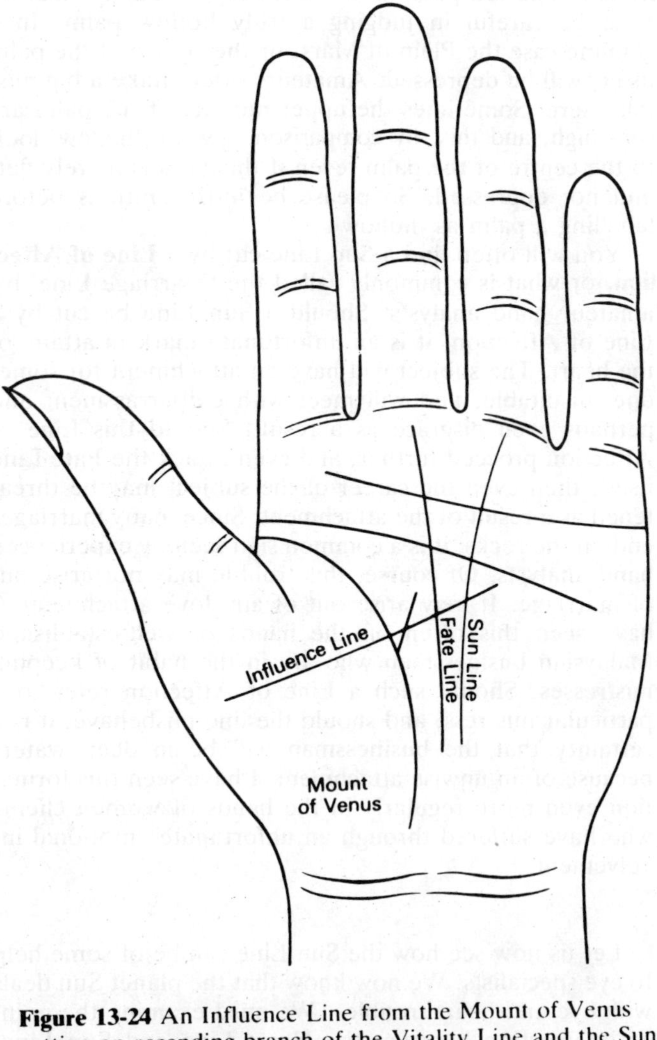

Figure 13-24 An Influence Line from the Mount of Venus cutting an ascending branch of the Vitality Line and the Sun Line. The subject will lose a lawsuit to a relative.

there is a hollow palm in the hands of the subject? But we must be careful in judging a truly hollow palm. In a genuine case the Plain of Mars, or the centre of the palm itself, will be depressed. Amateurs often make a big mistake here. Sometimes the upper mounts of the palm are very high, and this, by comparison, gives a 'hollow' look to the centre of the palm, even if this area is merely flat, and not depressed. So please be most cautious before labelling a palm as 'hollow'.

You will often find a Sun Line cut by a **Line of Affection,** or what is commonly called the 'Marriage Line' by amateur hand analysts. Should a Sun Line be cut by a Line of Affection, it is an unfortunate mark in affairs of the heart. The subject will have an attachment for someone unsuitable, and will meet with embarrassment and perhaps even disgrace as a result. Should this Line of Affection proceed further, and even attack the Fate Line itself, then even the career of the subject may be threatened as a result of the attachment. Since many marriages end on the rocks, it is a common sign seen by experienced hand analysts. Of course, this trouble may not arise out of marriage. It may arise out of any love attachment. I have seen this often on the hands of well-established Malaysian businessmen who are in the habit of keeping mistresses. Should such a Line of Affection refer to a particular mistress, and should the line misbehave, it is a certainty that the businessman will be in deep waters because of an unwise attachment. I have seen this formation even more regularly in the hands of women clients who have suffered through an unfortunate emotional involvement.

Let us now see how the Sun Line can be of some help to eye specialists. We now know that the planet Sun deals with eye and heart troubles. We must examine the point of intersection between the Heart Line and Sun Line.

Should a black dot be seen at this point, the subject will have a tendency towards blindness. Please notice the emphasis on the word black. Eye trouble is also shown by an island on the Sun Line. But an island has got various meanings, such as loss of reputation and loss of money. So how do we find out if this particular island refers to eye trouble rather than to loss of reputation? Examine the Vitality Line, and if at the corresponding age this line is also defective, e.g. having an island on it as well, the subject will undoubtedly tend to suffer from some eye trouble at that particular age. There are various other ways in which eye trouble, including cataracts, can be detected by a good hand analyst. But this is outside the scope of a book intended for beginners, and to whet the appetites of healthy sceptics.

I have examined the hands of blind people, and I have confirmed unfavourable marks on the Sun Line, indicative of eye trouble. Sometimes these unfavourable signs were found on the Line of Mentality as well. The fact that a really good analyst can forecast eye trouble several years ahead of time will give the subject a fighting chance to minimize the affliction, or perhaps, by a stroke of very good fortune, avoid it altogether. For those who believe in Naturopathy or Nature Cure, I can recommend an excellent book called *Better Sight Without Glasses* by Harry Benjamin.[1] Should you find a formation on the Sun Line indicative of possible eye trouble, please read this book and perhaps you will be able to nip the trouble in the bud by practising preventive medicine. Of course, it is also most important to see a really good eye specialist. Harry Benjamin has also written an excellent book called *Everybody's Guide to Nature Cure*.[2] In this book he has a

---

[1] Benjamin, Harry: *Better Sight Without Glasses*, Thorsons Publishers, Wellingborough, England, 1979.

[2] Benjamin, Harry: *Everybody's Guide to Nature Cure*, Thorsons Publishers, Wellingborough, England, 1975.

good section on 'Diseases of the Eye'. This is worth reading and would be of great help to a subject likely to suffer from eye trouble. There are specific exercises in Yoga which are most beneficial for eye trouble. But Yoga exercises must only be done under expert supervision.

The **calculation of age** on the Sun Line is done in exactly the same way as that for the Fate Line. A good hand analyst will make it a point of honour always to consult both lines when studying aspects such as loss of money, reputation, business partnership, and the outcome of court cases.

There are countless combinations of the Sun Line, but the important thing is to grasp the principles. The combinations can then be worked out and understood fairly easily. The Sun Line is definitely an important line. As long as the hand analyst does not misunderstand the functions of the Sun Line, a close study of this wonderful line will give a deep insight into your potential for success and happiness.

Chapter Fourteen

Health and Business Prospects as Revealed by the Line of Health or Mercury Line

Doctors and scientists will be studying the **Line of Health** intensively in the future. The author has been gratified to note that more and more doctors are becoming open minded about hand analysis. It is a fact that some years ago, the government of Kerala State in India announced the inauguration of a unique scheme under which research was to be carried out in the diagnosis of diseases by hand analysis at the Medical College Hospital at Trivandrum. The training camp was for a period of one month for the hand analyst-doctors. The State Health Minister, Mr. Balakrishnan, who declared open this camp, stated later that the research had been successful, and that the original research period of six months allowed to the hand analyst-cum-physician had therefore been extended by another six months. The Health Minister further stated that the hospital doctors were satisfied that diseases could be accurately diagnosed by studying the lines of the palm. It is significant that a whole team of doctors belonging to the topmost medical college hospital of the state of Kerala researched for six months in a new area considered worthy of their investigation, and having found some success, had asked for an extension to their period of research.

On 2 February 1977, I gave a lecture on 'Medical Hand Analysis' at the Institute of Medical Research (I.M.R.) in Kuala Lumpur, which is considered one of the foremost in the world as regards research in tropical medicine. The lecture[1] was in connection with the Eighteenth I.M.R. Monthly Scientific Meeting. The lecture was well received and an abstract of the talk was requested by one of the doctors present. This seems to indicate that there is a welcome wind of change, and more and more scientists are opening their minds to new disciplines and new ideas. Mankind in general, and patients in particular, will be the gainers.

Let us now study the **Line of Mercury** in some detail. The Mercury Line is also called the Health Line, Line of Liver, or Line of Hepatica. Some authorities say it starts from the Mount of Mercury and runs downwards to the Mount of Moon. The line reflects the condition of the digestive system, the workings of the liver, and it further reveals the presence of various maladies and conditions which arise from the malfunctioning of these important organs. Should you see defects in other parts of the hand, a poor Line of Mercury will often be the cause. It is common knowledge that a good, sound digestive system is vital to robust health. Many diseases of mankind would make a hasty exit should the digestive system be in perfect condition, and the bile flow normally. In many cases, once the digestive system works properly and the bile flows normally, the subject is restored to health. Since good health is normally necessary for business success, a well-formed, favourable Line of Mercury could well be an asset.

Should defects be shown in the Line of Mentality, the Line of Mercury could furnish an explanation. This is because the condition of the stomach and liver influences

[1] I wrote two articles on *Medical Hand Analysis* for the Malaysian Medical Association (M.M.A.), which appeared in the M.M.A.'s newsletter *Berita MMA*. (July/August and Sept/Oct 1976 issues.) Both articles were well received by Malaysian doctors.

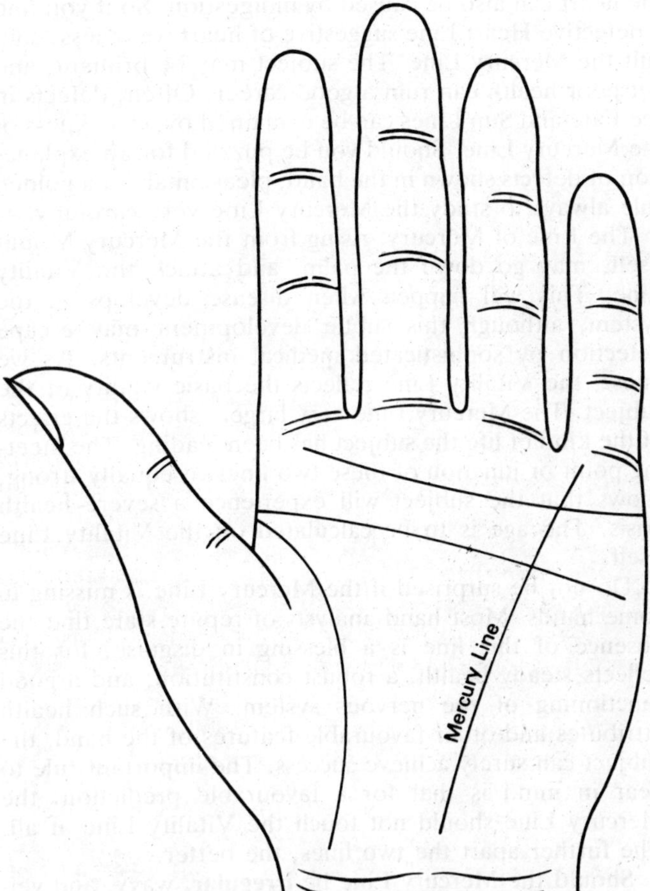

Figure 14-1 A deep, well-formed Line of Mercury

the health of the brain itself. Functional disturbances of the heart can also be caused by indigestion. So if you find a defective Heart Line suggestive of heart weakness, consult the Mercury Line. The subject may be brilliant, and yet poor health can ruin a good career. Often, defects in the Fate and Sun Lines can be explained by a weakness of the Mercury Line. Should you be puzzled for an explanation of defects shown in the hand, please make it a golden rule always to study the Mercury Line very carefully.

The Line of Mercury, rising from the Mercury Mount itself, may go down the palm, and attack the Vitality Line. This will happen when disease develops in the system, although this subtle development may escape detection by sophisticated medical instruments. As we know, the Vitality Line reflects the basic vitality of the subject. The Mercury Line very largely shows the effects of the kind of life the subject has been leading. The meeting point or junction of these two lines, if equally strong, shows that the subject will experience a severe health crisis. The age is to be calculated on the Vitality Line itself.

Do not be surprised if the Mercury Line is missing in some hands. Most hand analysts of repute state that the absence of this line is a blessing in disguise, for this reflects steady health, a robust constitution, and a good functioning of the nervous system. With such health attributes and other favourable features of the hand, the subject can surely achieve success. The important rule to bear in mind is that for a favourable prediction, the Mercury Line should not touch the Vitality Line at all. The further apart the two lines, the better.

Should the Mercury Line be **irregular,** wavy, and yellow in colour, the subject will have a very strong tendency to suffer from biliousness and liver complaints.

Sometimes you will find the Mercury Line **heavily marked** and traced from the Line of Mentality downwards towards the Vitality Line. This will reveal that the

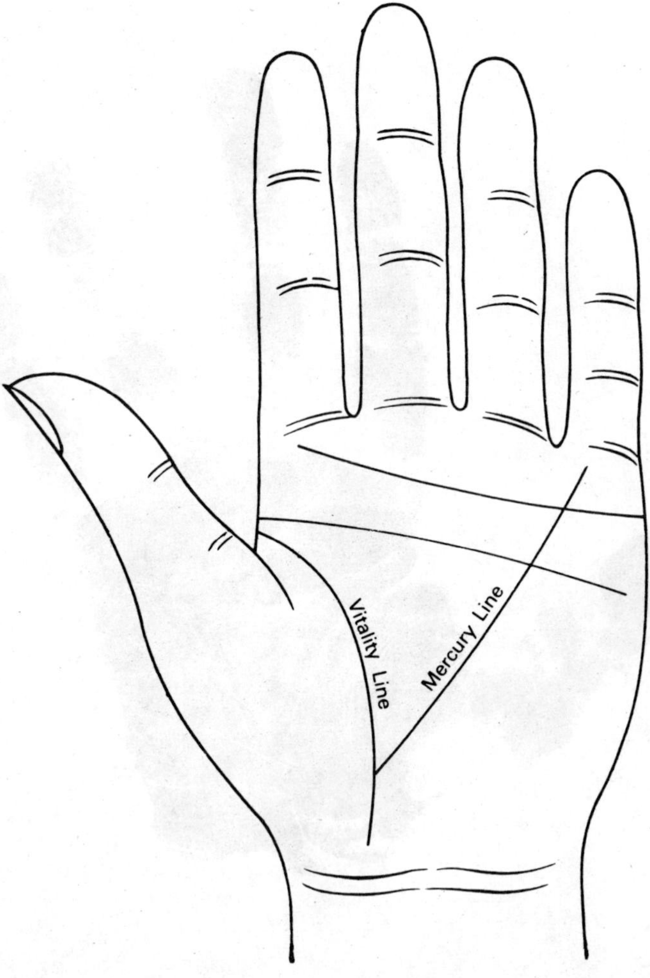

Figure 14-2 The Mercury Line touching the Vitality Line

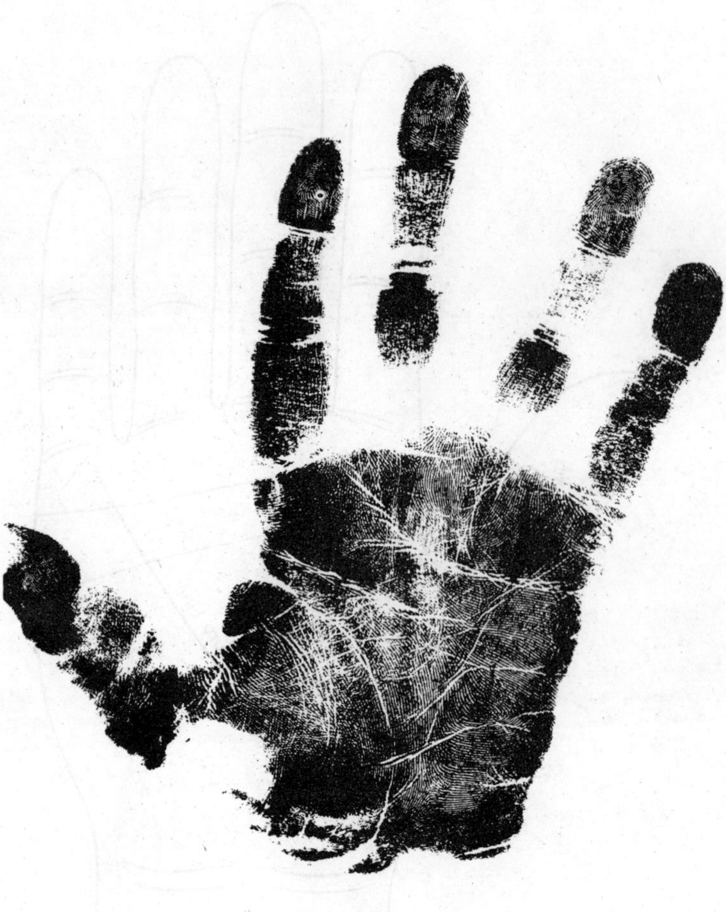

Figure 14-3 The right handprint of a polio victim. Notice the badly formed Lines of Mercury, Mentality and Vitality.

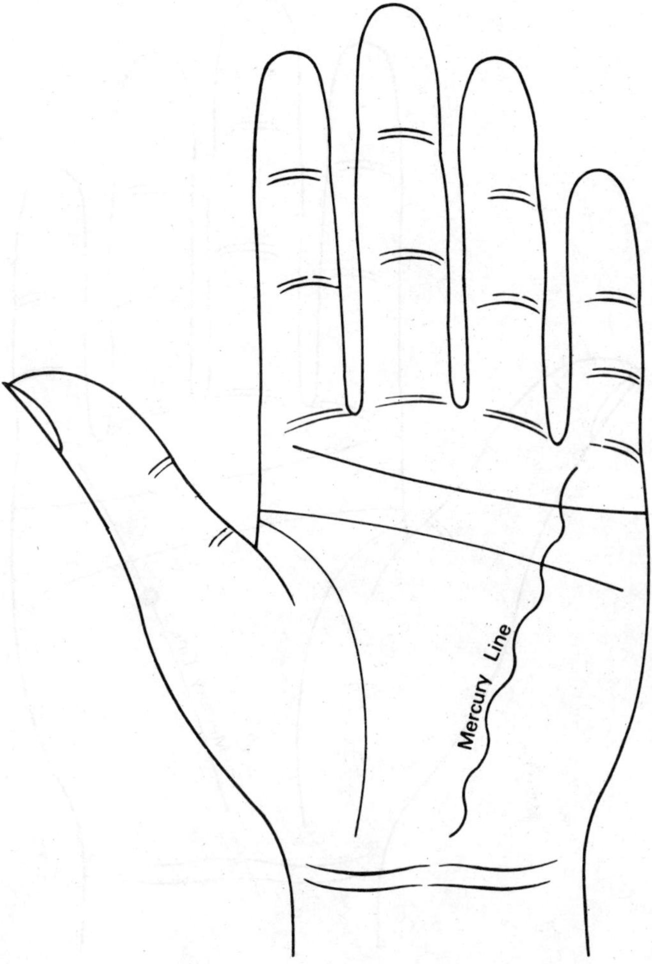

Figure 14-4 A wavy, twisted Line of Mercury

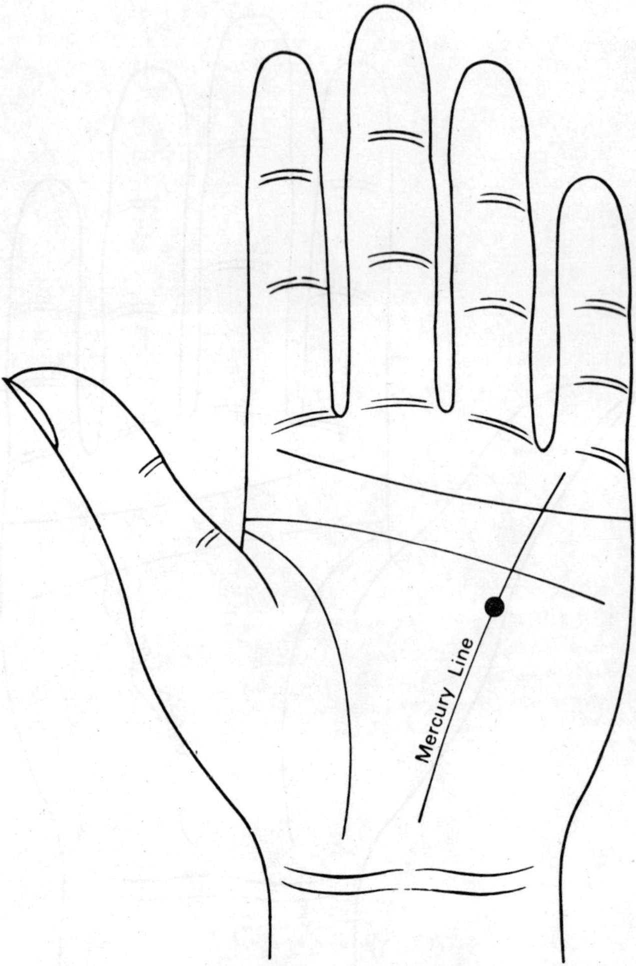

Figure 14-5 A Dot on the Mercury Line

nervous system has been overstrained, so the subject should guard his health with a watchful eye.

Rheumatic fever is shown by **red spots** or **dots** on the Mercury Line. Often you will find the line connected with the Heart Line and stopped by the Heart Line itself. This is a confirmatory indication of heart trouble.

There is yet another way in which the Mercury Line can show heart disease. This is shown when it is **irregular** in its course, with **red** or **bluish spots** on the line.

Sometimes, you will find a branch of the Mercury Line itself touching the Vitality Line. This is also unfavourable, and it foreshadows a severe illness at the age where the two lines meet. Calculate the age on the Vitality Line itself. The warning of a severe illness may help the subject to escape the worst results.

A **chained** Line of Mercury will sometimes be found on examination of this line. The chain will be formed of short loops. This indicates a serious health defect. The subject will have a strong tendency to suffer from inflammation of the gall duct, gall stones, cirrhosis of the liver, and other liver difficulties. Since mind and body are interrelated, the subject having this formation will also suffer from the consequent mental depression and slothfulness. Be very careful not to confuse islands on the Mercury Line with a chained formation. Should the Mercury Line be truly chained, the subject will indulge in negative thinking, become nervous and suspicious, and will find no joy in living. With all these host of troubles, the subject will have a confused brain, lack foresight and mental strength. Hence, if he is a businessman, he will find the going pretty tough with all these negative attributes to handicap him. Life will be an arduous, uphill struggle.

You will frequently find an **island** on the Mercury Line. This shows a period of delicate health during its presence. The island is a consequence. The cause could be due to health trouble associated with the liver, stomach, appendix, or the intestines. It might also be caused by weakness

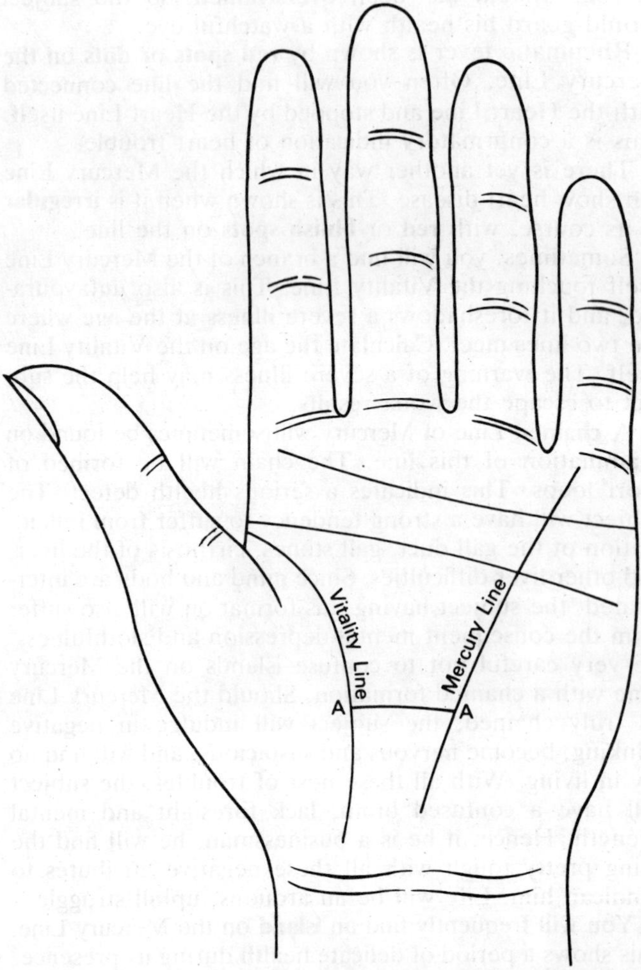

Figure 14-6 A branch (A-A) from the Mercury Line touching the Vitality Line

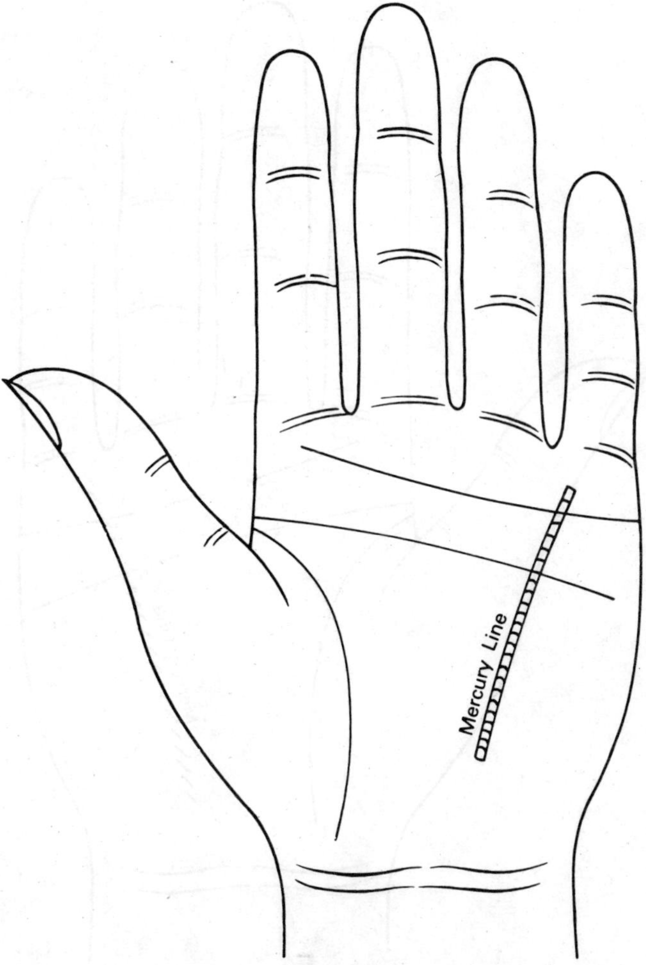

Figure 14-7 A chained Line of Mercury

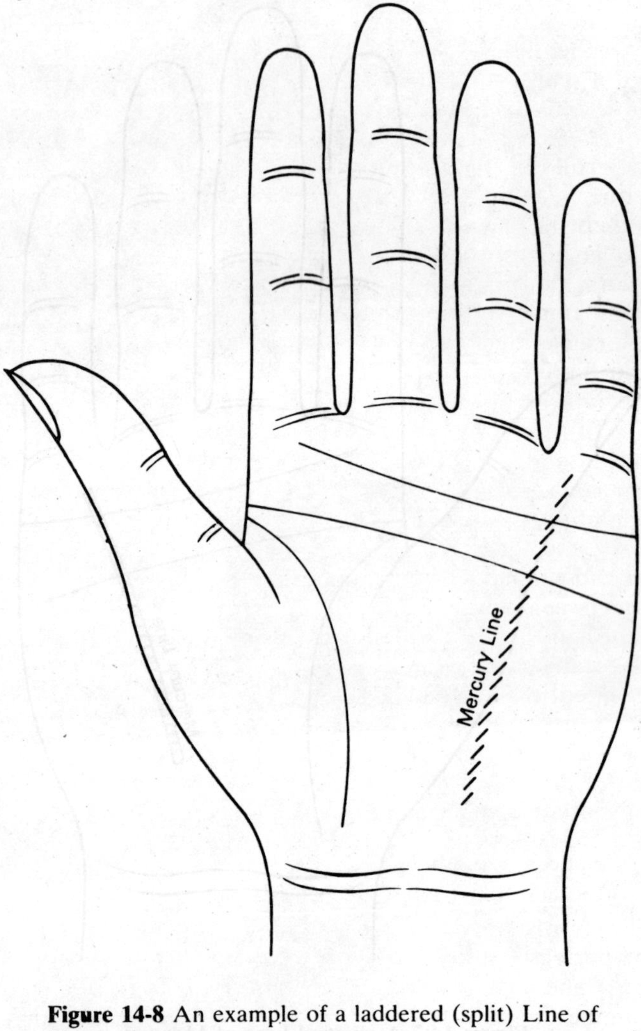

Figure 14-8 An example of a laddered (split) Line of Mercury

of the heart or some other organ. The technique to find out the cause of the island is to examine the mounts and the other lines of the hand. Please always bear in mind that a really good hand analyst is an occult detective. He is the Sherlock Holmes of the hand. Whenever you find defects and weaknesses in the hand, always ask the most powerful question in the English language: WHY? There is one peculiar fact about the Mercury Line that should be kept in view: the harmful effect of the island on this line is not always restricted to stomach and liver disorders, but extends to other types of illnesses. A single island must be interpreted as a sign of delicate health. The cause must be analysed by examining other parts of both hands.

The Line of Mercury with an island near but above the Line of Mentality shows trouble with the nose and throat, and a tendency towards catarrh. The Line of Mercury with an island stretching below and above the Line of Mentality is a sure mark of delicacy and danger from the chest and lungs, especially when the **nails** are long, almond-shaped, narrow and fluted. This combination reveals a general inflammation of the nerves. A really good hand analyst will always include the nails as a very important part of the examination. Chest specialists will be aided in their diagnosis by a close study of the Mercury Line for islanded formations. Let us use every scientific, reliable technique to give a sharp, precise diagnosis in that noble art and science — Healing.

Another combination to be found is that of two, three or more islands, well-formed or fairly large, on the Mercury Line. Sometimes practically the entire Mercury Line may be islanded. This is surely an indication of extreme delicacy of the throat and lungs. Even if the islands are not perfectly formed, they will be very reliable indications. The next step for a conscientious hand analyst is to examine the nails at once. Examine them to see whether they tend to have a bulbous condition. Finally, examine

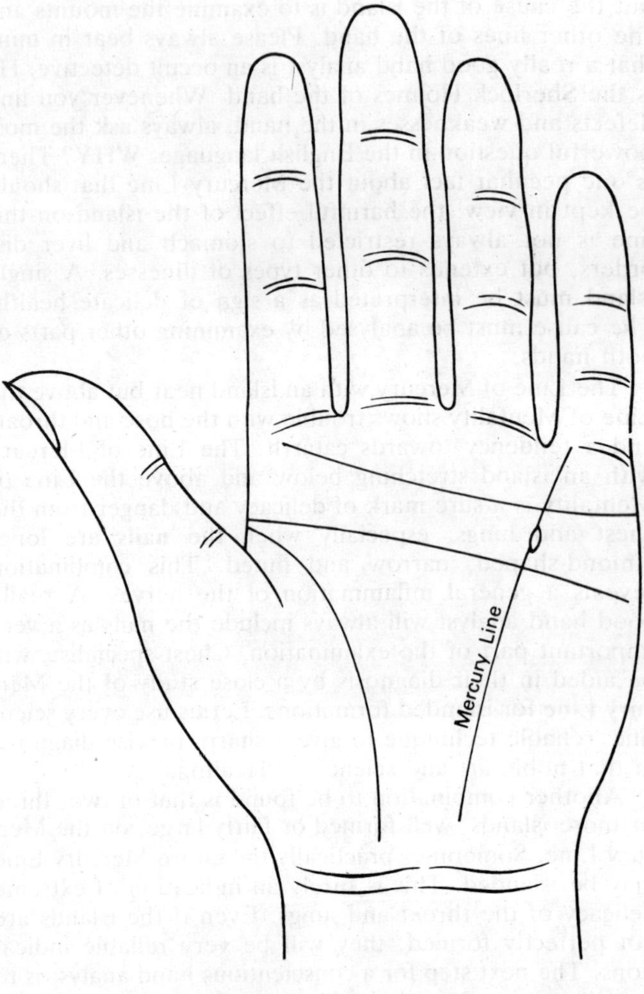

Figure 14-9 An Island on the Line of Mercury

the upper Mount of Mars to see whether it is grilled or crossbarred. Should these confirmatory markings be present as well, this is a really strong case. The hand analyst should suggest that the subject go to a good chest specialist for a check-up. If, in addition, an island is seen on the Mount of Jupiter, the subject must take great precautions to avoid any exposure, possibly leading to the development of consumption, bronchitis, pneumonia, or any delicacy of the throat, bronchia or lungs. Subjects with such an unhealthy combination may be weak at business dealings because of shaky health. However, even if they are not having lean times in the business sphere, they will be bankrupt in health. Other confirmatory indications can show bankruptcy or weak financial circumstances — the subject will be in such a condition if the Mercury Line is badly islanded, the Fate Line badly formed, with repeated crossbars attacking it, the Sun Line absent or severely afflicted, and the Upper Mounts of Mercury, Sun, Saturn and Jupiter flat or depressed.

Now we come to a sign which you will find many times on the hands of women. I am referring to a **Star** seen on the Line of Mercury in a women's hand. This is an indication of some kind of female trouble, but always look for confirmatory indications. With other confirmatory indications, this Star could be an indication of sterility. Often the Star will be found where the Mercury Line meets the Line of Mentality, but even if the Star is merely somewhere around this region, it will still give the same indication. In a fair number of cases, I have found women with such a star to be sterile; in a few cases, I found that they had finally given birth after being married for periods from nine to twelve years, and after having consulted the best gynaecologists. In other cases, women with this mark told me that they conceived easily, but had a difficult time during childbirth. I came across one case which intrigued me: a client with this star told me that she had become pregnant easily, had had a normal delivery, but strangely

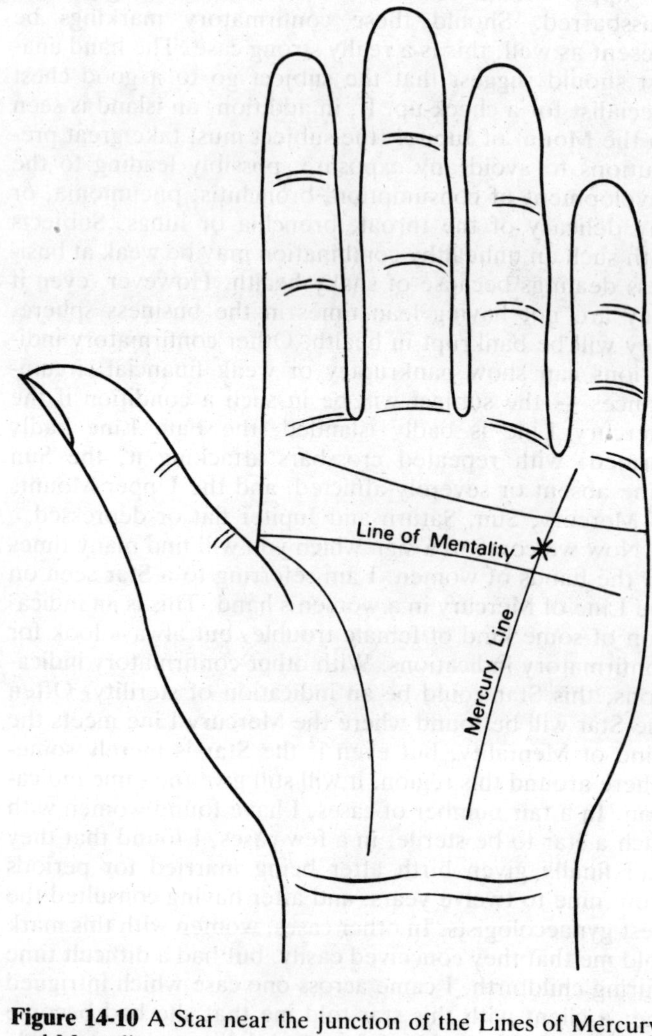

Figure 14-10 A Star near the junction of the Lines of Mercury and Mentality

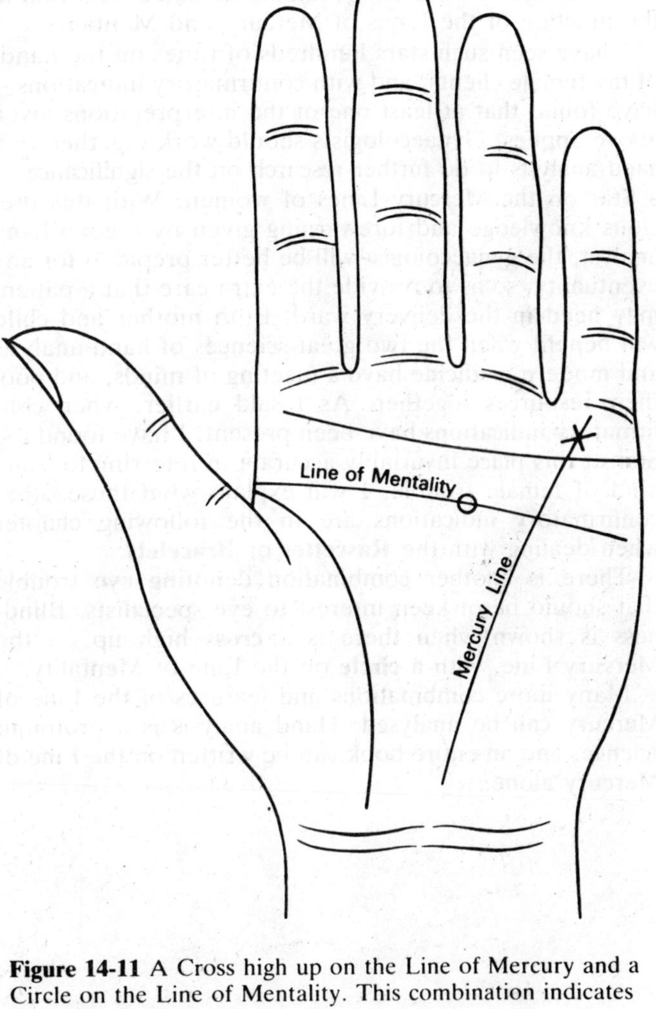

Figure 14-11 A Cross high up on the Line of Mercury and a Circle on the Line of Mentality. This combination indicates blindness.

enough, had developed very severe complications afterwards, and in fact had almost died. She had a clear Star at the junction of the Lines of Mercury and Mentality.

I have seen such stars hundreds of times on the hands of my female clients, and with confirmatory indications, I have found that at least one of the interpretations given above applies. Gynaecologists should work together with hand analysts to do further research on the significance of a Star on the Mercury Lines of women. With this precious knowledge and forewarning given by a good hand analyst, the gynaecologist will be better prepared for any eventuality, so as to provide the extra care that a patient may need in the delivery ward. Both mother and child will benefit when the two great sciences of hand analysis and modern medicine have a meeting of minds, and pool their resources together. As I said earlier, when confirmatory indications have been present, I have found the Star at this place invariably accurate in referring to some kind of female trouble. I will explain what these other confirmatory indications are in the following chapter when dealing with the **Rascettes** or **Bracelets.**

There is another combination denoting eye trouble that should be of keen interest to eye specialists. Blindness is shown when there is a **cross** high up on the Mercury Line, with a **circle** on the Line of Mentality.

Many more combinations and features of the Line of Mercury can be analysed. Hand analysis is a profound science, and an entire book can be written on the Line of Mercury alone.

Chapter Fifteen

The Minor Lines
The Girdle of Venus, Medical Stigmata, Ring of Saturn, Mystic Cross, Line of Mars, Ring of Solomon, Line of Intuition, Via Lascivia, Quadrangle, and the Rascettes or Bracelets

Why Every Husband Should Know the Significance of the Girdle of Venus on His Wife's Hands

There are some lines in the palm, commonly called the **Minor Lines,** which are not always found in every hand. Since when present they are always found in the same place, they can't be regarded as chance lines. These lines are in a category by themselves. The Minor Lines are the Girdle of Venus, the Medical Stigmata, Ring of Saturn, Mystic Cross, Line of Mars, Ring of Solomon, Line of Intuition, Via Lascivia, the Quadrangle, and the Rascettes or Bracelets. With regard to the Minor Lines, we must always bear in mind that the entire hand has to be studied before a correct interpretation can be given as to their significance. At the risk of repetition, we must know that this is the golden rule in scientific hand analysis.

The Girdle of Venus

This line is very frequently found in the hands of women. I have seldom found it in the hands of men. It generally starts from between the first and second fingers (Jupiter and Saturn fingers) and curves around to end between the

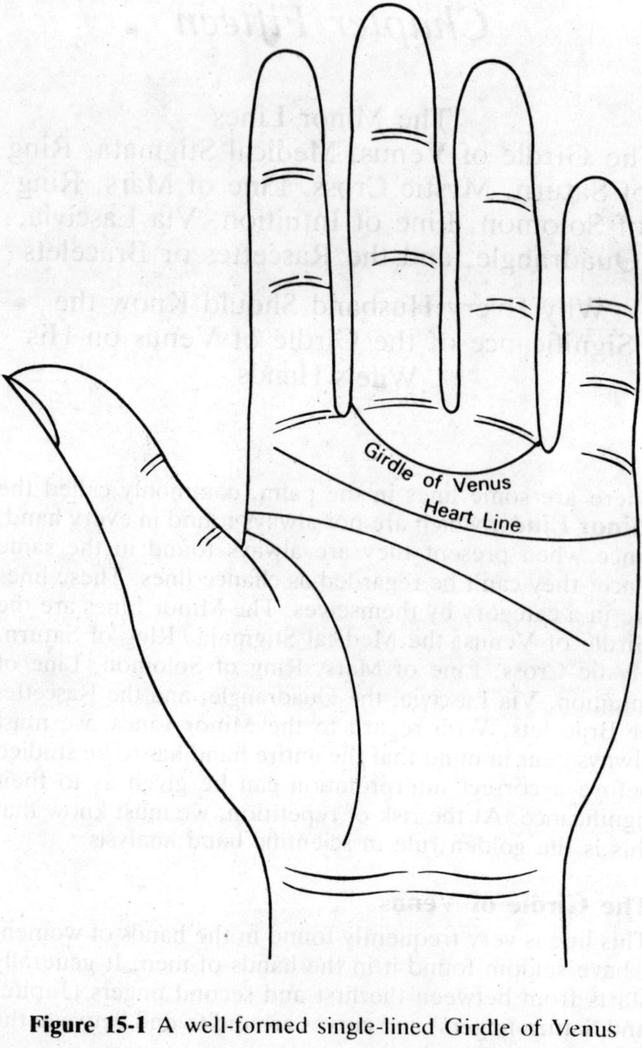

Figure 15-1 A well-formed single-lined Girdle of Venus

second and third fingers (Saturn and Sun fingers) and occasionally between the third and fourth fingers (Sun and Mercury fingers). The line curves like an arc. It is therefore parallel to the Line of Heart.

This is a very much misunderstood line. The older hand analysts were not very strong in the realm of logic, and jumped to the conclusion that this line always symbolizes coquetry and sexual licence. They regarded it as an evil mark. It is true that if the line is badly formed or fragmented, it is an unfavourable mark; but the Girdle of Venus need not necessarily mean sexual licence, especially if it is well-formed and if the other features of the hand are favourable.

Here is a very important rule when interpreting this particular sign. Fit the line to the subject, not the subject to the line. In other words, see the type of hand, and the character of the subject on whose hand or hands the line is found — *then* try to analyse the significance of the line. Do not take the line in isolation, for then it will be interpreted out of context. See the mounts, the other lines, the shape of the fingers, the strength of the thumb, and then pass judgement on the Girdle of Venus. The most important mount to study in connection with this line is the **Mount of Venus.**

You will often find the line badly fragmented, and having two or three lines parallel to it. This is certainly unfavourable, for it means that the subject will suffer humiliation, embarrassment and have no peace of mind in his relationships with the opposite sex. The subject may also be deprived of material assets or possessions by an unscrupulous lover. Such a formation is always an indication of nervousness, and if the fragmentation is very clearly marked, the Line of Mentality weak and the thumbs deficient, the subject may even tend to be hysterical. When such an unfavourable Girdle of Venus is found on the hand, the subject should be advised to marry later in life, preferably after the age of thirty or thereabouts.

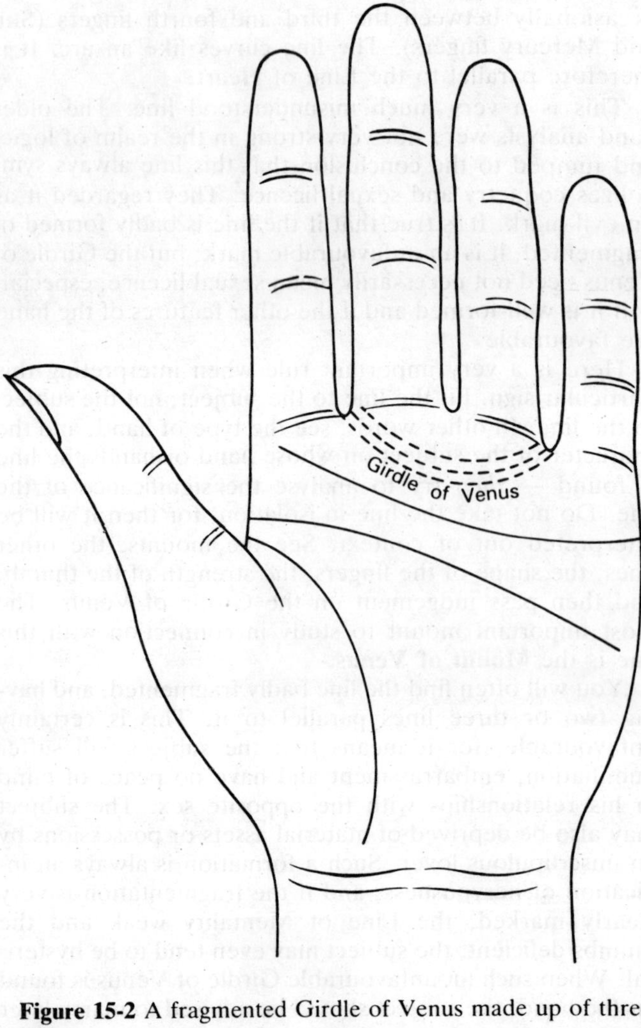

Figure 15-2 A fragmented Girdle of Venus made up of three layers

This is because the effect of the Girdle of Venus is minimized or subdued after the age of thirty. Such subjects cannot afford the luxury of a love marriage. They should consult a brilliant hand analyst or astrologer, and check the hands of their spouse-to-be for marriage compatibility if they wish to have a fighting chance of a reasonably happy marriage. Thousands of times I have seen great sorrow in the love lives of subjects having such a badly formed Girdle of Venus. These indications are heightened if there is a double or triple Girdle of Venus. Such an unfavourable indication will make the subject moody, whimsical, and temperamental by nature, and it could be one reason why the married or love life will not be smooth.

Should the Girdle of Venus cut the Marriage Line or Line of Affection, the subject's married life will be marred or disturbed because of his difficult temperament. This subject will find it difficult to have a balanced approach towards matters of love and affection. It is even worse if there is a well-formed **island** in the body of the Girdle of Venus, as this indicates that the subject will tend to be sexually promiscuous. This will be all the more certain if the Mount of Venus is very much elevated, red in colour, and badly grilled. It will be worse still if there are repeated islands in the body of the Girdle of Venus.

However, the Girdle of Venus has a good side to it. When it is a single well-formed line, the subject will have a good aesthetic judgement, be sensitive by nature, and capable of a healthy response to the opposite sex. However, he will still tend to be flirtatious and indiscreet, but will not be likely to come to any great harm as a result of these tendencies.

If the Line of Mentality is sloping and well-formed, together with a favourable Girdle of Venus, the subject will have an interest in aesthetic pursuits, as well as a talent for literary work. Such a formation is frequently seen on the hands of authors of repute.

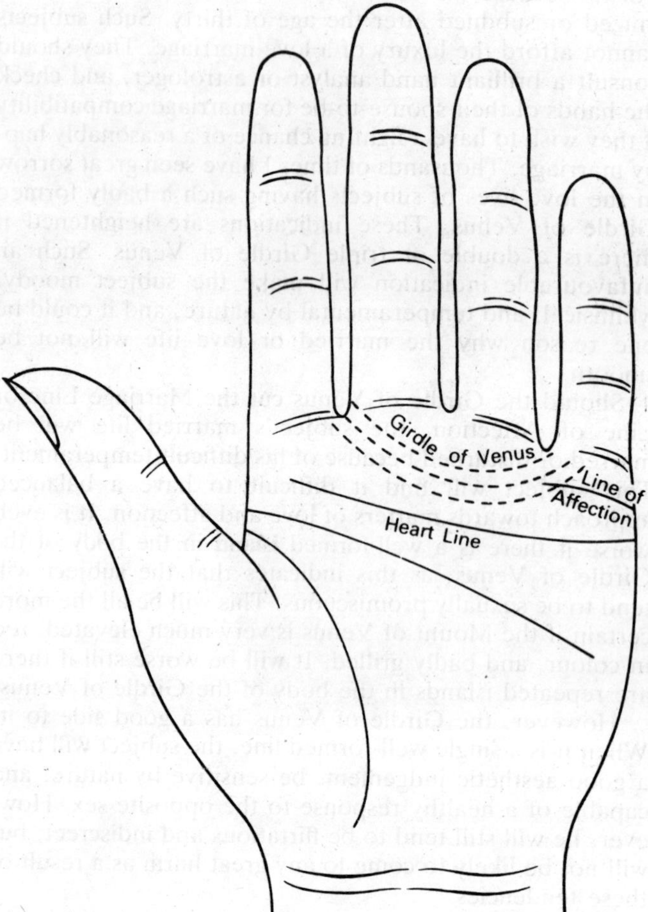

Figure 15-3 The Girdle of Venus cutting the Marriage Line or Line of Affection

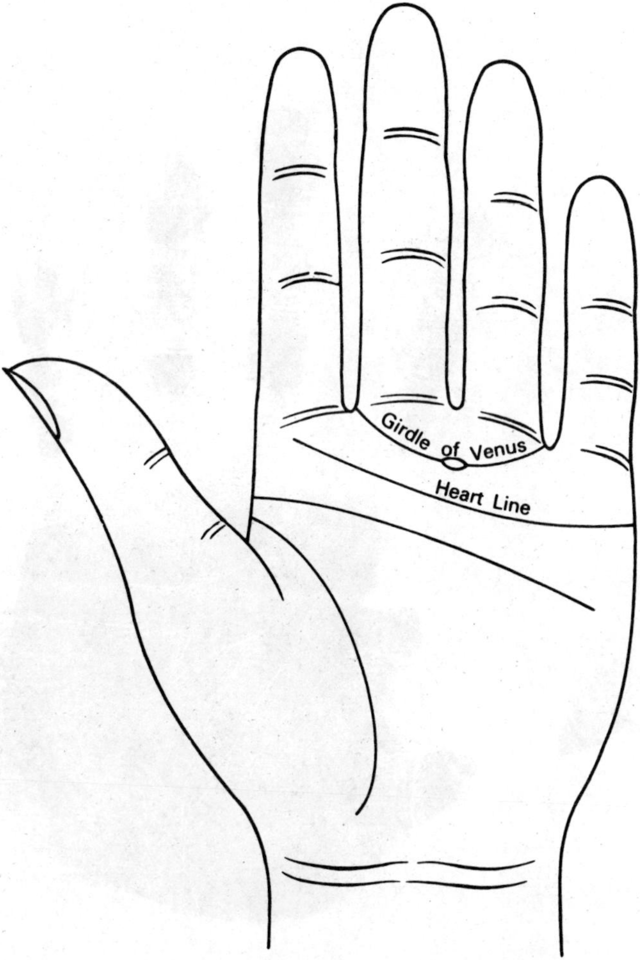

Figure 15-4 An Island in the body of the Girdle of Venus

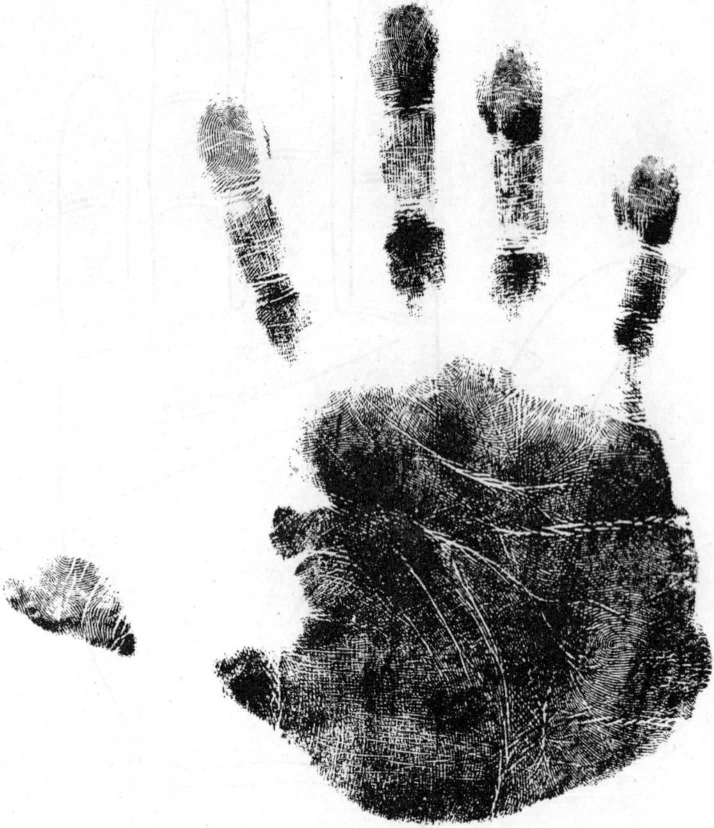

Figure 15-5 A handprint showing Islands in the body of the Girdle of Venus. Notice also the abnormally short Heart Line.

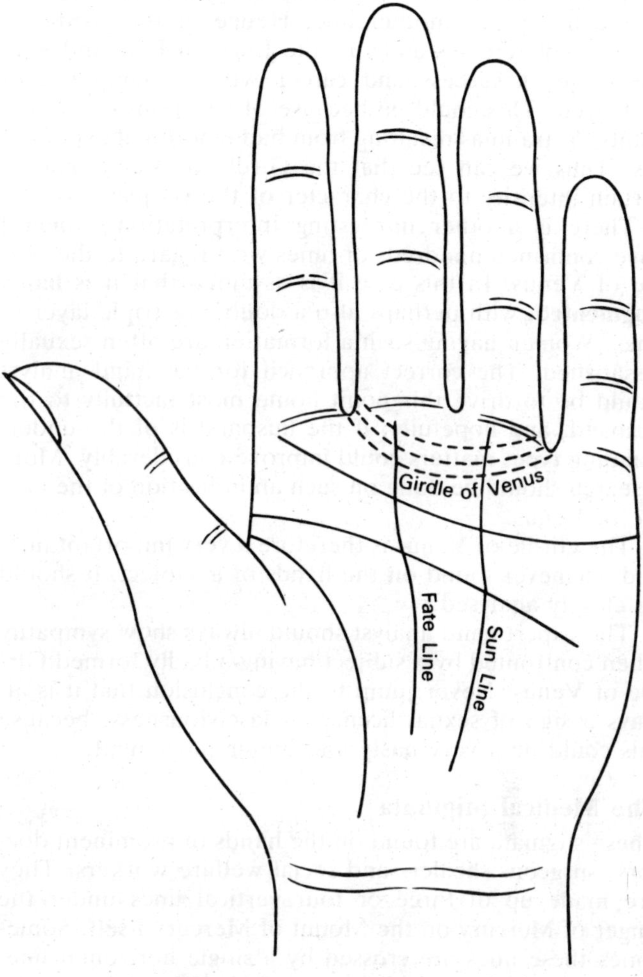

Figure 15-6 A fragmented Girdle of Venus cutting the Fate and Sun Lines

It is a rule of scientific hand analysis that one line should never cut another line. Hence, if the Girdle of Venus badly crosses and cuts the Lines of Fate and Sun, the subject's success and career will be hampered or destroyed. This could be because of irresponsible sexual habits, or traumas resulting from bad emotional experiences. Thus we can see that the Girdle of Venus adds a certain intensity to the character of the subject.

There is another interesting interpretation, which I have confirmed hundreds of times with regard to the Girdle of Venus. In this case it is assumed that it is **badly fragmented,** with perhaps also a double or triple layer of lines. Women having such a formation are often sexually dissatisfied. The correct approach for the hand analyst would be to drive this point home most tactfully to the husband, and hopefully, if the husband is of the understanding type, matters could improve considerably. More research should be done on such an indication of the Girdle of Venus.

The Girdle of Venus is therefore a very important line, and whenever found on the hands of a subject, it should be closely analysed.

The expert hand analyst should always show sympathy when confronted by a subject having a badly formed Girdle of Venus. Never jump to the conclusion that it is always a sign of sexual licence or lasciviousness, because this could be a very hasty and unfair judgement.

The Medical Stigmata

These stigmata are found on the hands of prominent doctors, surgeons, healers and social welfare workers. They are made up of three or four vertical lines under the finger of Mercury on the Mount of Mercury itself. Sometimes these lines are crossed by a single horizontal line. These lines are sometimes called the Good Samaritan lines. They show a latent aptitude for Medicine, or some form of healing. If the Medical Stigmata are well formed

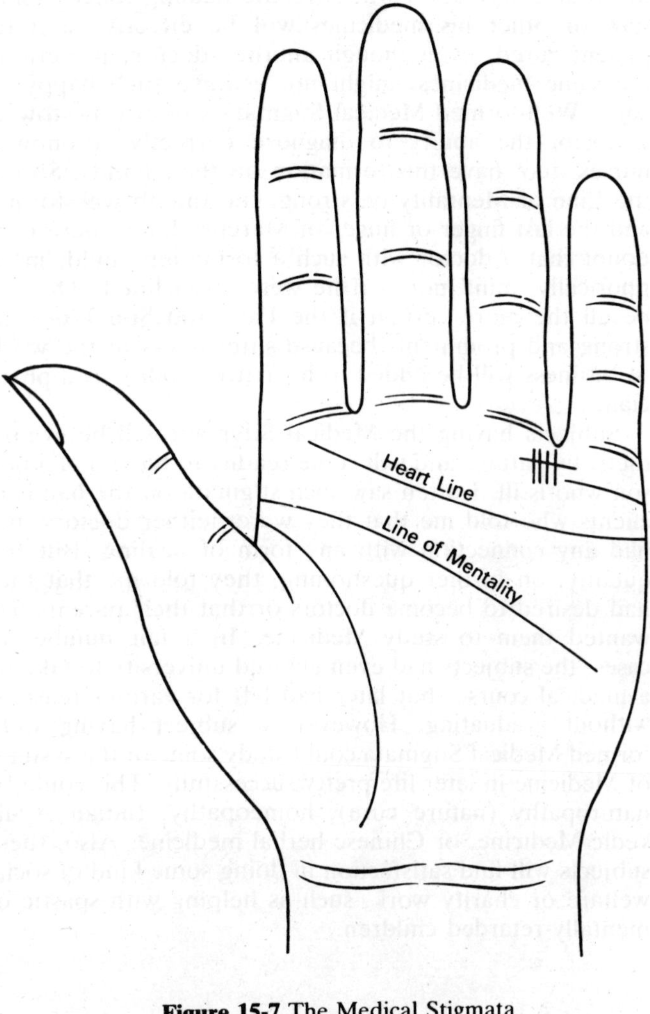

Figure 15-7 The Medical Stigmata

on both hands, and bright and clear, a doctor with such a favourable formation will have the healing touch: somehow or other his medicines will be effective and the patient cured, even though another doctor, prescribing the same medicines, might not achieve such happy results. Well-formed Medical Stigmata will also bestow on a doctor the ability to diagnose correctly. Prominent nurses, too, have this formation on their hands. Should the Line of Mentality be strong, the thumb well-formed and the last finger or finger of Mercury long, there is no doubt that a doctor with such a formation could, metaphorically, mint money if he were so inclined. This will be all the more certain if the Fate and Sun Lines are strong and prominent, because shrewdness in the world of business will be added to his native ability as a physician.

Subjects having the Medical Stigmata will be sympathetic by nature, and will come readily to the aid of a person who is ill. I often saw such stigmata on the hands of clients who told me that they were neither doctors, nor had any connection with any form of healing. But frequently, on further questioning, they told me that they had desired to become doctors or that their parents had wanted them to study Medicine. In a fair number of cases, the subjects had even entered university to take up a medical course, but later had left for various reasons, without graduating. However, a subject having well-formed Medical Stigmata could study some of the systems of Medicine in later life pretty successfully. This could be naturopathy (nature cure), homeopathy, Indian Ayurvedic Medicine, or Chinese herbal medicine. Also, these subjects will find satisfaction in doing some kind of social welfare or charity work, such as helping with spastic or mentally-retarded children.

The Mystic Cross

This is a clear-cut cross found in the Quadrangle between the Line of Mentality and Heart Line. Generally, it is found beneath the middle finger and below the Mount of Saturn. It should be well marked and bold. When thus formed, the subject will be very interested in mysticism, and will have the makings of a great occultist or seer of repute. With other good indications, such as a powerful Line of Mentality, a strong thumb, and firm, elastic palms, he can attain a very high standard in the art of analysing the future. Famous hand analysts and astrologers have such markings on their hands.

Another indication of such a mark is that the subject will suddenly become famous. One hand analyst has a very well-marked Mystic Cross in his hands: from being an unknown teacher, he became a world-famous hand analyst in the middle part of his life. He had always been interested in occult sciences, but pursued this interest seriously only a few years before the age of thirty-five. Should the Mystic Cross be ill-defined or small, the subject will have a longing to know more about the occult sciences but will probably not put in sufficient effort to reach a high standard.

The Ring of Saturn

This is a rare mark, which I have seen only about fifteen times so far in my professional career as a hand analyst. It is found at the base of the second finger, forming a half-circle in the hand. The Ring of Saturn is a destructive mark, because it prevents a smooth exit of the Vital Current from the Fate Line to the finger of Saturn. Thus, it acts as a sort of barrier to the Fate Line.

The Ring of Saturn weakens the Mount of Saturn. It is an unfavourable marking, especially if the ring is completely formed beneath the base of the middle or Saturn finger, thus making a perfect half-circle. Its presence indicates that the subject may have a tendency to jump from

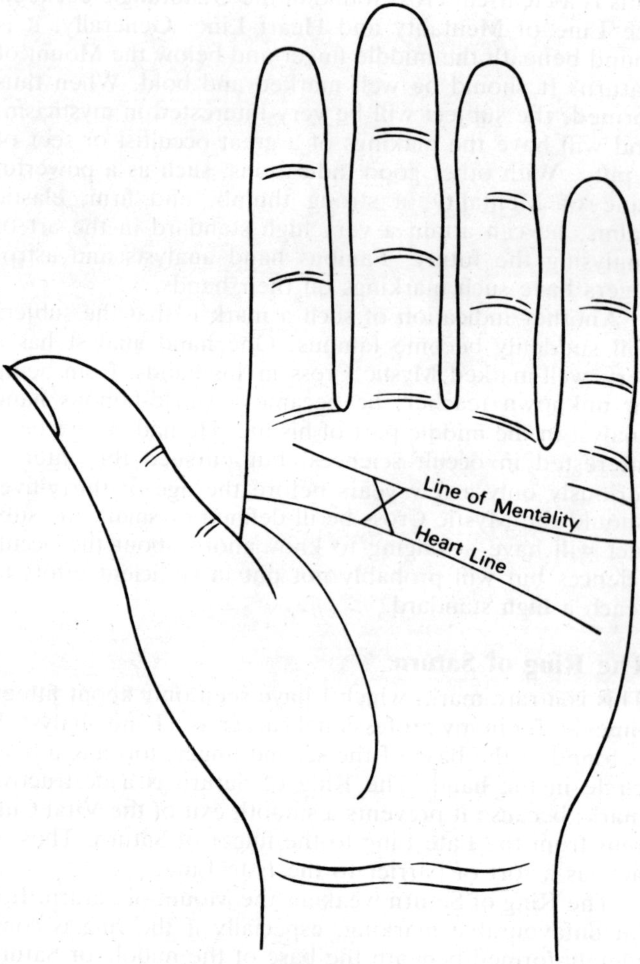

Figure 15-8 The Mystic Cross

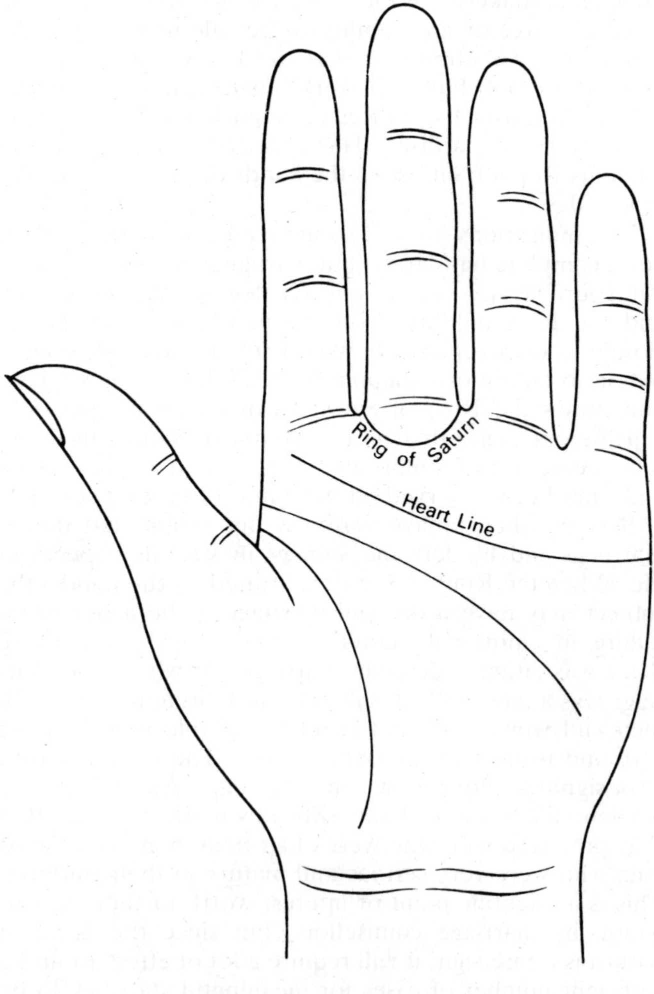

Figure 15-9 The Ring of Saturn

one job to the other. There will be something wrong in the mental make-up of the subject which will lead to persistent failure, or an inability to get along with people. Nowadays, it is often not *what* you know but *whom* you know that contributes to worldly success, so, with this defect, the subject's chances of acquiring influential contacts will be jeopardised. Hand analysts have found this ominous Ring of Saturn on the hands of prisoners as well as suicides.

The indications are not so unfavourable if the Ring is not a complete half-circle, but is fragmented. It is still an unfavourable sign, but to a lesser degree. Whenever you find the Ring of Saturn on the hand, examine it very closely to discover exactly what is its unfortunate contribution to failure or unhappiness in the life of the subject. Sometimes the Ring of Saturn is made up of two lines which cross each other on the Mount of Saturn itself. In such a case, it looks more like a cross than a ring. Such a mark has been observed on the hands of several suicides.

Saturn, when unfavourable, is the planet that delays marriage and hinders the subject in various aspects of life. When the Ring of Saturn is formed on the hands, the subject may have a delayed marriage or be a persistent failure in emotional matters. I have seen cases where there was either a delay in marriage, or where the marriage was a failure. Such subjects, and this applies to both men and women, do not seem to be able to retain the love and respect of the opposite sex. The planet Saturn also signifies old people, in astrology. Almost all the women clients whom I saw with this mark, told me that they preferred men who were older than them, or at least men who were very serious and mature in their outlook. This is a scientific point of interest worth further investigation by marriage counsellors, but since the Ring of Saturn is a rare sign, it will require a lot of effort to find a sufficient number of cases for meaningful statistics to be drawn up.

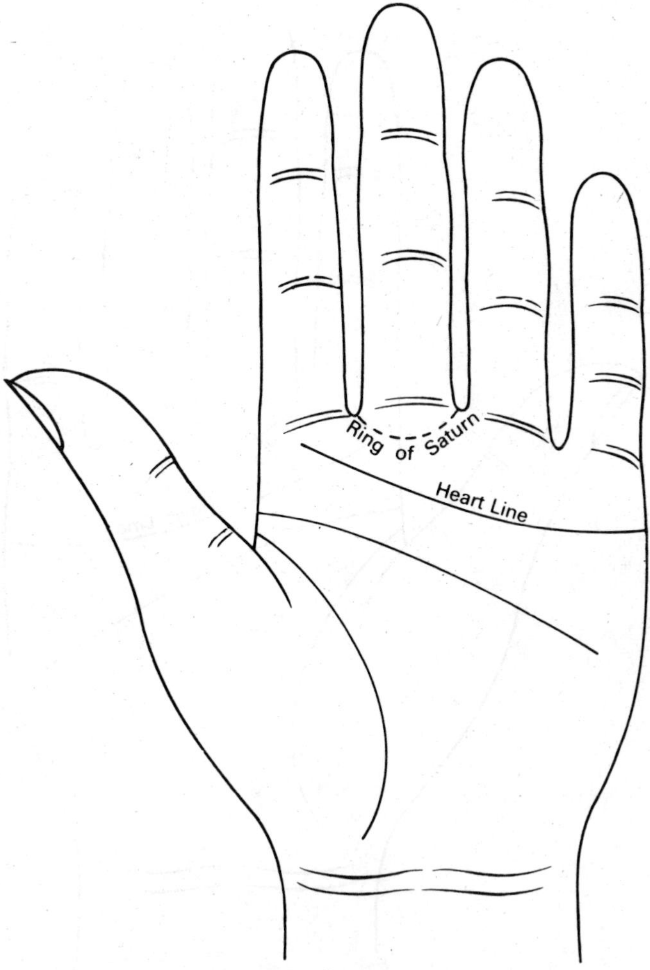

Figure 15-10 A broken Ring of Saturn

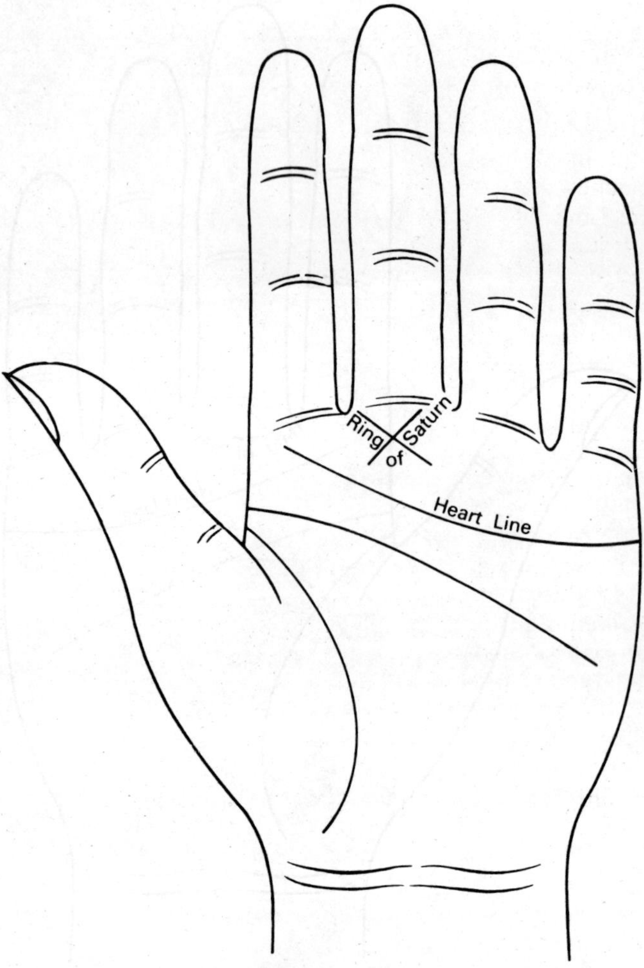

Figure 15-11 A Ring of Saturn shaped like a Cross

When the Ring of Saturn is found in the hands, it will be certain that Saturn is badly placed on the hands as well as in the subject's horoscope; or at least, in the horoscope, the planet Saturn will be aspected by, or conjoined with, some malefic planet.

The Line of Mars

This line runs parallel to the Line of Vitality. It never touches it. It is regarded as a sister or protective line to the Line of Vitality. In astrology, Mars deals with physical stamina, courage, and muscular strength. Mars is a war-like planet, and if the Line of Mars is well formed, long and clear, the subject will definitely be martial in outlook. Such subjects will have a lot of push and drive, and will regard obstacles as opportunities to further their careers. Prominent generals, with a reputation for being aggressive in warfare, will have a prominent Line of Mars. I saw such a well-marked Line of Mars on the hands of a very high-ranking police officer who was a holy terror to the gangsters of Penang, Malaysia. Aristotle found this mark on the hands of several Greek generals who consulted him. A well-formed Line of Mars is a sign of great physical vitality. Should the Vitality Line be broken, and the Line of Mars go past it, the subject will be saved from serious illness or an accident at that particular age. Death will surely not strike the subject with such a protective indication. Therefore, the Line of Mars is truly a sister line to the Line of Vitality.

However, should the Line of Mars be very close to the Vitality line, the subject will tend to be rather quarrelsome by nature and perhaps get involved in court cases unnecessarily, as a result of his over-aggressiveness. Should the Line of Mars be very long, well-marked, and very close to the wrist area, the subject will spend his last days in a distant country. The Line of Mars is favourable on a broad hand with a strong thumb because in such a case it will show strength of will, good judgement, and

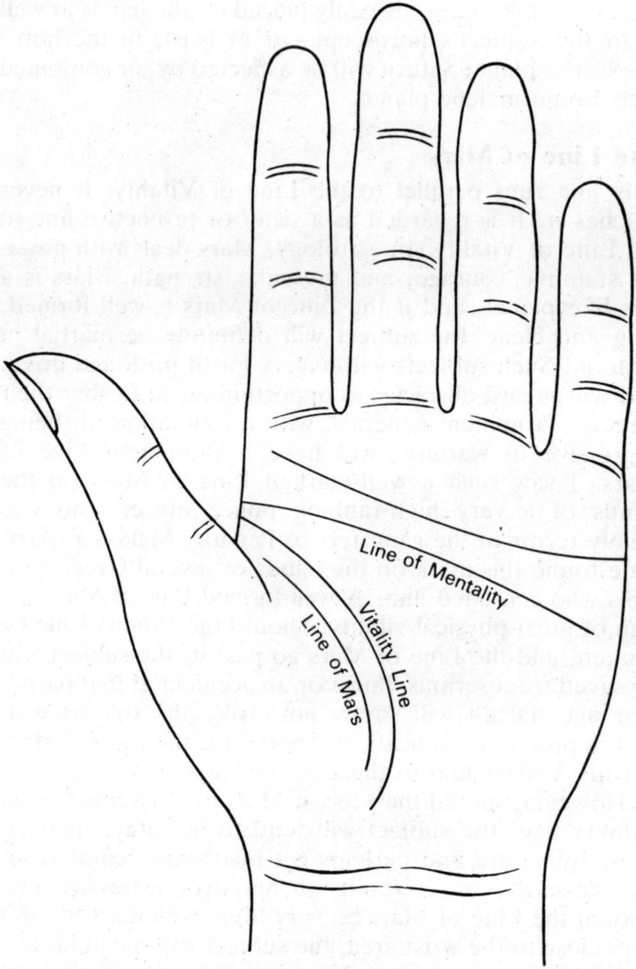

Figure 15-12 The Line of Mars

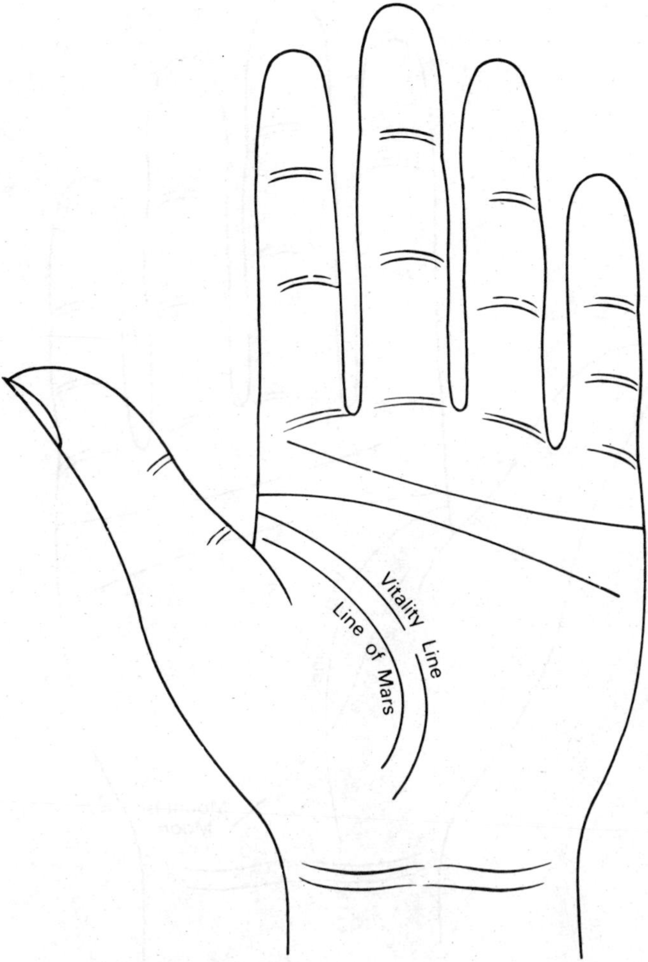

Figure 15-13 The Line of Mars protecting a break in the Vitality Line

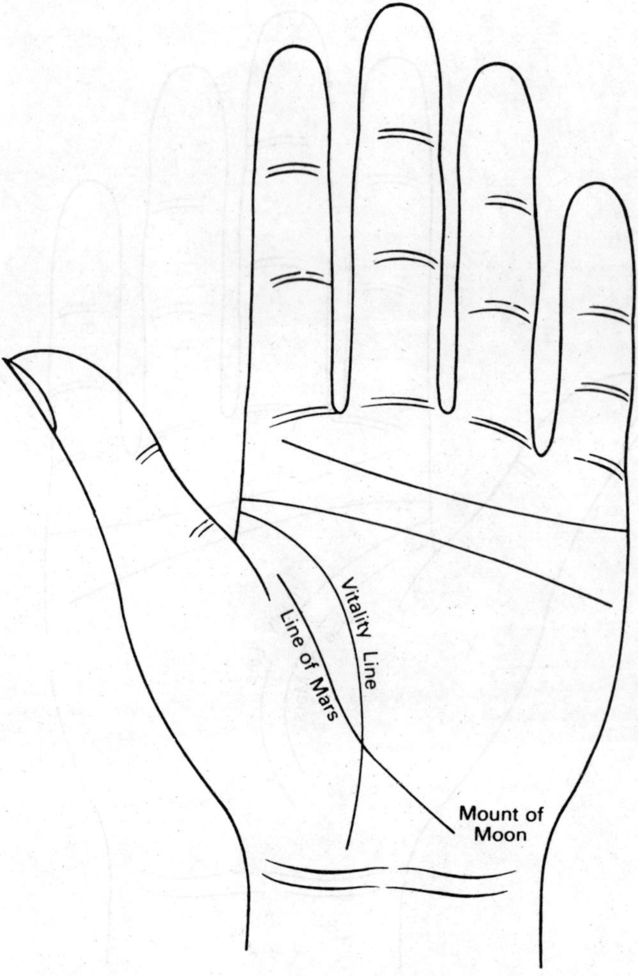

Figure 15-14 The Line of Mars cutting the Vitality Line and crossing over to the Mount of Moon

courage, but not to the extent of being unnecessarily aggressive or pugnacious. Should the Line of Mars cross the Vitality Line and go over to the Mount of Moon, the subject will indulge in some undesirable excesses. These excesses could be due to a love of alcohol, or an excessively strong sexual appetite. The tragic effects of alcoholic excesses are shown most accurately in the palms. Compulsive drinkers will have such a marking on the hands, and it is possible that the subject will with such an unfortunate mark have very bad habits, and suffer from some disease. Those addicted to alcohol should seriously take up the practice of meditation and fasting; these help to strengthen the mind. Furthermore, if the wearing of the gem Amethyst is found to cause no physical ill-effects after a test of three days, it will help the unfortunate subject to curb excesses in drinking.

The Ring of Solomon

This line starts from between the first and second fingers (Jupiter and Saturn), grows downwards, circles the Mount of Jupiter, and ends near the start of the Vitality Line. It is therefore a semi-circular line, and very rarely is it seen to be a flawless, complete line. Generally, it is not formed perfectly in the palm. This line shows a latent ability for occult studies. With other favourable indications, the subject can become a good hand analyst, astrologer, or numerologist. It is of course ideal if the Ring of Solomon is well-marked and perfectly formed on the Mount of Jupiter. Almost invariably this mark reveals that the subject has a liking for the study of psychology, and hence the probing of the human mind. By itself, however, the Ring of Solomon will not indicate high development in the field of the occult sciences. A good Line of Mentality, a strong thumb, and a well-marked Fate Line are very helpful or even necessary complementary indications, as a very great deal of study is necessary before the subject can develop his native ability in this field. On the

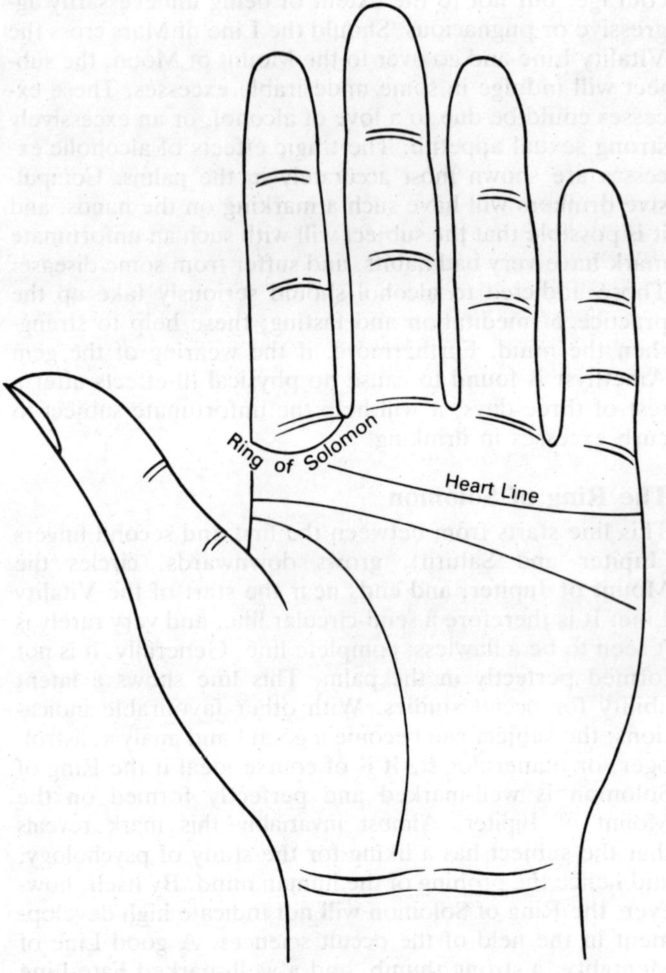

Figure 15-15 The Ring of Solomon

hands of businessmen, the mark has a different meaning. They will be blessed with a keen business intuition which will help them when making major business decisions.

The Line of Intuition

This is a rare mark. It indicates the gift of Intuition. Normally, it starts from the lower third of the Mount of Moon, travels up the palm, and ends on or near the Mount of Mercury in a curved formation. When well-formed, long, deep and clear, the subject will have a sensitive mind. His dreams and presentiments will generally be accurate. He will frequently receive vibrations on meeting people. It is also a fact that a favourable Line of Intuition will give the subject a flair for eloquence and a love of literature. In 1977 I analysed the hands of a famous Indian actor who has made a name for himself in Italian films and who is also a gifted writer. I saw a really long, beautiful, prominent Line of Intuition on one of his hands. He is also most sensitive by temperament, and cultured in outlook, and the temperament and gifts that we expect from a first class Line of Intuition are portrayed in his life.

It is most useful for hand analysts and astrologers to have a really good Line of Intuition. Of course, this line must be backed up by a strong Line of Mentality. Intuition must always be based on a deep knowledge and vast practical experience of the sciences of hand analysis and astrology.

A wavy, twisted Line of Intuition is an unfavourable sign. The subject will be erratic, mentally restless, and have some major flaw in his mental make-up. A broken Line of Intuition will mean that the subject's intuition will not work constantly, but will reveal itself only now and then, and will also often be misleading as well.

Clairvoyants also have a Line of Intuition on their hands. If their clairvoyance is of a really high order, then the Line of Intuition will be long, clear and deep.

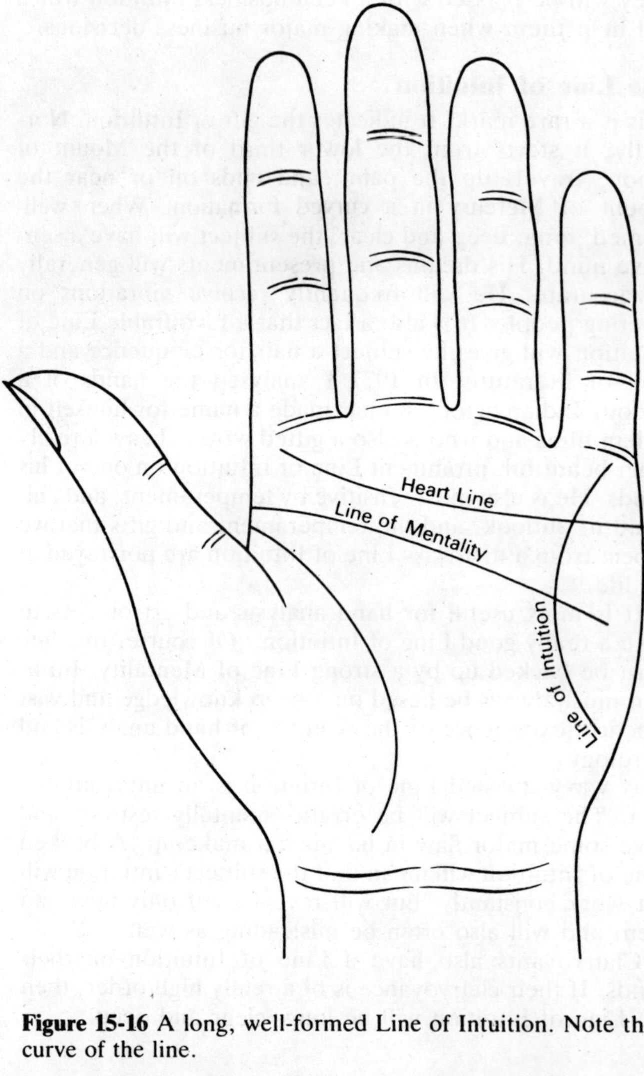

Figure 15-16 A long, well-formed Line of Intuition. Note the curve of the line.

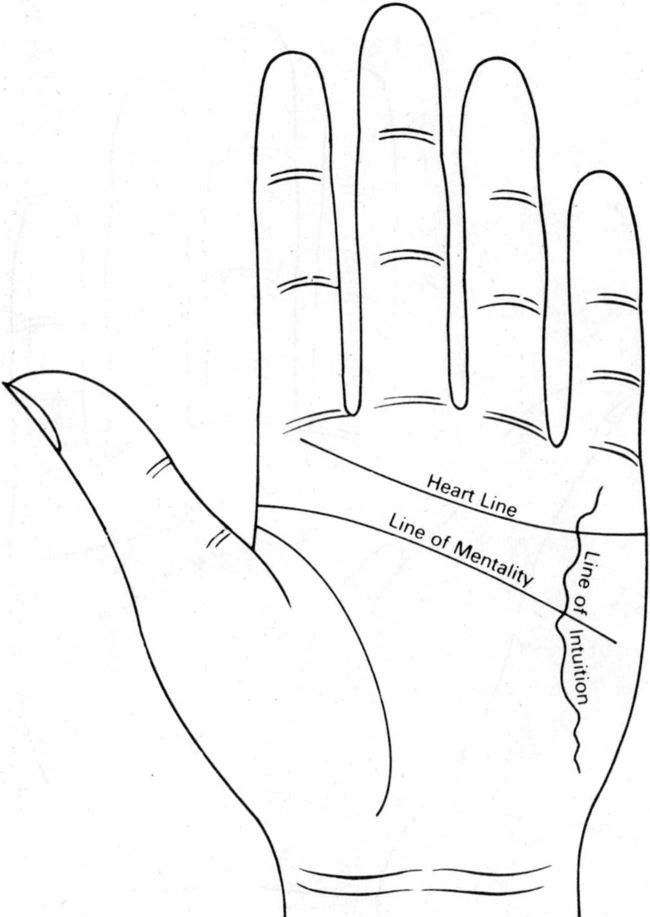

Figure 15-17 A wavy, twisted Line of Intuition

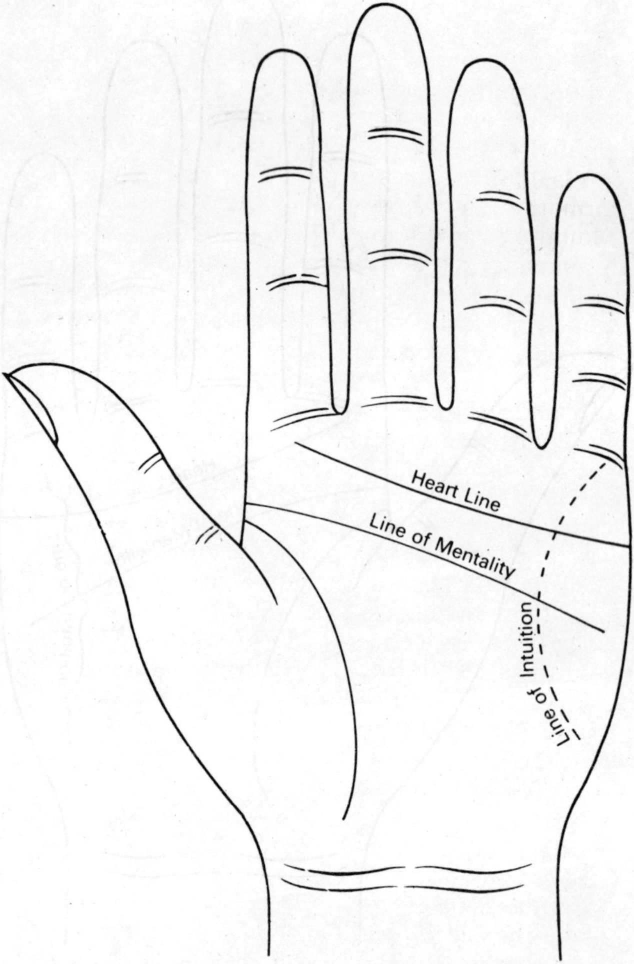

Figure 15-18 A broken Line of Intuition

The Via Lascivia

This line is regarded as a sister line to the Line of Mercury. In its ideal formation, it has a slanting position, starting from the inner part of the base of the Moon Mount, and ending on the lower part of the upper Moon Mount near the percussion. It should, therefore, run parallel to the Line of Mercury, but I have seldom found a Via Lascivia formed thus. It is generally curved in its formation and forms a semi-circular formation from the Mount of Venus to the Mount of Moon. The Via Lascivia is a menace if it is strongly curved thus, and broken up as well. It will tend to demean the subject in some way, usually causing him to be more susceptible to temptation. He will tend to pursue pleasure regardless of its consequences. This will be all the more certain if his hands are soft and flabby. Some subjects with such a combination generally have told me that they were either addicted to sex or to alcohol.

However, before judging the effect of the Via Lascivia, estimate the type of hand on which it is found. Should the rest of the hand show a fine, well-balanced personality, then the Via Lascivia should be given a favourable interpretation. In this case, it will mean that it will bestow added physical or mental energy to the subject, helping him to succed in some worthy ambition in life. Thus the Via Lascivia also has a good side. But in general, I have found it to have a sinister interpretation. Let us suppose that the hand shows a grasping, acquisitive nature. Then a badly formed Via Lascivia will make the subject pursue money along unethical lines, with 'Let the consequences be damned' as his motto.

Lascivia and the English word 'lascivious' both stem from the same Latin root-word. A bad Via Lascivia will make the subject short-sighted, not caring for the long-term consequences of his actions. Should the Via Lascivia be curved and wavy as well, the subject will definitely have many love affairs. I have seen such a formation

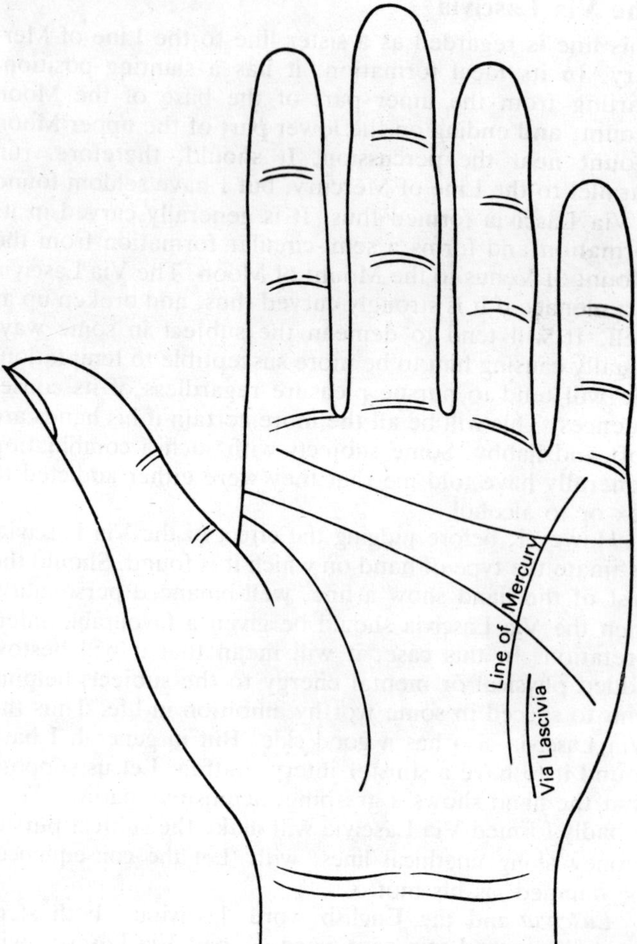

Figure 15-19 The ideal formation of the Via Lascivia. Here it is parallel to the Line of Mercury.

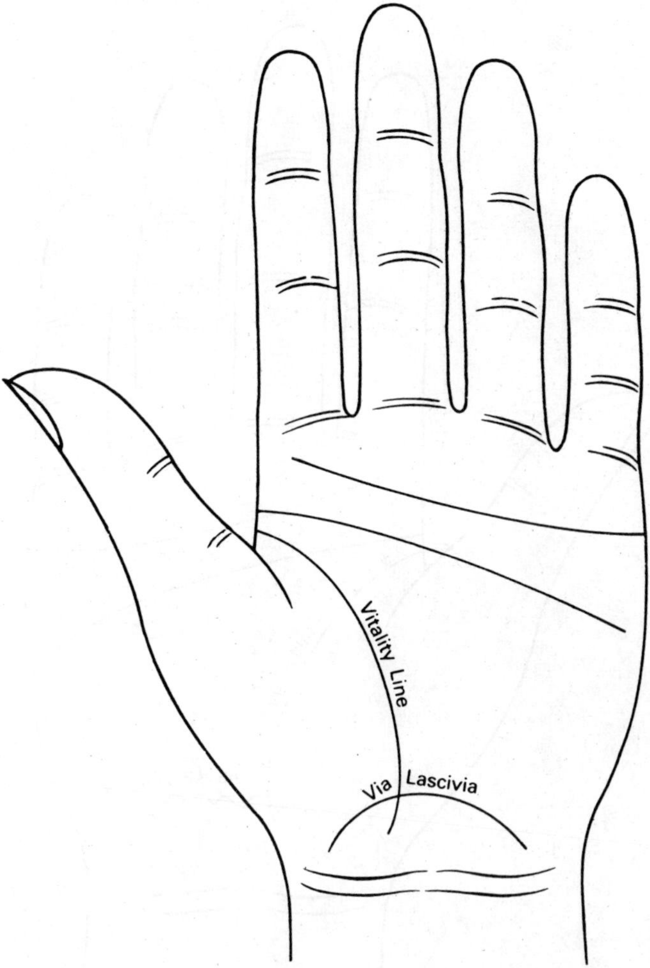

Figure 15-20 The Via Lascivia as it is normally found

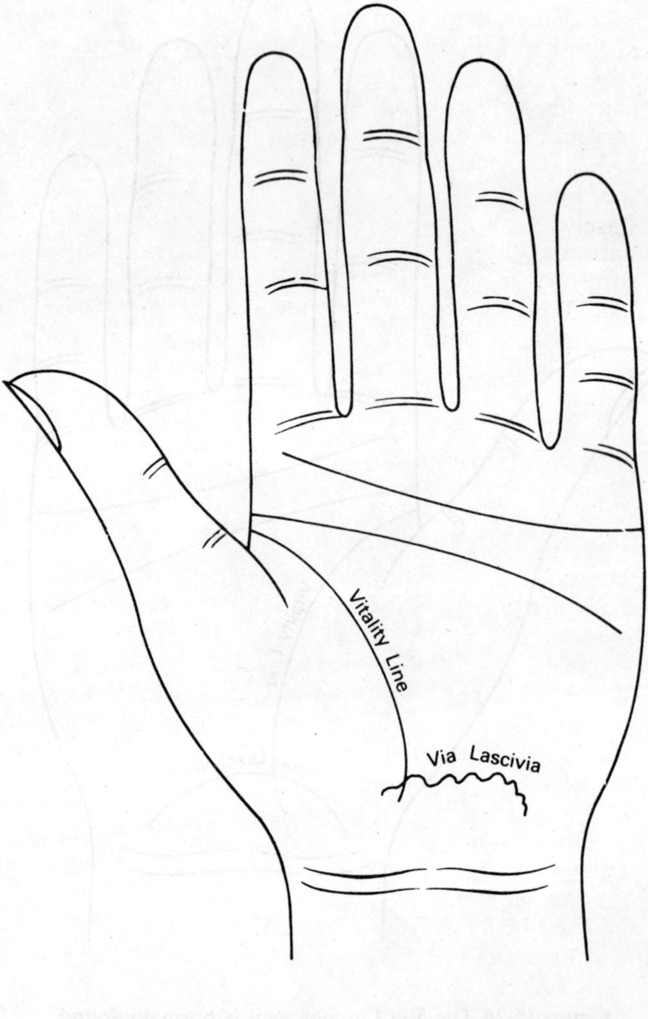

Figure 15-21 A curved and wavy Via Lascivia

many times on the hands of both men and women. However, I must state that I have found it slightly more often in the hands of women. Psychologists tell us that women have a more abiding interest in sex than men do, and perhaps this is the reason for the slightly more frequent occurrence of the Via Lascivia in the hands of women.

Whenever some major defect is found in lines such as the Line of Vitality, Fate and Sun, consider the Via Lascivia as a probable cause of these defects. The explanation could be that an excessive indulgence in the pleasures of the senses will jeopardise the career of the subject. With other unfavourable indications, even the reputation of the subject may be affected.

I have questioned many subjects with well-marked Via Lascivias on their palms, and have frequently been told that they were very fond of sexual pleasures and had a craving for variety and excitement in their sexual lives.

The Rascettes or Bracelets

These are found near the wrist at the bottom of the palm. They are horizontal lines, normally three, and sometimes two. It is very rare to find four Rascettes on one hand. According to the Western school of hand analysis, the Rascettes have very little meaning. However, the Indian school of hand analysis has done tremendous research on the Rascettes and has discovered a detailed significance for each rascette on the hand. It is favourable if there are three flawless, well-formed Rascettes on a subject's hand.

The first rascette is the one nearest the palm. If this rascette is well-formed and clear, it suggests good health for the subject. Often on the hands of women, you will find the first rascette invading the palm in the form of a convex arch. There is a very interesting meaning to this — it signifies that the subject will find it difficult to have children, or will experience delay in having children. I have seen this hundreds of times in my professional practice, and found this interpretation to be substantially true. By itself, this marking is not an indication of sterility, but with other unfavourable indications it could suggest that affliction. Should the first rascette be shaped like a convex arch, and should there be a star at the junction of the lines of Mentality and Mercury, with the Mount of Venus being flat, narrow and badly formed, it is practically certain that the woman will be sterile.

A **cross** on the Mount of Saturn can also suggest difficulty in having children, although I must confess that I have confirmed such an indication only once on the hands of a woman. She was married but unable to have children, and had been told by her gynaecologist that she was suffering from sub-fertility. This is very interesting, but expert hand analysts must confirm this marking on the Saturn Mount a couple of thousand times before we can say with confidence that a cross on the Mount of Saturn on the hands of a woman bears this significance. I have mentioned this as a point of research for the serious research-minded students of scientific hand analysis.

On the hands of a man, if the first rascette rises sharply like a convex arch into the palm, it suggests a sexual weakness or some deformity of the generative organs.

The Quadrangle

The Quadrangle is that part of the hand found between the Lines of Heart and Mentality. It should be well-formed, and beautifully proportioned. Such a Quadrangle will suggest a subject who is honest and straightforward, has a clear mind, and solid powers of judgement. He will generally have a calm temperament. It is not favourable if the Quadrangle is missing. Such would be the case if **a Simian Line** is found on the hands. In that case, the Lines of Heart and Mentality are merged into a single line running across the palm, from one side to the other. With a missing Quadrangle, there will definitely be a certain element of psychological imbalance in the character of

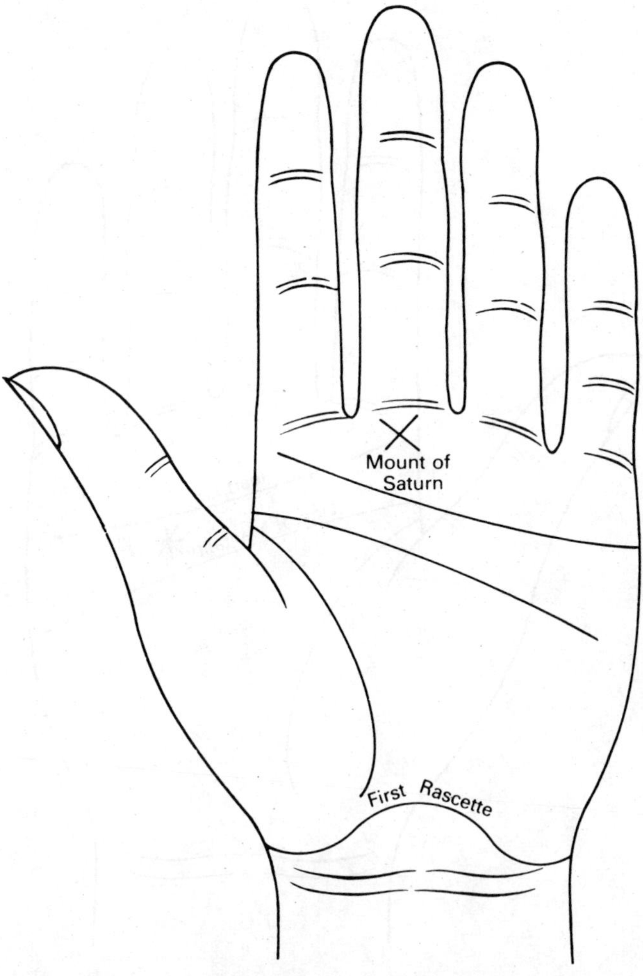

Figure 15-22 The First Rascette rising like a convex arch into the palm. Note the Cross on the Mount of Saturn.

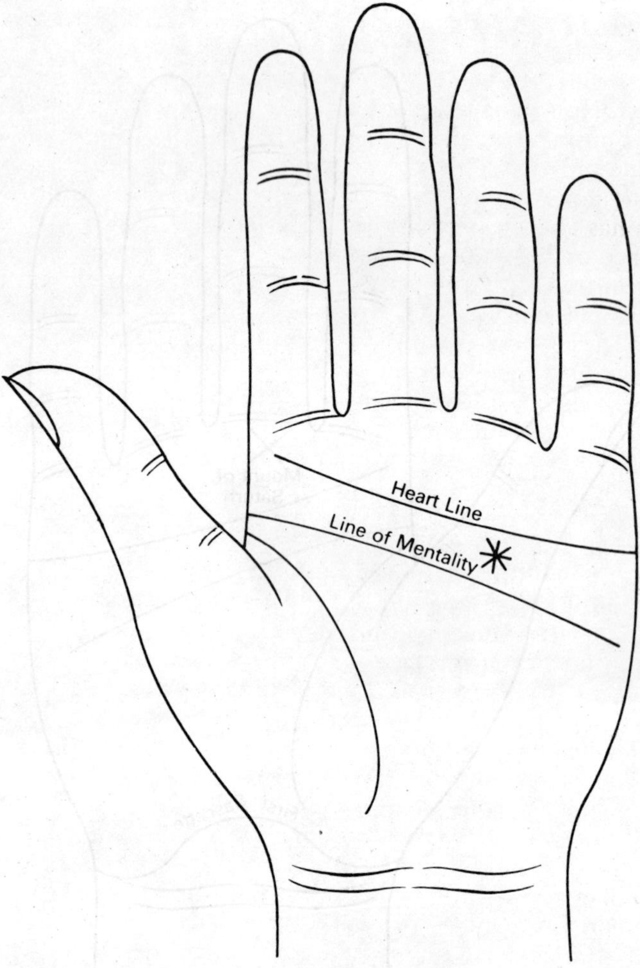

Figure 15-23 A well-formed Quadrangle with a Star inside

the subject.

The Quadrangle should neither be too broad nor narrow, but should strike a happy medium. If it is excessively wide, the subject will be very independent in disposition. He will be less cautious and will be apt to make serious mistakes. Quite often you will find a narrow Quadrangle on your subject's hands. In this case, the Lines of Heart and Mentality will be close together. This formation has two meanings. It can indicate some health significance or reveal psychological traits. If it shows psychological traits, the subject will be mean, self-centred, and will approach everything from the point of personal interest. These subjects can be utterly ruthless in love.

The Quadrangle should be free of **criss-cross lines,** and defects such as **islands** or **crossbars.** If this is the case, the middle age of the subject will be steady and favourable. Also, the subject will have a calm temperament and be reliable in nature.

It is very favourable to have a **star** in the Quadrangle. The star will suggest some significant success for the subject. Should the star appear in the Quadrangle under the Mount of Saturn, the subject will undoubtedly have some brilliant achievement in his career. If the same star be found in the Quadrangle under the Mount of Sun, the subject will achieve name and fame in the field of art or literature. This is easy to understand as the Mount of Sun is devoted to art, literature, and fame.

The planet Mercury represents science, business and commerce in hand analysis and astrology. Therefore if the star is found in the Quadrangle under the Mount of Mercury, the subject will be able to achieve some outstanding success in science, or the subject may be exceptionally successful in the world of business.

The **triangle** is always a favourable sign in the palm, and refers either to mental brilliance or material gains. It is favourable if a triangle is found in the Quadrangle, as this indicates that the subject will have the capacity to do

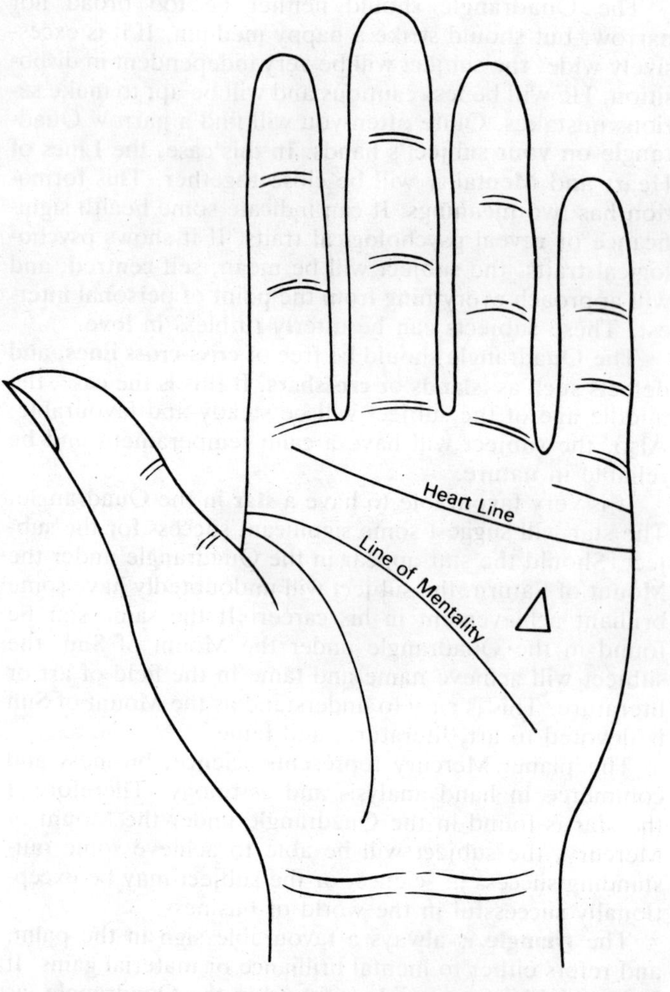

Figure 15-24 An excessively wide Quadrangle with a Triangle inside

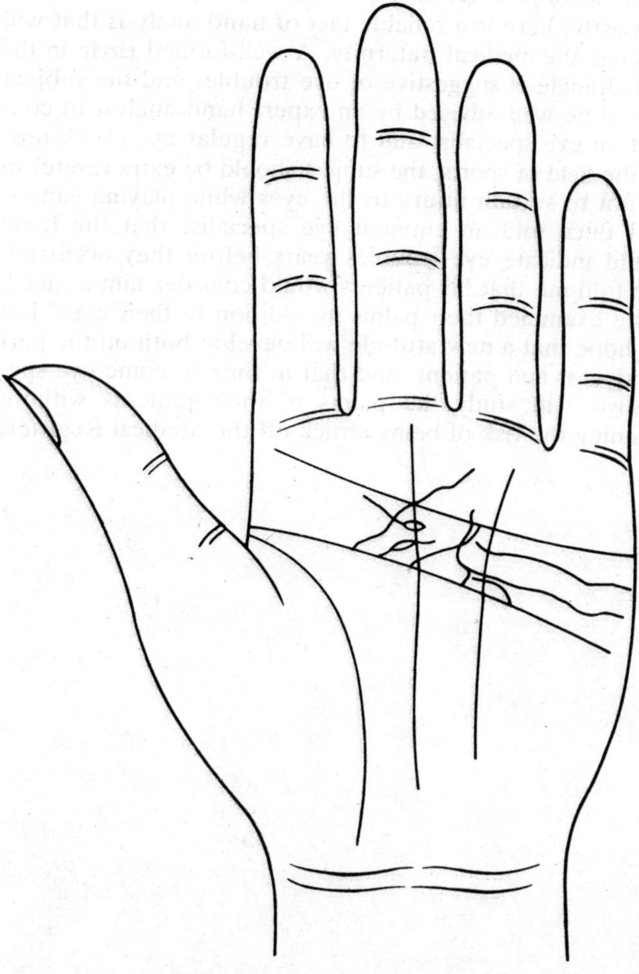

Figure 15-25 A disturbed Quadrangle

some solid research in a particular discipline.

Lastly, here is a reliable fact of hand analysis that will interest the medical fraternity. A well-formed **circle** in the Quadrangle is suggestive of eye trouble, and the subject would be well-advised by an expert hand analyst to consult an eye specialist and to have regular eye check-ups. In the field of sports, the subject should be extra careful so as not to sustain injury to the eyes while playing games.

I once told an eminent eye specialist that the hand could indicate eye troubles years before they occurred. He told me that his patients would consider him a quack if he examined their palms in addition to their eyes! Let us hope that a new attitude will develop both on the part of doctor and patient, and that in time to come eye specialists will study the palms of their patients without running the risk of being struck off the Medical Register.

Chapter Sixteen

The Line of Affection is an Indicator of the Major Affairs of Your Heart

The **Line of Affection** is wrongly called the Line of Marriage by amateur hand analysts. This line is also called the Line of Union by some eminent Indian hand analysts. The Lines of Affection, or the so-called Marriage Lines, are found on the side of the hand, transversing the Mount of Mercury. They are usually found between the Heart Line and the base of the little or Mercury finger. They start from the edge of the hand and progress inwards on the Mount of Mercury. These lines should be regarded as beginning from the area of the Heart Line and ending below the base of the little finger.

It is wrong to jump to the conclusion that each line refers to a legal attachment. Scientific hand analysis does not recognize a legal union — marriages are man-made institutions. When two people love each other, and there is an emotional impact, this event will be recorded by a strong Line of Affection, even though the couple may never legally marry in their lifetimes.

Nowadays, the concept of free love has complicated matters for hand analysts. When scientific hand analysis began thousands of years ago, a Line of Affection could confidently be analysed as a legal marriage, but in these days of free love, we must not jump to such a conclusion without a careful study of the palms. The Lines of Affection usually refer to attachments with members of the opposite sex, but in my professional practice I have analysed the hands of homosexuals and lesbians, and in their cases, the Lines of Affection will indicate an attachment to a member of the same sex. The Lines of Affection never refer to attachments towards brothers, sisters, mother or father.

The Lines of Affection should always be analysed in conjunction with other lines and features of the hand. Only then can accurate results be obtained as regards the probability of a marriage or a strong emotional attachment. Especially when considering emotional attachments, we must always consider the **Influence Lines** which start from the Mount of Moon and travel towards the Fate Line or Sun Line. The Influence Lines which drop from the Vitality Line are also of great importance in considering matters of the heart. Certain mounts of the hand are extremely important in considering the likelihood of a legal union. It takes years of experience and a really skilled hand analyst to state that a legal marriage will take place. It is difficult to determine from the palms whether the subject is legally married or not, but if the subject is not married, then certain features of the hand will show the likelihood of a legal union. For this we have to turn to the mounts of the hand, so as to see which ones are well-developed and prominent.

The Apollonian would have a well-developed Mount of Sun, and so on for the Jupiterians, Lunarians, Saturnians, Venusians and Mercurians respectively. The Apollonians, Venusians, Jupiterians, Martians and Mercurians tend to marry early. The Saturnian is under the restrictive influence of the planet Saturn. In astrology, the seventh house deals with marriage. Saturn badly placed in the seventh house, or aspecting the seventh house malefically, can delay marriage. In scientific hand analysis, the Saturnian will have a dislike for the opposite sex, so the chances of the subject saying 'Walter, Walter, lead me to the altar' will be considerably reduced! (This, of course, applies to the male subject as well.) The Lunarian is under the influence of the planet Moon. Moon is a fickle planet and these subjects can also be fickle in their temperaments. So, with Lunarians, it is difficult to tell whether they will marry young or late in life, although experience has shown that Lunarians tend to make strong alliances in the arena of love and marriage.

I have rarely seen happy marriages in my professional experience. Having a happy marriage is like striking the first prize in the Big Sweep, or in the Social Welfare Lottery Sweep which we have in Malaysia. My experience has shown that marriages fail for two reasons: (a) the choice of a wrong partner (b) the choice of a right partner, but selection of the wrong time to get married.

Many women lament when they are fated to have a late marriage, but little do they realize that sometimes it is better to have a late marriage. An early one could spell disaster.

Should the Lines of Affection be heavily afflicted, suggesting unhappiness in love or marriage, the subject should take recourse to remedial measures. The wearing of certain astrological gems may help to lessen the influence of evil planets. Also, Indian astrology has developed the science of *Mantras* or the incantation of certain forms of sound vibrations to a high degree. Sometimes the name of the subject should be changed — this aspect of change of name comes under the science of numerology. By changing the name, or altering the spelling of the name, the vibration of the name can be altered to that of a beneficent planet. Many famous singers and actors and actresses rose to prominence only after they had abandoned their original names. Among some Hindus in India, the name of the bride is altered after the wedding, the idea being that her name should be in harmony with that of her husband's. The rule among these Hindus is that the wife's name should have the first letter or syllable agreeing with that of the husband. The real name of the author is *Jaspal Singh.* He only came into prominence as a hand analyst when a new name, YASCHPAULE, was adopted after a careful study of numerology. This aspect of change of name should only be handled by an expert numerologist.

In a later chapter, the scientific basis of gem therapy will be explained. Finally, certain gifts or actions to appease the planets are most useful in the case of bad, troublesome marriages. Some of these remedies have been prescribed to my clients, and they have certainly helped to lessen the influence of evil planets.

It is very important to choose an auspicious time to get engaged and married. In this way, with a favourable planetary position, the chances of a happy marriage will be enhanced. This is all the more essential when the hands suggest an unhappy union. By choosing an auspicious time to get married, the marriage may still not be a bed of roses, but at least, in all probability, the unhappiness will be diminished to some degree.

The general idea is to increase the chances of suitability and compatibility so that a happy marriage can result. In this way, not only will the couple be happy, but society will also benefit. Nowadays, a doctor may examine the would-be couple to see whether the chances of a good marriage are present. He will examine the couple on the basis of past medical history, heredity, health at the time of medical examination, age and nationality. The method of marriage compatibility in scientific hand analysis is an advancement on the principles adopted by the medical doctor.

Let us suppose that a young couple are examined by the doctor. The young man and his fiancée are both given a thorough medical check-up. The lady is delighted to learn from the doctor that her future husband is in the pink of health. Only an expert hand analyst or astrologer would know that in three years' time this young man, so obviously fit as a fiddle, will succumb to that terrible disease called cancer, so that the young bride of barely three years will be widowed. This is possible to predict as the sciences of hand analysis and astrology have the capacity to transcend time and space. Now if the doctor was also a master of hand analysis, he could examine the young man's palms. Signs of a fatal disease terminating the life of the subject could be discerned three years ahead of time. The doctor could place the cards on the table, and let the couple decide. Of course, the couple might still decide to go on with the marriage ceremony, but at least they would know where they stood as regards the future of their marriage. So it is perfectly logical to combine the techniques of marriage suitability as practised by modern medicine with those of scientific hand analysis. Modern medicine is very highly advanced, but it has its limitations. Scientific hand analysis also has its limitations. Let there be a marriage between the two sciences, and definitely, there will be more happy marriages in the future. This is a point worthy of the earnest consideration of serious thinkers.

Let us now go back to the Lines of Affection. It has been clearly explained that these lines do not necessarily or always refer to a legal marriage, but for the sake of convenience, and to save unnecessary repetition, these lines will be called the **Lines of Marriage** in this chapter.

The most important mounts to study in analysing the probability of a legal marriage are Jupiter and Venus. The Mount of Jupiter is the more important of the two. In Indian astrology, Jupiter is regarded as a divine planet. It likes to do things in a legal, honest, above-board manner if it is favourably placed in the palms. In Indian astrology, Jupiter is regarded as the husband to all girls, and is a priest officiating at marriage and legalizing it. Hence, it is easy to understand why Indian hand analysts place so much importance on the development of this Mount when assessing the chances of a legal union. Of course, it is essential that the Mount of Jupiter must be strong, well-placed, and favourable in the palms.

It is stated by many eminent hand analysts that the nearer the Marriage Line is to the Line of Heart, the earlier marriage will take place. After observation of thousands of hands, I can confidently state that this interpretation can be misleading. The time factor as regards when a deep attachment took place can be elusive and tricky as regards the Marriage Line on the Mount of Mercury. For example, it is said that if the Marriage Line is found in the centre of the space between the Heart Line and the base of the little finger, then marriage will take place in middle age, probably around the age of thirty-five. However, I have seen cases where the Marriage Line was in such a position, yet the marriage took place around the age of twenty-one, and in a few cases, as early as eighteen. A more accurate assessment as regards this aspect of finding out the **Time of marriage** or a major emotional relationship is shown by the Influence Lines rising from the Mount of Moon and touching the Fate and Sun Lines; also, by the Influence Lines found on the mounts of Lower Mars and Venus, and dropping from inside the Vitality Line or running parallel to it. Mercury is a very fast planet. Maybe that is why the Marriage Lines on the Mount of Mercury do not reveal the time of marriage so accurately. However, they do record the event of marriage or a major emotional involvement with astonishing accuracy.

The **ideal Line of Marriage** should be long, clear, well-formed, and free of defects such as islands, breaks, chains or stars. Such a line could suggest a happy marriage but only if there are confirmatory indications of this in the rest of the hand. Always consult both palms. This is a crucial point to bear in mind. I have seen cases of great sorrow in marriage, even when the Marriage Line was flawlessly formed, where on a closer examination of the hands major defects were apparent in the rest of the palms. Generally, these major defects are found on the Heart Line. The Heart Line may have several drooping lines, or the Heart, Vitality and Mentality Lines may all be joined together at the start on or just below the Mount of Jupiter. Many a time, these major defects have nullified the effects of a good Line of Marriage on the Mount of Mercury.

Thus, the ideal Marriage Line or Line of Affection merely shows the *possibility* of a happy union: nothing more, nothing less. This line should not be too long or too short. It is a defect if the Marriage Line is extra long, and thus invades the palms. In such a case, it will cut the Line of Mercury, Line of Sun and perhaps the Line of Fate as well. It is a well-known principle of hand analysis that one line should not cut another, therefore such an extension of the Marriage Line will show an inconstant state in love prospects. Further, the unfortunate subject will have his reputation and peace of mind adversely affected. It is common to find such a formation on the palms of unhappily married subjects.

Let us assume that a subject comes to consult a good hand analyst. She is unmarried and is anxious to know when marriage will take place. Let us suppose that the Marriage Line is deep and clear, and that the subject is twenty-seven years old at the time of consultation. Round about the age of twenty-seven, a strong Influence Line rises from the Mount of Moon to touch the Fate Line favourably. Also, an Influence Line starts in a well-marked manner from inside the Vitality Line at about the same age. So we know that in all probability a deep emotional attachment with a man will occur when the subject is about twenty-seven years old. But the subject wants to know if a legal marriage is going to occur. How are we going to decide this? The key to this problem is to examine the Mount of Jupiter on both hands, but to pay more attention to the Jupiter Mount on the left hand. Now, if the Jupiter Mount is well-developed, elevated, promi-

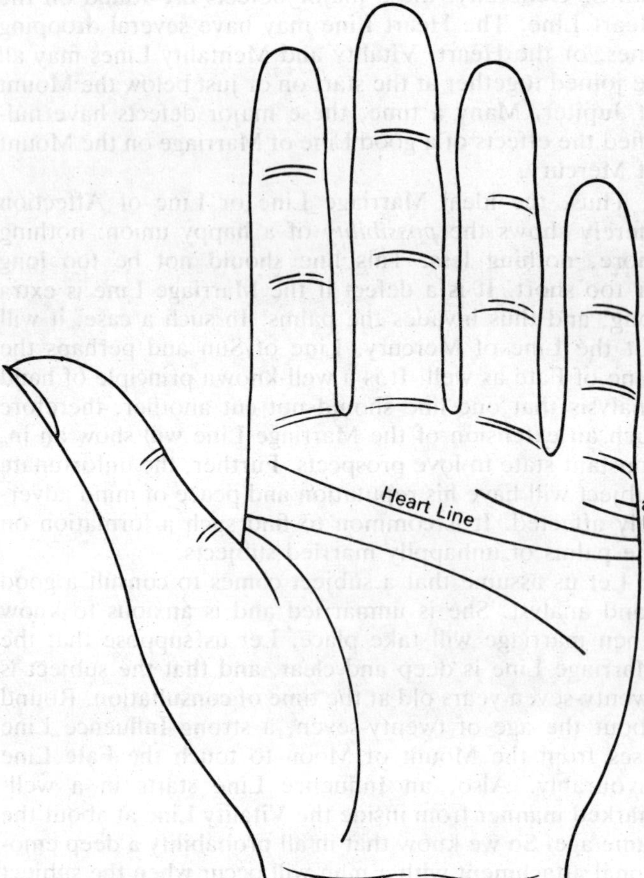

Figure 16-1 (a) a short Affection Line (b) an ideally long Affection Line (c) an excessively long Affection Line

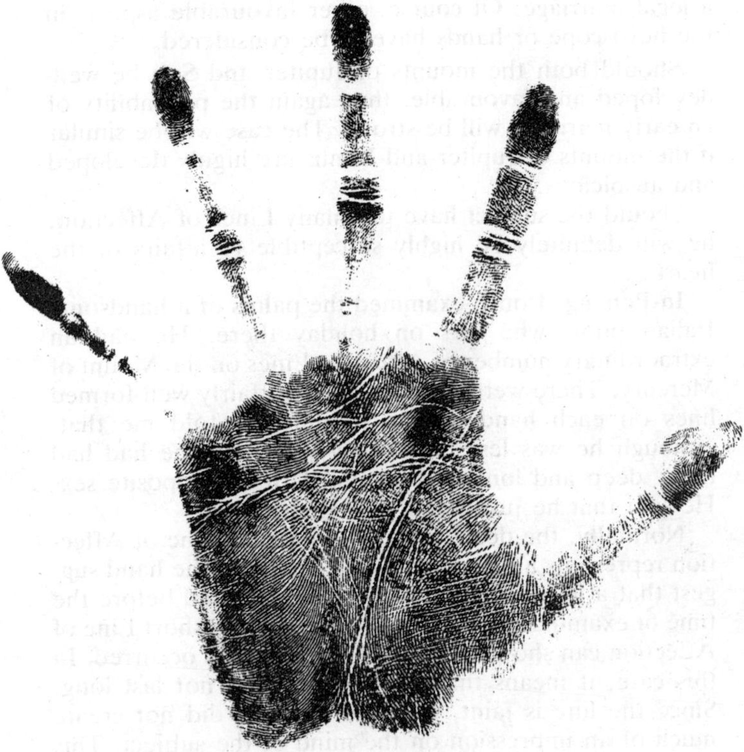

Figure 16-2 An example of an excessively long Line of Affection. Note also the abnormally short Heart Line.

nent, has favourable lines and signs on it, it is a very strong indication that a legal marriage will take place soon, and that the subject will be married around the age of twenty-seven. Let us bear in mind that a favourable Jupiter planet in the horoscope or palm tends to indicate a legal marriage. Of course, other favourable aspects in the horoscope or hands have to be considered.

Should both the mounts of Jupiter and Sun be well-developed and favourable, then again the probability of an early marriage will be strong. The case will be similar if the mounts of Jupiter and Venus are highly developed and auspicious.

Should the subject have too many Lines of Affection, he will definitely be highly susceptible to affairs of the heart.

In Penang, I once examined the palms of a handsome Italian pilot, who was on holiday there. He had an extraordinary number of Affection Lines on the Mount of Mercury. There were about nine clear, fairly well-formed lines on each hand on the Mount. He told me that, although he was less than thirty years old, he had had many deep and long associations with the opposite sex. He said that he just could not resist women.

Normally, the deep, long, well-marked Line of Affection represents a marriage, if other parts of the hand suggest that a legal union probably had occurred before the time of examination. But sometimes a faint, short Line of Affection can show that a legal marriage has occurred. In this case, it means that the marriage did not last long. Since the line is faint, the other partner did not create much of an impression on the mind of the subject. This state of affairs can be seen when the marriage has lasted for only a short time, let us say, a year or so. Thus there could not have been much depth of feeling for the partner on the side of the subject.

The deeper the line, the deeper the emotional impact of the partner on the mind of the subject. The fainter the

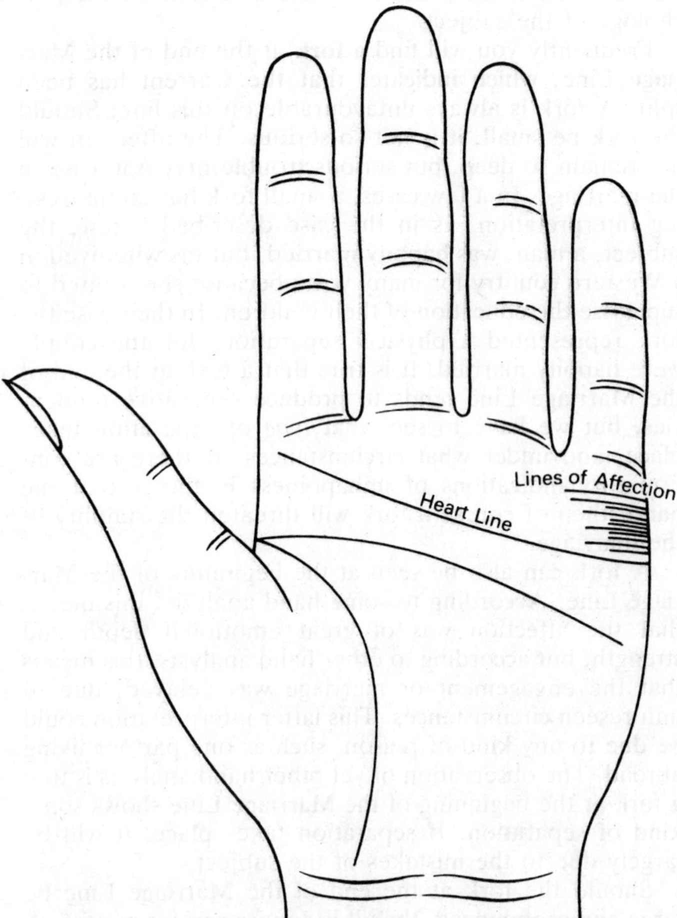

Figure 16-3 Too many lines of Affection show susceptibility to affairs of the heart.

line, the less marked the mental impression on the psychology of the subject.

Frequently you will find a **fork** at the end of the Marriage Line, which indicates that the Current has been split. A fork is always unfavourable on this line. Should the fork be small, it is not so serious. The affection will not remain so deep, but serious trouble may not arise in the marriage. In a few cases, a small fork has an interesting interpretation, as in the case described below: the subject, a man, was happily married, but his wife lived in a Western country for many years because she wanted to supervise the education of their children. In their case the fork represented a physical separation, for the couple were happily married. It is true that a fork at the end of the Marriage Line tends to produce separative tendencies, but we have to see what *type* of separation takes place, and under what circumstances. If there are confirmatory indications of unhappiness in the rest of the hand, then of course a fork will threaten the stability of the marriage.

A fork can also be seen at the beginning of the Marriage Line. According to some hand analysts, this means that the affection was of great emotional depth and strength, but according to other hand analysts, this means that the engagement or marriage was delayed, due to unforeseen circumstances. This latter interpretation could be due to any kind of reason, such as one partner living abroad. The observation of yet other hand analysts is that a fork at the beginning of the Marriage Line shows some kind of separation. If separation takes place, it will be largely due to the mistakes of the subject.

Should the fork at the end of the Marriage Line be large and pronounced, then it is a more serious matter. A big fork will suggest either a physical or a legal separation. Obviously, the marriage will be unhappy. Such a well-marked fork suggests a basic lack of compatibility between husband and wife. The couple will have different

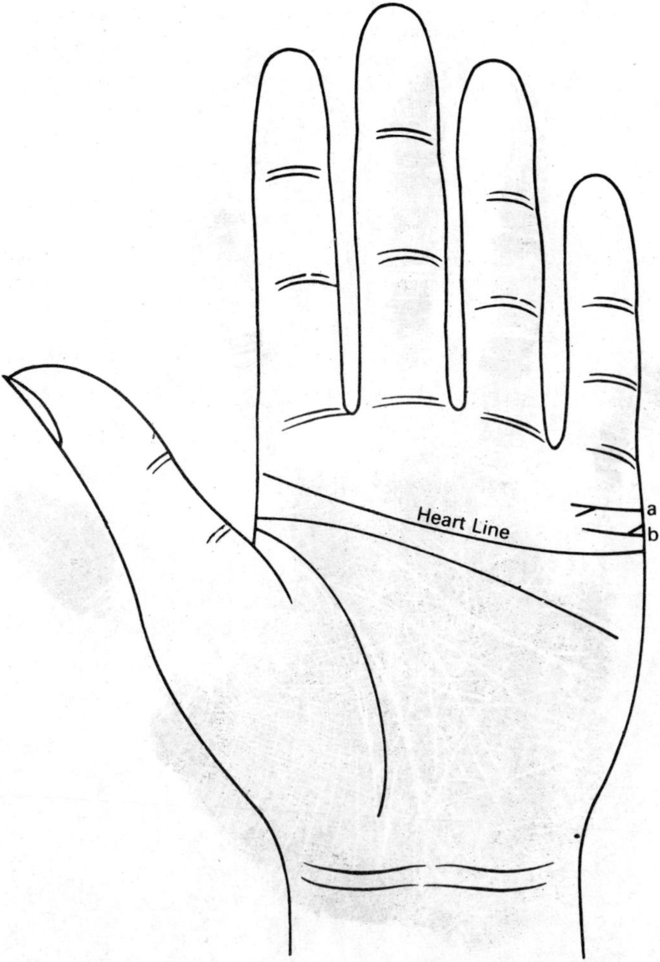

Figure 16-4 (a) a Fork at the end of the Affection Line
(b) a Fork at the beginning of an Affection Line

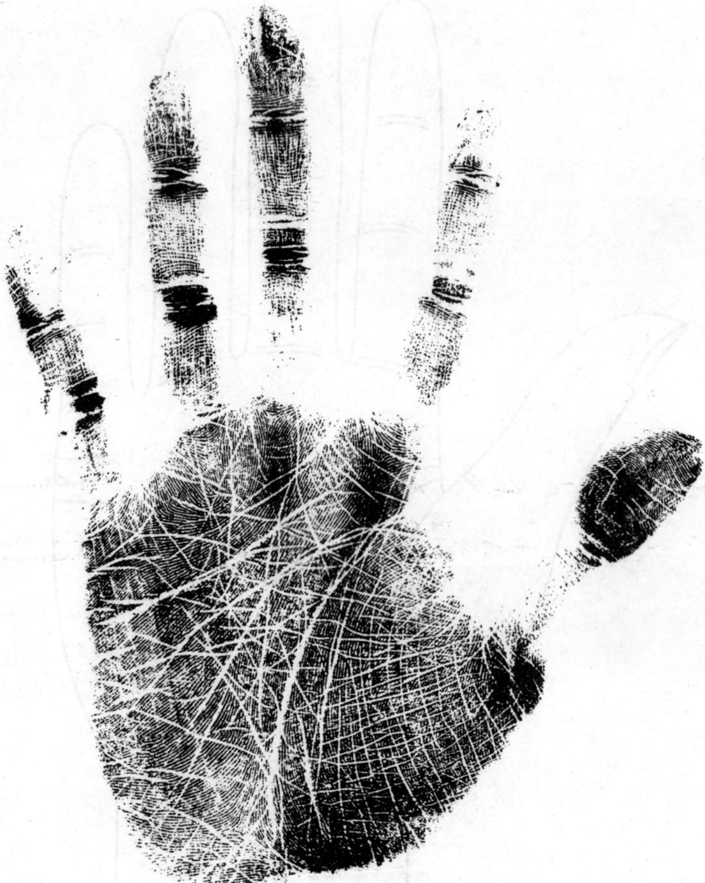

Figure 16-5 The handprint of a subject, married but separated from his wife for several years. Note the Fork at the end of the Line of Affection.

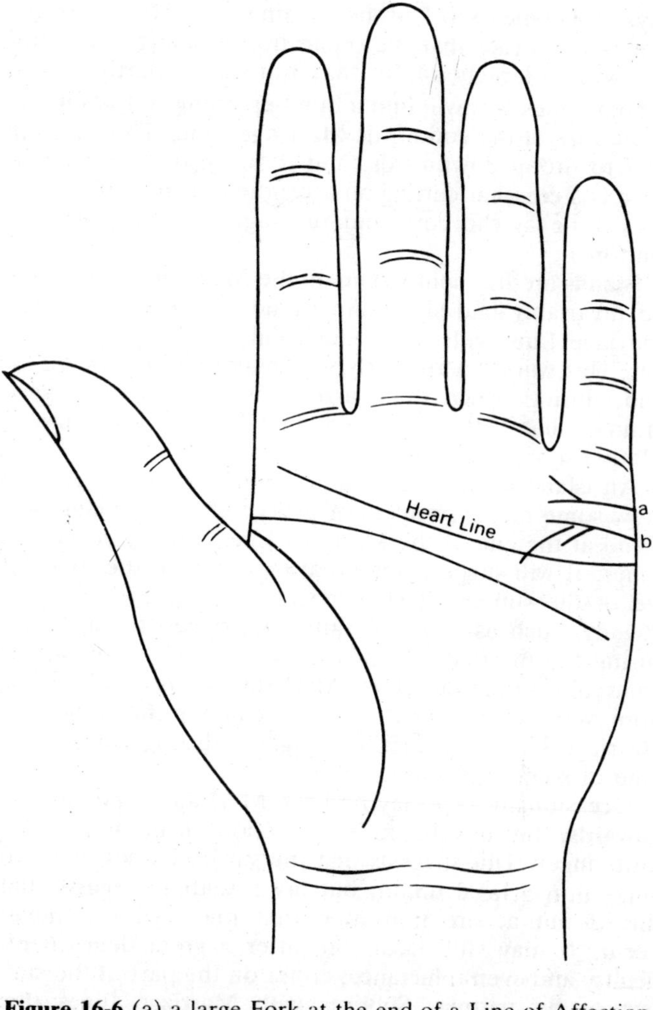

Figure 16-6 (a) a large Fork at the end of a Line of Affection (b) this usually indicates divorce

intellectual interests, and will tend to go their separate ways. This type of fork at the termination of the Marriage Line will indicate that the separation or major unhappiness will be largely due to the fault of the partner.

Sometimes you will find a **line** beginning in the middle of the fork at the end of the Marriage Line. This line will tend to droop downwards, and it suggests a divorce. If there is a **crossbar** cutting an ascending branch of the Vitality Line at the corresponding age, the case will be confirmed.

Islands are frequently seen on the Marriage Line. They are invariably bad signs. An island in the body of the Marriage Line will cause emotional distress to the subject. This will be particularly so for the duration of the island, during which the marriage will be under severe strain — that is, the other party may have an extramarital relationship.

An island at the beginning of the Marriage Line may show some major problem or delay before marriage. An island at the end of the Marriage Line is not a good sign either. It will suggest some major sorrow in the married life of the subject. The marriage will experience some tragedy, such as a divorce after prolonged unhappiness during the married life, or a bitter divorce case. Sometimes this formation shows that the partner will suffer from some severe illness. Thus an island at the end of the Marriage Line is invariably a sign of disaster or misfortune of some kind.

Occasionally you may find the Marriage Line **curving upwards,** thus heading in the direction of the base of the little finger. This suggests that the subject is not likely to enter into a legal union, but my research suggests that this is not a sure indication that marriage will never occur. It may still occur, but after a great deal of difficulty, and even reluctance, either on the part of the subject or his partner. Subjects with Marriage Lines that curve upwards may be pretty agreeable to a love affair;

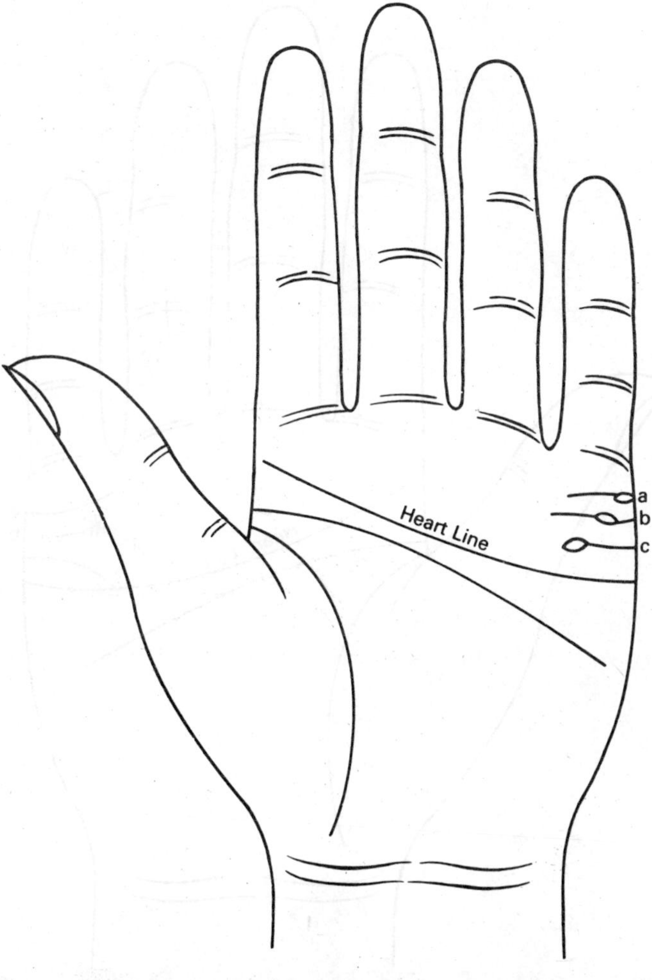

Figure 16-7 (a) an Island at the beginning of an Affection Line (b) an Island in the centre of the Line (c) a Line of Affection ending in an Island

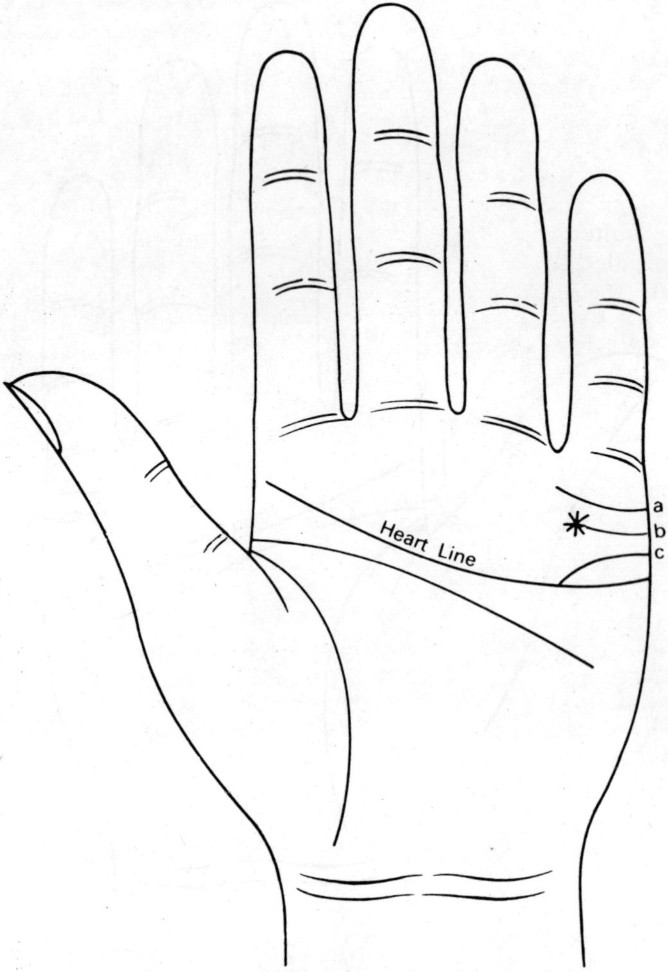

Figure 16-8 (a) the Line of Affection curving upwards (b) a Star at the end of the Line of Affection (c) Affection Line bending downwards to touch the Heart Line

however, they may show a clean pair of heels at the mention of the word marriage!

Another unlucky sign is the mark of a **star** at the end of the Marriage Line. It will suggest a sudden termination of the marriage, due to divorce or death. In this position, the star is an explosion that destroys married life. I saw this in the hands of an Australian woman client who consulted me in 1977 after having lost her husband. She revealed to me that two years previously her husband had left the house in the afternoon for a stroll down the beach. He never returned, and the police could not solve the mystery, although the possibility of his having drowned was not ruled out. I informed her that her husband was dead, as there were strong confirmatory indications of widowhood on her palms and feet. The star at this position will show sudden tragedy over which the subject has no control or previous warning.

The Line of Marriage can **bend downwards** to touch the Heart Line. This will suggest that the subject's partner will pass away first.

It is most favourable indeed if the Marriage line **touches the Sun Line.** The subject will definitely marry someone rich and famous. This sort of mark is seen on the hands of men who marry women of high social status and wealth or vice versa. This auspicious mark was present on the hands of an American woman who, through marriage, gained wealth and reputation.

However, it is very unfavourable if the Marriage Line touches the Sun Line, and then cuts it. This bad effect will be magnified if the Marriage Line slopes downwards while cutting the Sun Line. This is because a descending line is always bad in this science. Such a formation will reveal that the subject will lose honour, wealth, and peace of mind because of a bad alliance.

A **break** in the Marriage Line will mean a very serious interruption in the married life. This is because a short-circuit has taken place as regards the Vital Current cours-

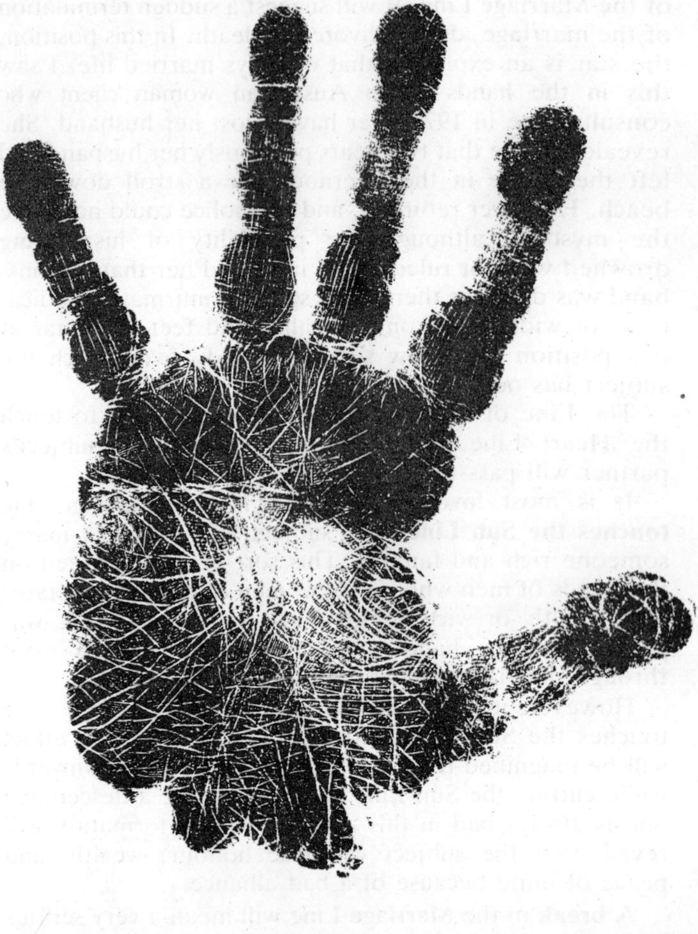

Figure 16-9 An example of a hypersensitive person. Notice the Line of Affection bending downwards to touch the Heart Line

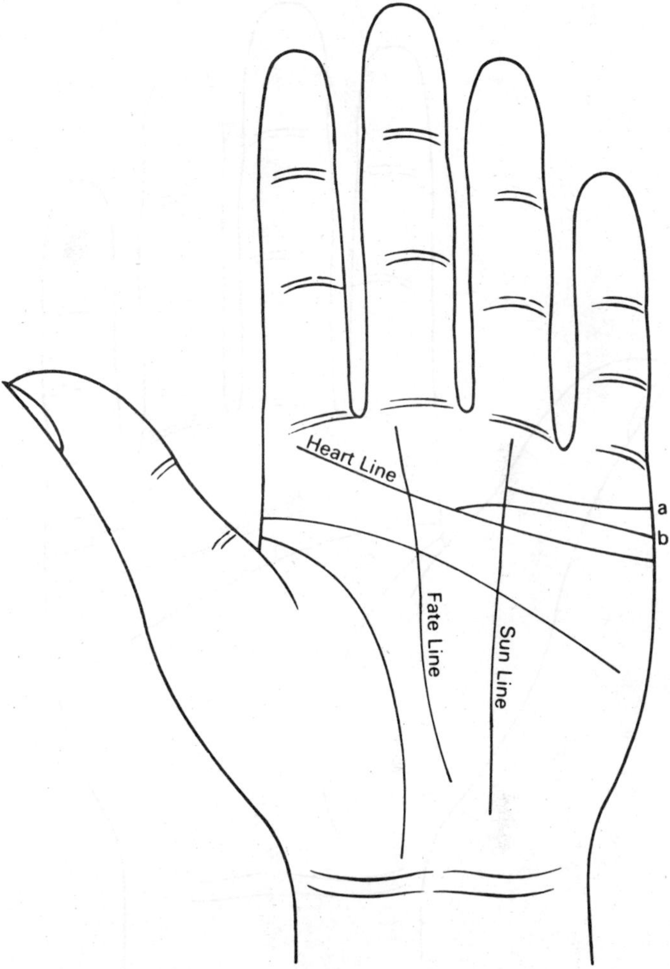

Figure 16-10 (a) Affection Line touching the Sun Line (b) Affection Line cutting the Sun Line

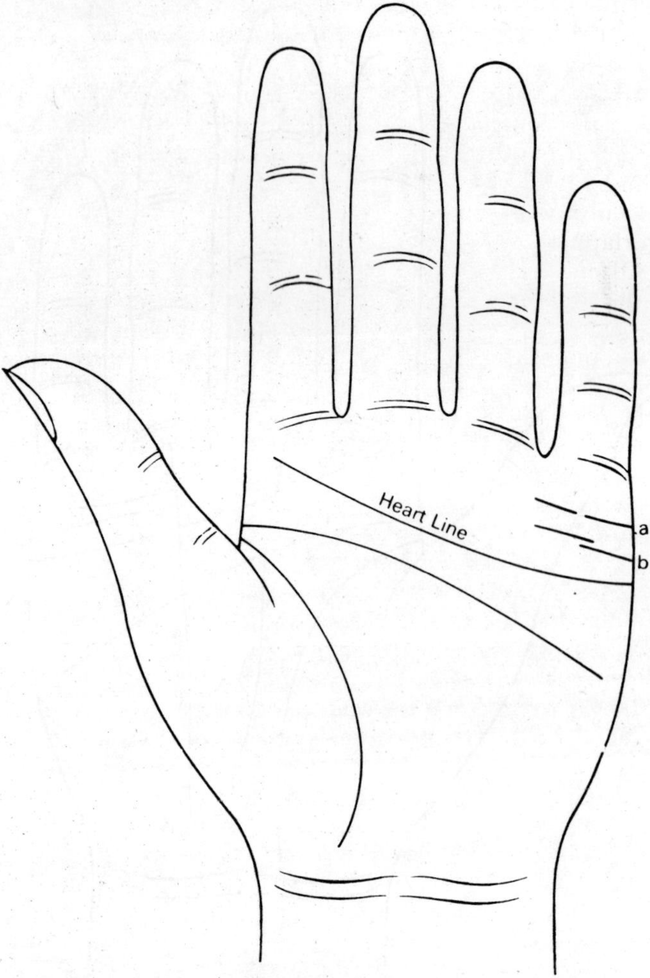

Figure 16-11 (a) a Break in the Line of Affection
(b) an overlapping Break in the Affection Line

ing through the Marriage Line. Generally, such a mark signifies a serious break or a divorce. But should there be an overlapping break, then the situation has been saved, as the overlapping break is a sign of repair. The couple will be reconciled and thus the marriage will continue. Should the overlapping line continue long and firmly, the reunion could prove to last a long time. We must always bear in mind the vast difference between a break and an overlapping break in the Marriage Line.

Often, you will find a clear line dropping from the base of the little finger and cutting the Marriage Line. This is a mark of obstruction. Generally, this marking suggests some opposition to the contemplated marriage by relatives or others. I have found this mainly on the hands of fellow Asian clients. This makes sense, as among Asians the family still has a large say in matters of marriage. I have seldom found this mark in the hands of clients from Western countries. In these countries, the environment is different, and parents generally do not interfere in the choice of a marriage partner. In Asian families the family structure is in general well-knit and close. It is interesting to note that the Line of Marriage reflects the social and cultural conditions of the subject's environment, a point which is worthy of further research by sociologists.

Let us assume that the Marriage Line has been correctly identified by the hand analyst. Lines before the Marriage Line will then refer to earlier attachments, before marriage took place. These previous attachments need not be sexual. They could be platonic as well. Lines of Affection after the Marriage Line will suggest attachments after marriage. In this case, the lines will be nearer the base of the little finger. Confirmatory indications on other parts of the hand will show whether there was a real affair after marriage. Experienced hand analysts see such lines many a time on the palms of distinguished men and women who hold very respectable positions in society, so the mature hand analyst will only reveal this fact to the

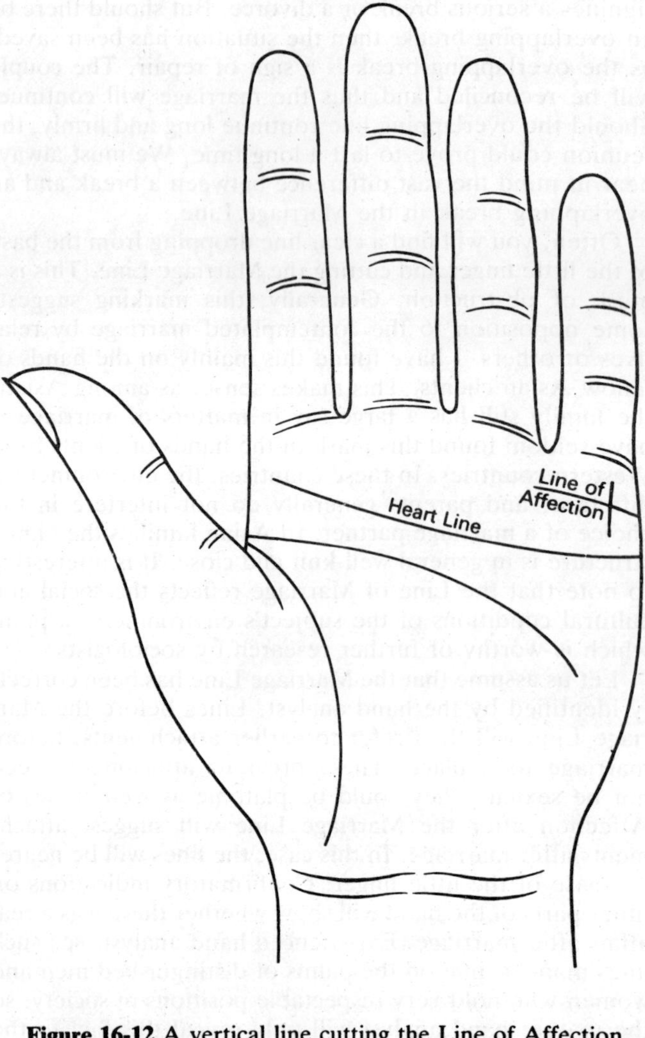

Figure 16-12 A vertical line cutting the Line of Affection

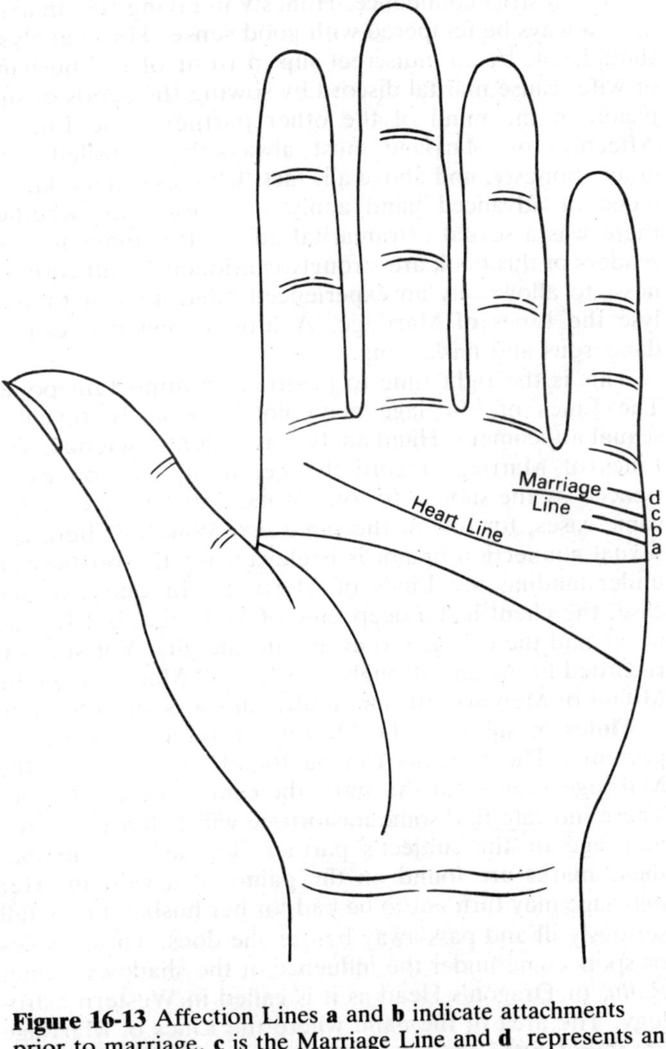

Figure 16-13 Affection Lines **a** and **b** indicate attachments prior to marriage. **c** is the Marriage Line and **d** represents an attachment after marriage.

subject in strict confidence. Honesty in giving the analysis must always be tempered with good sense. Hand analysts should not, by an indiscreet slip in front of the husband or wife, cause marital discord by sowing the seeds of suspicion in the mind of the other partner. The Line of Affection or Marriage must always be handled with grace, honesty, and above all, tact. It takes a deep knowledge of advanced hand analysis to ascertain whether there was a sexual extramarital affair after marriage. So readers of this book are strongly cautioned, in all earnestness, to allow only an experienced hand analyst to analyse the Lines of Marriage. A little knowledge can be dangerous and misleading.

This is the right time to mention an important point. The Lines of Marriage need not necessarily reveal a sexual attachment. Hand analysis is a mental science. The Lines of Marriage record the depth of emotion experienced by the subject for one of the opposite sex, and in some cases, for one of the same sex. Whether there is a sexual connection or not is irrelevant for the purpose of understanding the Lines of Marriage. In one extreme case, the client had a deep Line of Marriage, but he had never had the courage to even date the girl. Yet she was recorded firmly and strongly as a Line of Marriage on the Mount of Mercury. But, naturally, this was an exception.

Moles or **spots** on the Marriage Line are always evil portents. These marks can be found anywhere on the Marriage Line — at the start, the centre, or at the end. These indicate that some misfortune will either befall the marriage or the subject's partner. Let us assume that these marks are found on the palms of a woman. Her marriage may turn out to be bad, or her husband may fall seriously ill and pass away before she does. These moles or spots come under the influence of the shadowy planet *Rahu*, or Dragon's Head as it is called in Western astrology. The area of the palm where the Lines of Marriage are found in the Mount of Mercury is symbolic of the sev-

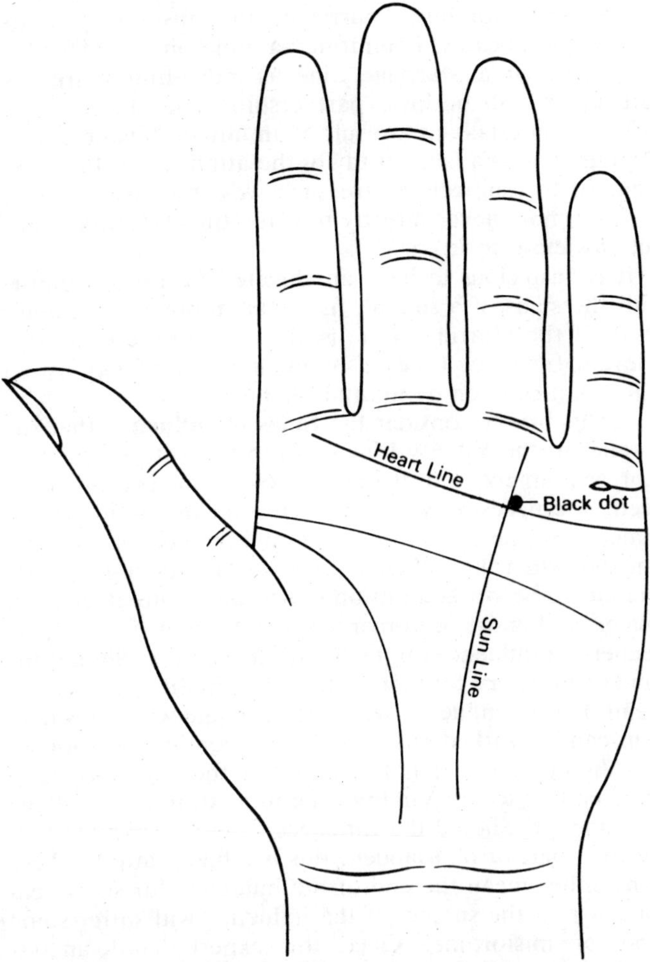

Figure 16-14 An Island on the Marriage Line and a black Dot near the Sun Line is suggestive of emotional trouble or even scandal after marriage.

enth house in astrology. In Indian astrology, the seventh house stands for love, marriage, and business partnership. In some cases, I confirmed a mole on the Mount of Mercury near a Marriage Line as indicating sharp disagreement in a business partnership. The subjects had suffered materially as a result of an unwise business partnership. This is a fact worthy of the attention of businessmen. In the subjects where such was the case, I found that the mole never directly touched the Affection Line, but was close to it.

It is auspicious to have an elevated **Mount of Jupiter** with the signs of a square, fish, star, temple, or triangle on it. If the Marriage Line is also well-formed, and the relevent Influence Lines also beneficial, the lucky owner will doubtlessly enjoy marital bliss.

Let us briefly consider the **Lines of Influence** that run parallel to the Vitality Line or drop from it. These lines represent an event, or the influence of some person. They need not necessarily always refer to the influence of someone of the opposite sex, but in many cases, they do. The age when the Influence Line starts affecting the subject has to be worked out on the Vitality Line itself. The longer and more well-marked the Influence Line, the deeper the influence on the life of the subject. Should the Line of Influence turn away from the Vitality Line, it will mean that the influence will fade. The age when this happens can be worked out on the corresponding position on the Vitality Line. It is favourable if the Influence Line runs parallel to the Vitality Line in a strong, clear, flawless manner. Should the Influence Line itself be starred, cut by a bar, or be islanded, this is a bad feature. These signs either mean the end of the influence for some reason, or that the subject of the influence will suffer some kind of misfortune. Once the expert hand analyst confirms that the Influence Line represents the lover, wife, or future spouse, it will be easy to analyse the future influence of this person on the emotional life of the subject.

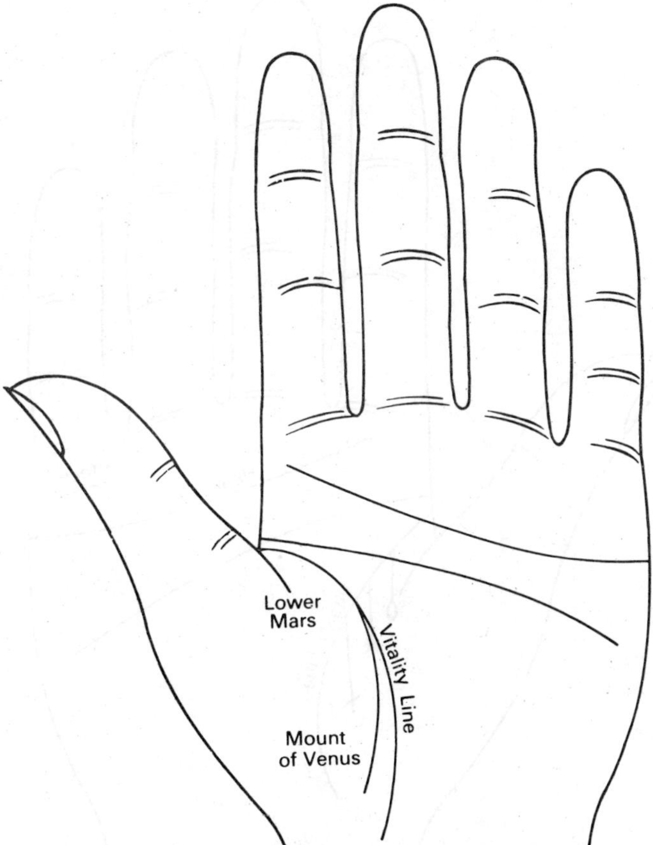

Figure 16-15 An Influence Line parallel to the Vitality Line

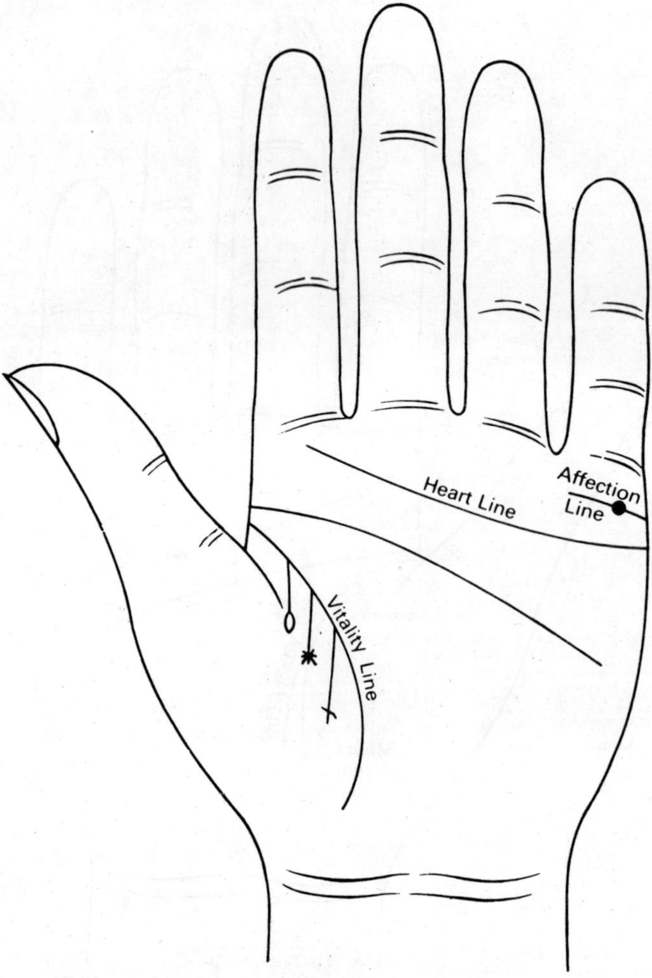

Figure 16-16 Influence Lines islanded, starred and cut by a crossbar. Note the mole on the Affection Line.

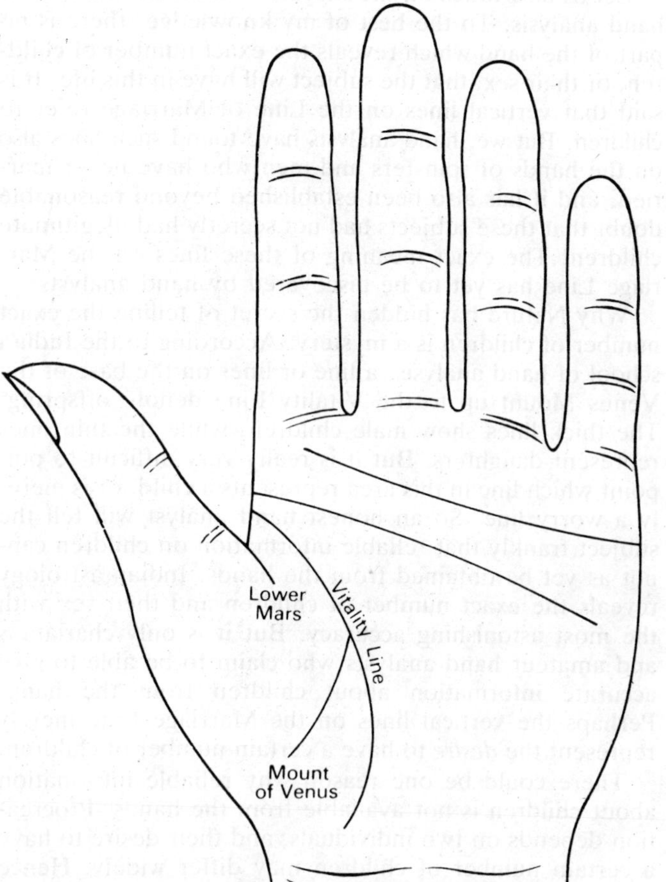

Figure 16-17 An Influence Line turning away from the Vitality Line on the Mount of Venus

Let us now touch on the subject of **children** in scientific hand analysis. To the best of my knowledge, there is no part of the hand which reveals the exact number of children, or their sex, that the subject will have in this life. It is said that vertical lines on the Line of Marriage refer to children. But we, hand analysts have found such lines also on the hands of spinsters and men who have never married, and it has also been established beyond reasonable doubt that these subjects had not secretly had illegitimate children! The exact meaning of these lines on the Marriage Line has yet to be discovered by hand analysts.

Why Nature has hidden the secret of telling the exact number of children is a mystery. According to the Indian school of hand analysis, a line or lines on the base of the Venus Mount up to the Vitality Line denote offspring. The thick lines show male children, while the thin ones represent daughters. But it is really very difficult to pinpoint which line in this area represents a child, or is merely a worry line. So an honest hand analyst will tell the subject frankly that reliable information on children cannot as yet be obtained from the hands. Indian astrology reveals the exact number of children and their sex with the most astonishing accuracy. But it is only charlatans and amateur hand analysts who claim to be able to give accurate information about children from the hand. Perhaps the vertical lines on the Marriage Line merely represent the *desire* to have a certain number of children.

There could be one reason why reliable information about children is not available from the hands. Procreation depends on two individuals, and their desire to have a certain number of children may differ widely. Hence the mental influences of the two individuals concerned are shown in a haphazard manner on the palms. Occasionally, it is true that these vertical lines do reveal the exact number of children. But in such cases, I have always found the vertical lines to be clear and well-formed. At any rate, it is best to be ruthlessly honest with

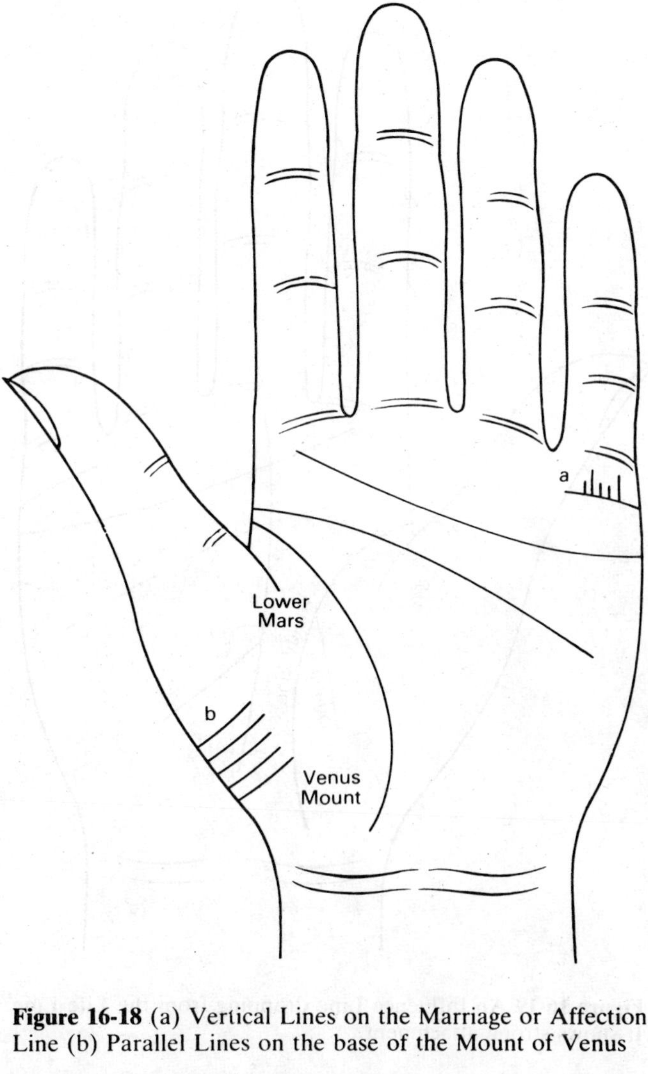

Figure 16-18 (a) Vertical Lines on the Marriage or Affection Line (b) Parallel Lines on the base of the Mount of Venus

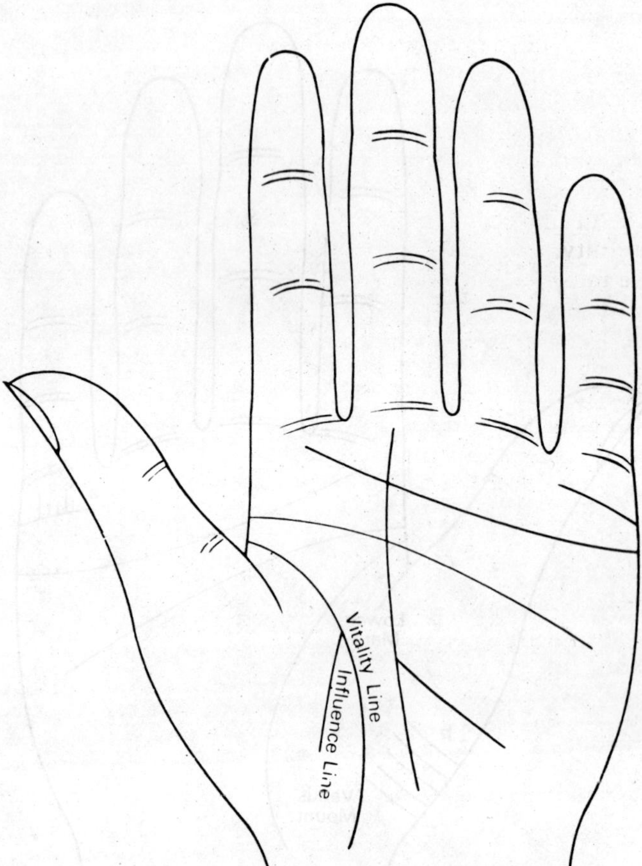

Figure 16-19 An Influence Line dropping from the Life Line. It shows strong attachment.

the subject, and explain lucidly the truth of the matter. Just for passing interest, as regards the vertical lines on the Marriage Line, the thick lines are supposed to represent male children, while the thin ones reveal the birth of daughters. Broken or cut lines are supposed to denote children who will suffer a premature death. However, this aspect of hand analysis still awaits further research.

But the hand does give reliable information as to sterility, which has been discussed earlier. In this science, we must test each line thousands of times, and see whether it shows what has actually happened in the experience of the subject whose palms are being analysed. This is the hallmark of the first-class scientist. Observe, experiment, and test each law of scientific hand analysis. Do not be awed by the reputation of any author or world-famous hand analyst. The only criterion is that the laws of scientific hand analysis are founded on the bedrock of TRUTH.

Chapter Seventeen

Scientific Hand Analysis, Your Sexual Attitude and Sex Potential

Experienced hand analysts know that sex plays a vital role in the happiness of a marriage. Many marriages break down because of sexual dissatisfaction, incompatibility and frustration. A really competent hand analyst can assess sexual compatibility or otherwise with a surprising in-depth analysis that would be the envy of psychologists. In this chapter, let us look at a few important guide-lines regarding sex and scientific hand analysis. Dr. Sigmund Freud made the world aware of the truth that many emotional disorders can be traced to sexual difficulties and problems.

The **Mount of Venus** is the barometer of sexuality. Should this mount be flat, white, narrow, soft or flabby, it will reveal a sexual weakness. The situation will be aggravated if the Mount is depressed. We must bear in mind that Venus represents sexual desire, music, and grace in both hand analysis and astrology. A woman with such a weak formation would probably be frigid. A man, too, would tend to lack sexual ardour, and with other unfavourable indications, such as a rising first rascette, will also be impotent.

It is also unfavourable if the Mount of Venus is over-elevated, red, and heavily grilled. This subject would be excessively passionate.

Let us consider the case of a man with an over-elevated Mount of Venus. We will now assume that his Heart Line and Line of Mentality are not strong. This would suggest a lack of self-control, and would thus be an added danger to the over-elevated Mount. This sort of man would hanker after sexual pleasures, throwing caution to the winds.

There are certain signs on the Mount of Venus which heighten sexual ardour and heat. These are the cross, the island, grille, or star on the Mount itself.

It is very revealing if the Heart Line stops below the Mount of Saturn. This will indicate that sex will surely play a very important role in the love or married life of the subject. Let us bear in mind again that Saturn is basically an unfavourable planet in hand analysis. Let us assume that with such a Heart Line, the Mount of Venus is also over-elevated with unfavourable signs such as a cross or grille on it. Such a subject would be obsessed by sex. Should the quadrangle, the space between the Lines of Mentality and Heart, also be narrow, the subject would be very selfish in his sexual behaviour and attitude.

The junction of the Lines of Heart, Vitality and Mentality below or on the Mount of Jupiter is also revealing. Some sort of sexual disharmony is indicated by this formation. This is all the more certain if the Mount of Venus and the Line of Heart are afflicted. The subject may be promiscuous, especially if there is an islanded Girdle of Venus.

A red Mount of Venus shows more sexual ardour than a pink, yellow or white formation. The normal colour is a healthy pink. Red is a sure sign of excess of sexual ardour. So we have to analyse the following aspects when we study sex and scientific hand analysis:

(a) The Girdle of Venus
(b) Influence Lines found on the Mount of Venus
(c) The colour of the palm, and especially the colour of the Line of Heart and Mount of Venus
(d) The terminations of the Lines of Heart and Mentality
(e) Islanded formations or other malformations on the

Lines of Mentality and Heart
(f) The Mount of Venus
(g) The colour of the nails
(h) The Thumb
(i) The first Rascette or Bracelet
(j) Afflictions to the Lines of Affection or Marriage Line below the little finger on the Mount of Mercury, and
(k) The length of the little finger or finger of Mercury.

With other indications, the colour of the **nails** also reveals sexual ardour. Red-coloured nails will show an excess of sexual heat. Pink-coloured nails are suggestive of good health, as well as a desirable sexual potential and outlook. Similarly, should a woman's Mount of Venus be well-developed, and preferably pink in colour, as well as elastic in its consistency, she will surely have a healthy sexual response.

The ideal sexual partner must not only be passionate, but must also know how to communicate effectively. The planet Mercury stands for communication. So to study this aspect of communication, we must examine the Mount of Mercury, and the little finger, the **finger of Mercury.** I have often noticed that when the little finger is abnormally short,[1] that there frequently is trouble in the married life. Among mongoloids, the little finger is short, undeveloped, and also pointed. In scientific hand analysis, it is a profound truth that the length and shape of the small finger gives valuable clues as to the sex life of the subject.

Should the little finger be short and pointed, it will show a low sex drive. This will be all the more certain if the Mount of Venus is also weak and undeveloped. It has also come to my notice that subjects of both sexes, with abnormally short little fingers, find it difficult to communi-

---

[1] The fingers are considered small if the small finger does not reach the middle or second phalange of the ring or third finger.

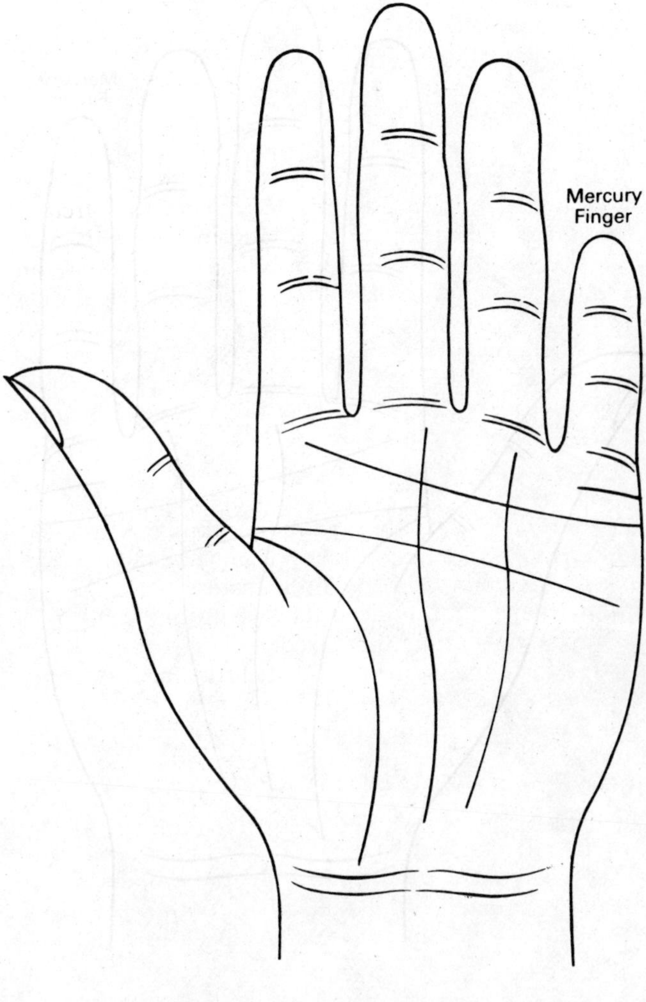

Figure 17-1 A short Little (Mercury) Finger

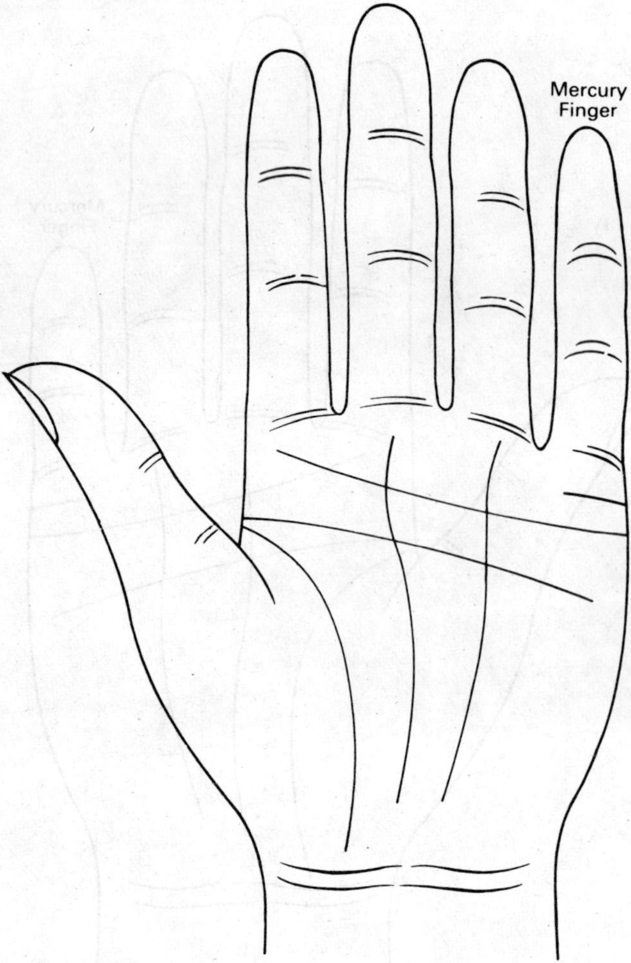

Figure 17-2 A long Little (Mercury) Finger

cate effectively with the opposite sex. Such subjects have said that frequently they are at a loss for the right words at the right time. Among Indian hand analysts, there is a saying that a man with a short little finger will have a shrew for a wife. This is, of course, assuming that the wife has a normally developed little finger. This situation will arise because generally the wife will out-talk her husband. Physically, a woman with a short Mercury finger may have an underdeveloped uterus, and may also tend to frigidity. On the other hand, a long little finger will suggest that the sex drive is good, and that the sexual organs are healthy and in a normal state of development.

What is to be done if the little finger is short? There are various astrological remedies, such as the wearing of selected gems, to correct this deficiency. But this is an intricate process, involving a deep knowledge of advanced hand analysis, as well as astrology. But here is a **simple remedy: grow the nails of both the little fingers.** The nails of the other fingers can be cut and kept trim. When the little finger is short, not enough of the Vital Current enters this particular finger, so not enough energy flows through it, due to its defective length. Thus, to lengthen the finger metaphorically, the simple remedy will be to grow the fingernail. In this way, to some degree, the deficiency of the flow of the Vital Current will be corrected. Of course, there are more effective astrological remedies, but these are outside the scope of this elementary work on scientific hand analysis.

Psychologists point out that marriages often break down when there is no communication between the couple. The great seducers of history, male and female, probably had long Mercury fingers. In this way, they were able to mentally seduce the object of their affection, and soften the resistance of the other party.

Let us now study this aspect of **sexual compatibility** in some depth. Let us suppose that a woman has a weak Vitality Line, with a restricted, flat Mount of Venus.

Clearly, this woman will have a weak sex drive. This will be all the more evident if the little finger is also short. Especially if the Heart Line is straight, this woman will rarely be able to think of sex outside a romantic framework. It is therefore advisable for her to choose a husband with a similar outlook on sex. Should the husband be very physical and aggressive in his sexual make-up and approach, clearly there will be trouble. Such a woman as the one described above will require the emotion of love to be present if she is to derive pleasure from the sexual act.

Let us now consider another example. Here we have a man whose palms are thick, the Mount of Venus highly developed, the Heart Line strongly curved, and the texture of the skin coarse. This man will be burning with sexual desire. His sexual appetite will be strong and physical. He will enjoy sex tremendously, without the emotion of love being necessarily present. This man must be as wise as a serpent, and choose a woman with a similar type of hands. Such a woman will have a similar sexual outlook towards males, so there will be a large element of sexual compatibility between the couple. This is scientific hand analysis in practice.

In my professional career I have come across several cases of men and women who believed in the philosophy of **sexual conquest.** I must say that I have found more men than women having this undesirable attitude. Some of the men were prepared to resort to highly unethical means to seduce unwilling females. How do we recognize the person who believes in sexual conquest?

For this, we must examine the Index (Jupiter) and Middle (Saturn) fingers. When the tip of the Jupiter finger leans towards the Saturn finger, the subject will believe in the philosophy of "What I want, I must get at all costs." To have a deeper understanding of the strength of determination, we must also examine the thumb. If the thumbs and other features of the hand also reveal selfish-

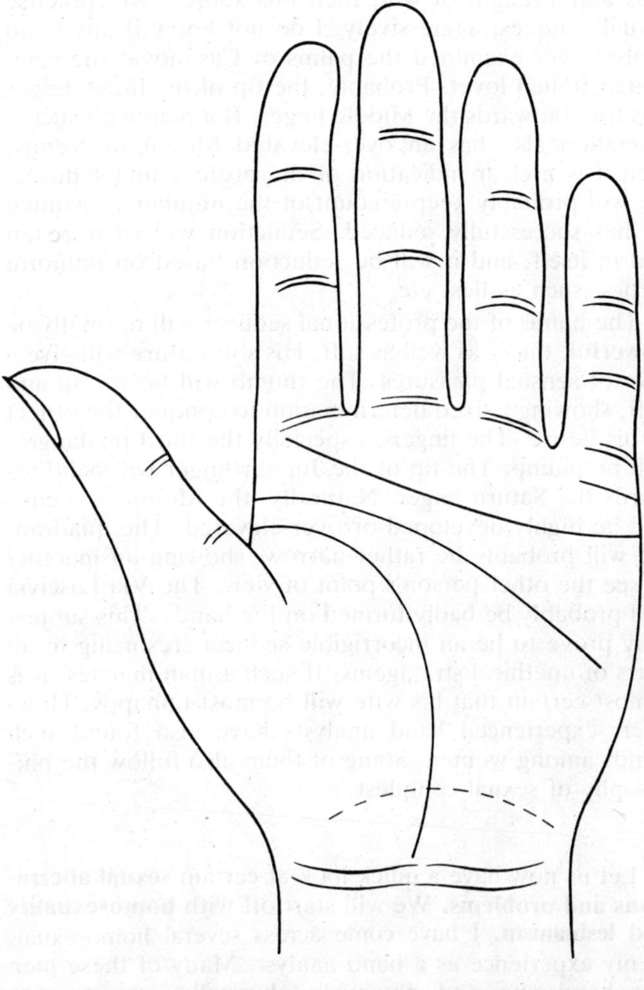

Figure 17-3 The handprint of a subject who strongly believes in sexual conquest. Note the tip of the First (Jupiter) Finger and the prominent Venus Mount.

ness and strength of will, then this subject will practise sexual conquest aggressively. I do not know if any hand analyst ever examined the palms of Casanova, the celebrated Italian lover. Probably, the tip of his Index finger was tilted towards the Middle finger. If a man with such a formation also has an over-elevated Mount of Venus, then it is a clear indication of the professional seducer. He will probably keep a count of the number of women he has successfully seduced. Seduction will then be an end in itself, and it will be seduction based on immoral tactics, such as lies, etc.

The hands of the professional seducer will normally be powerful, thick, as well as soft. His soft nature will give a love of sensual pleasures. The thumb will be strong and stiff, showing a fixed determination to conquer the object of his desire. The fingers, especially the third phalanges, will be plump. The tip of the Jupiter finger will bend towards the Saturn finger. Naturally, the Mount of Venus will be highly developed or over-elevated. The quadrangle will probably be rather narrow, showing an inability to see the other person's point of view. The Via Lascivia will probably be badly formed on the hands. This subject may prove to be an incorrigible seducer, resorting to all sorts of unethical stratagems. If such a man marries, it is almost certain that his wife will be most unhappy. However, experienced hand analysts have also found such hands among women. Some of them also follow the philosophy of sexual conquest.

Let us now have a quick look at certain **sexual aberrations and problems.** We will start off with **homosexuality** and **lesbianism.** I have come across several homosexuals in my experience as a hand analyst. Many of these men are handsome and obviously physically attractive to women, and under different circumstances, many women would be interested in them.

The homosexual generally has a very sensitive mind. On the hands of most homosexuals, I have observed the Girdle of Venus. As stated earlier, the Girdle of Venus is seldom found on the hands of men. But let us be logical in thought. Please do not jump to the conclusion that every man who has a Girdle of Venus must be a homosexual. In some cases, the homosexuals I have examined did not have the Girdle of Venus marked on their hands, but a high percentage of them, easily over fifty percent, did have this formation.

On close questioning, I discovered that there had been some form of early repression in the lives of most of these subjects. Sometimes the father had been repressive, and at other times it had been the mother. There is one indication in hand analysis that shows early repression. The Fate Line or the Line of Saturn is tied to the Vitality Line for quite some distance; the Fate Line does not start away from the Vitality Line, or from the Mount of Moon, in such cases. I encountered this tied formation in the majority of cases. It is interesting to note that in the Indian School of Hand Analysis, the Vitality Line is called the Line of Heredity, or the Line of Father. This tied formation symbolizes some early restrictive factors, causing psychological repression in most cases. It can be confidently stated that this is in accordance with the learned views of eminent psychologists as being one of the major causes of homosexuality.

There are two types of homosexuals — the passive, and the active type. The passive type of homosexual will generally have a straight Heart Line. Occasionally, the Line of Heart will descend to touch the Line of Mentality. Furthermore, the texture of the skin will tend to be smooth and fine. In the case of the active, aggressive type of homosexual, the Mount of Venus is generally highly developed, but a more significant clue is the curve of the Heart Line, showing an aggressive sexuality. This I confirmed repeatedly after questioning subjects in the strictest confidence.

In astrology, homosexuality is shown by afflictions from the planet Uranus to Mercury and Moon. Mercury and Moon affect the human mind strongly. Eminent Indian astrologers regard homosexuality as the chief of the Uranian type of abnormalities. Should the subject require a cure, a complete horoscope, preferably based on Hindu Astrology, must be cast. Then remedies can be prescribed, based on which planets are afflicted and have to be appeased. But in general, I have found that most homosexuals were happy as they were, in which case, it is my opinion that they should be left to lead their own lives in peace, as long as they do not harm others, emotionally or physically. If a homosexual wishes to get rid of this sexual trait, however, meditation should help tremendously.

Let us now consider **Satyriasis** and **Nymphomania.** If a male has an excessive sexual appetite, the condition is known as satyriasis, while a similar condition in a woman is called nymphomania. I have encountered such men and women in my professional practice several times. How do we recognise the subject with an excessive sexual appetite?

Generally, there will be a consistent pattern. The hands will be thick and flabby. The flabby consistency of the palms will give the subject an extreme love of sensual pleasures. The fingers will tend to be short and plump. The thumb will be supple. Also, most of these subjects will have both the Girdle of Venus and the Via Lascivia well marked. Between the two, the Via Lascivia will be more frequently present.

I saw such indications on the hands of a man from a different country. He confessed that women were his very serious weakness. A pretty local girl, barely twenty-seven years of age, confessed that she had had sexual relations with about two hundred men. She consulted me in 1977, and complained that keeping track of the men with whom she had sexual relations was becoming increasingly difficult!

Lastly, let us have a look at a problem which is universal among men. This is the problem of **premature ejaculation,** although strictly speaking, this is not an abnormality. In hand analysis, what are the features which indicate this problem?

The thumbs will be supple, the hand weak, the mounts will be flat or depressed, and the lines of the hand will be fine and numerous. Also, the Girdle of Venus will be prominent. The Lines of Mentality and Heart may be tied together excessively at the beginning. Or they may be widely separated at the beginning. A subject having these hand features will tend to suffer from premature ejaculation. Should the skin texture be smooth and soft, this condition will be aggravated. This problem of premature ejaculation will be more difficult to correct should the Fate Line (Saturn Line) be tied to the Vitality Line. A deeply hypersensitive nature is one of the causes of premature ejaculation. The presence of the Girdle of Venus will reveal swift psychic or mental stimulation This mental stimulation will speed up the process of premature ejaculation.

Let us assume that these features are present and that the crucial point is the excessive separation between the Lines of Vitality and Mentality. This subject will be a 'bluffer'. He will outwardly make bold advances towards the opposite sex, but inwardly he will feel both insecure and inadequate sexually. The outward boldness will be caused by a certain impulsiveness, associated with a wide gap between the Lines of Mentality and Vitality. Such an attitude will reveal a deep-rooted inferiority complex, parading as a misleading sense of superiority.

What is the cure for this? Yoga physical exercises will be a boon to such a subject. There is a brilliant book called *Yoga* and *Sex* by the late Pandit Shiv Sharma. There are many effective Yoga postures to cure this affliction. Furthermore, the Indians have a sophisticated sex cult called Tantra and there is a good elementary book on the subject called *Tantra, The Secret Power of Sex.*[3]

Needless to say, the Yoga physical exercises must be practised under expert guidance. This is partly because some of the Yoga Sex exercises are meant to promote celibacy. Hence they are not suitable for married couples. Tantric Sex should also be practised under expert guidance.

This has been a brief survey of sex and scientific hand analysis. A deeper study of the subject requires a book by itself.

---

[2] Pandit Shiv Sharma, *Yoga and Sex*, G.G. Harrap & Co, London, 1973.

[3] Arvind & Shanta Kale, *Tantra, The Secret Power of Sex*, Jaico Publishing House, Bombay, 1976.

Chapter Eighteen

Luck and Good Fortune as Revealed by Scientific Hand Analysis

This is a materialistic world. Most clients are interested to know about their financial position, when they will join the Millionaire's Club, and their chances of sudden wealth. They are concerned about having a healthy bank balance. Being rich is good fortune and luck to them. I have seen the hands of extremely rich clients from various parts of the world. To my surprise, however, I have found that most of these people are pretty unhappy. In their pursuit of Mammon they have sacrificed the interests of the family. A large number have also paid the penalty for an excessive drive for money by suffering from ruined health.

Hand analysts believe that health is wealth. Having a very strong bank balance is only one aspect of good fortune. Our concept of good fortune and luck is comprehensive. To have true blessedness, the subject should be financially sound, have excellent health, a happy married life, as well as peace of mind. He must basically be a happy, well-adjusted personality.

But in this elementary work on hand analysis, let us limit the scope of the discussion to signs of wealth in the hand. After having examined the hands of hundreds of really wealthy clients, certain laws of wealth in this science can be worked out accurately.

First of all, let us study the position of the **Line of Mentality.** This line, in normal circumstances, divides the palmar area into two zones. When we talk of the palmar area, we do not include the fingers. The palm is that area between the wrist and the base of the fingers. This is the area divided into two halves by the Line of Mentality. There is the upper active zone, and the lower passive zone. The upper zone, being nearer the fingers, refers more to concern for the future and planning for a rainy day. In general, the upper zone refers to the nobler aspirations. The lower zone contains the pleasure-loving planets and mounts, the Mounts of Moon and Venus. Let us assume that the lower zone is prominent in the palm. In this case, the subject will not be thrifty, and will tend to spend excessively. So even if this subject earns a lot of money, his savings will tend to be meagre. The reverse will be the case should the upper zone be prominent. Of course, other factors of the hand have to be taken into consideration.

Then there is another important factor of assessment as regards acquisition of wealth. In this case, we consider the **back of the hand.** We must measure the length of the fingers, as well as the length of the palm. The important finger length to consider is that of the middle or Saturn finger. We measure this finger from the base to its tip. In an earlier chapter, we have learnt that the fingers refer more to the spiritual or mental side of the individual. The palm area of the back of the hand symbolises the materialistic aspect of the subject's life. Let us now assume that the back of the palm is longer than that of the fingers. Then we can easily deduce that this subject will have a materialistic mentality. He will be more interested in money-making than in intellectual and spiritual attainments. On the other hand, the subject whose fingers are longer than the length of the back of the palm will not be so interested in material wealth.

We must analyse both these points carefully before we can assess the attitude of the subject towards material gains.

The hands of very wealthy subjects have certain com-

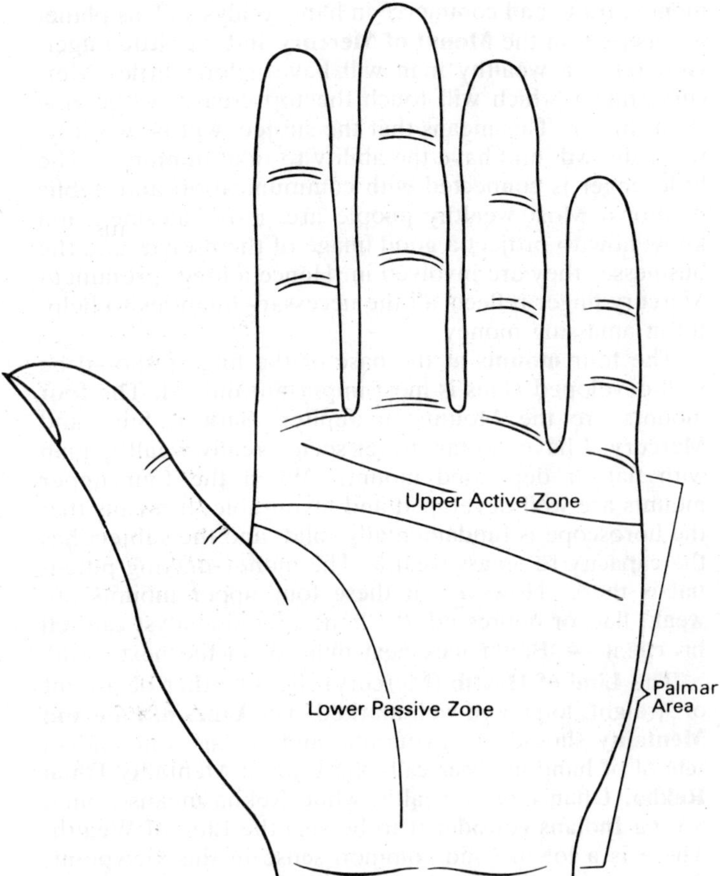

Figure 18-1 The Line of Mentality dividing the palm into two zones

mon characteristics. The planet Mercury stands for money, trade and commerce in hand analysis. This planet has its seat on the **Mount of Mercury** and the little finger. Generally, a wealthy man will have a long little (Mercury) finger which will touch the top crease of the ring (Sun) finger. This means that the subject will be worldly-wise, shrewd, and have the ability to rake in money. The little finger is connected with communication and public relations. Most wealthy people are good salesmen and know how to project a good image of themselves and the businesses they are involved in. Hence a long, prominent Mercury finger reflects all the necessary qualities so helpful in amassing money.

The four **mounts** at the base of the fingers should be well-developed. This is most important indeed. The four mounts are the Mounts of Jupiter, Saturn, Sun, and Mercury. I have, so far, never seen a really wealthy man with flat or depressed mounts. When the four upper mounts are well-developed and favourable, it means that the horoscope is fundamentally solid, and the subject has the capacity to amass wealth. The money-making potential is there. However, if these four upper mounts are weak, flat, or depressed, the honest hand analyst can tell his client — 'Better luck next time, or in the next birth!'

The **Line of Health** (Mercury) should either be absent or straight, long, and well-marked. The **Lines of Fate and Mentality** should be favourable and strong. The Indian school of hand analysis calls the Line of Mentality **Dhan Rekha.** Dhan means wealth, while Rekha means a line. So the Indians consider it to be also the Line of Wealth. There is a lot of solid common sense in this viewpoint. Success in business and money matters depends largely on a healthy, positive attitude, plus lots of self-confidence. These essential qualities are reflected by a prominent, deep, long, well-marked Line of Mentality. With other favourable supporting features on the hand, a good Line of Mentality will help substantially in accumulating wealth.

The possession of a good, strong **Sun Line** is most important in this aspect. The Sun Line is the barometer of wealth. The subject without a good Sun Line will not have Luck in worldly matters, while the presence of a favourable Sun Line means that success will smile upon the subject. His efforts will be crowned with success from the time the Sun Line makes its appearance in the hand. In my experience, all my extraordinarily rich clients have had good Sun Lines in their hands.

It is also favourable when the Sun Line rises from the Fate Line, and joins up with a Line of Sun on the Mount of Sun (Apollo). The age has to be worked out on the Fate Line itself. From that time, the subject will attain wealth, and probably social prominence as well. All international celebrities have favourable Sun Lines. Without a good Sun Line, the talents of the subject will not be recognized by society.

The **palm** should be broad. Also, the **fingers** should be evenly set on the palm. This means that there will be no major defects in the strength of the four upper mounts. After all, the fingers partake of the qualities of the mounts at their base.

A **trident** formation of the **Heart Line** on the Mount of Jupiter is an indication of wealth or fame. This is a sign very often seen on the hands of rich people. I have confirmed this indication hundreds of times. A **star** on the mount of Jupiter is also a most desirable sign to have. It is a mark of wealth. The subject may have a sudden rise in wealth as a result of this sign. We must note that Jupiter is a planet of expansion. A star on the Mount of Jupiter shows that the subject will think of expanding his business, and be outstandingly successful.

According to the Indian school of hand analysis, certain signs are indicative of wealth or great riches. The signs of the **Conch, Temple, Crocodile** and **Fish** are symbolic of great wealth. A few years ago, an extremely rich

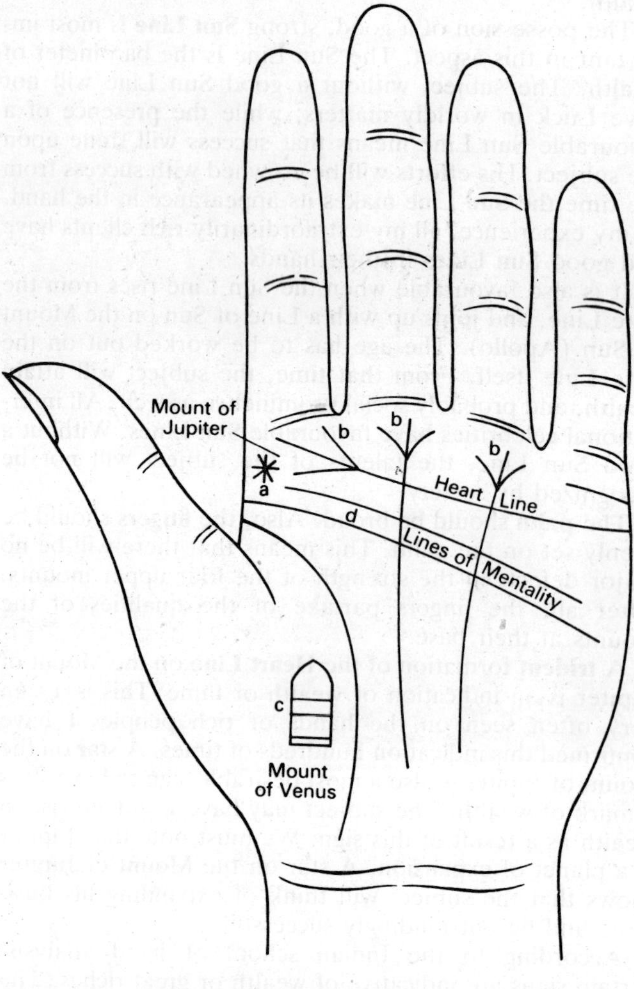

Figure 18-2 Some features of Wealth (a) a Star on the Mount of Jupiter (b) a Trident (c) a Temple on the Mount of Venus (d) Double Lines of Mentality

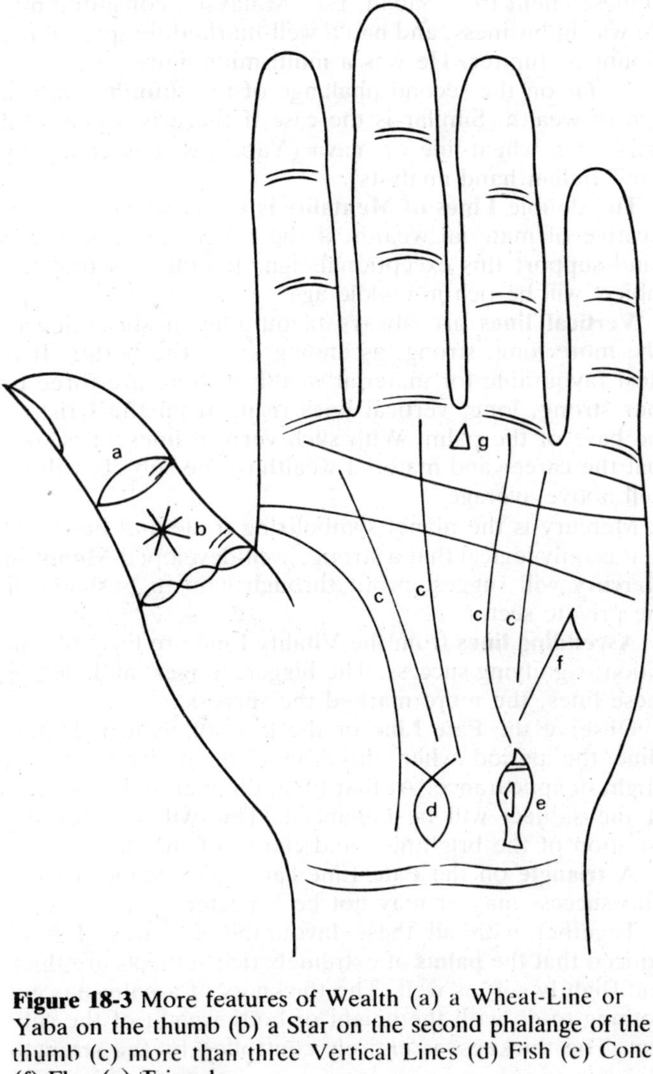

Figure 18-3 More features of Wealth (a) a Wheat-Line or Yaba on the thumb (b) a Star on the second phalange of the thumb (c) more than three Vertical Lines (d) Fish (e) Conch (f) Flag (g) Triangle

Chinese client from Sabah, East Malaysia, consulted me. He was in business, and had a well-marked temple on the Mount of Jupiter. He was a multi-millionaire.

A **star** on the second phalange of the **thumb** is also a sign of wealth. Similar is the case if there is a beautiful mark of a wheat-line or Yava (Yaba, as it is called by some Indian hand analysts).

The double **Lines of Mentality** is a rare mark. It is indicative of material wealth, if the other features of the hand support this exceptional sign. It indicates that the subject will be rich in middle age.

Vertical lines are always favourable in this science. The more long, strong, ascending lines, the better. It is most favourable for material wealth if there are three to four strong, long, vertical lines rising from the wrist or the base of the palm. With such vertical lines, it is sure that the career and material wealth of the subject will be well above average.

Mercury is the planet symbolizing trade and business, so it is only logical that a strong, well-developed **Mount of Mercury** will suggest profit through gain in business or the private sector.

Ascending lines from the Vitality Line are lines of ambition, signifying success. The bigger, longer, and clearer these lines, the more marked the success.

Observe the **Fate Line** or the Line of Saturn. Determine the period when this line is deep, well-cut and bright in appearance. At that time, the material prospects of the subject will be enhanced. This will last for the duration of the brightness and clarity of the line.

A **triangle** on the Fate Line can mean financial gain. This success may or may not be expected.

Together with all these favourable features, I have noticed that the **palms** of extremely rich subjects are thick and slightly soft as well. The thickness of a palm has got nothing to do with the height or body weight of the subject. The thickness is entirely controlled by the strength

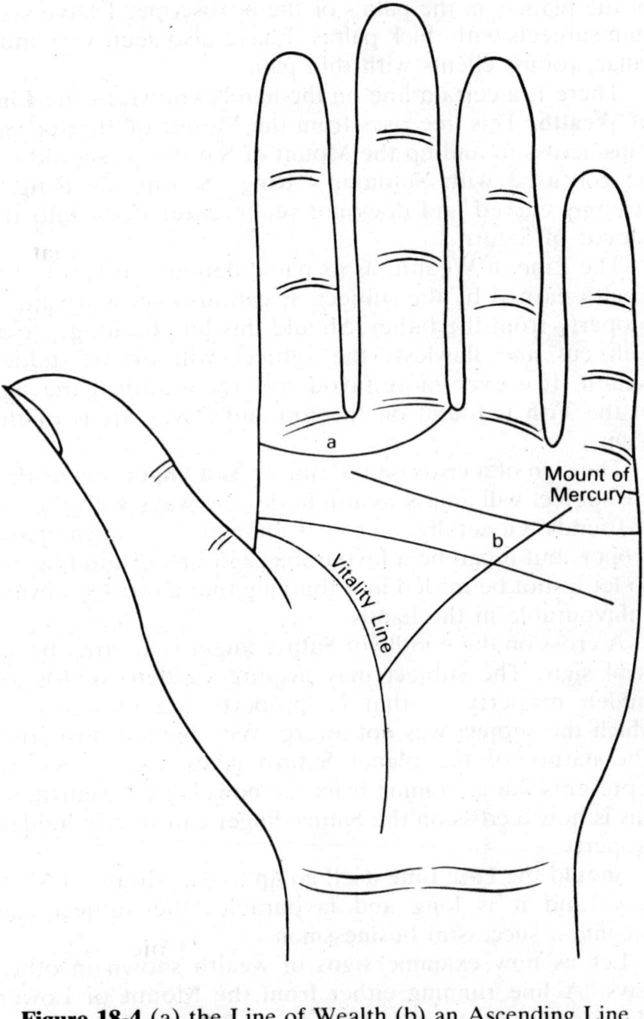

Figure 18-4 (a) the Line of Wealth (b) an Ascending Line from the Vitality Line reaching the Mount of Mercury

of the planets in the palms or the horoscope. I have seen thin subjects with thick palms. I have also seen very muscular, robust clients with thin palms.

There is a certain line on the hands known as the **Line of Wealth.** This line rises from the Mount of Jupiter and runs across to and up the Mount of Saturn. It should not be confused with Solomon's Ring. Solomon's Ring is strongly curved and does not really enter deep into the Mount of Saturn.

The Line of Wealth, as its name denotes, refers to the wealth earned by the subject. It can also show a gain of property from the father. Should this line be long, clear, well cut and flawless, the subject will attain sudden wealth. It is even more favourable for wealth if the sign of the **Fish** is found on the top and lower areas of the palm.

The sign of a **cross** on the ring or **Sun finger** means that the subject will amass wealth in diverse ways with the aid of friends. Generally, a cross is unfavourable in the palm proper, but it can be a favourable sign on certain fingers. So let us not be misled into thinking that a cross is always unfavourable in the hands.

A cross on the middle or **Saturn finger** is another beneficial sign. The subject may acquire sudden wealth, or hidden property — that is, property the existence of which the subject was not aware. Why hidden property? The nature of the planet Saturn gives a clue. Saturn represents things coming from the bowels of the earth, so this is how a cross on the Saturn finger can signify hidden property.

Should the **Fate Line** itself go up to the Mount of Mercury, and it is long and favourable, the subject can become a successful businessman.

Let us now examine signs of wealth shown in other ways. A line running either from the Mount of Lower Mars (under the Jupiter Mount) or Mount of Venus towards the Mount of Jupiter is a good sign for money

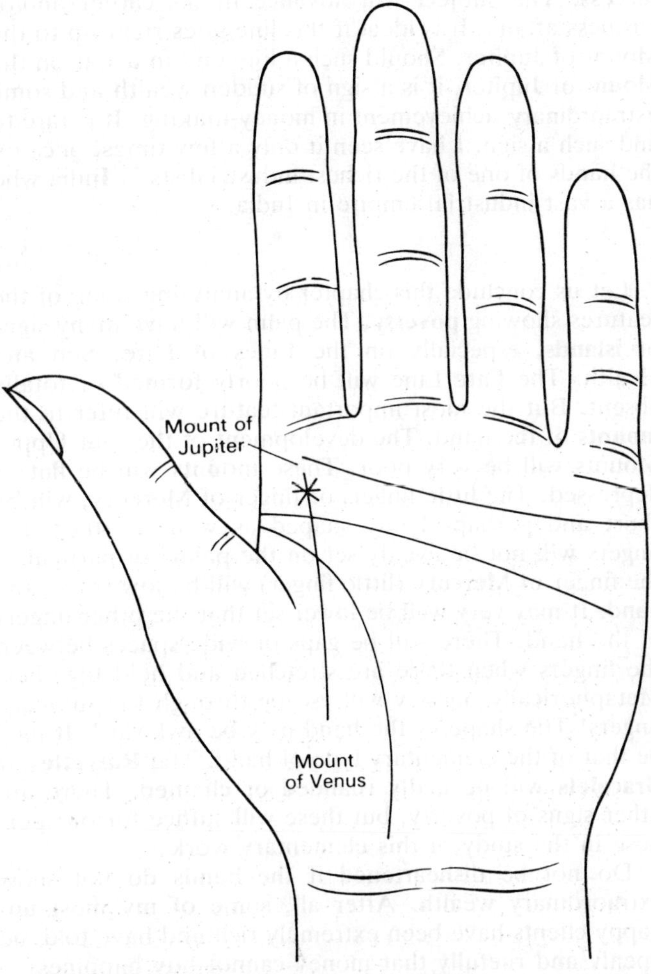

Figure 18-5 An ascending line from the Mount of Venus ending in a Star on the Mount of Jupiter

success. The subject will advance in his career and/or business affairs. It is ideal if this line goes right up to the Mount of Jupiter. Should such a line end in a star on the Mount of Jupiter, it is a sign of sudden wealth and some extraordinary achievement in money-making. It is rare to find such a sign. I have seen it only a few times, once on the hands of one of the richest industrialists in India who has a vast industrial empire in India.

Let us conclude this chapter by analysing some of the features showing **poverty.** The palm will have many signs of **islands,** especially on the Lines of Fate, Sun and Health. The Fate Line will be poorly formed or totally absent. But the most important feature will refer to the **mounts** of the hand. The development of the four Upper Mounts will be very poor. These mounts will be flat or depressed. The little finger, or finger of Mercury, will be short and perhaps badly shaped as well. Further, the fingers will not be evenly set on the palm. In particular, the finger of Mercury (little finger) will be low-set on the hand. It may very well be lower set that the other fingers of the hand. There will be gaps or wide spaces between the fingers when these are stretched and held together. Metaphorically, money will escape through the subject's fingers! The shape of the hand may be awkward. It may be that of the elementary type of hand. The **Rascettes or Bracelets** will be badly islanded or chained. There are other signs of poverty, but these will suffice for our purpose in the study of this elementary work.

Do not be disheartened if the hands do not show extraordinary wealth. After all, some of my most unhappy clients have been extremely rich and have told me openly and ruefully that money cannot buy happiness.

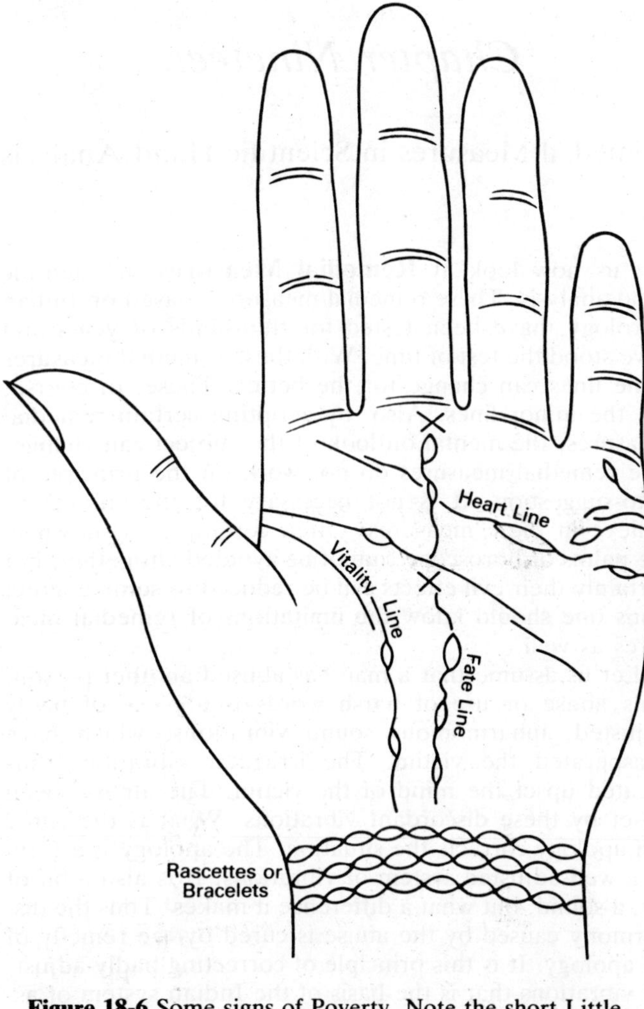

Figure 18-6 Some signs of Poverty. Note the short Little Finger, malformed Rascettes and the badly islanded Fate Line.

Chapter Nineteen

Remedial Measures in Scientific Hand Analysis

Let us now look at **Remedial Measures** in scientific hand analysis. These remedial measures, based on Indian astrology, have been tested for thousands of years and have stood the test of time. With these remedial measures some lines can change for the better. These, of course, are the minor lines. Also, by adopting certain remedial measures, the mental outlook of the subject can change. The remedial measures do not work on the principle of auto-suggestion. It is not necessary for the subject to believe in these measures. Often certain evils shown in the palms or horoscope cannot be avoided altogether, but certainly their evil effects can be reduced to some degree. Thus one should know the limitations of remedial measures as well.

Let us assume that a man has abused another person. This abuse or use of harsh words is a piece of badly adjusted, inharmonious sound vibrations, which have exasperated the victim. The irregular vibrations thus created upset the mind of the victim. The air has been upset by these discordant vibrations. What is the cure? An apology corrects the situation. The apology is a form of a well-adjusted system of vibrations. It is also a bit of air, a sound, but what a difference it makes! Thus the disharmony caused by the abuse is cured by the remedy of an apology. It is this principle of correcting badly-adjusted vibrations that is the basis of the Indian system of astrological remedies.

There are a variety of astrological remedies. There are

medicines, *mantras* or specially worked out sound vibrations, the wearing of selected gems, change of name or change of spelling of name, meditation, Yoga physical exercises, fasting, nature cure (naturopathy), colour therapy, and the performance of special kinds of astrological charities.

Let us now consider **the use of gems** to correct the weaknesses of certain lines in the palms. Why do gems work? Thousands of sceptics have been convinced of the truth of scientific hand analysis, but this science of gem therapy is relatively unknown to the Western world. Certain gems have radioactive properties in them. They are formed by the cosmic rays of certain planets, and it has been confirmed that some gems have radioactive properties in them. A gem responds to the body temperature, and it also possesses properties of refraction and dispersion. The colour of the gem sends out light rays, and chemical reactions take place while the gem is used on the body. The gem has the same elements as those found in the stars and the planets. It is not superstitious but entirely logical to say that the human body can react in a helpful or obstructive manner to the cosmic radiations and vibrations generated by the gem. The science of Yoga says that there is an electrical field called the human aura. A red band is found about an inch from the body, and this is followed by bands of orange, yellow, green, blue and purple. Dr. Crile of the National Academy of Sciences, Cleveland (USA), has proved that the human aura is a magnetic field. He has also shown that colour vibrations work through the aura. So gems, selected after a careful study of the palms or horoscope, can be healing colour agents as well as helpful magnetic fields. Gems are nature's storehouse of energy, and correctly used, they give rise to helpful vibrations against malefic vibrations causing disease. The evil powers released by the planets are always negative, while the cosmic forces released by gems are invariably positive. When the positive rays meet the negative rays, both are neutralized. This is how gem therapy works.

Here are the radiation wave-lengths of selected gems: (a) ruby (70,000); (b) pearl (70,000); (c) red coral (65,000); (d) emerald (70,000); (e) yellow sapphire (50,000); (f) diamond (80,000); (g) blue sapphire (70,000); (h) 'gomed' (hessonite or hyacinth) (70,000); (i) cat's eye (70,000).

Let us now see the wave-lengths of planetary radiations: (a) Sun (65,000); (b) Moon (65,000); (c) Mars (85,000); (d) Mercury (85,000); (e) Jupiter (130,000); (f) Venus (130,000); (g) Saturn (65,000); (h) Rahu (35,000) (a shadowy planet called the Ascending Node of the Moon in Western astrology); and (i) Kethu (35,000) (Kethu is also a shadowy planet, called the Descending Node of the Moon in Western astrology).

The vibrations of the evil planets are both negative and destructive. Thus they have to be neutralized. This can be done through the positive vibrations of either suitable medicines or gems. When a gem is worn next to the skin, it gives out its vibratory power all the time and this power is absorbed into the aura of the subject. This protective aura becomes strong enough to overcome any malignant vibrations from outward sources. It is most important to select the correct gemstone. A single beam of sunlight contains a thousand millionth part of the energy of the sun. A single beam of this energy is sufficient to destroy an entire town when such energy is concentrated through lenses. Likewise, you can imagine the misfortune that will befall a subject who is wearing a wrong gem out of sheer ignorance. A beam of light passed through a prism will change its course. This change differs in various types of prisms. The rays of a planet at a certain angle are of benefit to the subject, but the very same rays at a different angle are a source of danger. So if the angle can be corrected artificially, the evil effects can be minimized to a substantial degree. A gem is like a prism, and we can use this principle to explain the effect of gems on the human body and mind. We cannot possibly change the positions of the planets! They are simply too far away for us mortals to do such a thing, but what is possible is to change the angle of the rays by wearing correctly prescribed gems. This technique will surely lessen the evil effects of the stars and planets.

When the British ruled India, many Englishmen who were critically ill were brought round to health by Indian astrologers who prescribed gems, based on a deep study of the palms and horoscope. The English patients and their Western trained doctors were at first sceptical of such unorthodox methods. However, they were astounded when the gems showed remarkably favourable effects on the health of the patients. Many Englishmen irrationally dismissed this as sheer coincidence. Gem therapy will work if the palms and the horoscope show that death is not at hand. Also, the horoscope must show that the disease or illness is curable. Then, if orthodox techniques of modern medicine fail, unorthodox techniques of 'fringe' medicines such as gem therapy will work. So gem therapy, too, has its limitations.

I once had a dramatic personal experience of gem therapy at work. An education officer fell critically ill, and was bleeding profusely from the stomach. In the hospital he was given a transfusion of twelve pints of blood. The physician in charge was a brilliant man with a great reputation for having the healing touch, yet he was not able to reach a diagnosis and privately told the relatives that the patient probably had only forty-eight hours to live. The patient, though not told this, sensed that his end was near. He made arrangements for his car to be sold, and money to be withdrawn from the bank. I happened to know him well, and a few days after he was warded, I went to donate blood for him. He told me that he was dying and had lost hope of recovery. I suggested that he show his palms to me. I examined both palms thoroughly and informed him that he had a normal life-span. The patient at that time was about forty years of age. He was most sceptical, and asked me whether I would write down this prediction on a piece of paper and sign it. Incidentally, he was a science graduate and did not have faith in anything besides modern science. I asked the nurse for a piece of paper, and wrote on it that the patient would definitely recover from the present critical illness. I signed this statement, dated it, and gave the paper to the patient for safekeeping. His wife was present as a witness.

In the meantime, a famous *bomoh* had been contacted for help. The *bomohs* are village medicine men who practise traditional herbal medicine. They are Malays, and practise a form of herbal medicine akin to Hindu Ayurvedic medicine. The *bomoh,* an old man, was living about a hundred miles away from the hospital, and the symptoms of the patient's illness were described to him by a relative. The *bomoh* gave a ring set with a gem to the relative, and said that the patient must wear the gem on his finger. At the time I visited the patient, he was still bleeding internally.

One or two days later, the ring was given to him by the relative. Within twenty-four hours the bleeding stopped. Within a week the patient was up and about. No one was more thunder-struck than the brilliant physician in charge of his case. A few days later the patient was discharged from the General Hospital. He was able to resume his duties as an education officer. I examined the gem prescribed by the *bomoh,* and I think it was a red coral. Indian gem therapists prescribe red coral to stop bleeding. I also advised the discharged patient never to take off the ring, but always to have the gem touching his skin. Incidentally, just before being discharged, the patient asked the physician what he had been suffering from. The physician said that despite extensive tests, he was in the dark himself.

The *bomoh* had set the gem on a silver ring. The education officer did not like this, and wanted to mount the gem on a gold ring, as the silver ring became dark and dirty after some time. So the ring was given to a Chinese jeweller for resetting. Within forty-eight hours, my friend became very ill, started bleeding profusely again from the stomach, and was readmitted to the same hospital. This happened about nine months after he had recovered from the first illness.

I again went to the hospital to donate blood, and when I visited the patient I noticed that the ring was missing from his finger. On questioning, he explained that it had been sent for resetting in a gold ring. I informed the patient that the second attack had occurred because he had removed the gem from his body, and the protective influence of the gem was gone. He told me at once that he was sceptical of this. His training as a science graduate would not allow him to believe this. However, I persuaded him to put on the ring as quickly as possible. His wife accordingly saw the jeweller, and asked him to complete the setting swiftly, and within a day or two the ring was put on the ring finger of the patient's right hand. Within twenty-four hours the internal bleeding stopped. I then asked him whether he believed that the gem had helped to stop the bleeding. He said that he was now no longer sceptical, and that he had no choice but to believe in the remedial influence of gems. The fact that the same gem had twice stopped internal bleeding within twenty-four hours could not possibly be sheer coincidence. I then advised him again never to take off the gem from his finger. He followed my advice faithfully, and has been keeping excellent health since then. At the time of writing, he is a very active man, in good health. He also holds a high position in the educational field. He is still keeping the piece of paper, on which I assured him previously that he would survive his illness, as a souvenir.

Many of my European female clients buy blue sapphires from Thailand. **Blue sapphire** comes under the influence of the essentially malefic planet Saturn, the dispenser of Justice and Divine Punishment. For many people Saturn is an evil planet. I deliberately asked my female clients whether any sorrow or illness had struck them after they had worn blue sapphires on their fingers. The vast majority of them said yes. They had lost their passports, fallen very ill, had had major quarrels for no apparent reason with their husbands, lost money, and narrated many other incidents of sorrow and grief. I then informed them seriously that the blue sapphire had brought them bad luck, and advised them to get rid of the gem swiftly. Practically all the women were incredulous and asked me whether I was serious. On seeing that I was not joking, some of them took my advice. I followed up a few cases, and the women told me that everything returned to normal once they had removed the blue sapphire from their fingers. I have confirmed incidents of bad luck created by wrong use of blue sapphires hundreds of times. Here's a point worth noting. Until the women consulted me, they had never heard of gems influencing the body and mind. The incidents of bad luck occurred after they had started wearing the gem and before they met me, so it cannot be argued that I had put the idea of bad luck into their minds. They were, however, able to correlate the incidents of sorrow from the time they wore the blue sapphires. In Indian gem therapy, the blue sapphire is regarded as an extremely dangerous gem. If unfavourable, it can bring untold sorrow to the unfortunate victim. If favourable, it can be a blessing in many spheres of life. The effect of gems is chemical and planetary, not psychological. As a result of chemical reaction, certain gems such as pearls and corals can change colour when worn next to the skin.

Each gem is under the influence of a particular planet. Thus yellow sapphire is under the influence of the planet Jupiter. The rays of the planet Jupiter help to produce the gem yellow sapphire. Gems are storehouses of cosmic rays, and their cosmic colours are violet, indigo, blue, green, yellow, orange and red. Gems release these colours, especially when brought into contact with the human skin. When the human body lacks three or more of these coloured rays, there is disease or illness. When all seven colours are affected, then we get very dangerous diseases such as paralysis, poliomyelitis and leukaemia. The wearing of selected gems will correct the colour imbalance in the human body and aura.

Various illnesses arise when the brain cells are weak. The use of the correct gems strengthens the brain cells. It is a fact that gems affect the brain cells, and these brain cells are affected adversely if the wrong gem is worn. Doctors sometimes ask patients to go to hill resorts or other places of a different environment so that they can regain their health. There is something in the atmosphere or environment of certain places that is conducive to the health of the patients. Gem therapists believe that these places have cosmic rays which the body of the patient lacks. Hence, the required cosmic rays are absorbed by the body of the patient, colour hunger is appeased, and health is regained. But by wearing a suitable gem, it is not necessary to go to a hill resort. The necessary cosmic rays can be absorbed into the body by wearing the correct gemstone.

Diseases can result from wearing the wrong gem. A certain businessman in India wore a **ruby** out of sheer ignorance. After three months he become paralysed. He also had a constant temperature. The poor victim saw many good doctors, but they were unable to help him, and he suffered for two years. Then an astrologer examined his horoscope and saw that it was wrong for him to wear a ruby. The patient was asked to get rid of the ruby ring, and, deliberately, no medicines were given to him. The idea was to see whether the ruby ring was the cause of the constant temperature. Within twenty-four hours the temperature of the patient had disappeared and he was soon completely recovered. The sceptics were at a loss to explain this.

In Indian Astrology, nine gems are used. They are (a) ruby, (b) pearl, (c) red coral, (d) emerald, (e) yellow sapphire, (f) diamond, (g) blue sapphire, (h) gomed (hessonite), and (i) cat's eye.

Ruby is under the influence of the Sun, pearl under Moon, red coral under Mars, and emerald under Mercury. Yellow sapphire comes under the influence of Jupiter, diamond under Venus, blue sapphire under Saturn, gomed under Rahu and cat's eye under Kethu.

Before wearing gems, we must see carefully which planet is giving out malefic vibrations, thus damaging the prospects of the subject. The correct gem will act as a powerful antidote.

Certain conditions must be observed before gems are worn on the fingers. The gems should be GENUINE, and not synthetic. They should not be heat treated, dyed, or irradiated. No dyes or injections should be introduced in the gems. By not being heat treated, means that the gems should not have been put in an electric oven to heat the gem at very high temperatures. This will kill the basic energy, prana, or 'chi' of the gems. 'Chi' is a Chinese word that refers to the Vital Force in the human body as well as in gems. By not being irradiated, it means that the gems should not have been put in a nuclear reactor to be bombarded with gamma rays. This will also kill the basic vitality of the gems. Such artificial processes make the gems sparkle. This process is called enhancing the colour of the gems.

If this is done, the gem would be useless astrologically. Such a gem cannot bring LUCK to the wearer. This is because the gem would be 'DEAD' astrologically. No doubt, the gem would look more beautiful, but a competent, highly professional, ethical astrologer would warn the client to buy ONLY gems which have not been dyed, heat treated, or irradiated.

In hand analysis, the thumb is not regarded as a finger. The gems should be worn on certain days within one hour of sunrise. Each gem should be tested for three days. The subject should watch for ill effects within three days. The ill effects could be sickness, disease, loss of money, accident, a major quarrel, acute mental worry, bad news, etc. If there are not ill effects within three days, the subject can safely wear the gem. But if there are ill effects, the gem must be removed at once from the body. In that case, the subject should not wait for three days. Then another piece of the same gem should be tested for three days. If this again proves unfavourable, the subject should consult a learned hand analyst or astrologer. The practitioner will then recommend a different gem or a substitute. If the gem is found suitable, the subject should wear it on the finger continuously. Generally, it takes three to four months for the stone to show favourable effects. Continuously removing the gem, after it has been found to be favourable for three days, will upset the vibrations of the planet influencing the gem.

A gem should generally weigh at least 4 carats in weight if it is to be effective for astrological purposes. If it weighs less than this, the gem could be too weak to show marked beneficial effects. It is a must that every gem should be tested for three days. This applies especially to blue sapphires, cat's eye, and gomed. These gems are very powerful, either for good or evil. It is bad if a gem has artificial flaws and major artificial chips or cracks. In such a case, the vibrations of the planet influencing the gem become irregular and malefic. Many of the female clients mentioned earlier who bought blue sapphires from Bangkok, had flawed gems. No wonder ill luck struck these unfortunate victims! Also, husbands will be pleased to note that diamonds need not necessarily be a lady's best friend. It all depends on the individual's horoscope.

But as diamonds are very expensive, the client can wear a diamond of any weight he can afford. Later, when the client has more money, he can upgrade the diamond. But the client is warned to be careful of SYNTHETIC diamonds. Nowadays, there are synthetic gems like cubic zirconian and moissanite. In particular, the moissanite is a very brilliant SYNTHETIC diamond. It is very hard to detect this gem unless the gem undergoes very sophisticated gemological tests. This is because the moissanite sparkles better than a real diamond. It behaves like a diamond. But it is NOT a real diamond.

Also many real diamonds have been heavily irradiated. This high dosage could very well lead to the much dreaded disease called cancer in the long run.

Also, the synthetic Blue Topaz has been heavily irradiated. Women clients are advised to be careful of all these factors before investing in a diamond ring. In the future, it is going to be very difficult indeed to tell the difference between a real diamond and the synthetic variety. A viable suggestion is to buy the gem from a highly reputable jeweller and get a certificate stating that the gem is genuine, and has not been dyed, heat treated, or irradiated. Nowadays the synthetic gems are such clever fakes that even reputable jewellers can be fooled at times.

A gem should ONLY be selected after a careful study of the horoscope. A proper horoscope, preferably based on Indian astrology, should be cast by a competent astrologer. The basic chart called the RASI chart should be cast scientifically. This chart should be based on the correct date, time and place of birth of the client. Then a very important chart called the NAVAMSA chart should also be worked out. The Navamsa chart is a divisional chart known only to Indian Vedic astrology. This sophisticated chart reveals the true strength of the planets. It is strictly an individual selection. The practice of wearing birthstones for good luck is unscientific and ridiculous. Millions of people are born in the same month. How could they possibly have the same malefic or benefic planets influencing them? A person born in the same month may have different malefic planets from someone else also born in the same month. Then how could the same birthstone have favourable effects for both? Selection of gems is a highly specialized task. It should only be handled by an experienced, learned hand analyst or astrologer. It is wrong to wear any gem without the expert advice from a hand analyst or astrologer.

Emerald or green jade should be worn on the little finger. The Planet Mercury influences the gems emerald and green jade, and the little finger is the Mercury finger, which is why emerald or green jade should be worn on this finger.

Yellow sapphire should be worn for the first time on a Thursday morning within one hour of sunrise; ruby or amber on a Sunday morning; moonstone or pearl on a Monday morning; and red coral on a Tuesday morning. Diamond should be worn on a Friday morning; gomed and blue sapphire on a Saturday morning, and finally, cat's eye on a Monday morning. All times are within one hour of sunrise.

How are we to find out which planets are malefic and obstructing the progress of the subject?

Certain astrological charities are useful in lessening the influence of weak or malefic planets. The evil Karmic effects of sins committed in the previous life or lives are thus mitigated. That is how these astrological charities work. I have recommended these astrological charities to sceptical clients of various races, and they have worked in lessening the effect of evil periods the clients were experiencing. Once again, the effect of these charities is not psychological at all. Whether one believes or does not believe in the efficacy of these astrological charities is irrelevant — they will certainly have some effect. The articles to be donated for charity should be presented personally. All the items listed need not be donated on the same occasion. One item may be donated to charity this week, and another the following week. These charities should be performed for at least nine consecutive weeks on the specific days mentioned. To the sceptics, all one can say is that the proof of the pudding is in the eating. By performing these astrological charities, the malefic planet or planets will be appeased to some degree.

The following table shows the items to be given in charity. The malefic or weak planets can be deducted by studying the evil marks on the mounts of the hand.

Sun: Give wheat, oranges, and something made of copper on Sundays, to a man. Should this man be a government servant, it would be better still. We know that in Indian astrology, the planet Sun represents Sunday and the government; hence it is easy to deduce why this charity should be done on a Sunday, and preferably to a government servant.

Moon: Give rice, white clothes, milk, or white flowers to a woman, on Monday. In Indian astrology the Moon rules on Mondays and is regarded a feminine planet.

Mars: Give red cloth, red flowers and a book with a red cover to a young man, on Tuesdays. In Indian astrology, Mars represents young people and the colour red. It is easy to give one of these items to a young student.

Mercury: Give anything green in colour, such as green cloth and green vegetable to a woman on Wednesdays. In Indian astrology, the planet Mercury rules on Wednesdays and signifies the colour green.

Jupiter: Give anything yellow in colour such as yellow cloth, yellow flowers, and yellow bananas to a middle-aged man on Thursdays. Should this person be a priest or a spiritual personality, so much the better. In Indian astrology, the planet Jupiter represents the colour yellow and the priestly class. It rules on Thursdays.

Venus: Give white silk cloth, sandal, and curd to a woman, on Fridays. In Indian astrology the planet Venus refers to articles of refined texture. It rules on Fridays.

Saturn: Give anything black in colour such as black sesame seeds and black cloth to an old man or woman on Saturdays. Shoes, cooking oil, coal, and any article made of iron can also be donated in charity. In Indian astrology, Saturn rules on Saturdays, and represents elderly people. It represents the colour black.

Rahu: The charity is essentially the same as that for Saturn. As Rahu is a foreign planet in Indian astrology, it would be more effective if charity were performed to persons shunned by society or regarded as outcasts.

Kethu: The charity is the same as that for Mars, but in addition, cloth of a smoky colour and coconuts can also be given to charity.

The planets rule various vegetables and minerals. Thus Saturn rules black sesame seeds, oil, iron and coal. That is why these articles have to be donated in charity to appease Saturn.

For more effective results, the subject under the influence of an evil planet should wear the correct gem, and also perform the appropriate charity to appease the malefic planet. This, then, will represent a double attack on the problem.

Some of my clients believe in gem therapy, but are reluctant to wear gems on their fingers. There is an alternative: the gem can be worn as a pendant on a chain round the neck, but in this case the gem should touch the skin of the chest.

These remedial measures will influence the lines in the palms for the better. Weak lines will be strengthened. Let us assume that a businessman has a large island on the Fate Line. This can mean heavy financial losses. An island on the Fate Line shows the evil influence of the planet Saturn. Perhaps there is also a grille, island, mole, cross, or spot on the Mount of Saturn. By adopting remedial measures to appease the malefic planet Saturn, the island on the Fate Line may not disappear, but it could become smaller in size; in other words, it may shrink. Thus, while the businessman will still suffer financial losses, these will not be to such a marked degree. Expert hand analysts have actually seen islands on the Fate Line shrink after remedial measures have been adopted by the subject. Prints have been taken before and after remedial measures were adopted. Subsequent prints, after remedial measures had been followed, showed a shrinking of the island on the Fate Line. Thus, the effectiveness of the remedial measures has been proved.

Chapter Twenty

The Modern Relevance and Promise of Scientific Hand Analysis

Scientific hand analysis has a brilliant future ahead of it. According to Dr. Louis Cohen, associate professor of medicine at the University of Chicago's Pritzker School of Medicine, every part of the body will at some time or other give an indication of something else going on in another part of the body. However, while the hand is a particularly rich source of information, it is not the only source.[1] Dr. Cohen goes on to say that changes of colour can be significant. Hands reveal both serious and minor health problems in distant parts of the body. A hand surgeon, Dr. J. Edward Flynn, says that changes in the fingernails alone — brittleness, thickening, spooning, discoloration — all these can show various health difficulties ranging from vascular diseases to disorders of the endocrine system, such as sex hormone, thyroid and pituitary deficiencies.

In the future, doctors will be using medical hand analysis and medical astrology on a massive scale. The Western countries will take to hand analysis in a big way. Australia, especially, will experience a great interest and belief in scientific hand analysis within the next fifteen years. Lectures in this science will be held at prestigious hospitals, clinics, and universities, and many thinkers and intellectuals will be convinced of the great value of this

---

[1] Don A. Schanche, *op.cit,* p.92

ancient science in the field of vocational guidance and preventive medicine.

Hand analysis and astrology should be included in the subjects taught in all the universities of the world. Inclusion of these sciences at university level will make them popular, and bestow on them the intellectual and academic dignity which they so richly deserve. Besides, further research in these sciences will be accelerated to a marked degree, and mankind will be benefited to a great degree.

The police should seriously take up the study of hand analysis. Hand analysis is used by the Crime Branch of police departments throughout the world. Police officials make use of thumb-prints in catching criminals. But in some countries, the police use a complete handprint to aid them in their work. Unfortunately, however, the full benefits and advantages of this great science have not been tapped by the police. All police departments should have a competent hand analyst to aid the police in their job of detecting criminals. A lot of precious time and energy could be saved in this manner, for it is perfectly possible for a really good hand analyst to inform the police accurately as to the motive of the suspect. Let us assume that a woman has been found murdered. The police will send their fingerprint experts to the scene of the crime. These experts will then try to match the finger prints with the available ones in their files. Yet this technique will not expose the motives of the criminal. Why was the woman murdered? Was it for lust or for money? These are very important questions indeed, and they deserve accurate answers.

A really good hand analyst can easily deduce the motive as to why the crime was committed. We will now assume that the police have been able to get a good set of handprints of the criminal. Let us assume the handprints show a clubbed thumb and short Lines of Mentality and Heart. A clubbed thumb with other adverse features of the hand, can show a brutal nature. A short Line of Mentality will mean that the subject is metaphorically shortheaded. A short Line of Heart will reveal a nature cold in disposition, lacking warmth of spirit. It is then easy to deduce that the subject must have committed murder because of sadistic tendencies. But with these indications, let us assume that the little fingers of both hands are naturally crooked, and the Line of Mentality curves in an upward direction towards the Mount of Mercury. We know that a naturally crooked little finger shows dishonest tendencies, while an upward curve of the Line of Mentality towards the Mount of Mercury shows a grasping disposition. It is therefore easy to deduce, with such signs, that the crime was committed for the sake of money.

If in addition to all these indications, the handprints also reveal a double Vitality Line, badly formed, a fragmented Girdle of Venus, and an excessively developed Venus Mount, the interpretation has another important significance. A badly formed Girdle of Venus, double Lines of Vitality, and an overdeveloped Mount of Venus are indications of very strong sexual instincts. A short Line of Heart, preferably ending on the Saturn Mount, will show an excessive preoccupation with the pleasures of the bed. With such additional signs, a competent hand analyst would know that the murderer also raped the victim. When the motives of a crime can be easily and accurately worked out, it becomes so much easier for the police to catch the criminal, and a lot of unnecessary, painstaking work can be eliminated.

Then, of course, we know that tendencies towards drug addiction can also be deduced from the features of the hand. A teenager, having such undesirable features in the hands, can be more closely supervised by parents and teachers. This would then be a shining example of preventive medicine.

The police could also use hand analysis to recruit personnel. The present methods of selection are haphazard.

The real mentality and character of the candidate are seldom revealed ruthlessly by a couple of tests on the ground and across the table. We are largely governed by the subconscious mind, and such tests are not penetrating enough to lay bare the workings of this part of the mind. The ideal police officer should have courage as well as mental and physical stamina. He should also have a clear mind. In astrology and hand analysis, the planet Mars stands for courage, both physical as well as moral. The ideal police officer should have a square-shaped hand or square finger tips. These will show a practical, realistic frame of mind. The Mounts of Mars should be well-developed. These mounts are the Mount of Lower Mars below the first or Jupiter finger, as well as the Mount of Upper Mars, found below the little finger and the Heart Line on the percussion. Such well-developed Mounts of Mars will show physical as well as mental bravery. A strong Line of Vitality, as well as a clear Line of Mars running parallel to it are sure signs of tremendous physical stamina. A straight, deep, clear Line of Mentality will show a clear-thinking, practical sort of man. Finally, the Fate Line or the Line of Sun should be favourable or at least fairly well marked. With all these features, it is sure that the candidate would be a real asset to the police force of any country. These indications of hand analysis are unerringly accurate. Should such favourable markings be found only on one hand, the subject could make a good police officer. But should these be found on both hands, then it is a foregone conclusion that the candidate would definitely make a really capable police officer. The reason is that favourable marks on both hands will make the analysis doubly sure.

In some countries, there are laws against the practice of hand analysis and astrology on a professional basis. These laws are obsolete, especially in these days of scientific thinking and progress. Instead, the government should have adequate safeguards to protect the public from quacks in these fields. Every professional astrologer and hand analyst should be tested and licensed. Barring the practice of hand analysis altogether is a short-sighted move.

Sceptics ask how the future can be revealed if it is true that the lines change in the palms. It is a fact that the lines can change in the palms, but we must note that around the age of fourteen, the major lines are stabilized. After that, only the minor lines change. Thus, for example, the course of the Line of Mentality, a major line, will not change. Changes in the minor lines of the palms are not fundamental in any sense of the word. That is why experienced hand analysts can make predictions accurately thirty to forty years ahead of time.

Latent talents can be seen in the hands. This is most useful for vocational guidance. Parents, though generally with the best of intentions, often mislead their children into pursuing the wrong careers. The vocation for which the subject is most suited can be correctly analysed by a thorough examination of the dominant finger and the Mount at its base. Of course, the shape of the tips, the course of the Line of Mentality and the consistency of the palms are very important factors. In astrology and hand analysis, the planet Jupiter represents law, administration, banking, diplomacy, teaching and religious pursuits. Let us assume that a boy of eighteen has got a very favourable dominant finger and Mount of Jupiter. Thus the subject could shine as a teacher, diplomat, banker, lawyer, judge, administrator or a priest. A most careful study of both hands, taking various other features into account, will pinpoint what vocation this particular subject should pursue. The mounts have to be analysed in combination with the strong, favourable Jupiter Mount.

We must be practical in outlook Knowledge is meant to be used to brighten our lives. Choose your marriage partners, business associates and friends by making full use of scientific hand analysis. In this way, there will be much more harmony in inter-personal relationships. Only a foolish mind will discard a reliable lamp of knowledge. Hand analysis is certainly such a lamp. Why discard or ignore it when all we have to do is to analyse our hands for reliable guidance in so many spheres of life? It is no use being sorry later on. Let us have our feet on the ground at the outset. Prevention is better than cure.

Let us consider one extremely important point. We shall assume that a really good hand analyst has predicted academic success for a university student in his final year examination. Now this does not mean that the student can stop studying, and will still pass the examination: what it means is that if the student continues to work hard and intelligently, his efforts will be crowned with success. A prediction will be fulfilled provided it is backed up by hard work. The predictions of an expert hand analyst should not be regarded as passports for laziness.

We have now come to the end of this elementary work on scientific hand analysis. It is my fervent hope that this book will open the eyes of many a sceptic or even a prejudiced mind. Hand analysis will help promote universal peace. The word *Guru* means a teacher. Let us hope that the following verse by *Guru* Arjan, one of the Ten Gurus of the Sikh religion, is suitable for sceptics reading this work:

> *The egg of superstition hath burst; the mind is illumined: The Guru hath cut the fetters off the feet and freed the captive.*[2]

---

[2] Max Arthur Macauliffe, *The Sikh Religion,* Clarendon Press, Oxford, 1909.